In Fashion

In Fashion

Fourth Edition

SHERYL A. FARNAN

METROPOLITAN COMMUNITY COLLEGE

KANSAS CITY, MISSOURI, US

ELAINE STONE

FAIRCHILD BOOKS

NEW YORK · LONDON · OXFORD · NEW DELHI · SYDNEY

FAIRCHILD BOOKS
Bloomsbury Publishing Inc
1385 Broadway, New York, NY 10018, USA
50 Bedford Square, London, WC1B 3DP, UK
29 Earlsfort Terrace, Dublin 2, Ireland

BLOOMSBURY, FAIRCHILD BOOKS and the Fairchild Books
logo are trademarks of Bloomsbury Publishing Plc

Second edition published 2012
Third edition published 2017
This edition published 2021
Reprinted 2022
© Bloomsbury Publishing Inc, 2021

For legal purposes the Acknowledgments on p. xiii constitute
an extension of this copyright page.

Cover design: Anna Perotti, www.bytheskydesign.com
Cover photo: Kirstin Sinclair / Getty Images

Bloomsbury Publishing Inc does not have any control over, or responsibility for,
any third-party websites referred to or in this book. All internet addresses given
in this book were correct at the time of going to press. The author and publisher
regret any inconvenience caused if addresses have changed or sites have
ceased to exist, but can accept no responsibility for any such changes.

Library of Congress Cataloging-in-Publication Data
Names: Farnan, Sheryl A., author. | Stone, Elaine, author.
Title: In fashion / Sheryl A. Farnan, Metropolitan Community
College, Kansas City, Missouri, US., Elaine Stone.
Description: Fourth edition. | New York : Fairchild Books, An Imprint of Bloomsbury
Publishing Inc, 2021. | Includes bibliographical references and index.
Identifiers: LCCN 2020018981 (print) | LCCN 2020018982 (ebook) |
ISBN 9781501362040 (paperback) | ISBN 9781501362002 (pdf)
Subjects: LCSH: Fashion—Textbooks. | Clothing trade—Textbooks.
Classification: LCC TT518 .S76 2021 (print) | LCC TT518 (ebook) | DDC 746.9/2—dc23
LC record available at https://lccn.loc.gov/2020018981
LC ebook record available at https://lccn.loc.gov/2020018982

ISBN: 978-1-5013-6204-0

Typeset by Lachina Creative, Inc.
Printed and bound in Great Britain

To find out more about our authors and books
visit www.fairchildbooks.com and sign up for our newsletter.

CONTENTS

EXTENDED TABLE OF CONTENTS

PREFACE

The fashion industry is a vibrant and vital part of our world, offering a wide array of challenging and engaging career opportunities. *In Fashion*, now in its fourth edition, has been developed to help students learn and understand the various fac-tors that come together to contribute, form, and shape the world of fashion.

Fashion is a business, and *In Fashion* brings a positive, fresh approach to helping students understand the art, business, and craft in helping and marketing the fashion product. *In Fashion* covers a broad scope of fashion topics, adding the newest, most up-to-date facts and figures used by industry professionals to keep the industry vital.

In Fashion reflects the survey nature of an introductory course and is structured so that the concepts and practices developed are equally applicable to all career paths. To keep the students current in the most recent happenings, each chapter concludes with a discussion of the latest developments and upcoming trends.

Organization of the Text

PART ONE
The Changing World of Fashion

The first part examines how and why fashion evolves and changes. It explains the principles around which fashion revolves and the role that economic, sociological, and psychological elements play in the cyclical nature of fashion. It also covers the business scope of the industry, including recent growth and expansion. The fashion industry operates in a far different way than it did years ago. It moves faster and reaches more people. To understand the changes that have occurred and will occur in the future, you must first understand the dynamics that underlie the fashion business.

PART TWO
The Primary Level:
The Materials of Fashion

The growers and producers of the raw materials of fashion, fibers, fabrics, leather, and fur are covered in this unit, along with the sustainability of products made from recycled materials. Technological advances in these industries coupled with an increasing variety of fashion goods using these materials are also discussed.

PART THREE
The Secondary Level:
The Producers of Fashion

The third part begins with a chapter on product development, explaining how each fashion product is developed and the systems that are used. Then, industry trends in apparel (for women, men, children, and teens) and accessories are highlighted. Each market sector is compared and contrasted with the factors that are common to all: supply chain management, licensing, private label, brand extension, specification buying, and offshore production, with examples and concepts to help students ground them into industry-relevant context. This unit explains how each industry functions and covers current and future practices and trends.

PART FOUR
The Retail Level:
The Markets for Fashion

This part focuses on the elements of fashion marketing and reveals how markets operate to help manufacturers sell their products and how retailers satisfy the needs of their target customer. It details both domestic and foreign markets and global sources. Different types of retailers and current trends are detailed. Also discussed are the many fashion services that work with all levels of the fashion industry, including magazines, newspapers, broadcast media, television, the Internet and social media, and fashion reporting, as well as trade associations.

Text Features

In Fashion includes a wide range of examples, photographs, diagrams, and images to help students learn the creative and business facets of the fashion industry in an engaging and dynamic manner. These features are appropriate for class discussion, library research projects, and group projects.

Spotlight on Innovators

The feature "Spotlight on Innovators" highlights people, products, and places that affect creative development and groundbreaking presentation of the fashion product. This feature is found in every chapter.

Spotlight on Careers

The feature "Spotlight on Careers" focuses on the education, background, and career path of a noted professional in the fashion industry. A wide variety of career areas are showcased, including bridal and formalwear, education,

research, costume design, textile design, children's product development and production, and more. This feature is found in every chapter.

Spotlight on Business

The feature "Spotlight on Business" explores the importance of technology, innovation, and business and marketing execution in this rapidly changing industry. Topics include social responsibility, customer service, textile and clothing recycling programs, social media, global retailing, and more. This feature is found in selected chapters.

Spotlight on Sustainability

The feature "Spotlight on Sustainability" explores topics related to the growing emphasis on the sustainability and transparency of fashion brands. Topics include environmental issues, textiles, water usage, recycling, and more. This feature is found in selected chapters.

Top 100 Fashion Influencers

This is a compilation of top designers, models, photographers, writers, editors, public figures, and society leaders, both old and new, who have significantly influenced fashion.

Glossary

The glossary contains industry terms called "Trade Talk." A knowledge and understanding of the language of fashion gives students a firm footing with industry terminology and concepts.

Summary and Review

Each chapter concludes with activities designed to reinforce the instructional material.

Summary and Review provides a quick review and reminder of key concepts covered in the chapter

For Review asks questions about key concepts of each chapter. These questions provoke thought, encourage classroom discussion, and develop recall of material presented in the text.

For Discussion asks students to explain the importance and significance of a major concept and to support the explanation with specific concepts from the chapter. This activity provides students an opportunity to apply theory to actual situations and to draw on their own background and experiences.

Trade Talk lists fashion and industry terms introduced throughout the text of the chapter. Students will recognize and build upon these terms as they appear in subsequent chapters. All Trade Talk terms are defined in the glossary.

Instructor's Resources

- The Instructor's Guide includes tips for integrating the STUDIO into a course.
- The updated test bank now includes 50% new questions and page references for easy course mapping.
- PowerPoint presentations provide a framework for lectures and include color images from the book.

In Fashion STUDIO

Fairchild Books has a long history of excellence in textbook publishing for fashion education. Our new online STUDIOS are specially developed to complement this book with rich media ancillaries that students can adapt to their visual learning styles. *In Fashion STUDIO* features:

- Online self-quizzes with scored results and personalized study tips
- Flashcards with terms/definitions and image identification
- Videos to help students master concepts and improve grades
- Timeline featuring the Top 100 Fashion Influencers appendix

STUDIO access cards are offered free with new book purchases and also sold separately through Bloomsbury Fashion Central (www.BloomsburyFashionCentral.com).

ACKNOWLEDGMENTS

In preparing the fourth edition of *In Fashion*, my sincere thanks and appreciation is extended posthumously to Elaine Stone for her dedication and work in the field of fashion and apparel education. Thank you to my colleagues and mentors who have provided encouragement and guidance throughout this process and throughout my academic career. And appreciation to my students, who, year after year, work very hard and overcome significant personal trials to learn, study, and follow their dreams. You are a continual inspiration to me.

I am indebted to industry professionals who have provided guidance and direction throughout this process. Comments from readers and educators selected by the publisher have also been very helpful. Thanks to reviewers Melinda K. Adams, University of the Incarnate Word; Mary Elliott, Wayne State College; Donna Reamy, Virginia Commonwealth University; Alyssa Adomaitis, The New York City College of Technology, City University of New York; Patsy Perry, The University of Manchester; Marissa Zorola, University of North Texas.

My gratitude and sincere appreciation go the staff at Fairchild Books. I would like to thank Emily Samulski, Acquisitions Editor, Joseph Miranda, Editorial Development Manager, Edie Weinberg, Art Development Editor, and Jenna Lefkowitz, Editorial Assistant. You are all professional, kind, and encouraging – it is an absolute joy to work with each of you!

On a personal note, I wish to thank the many teachers throughout my life who approached their work with passion, sincerity, and the desire to help students succeed. You not only taught subjects and information, but you taught me how to teach. I think of many of them often.

I would not, and could not, do this work without the support and encouragement of my dear husband, Jay Leipzig. He always sees possibilities where others usually see obstacles. He has taught me to lead with "yes!"

I welcome comments from students and instructors who use this book. You are welcome to send those through Fairchild Books.

This work is dedicated to my father and mother, Tom and Darlene Farnan, my first teachers, most truthful critics, and biggest cheerleaders. Thank you.

PART ONE

The Changing World of Fashion

In this part, you will learn how and why fashion evolves and changes. You will begin to develop a basic vocabulary and a working knowledge of the following:

- The principles around which the fashion world revolves are featured in Chapter 1.
- The environmental forces—the role that economic, demographic, sociological, and psychological elements play in the fashion business—are in Chapter 2.
- The cyclical forces—how fashions change and how an understanding of this constant cycle of change can be used to predict and analyze current and future fashion—are in Chapter 3.
- The business forces—the scope of the industry, including recent growth and expansion—are in Chapter 4.

The world of fashion operates in a far different way today than it did years ago. It moves faster and reaches more people. To understand the changes that have occurred and that will occur in the future of the fashion industry, you must first understand the dynamics that underlie the fashion business.

1

The Nature of Fashion

Key Concepts

- Marketing and merchandising in the fashion business

- The terminology of the fashion business

- The stages of the fashion cycle

- The intangibles of fashion

Behold the many faces of fashion—fun, fantastic, frivolous, frantic, fabulous, futuristic, flirtatious, fresh, and financial. Fashion is all of this, and much more. Fashion is the most dynamic of American businesses. It thrives on change—and change is the engine that fuels it. Life might be easier if we never had to change. However, if the fashion business did not change, it would not survive. Refer to Figure 1.1 for an example of fashion's constant evolution.

The Importance of Fashion

In recent years, general interest in fashion has increased. Fashion has a great impact on our country's economy. Changes in fashion result in new consumer goods. At the same time, such changes encourage consumers to purchase new products because the thought of being unfashionable is a fate worse than death to many people!

Figure 1.1 Flowing Bohemian-inspired layers modeled by Karlie Kloss at the Atelier Versace, Paris Fashion Haute Couture Fall/Winter 2015.

Webster's defines fashion as "prevailing custom, usage, or style,"[1] and in this sense, it covers a wide range of human activity. In this book, however, fashion is used in a narrower sense. Fashion here means the style or styles of clothing and accessories worn at a particular time by a particular group of people. It also includes fashion in cosmetics, fragrances, and home furnishings.

The Fashion Business

Fashion is big business, and millions of people are employed in fashion-related activities. The **fashion industries** are businesses that are engaged in manufacturing the materials and finished products used in the production of apparel and accessories for men, women, and children. The broader term **fashion business** includes all the industries and services connected with fashion: design, manufacturing, distribution, marketing, retailing, advertising, communications, publishing, and consulting—in other words, any business concerned with fashion goods or services.

Marketing

Today, marketing has become a major influence in the fashion business. The process of **marketing** includes many different activities that identify consumer needs; develop good products; and price, distribute, and promote those products effectively so that they will sell easily.

Fashion Marketing and Merchandising

Fashion marketing and merchandising is the business of selling products and services of the fashion industries. Marketing should be understood as the practice of identifying a target market and satisfying the product and service needs of those consumers. If the marketer understands consumer needs; develops products and services that provide superior customer value; and prices, distributes, and promotes them effectively, these products will sell.

We are also concerned with fashion merchandising. *Webster*'s defines **merchandising** as sales promotion as a comprehensive function, including market research, development of new products, coordination of manufacture and marketing, and effective advertising and selling.[2] It refers to the *planning* required to have the right fashion-oriented merchandise at the right time, in the right place, in the right quantities, at the right prices, and with the right sales promotion for a specified target customer. This is better known in the industry as the five Rs of merchandising.

Misconceptions about Fashion

The first and most common misconception about fashion is that designers and retailers dictate what the fashion will be and then force it upon helpless consumers. In reality, consumers decide what the fashion will be by influencing new designs and by accepting or rejecting the styles that are offered.

The second misconception is that fashion acts as an influence on women only. Men and children are as influenced by and responsive to fashion as women. Fashion is the force that causes women to raise or lower their skirt lengths from minis to maxis, straighten or curl their hair, and change from casual sportswear to dressy clothes. Fashion is also the force that influences men to grow or shave off their mustaches and beards, choose wide or "skinny" ties and lapels, and change from casual jeans into three-piece suits. And fashion is the force that makes children demand specific products and styles.

The third misconception is that fashion is a mysterious and unpredictable force. Actually, its direction can be determined and its changes predicted with remarkable accuracy by those who study and understand the fundamentals of fashion. Fashion was once considered an art form controlled by designers who dictated its content, but today fashion can be measured and evaluated.

The Terminology of Fashion

What are the differences among fashion, style, and design? Just what do *high fashion*, *mass fashion*, *taste*, *classic*, and *fad* mean?

Style

The first step in understanding fashion is to distinguish between fashion and style. In general terms, a **style** is a characteristic or distinctive artistic expression or presentation. Styles exist in architecture, sculpture, painting, politics, and music, as well as in popular heroes, games, hobbies, pets, flirtations, and weddings.

In apparel, style is the characteristic or distinctive appearance of a garment—the combination of features that makes it different from other garments. For example, T-shirts are as different from polo shirts as they are from peasant blouses. Riding jackets are as different from safari jackets as they are from blazer jackets.

Although styles come and go in terms of acceptance, a specific style always remains a style, whether it is currently in fashion or not. Some people adopt a style that becomes indelibly associated with them and wear it regardless of whether it is currently fashionable. Carmen Miranda's platform shoes, Gwen Stefani's fiery red lips, Madonna's bustier and layers of jewelry, Marilyn Monroe's white halter dress, Michael Jackson's glove, Mary J. Blige's sunglasses, and Snooki's pouf are all examples of personal style.

Some styles are named for the period of history in which they originated—Grecian, Roman, Renaissance, Empire, Gibson Girl (early 1900s), flapper (1920s). When such styles return to fashion, their basic elements remain the same. Minor details are altered to reflect the taste or needs of the era in which they reappear. For example, the flapper style of the 1920s was short, pleated, and body slimming (Figure 1.2). That style can be bought today but with changes for current fashion acceptance.

Figure 1.2 Mannequins dressed in 1920s flapper chic in the Costume Institute's "American Woman: Fashioning a National Identity" exhibit.

Fashion

Alternatively, a **fashion** is a style that is accepted and used by the majority of a group at any one time, no matter how small that group. A fashion is a result of social emulation and acceptance. Miniskirts, square-toed shoes, mustaches, and theatrical daytime makeup have all been fashions. And no doubt each will again be accepted by a majority of a group of people with similar interests or characteristics—for example, college students, young career men and women, retired men and women.

Fashions appeal to many different groups and can be categorized according to those groups. **High fashion** refers to a new style accepted by a limited number of fashion leaders who want to be the first to adopt changes and innovation in fashion. However, if the style can appeal to a broader audience, it is generally copied, mass-produced, and sold at lower prices. The fashion leaders or innovators who first accepted it then move on to something new.

To contrast with high fashion, **mass fashion or volume fashion** consists of styles that are widely accepted. These fashions are usually produced and sold in large quantities at moderate to low prices and appeal to the greatest majority of fashion-conscious consumers. Mass fashion accounts for the majority of sales in the fashion business. Mass fashion is the "bread and butter" of the fashion banquet.

Design

There can be many variations of detail within a specific style. A **design** is a particular or individual interpretation, version, or treatment of a style. A style may be expressed in a great many designs—all different, yet all related, because they are in the same style. A sweatshirt, for example, is a distinctive style, but within that style, variations may include different types of necklines, pockets, and sleeves. Another example is a satchel handbag, which may be interpreted with different closures, locks, or handles. These minor variations are the different interpretations that change the design of a style.

In the fashion industries, manufacturers and retailers assign a number to each individual design produced. This is the style number. The **style number** of a product identifies it for manufacturing, ordering, and selling purposes. In this instance, the term *style number* is used rather than *design number*, even though a design is being identified.

Taste

In fashion, **taste** refers to prevailing opinion of what is and what is not appropriate for a given occasion. Good taste in fashion, therefore, means sensitivity not only to what is artistically pleasing but also to what is appropriate for a specific situation. A style, such as an evening gown, may be beautiful. But if it is worn to a wedding breakfast, for example, it may not be considered in good taste.

While the time an individual fashion takes to complete this course may vary, the course is always a cyclical one. A new style is often considered daring and in dubious taste (see Figure 1.3). It is gradually accepted, then widely accepted, and finally gradually discarded.

Figure 1.3 Madonna's costumes for the 1987 "Who's That Girl Tour" sparked a long-lived 'underwear as outerwear' fad.

OUT-OF-THIS-WORLD: Designs of Iris van Herpen

Forget leaves, trees, or flowers for fashion inspiration. For Danish designer Iris van Herpen, that's just too earthly. Inspiration for her fantastical, whimsical designs comes from the extraterrestrial.

In her studio in Amsterdam, using somewhat traditional methods of sewing and construction, van Herpen takes unlikely materials to create her pieces. Ultra-light synthetic silks, bio-fabricated leather grown from cow cells, 3-D printed textiles, and textiles that shift in color and shape when exposed to varying temperatures are examples of the type of materials she likes to work with. She collaborates with architects, sources materials from military resources, and pays frequent visits to the European Organization for Nuclear Research.

"For me," van Herpen explains, "technology is not an inspiration and it's not a goal, it's just a tool." In a gadget-driven marketplace filled with "wearable technology" like smart watches, smart glasses, fitness-tracking gadgets, and more, van Herpen looks at the combination of clothing and technology in a new way. Rather than using technology in the more utilitarian way of creating clothing that multitasks for the wearer, she looks at using technology in creating and innovating fabrics. "I think the biggest potential is in the materials. I really think materials can revolutionize fashion in the future," she explains.

Luminous burn marks on metallic-embedded fabrics, shoes made from crystal collages, 3-D woven fabrics that look like celestial honeycombs—her creations take on shapes and silhouettes that abstract the human form. They are at once innovative, sculptural, elegant, and out of this world.

Haute Couture Collection 2020.

Iris van Herpen.

Crystal clog shoes designed by van Herpen.

Burned metallic fabric, one example of van Herpen's experimentation.

For many decades, Laver's cycle (see "The Fashion Cycle," p. 10) has been accepted as the movement of most fashions. However, in the past few decades some fashions have deviated from this pattern. The fashion cycles have become shorter and have repeated themselves within a shorter space of time. For the student of fashion, this presents an interesting challenge. What factors determine which fashions will follow the accepted cycles and which fashions will not? To understand the movement of fashion, it is important to understand that fashions are always in harmony with the times in which they appear.

Classic

A **classic** is a style or design that satisfies a basic need and remains in general fashion acceptance for an extended period of time. Classics are exceptions to the usual movement of styles through the fashion life cycle.

Depending upon the intended fashion statement, a person may have only a few classics or a wardrobe of mostly classics. A classic is characterized by a simple design that keeps it from being easily dated. The Chanel suit is an outstanding example of a classic because its simple lines have made it acceptable for many decades. Although it reappears now and then as a fashion, many women always have a Chanel suit in their wardrobes. In Figures 1.4a and 1.4b, the iconic Chanel suit is the centerpiece of the show. Other examples of classics

are denim jeans, blazer jackets, cardigan or turtleneck sweaters, button-down oxford shirts, and T-shirts. Among accessories, the pump-style shoe, the loafer, the one-button glove, the pearl necklace, and the clutch handbag are also classics. For young children, overalls and one-piece pajamas have become classics.

Fad

A fashion that suddenly sweeps into popularity, affects a limited part of the total population, and then quickly disappears is called a **fad**. It comes into existence by the introduction of some feature or detail, usually exaggerated to excite the interest of the customer. The fad starts by being quickly accepted and then imitated by others. Fads often begin in lower price ranges, are relatively easy to copy, and therefore flood the market in a very short time. Because of this kind of market saturation, the public tires of fads quickly, and they end abruptly.

Fads follow the same cycle as do fashions, but their rise in popularity is much faster, their acceptance much shorter, and their decline much more rapid than that of a true fashion. Because most fads come and go in a single season, they have been called "miniature fashions." In recent decades we have had the "punk" multicolored hair favored by certain pop stars, the "King Tut" design fad, the "Urban Cowboy" fad, and the "grunge" fad. Fads, like fashions, invade every field: sports, literature, religion, politics, and education.

Figure 1.4a A massive Chanel coat dwarfs models at the brand's Spring 2008 Haute Couture show at the Grand Palais in Paris.

Figure 1.4b A model poses at the hem of the show's iconic set piece.

Trend

A **trend** is a general direction or movement. For example, you will often read in fashion magazines that "there is a trend toward longer skirts"; it means that several designers, including some leading ones, are showing longer skirts, important retailers are buying them, and fashion-forward customers are wearing them. It is often difficult to tell a trend from a fad; even the experts get caught. However, marketers always want to know whether a new development is going to be a trend or a fad because they want to cash in on trends but avoid getting burned by fads.

Components of Fashion Design

Fashion design does not just happen, nor does the designer wave a magic wand to create a new design. Fashion design involves the combination of four basic elements or components: silhouette, detail, texture, and color. Only through a change in one or more of these basic components does a new fashion evolve.

Silhouette

The **silhouette** of a costume is its overall outline or contour. It is also frequently referred to as *shape* or *form*.

It may appear to the casual observer that women have worn countless silhouettes throughout the centuries. In the 1930s, Agnes Brooke Young's research showed that there are actually only three basic forms—bell-shaped, or bouffant; bustle, or back fullness; straight, or tubular—with many variations.[3] Today, most fashion experts include four variations on the tubular silhouette: slim, rectangle, wedge, and A-line (see Figure 1.5).

Details

The individual elements that give a silhouette its form or shape are called **details**. These include trimmings; skirt and pant length and width; and shoulder, waist, and sleeve treatment.

Silhouettes evolve gradually from one to another through changes in detail. When the trend in a detail reaches an extreme, a reversal of the trend takes place. For example, dresses and suits featured wide shoulders with much padding in the 1940s and 1950s. This was reversed in the late 1960s and 1970s, when the look became casual and unstructured. This casualness reached such extremes that by the start of the 1980s, structured clothing was back in fashion and dress and suit shoulders began once again to grow wider as padding was inserted. By the 1990s, the unstructured look was predominant again, and entering the 2000s, structured suits and wide shoulders were back on the runways.

Figure 1.5 Silhouettes are categorized as belonging to one of three basic groups (from left to right): (1) bell-shaped, or bouffant; (2) bustle, or back fullness; and (3) straight, or tubular. Variations of the straight silhouette are (4) slim, (5) rectangular, (6) wedge, and (7) A-line.

Texture

One of the most significant components of fashion is texture. **Texture** is the look and feel of material, woven or nonwoven.

Texture can affect the appearance of a silhouette, giving it a bulky or slender look, depending on the roughness or smoothness of the materials. A woman dressed in a rough tweed dress and a bulky knit sweater is likely to look larger and squarer than she does in the same dress executed in a smooth jersey and topped with a cashmere sweater.

Texture influences the drape of a garment. Chiffon clings and flows, making it a good choice for soft, feminine styles, while corduroy has the firmness and bulk suitable for more casual garments.

Texture affects the color of a fabric by causing the surface to either reflect or absorb light. Rough textures absorb light, causing the colors to appear flat. Smooth textures reflect light, causing colors to appear brighter. Anyone who has tried to match colors soon discovers that a color that appears extremely bright in a shiny vinyl, satin, or high-gloss enamel paint seems subdued in a rough wool, suede, or stucco wall finish.

Color

Color has always been a major consideration in women's clothing. Since World War II, color in men's clothing has been regaining the importance it had in previous centuries. Today, color is a key factor in apparel selection for both genders. Color is important in advertising, packaging, and store decor as well.

Historically, colors have been used to denote rank and profession. Purple, for instance, was associated with royalty, and in some periods, could be worn only by those of noble birth. Black became customary for the apparel of the clergy and for members of the judiciary.

Today, a fashion designer's color palette changes with consumers' preferences. In some seasons, all is brightness and sharp contrast, and no color is too powerful to be worn. In other seasons, only subdued colors appeal. Fashion merchants must develop an eye for color—not only for the specific hues and values popular in a given season but also for indications of possible trends in consumer preference.

Color forecasting services and organizations such as Pantone or the Color Marketing Group are essential to

Figure 1.6 Color palettes are updated seasonally to reflect current fashion trends.

the industry. (See page 99 to learn more about the Color Marketing Group and the color forecasting process.) They not only provide systems for consistent color communication between the different parts of the fashion development and marketing process, but they also help forecast key colors for each season. Figure 1.6 shows the Pantone palette for Spring 2016.

The Fashion Cycle

All fashions move in cycles. The term **fashion cycle** refers to the rise, wide popularity, and subsequent decline in acceptance of a style. The word *cycle* suggests a circle. However, the fashion cycle is represented by a bell-shaped curve.

Some authorities compare the fashion cycle with a wave, which shows first a slow swell, then a crest, and finally a swift fall. As with the movement of a wave, the movement of a fashion is always forward, never backward. As with waves, fashion cycles do not follow one another in regular, measured order. Some take a short time to crest, while others take a long time. The length of the cycle from swell to fall may be long or short. And, again like waves, fashion cycles overlap.

Stages of the Fashion Cycle

Fashion cycles are not haphazard; they don't "just happen." There are definite stages in a style's development that are easily recognized. These stages can be charted and traced, and in the short run, accurately predicted. Being able to recognize and predict the different stages

THE FASHION CYCLE

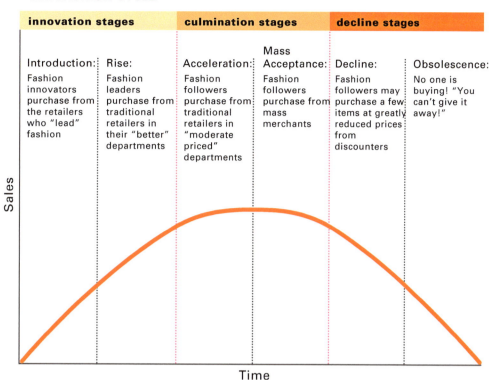

innovation stages		culmination stages		decline stages	
Introduction: Fashion innovators purchase from the retailers who "lead" fashion	**Rise:** Fashion leaders purchase from traditional retailers in their "better" departments	**Acceleration:** Fashion followers purchase from traditional retailers in "moderate priced" departments	**Mass Acceptance:** Fashion followers purchase from mass merchants	**Decline:** Fashion followers may purchase a few items at greatly reduced prices from discounters	**Obsolescence:** No one is buying! "You can't give it away!"

Figure 1.7 The basic life cycle of fashion can be represented by a bell-shaped curve.

is vital to success in the designer's buying and selling of fashion.

Every fashion cycle passes through five stages: (1) introduction, (2) rise, (3) culmination, (4) decline, and (5) obsolescence. Figure 1.7 illustrates these five phases of the fashion cycle.

The fashion cycle serves as an important guide for fashion merchandising. Fashion merchants use the fashion cycle concept to introduce new fashion goods, to chart their rise and culmination, and to recognize their decline and obsolescence.

Introduction Stage

The next new fashion may be introduced by a producer in the form of a new style, color, or texture. The new style may be a flared pant leg when slim legs are popular; vibrant colors when earth tones are popular; or slim, body-hugging fabrics such as knit jersey when heavy-textured, bulky looks are being worn.

New styles are almost always introduced in higher-priced merchandise. They are produced in small quantities because retail fashion buyers purchase a limited number of pieces to test the new styles' appeal to targeted

customers. This testing period comes at the beginning of the buying cycle of fashion merchandise, which coincides with the introduction stage of the fashion cycle. The test period ends when the new style either begins its rise or has been rejected by the target customer. Because there can be many risks, new styles must be priced high enough so that those that succeed can cover the losses on those that do not succeed. Promotional activities, such as designer appearances, institutional advertising, and charity fashion shows, all of which appeal to the fashion leaders of the community and also enhance a store's fashion image, take place at this point.

Rise Stage

When the new original design (or its adaptations) is accepted by an increasing number of customers, it is considered to be in its **rise stage**. At this stage, the buyer reorders in quantity for maximum stock coverage.

During the rise stage of a new original design, many retailers will offer line-for-line copies—or **knockoffs**, as they are referred to in the fashion industry. These are versions of the original designer style duplicated by manufacturers. These copies look exactly like the original except that they have been mass-produced in less expensive fabrics. Because production of the merchandise is now on a larger scale, knockoff prices are generally lower.

As a new style continues to be accepted by more and more customers, adaptations appear. **Adaptations** are designs that have all the dominant features of the style that inspired them but do not claim to be exact copies. Modifications have been made, but distinguishing features of the original, such as a special shoulder treatment or the use of textured fabric, may be retained in the adaptation. At this stage, the promotion effort focuses on regular price lines, full assortments, and product type ads to persuade the customer of the store's superiority in meeting his or her fashion needs.

Culmination Stage

The **culmination stage** of the fashion cycle is the period when a fashion is at the height of its popularity and use. At this stage, the fashion is in such demand that it can be mass-produced, mass-distributed, and sold at prices within the range of most customers. This stage may be long or brief, depending on how extended the peak of popularity is. The culmination stage of a fashion may be extended in the following two ways:

> If a fashion becomes accepted as a classic, it settles into a fairly steady sales pattern. An example of this is the cardigan sweater, an annual steady seller.
>
> If new details of design, color, or texture are continually introduced, interest in the fashion may be kept alive longer. Shoulder-strap handbags are a perfect example. Another example is the continued fashion interest in running shoes, fostered by new colors, designs, and comfort innovations.

Decline Stage

When boredom with a fashion sets in, the result is a decrease in consumer demand for that fashion. This is known as the **decline stage**. It is a principle of fashion that all fashions end in excess.

As a fashion starts to decline, consumers may still be wearing it, but they are no longer willing to buy it at its regular price. The outstanding fashion merchandiser is able to recognize the end of the culmination stage and start markdowns early. At this point, production stops immediately or comes slowly to a halt. The leading fashion stores abandon the style; traditional stores take a moderate markdown and advertise the price reduction. This will probably be followed in a short while by a major price-slash clearance or closeout. At this stage, the style may be found in bargain stores at prices far below what the style commanded in earlier stages.

Obsolescence Stage

When total lack of interest for a style has set in and it can no longer be sold at any price, the fashion is in its **obsolescence stage**. At this stage, the style can be found only in thrift shops, garage sales, or flea markets.

Lengths of Cycles

Predicting the time span of a fashion cycle is impossible because each fashion moves at its own speed. However, one guideline can be counted on. Declines are fast, and a drop to obsolescence is almost always steeper than a rise to culmination. At this point, as they say in merchandising: "You can't give it away." Figure 1.8 illustrates various cycle lengths in fashion products.

VARIATIONS IN THE FASHION CYCLE

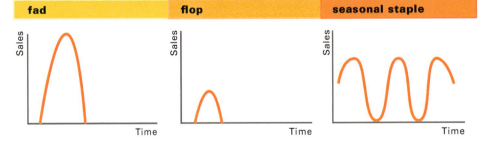

Figure 1.8 Variations can occur in the height to which a fashion rises at its peak and the length of time it takes to get to that point and then to decline in popularity.

JUDI DAWAINIS: Patternmaker and Historian

MEET JUDI DAWAINIS, PATTERNMAKER AND HISTORIAN. Dawainis's skill as a patternmaker has taken her through a fascinating career journey, including the theater, mass-production manufacturing, and ultimately historic research. Dawainis earned her BS and MS in clothing and textiles in apparel design from Southern Illinois University.

Dawainis began her career in theater design, working as a cutter/tailor (patternmaker) and draper in a series of costume shops for various professional and academic theaters across the country. She interpreted the designer's sketch, translating it into a pattern that can be cut and then sewn by a sewing operator. Most costumes are one of a kind. Knowledge of costume history, flat pattern making, draping, sewing, tailoring, and custom fitting are necessary skills. A sense of urgency to meet deadlines is essential, as well as the willingness to work long hours in a very creative environment.

After about ten years working in the theater, Dawainis transitioned to industry, where she worked for thirteen years as a production patternmaker for women's and girls' clothing before becoming a patternmaker/technical designer for Levi Strauss & Company. In industry there are two types of patternmakers: first and production. Working from a sketch or garment, first patternmakers create the pattern for samples. These patterns emphasize "hanger appeal," as the fit has not yet been perfected. This position is ideal for new graduates as they build their skills. Production patternmakers start with the first pattern and adjust it to fit the model selected to represent the company's target consumer. This position requires knowledge of grading, marking, cutting, costing, and sewing. The accuracy of the production pattern affects fabric utilization and sewing efficiency, directly affecting profitability. And in the denim category, fiber content and finish affect shrinkage and fit significantly, requiring a variety of pattern and construction variations depending on the fabric used. Pattern work in major companies is made on a computer, while smaller companies may still make it manually. To learn and help solve specific manufacturing challenges, Dawainis's job occasionally required travel to domestic and international factories.

With offshore manufacturing, the patternmaker role may be called technical designer (TD). This process begins with the initial sketch and detailed specifications, or a "tech pack." From this, contractors develop prototypes. Samples are evaluated to ensure design, fit, construction, and safety requirements are met. In this process, the TD needs to have the same skills as a patternmaker. But instead of doing the pattern work themselves, they must be able to direct someone else, often thousands of miles away, to make adjustments. For this, excellent written communication skills are essential, and diplomacy is helpful in navigating through different cultures.

The problem of finding a great-fitting pair of jeans is as old as the blue jean itself, especially for women. To help solve this problem, Dawainis worked on a special global development team for Levi Strauss & Company, studying scanned body measurements from over 60,000 women around the world. Using this data, different global body types of women were established and then new fits were developed for each body type. Dawainis traveled to test the new products on women in Tokyo, Shanghai, Hong Kong, and Bangalore, India. Interpreting real data into a series of new fits, seeing these through the production process, and watching the success of these efforts on people around the world was a true career highlight! The Levi Strauss & Company 150th anniversary "Celebration Jean" was also one of Dawainis's projects. Based on her copy of one of the oldest pairs of jeans in the Levi Strauss & Company archives, her pattern was put into a limited production of 501 pairs, selling for $501 each.

Now retired, Dawainis has switched her career focus to historic garment research. Theatrical costume design required research of the cut and construction of the costume time period. Dawainis found that while there were plenty of good resources for women's fashion, good resources for patterning period menswear were scarce. Her master's degree became the vehicle for increasing the resources for men's period costumes; she used her thesis as an opportunity to create a collection of patterns for men's clothing worn in America from 1850 to 1900. Dawainis plans to build on this research and publish a book on nineteenth-century men's patterns and construction.

The speed with which products move through their cycles is becoming faster and faster. Rapid technological developments and "instant" communications have much to do with this speedup, as do fast-changing environmental factors. The result is an intense competition among manufacturers and retailers to provide consumers with what they want and expect—constantly changing assortments from which to choose.

Consumers either give a new style enough acceptance to get it started or they immediately reject it. Because more new fashions are always ready to push existing ones out of the way, it is no wonder that with each passing year, the time required for a fashion to complete its cycle becomes shorter and shorter.

Studies recognize the importance of assortment rotation, universally called **fast fashion**. This strategy of keeping fashion fresh, as if it were a perishable good, has been successful for many retailers, including Zara, H&M, and Uniqlo. For any retailer with variety-seeking customers, some degree of fast fashion is important, and it allows retailers to develop ways to officially manage variety. [4]

Breaks in the Cycle

In fashion, as in everything else, there are always ups and downs, stops and starts. The normal flow of a fashion cycle can be broken or abruptly interrupted by outside influences. The influence can be as simple as unpredictable weather or a change in group acceptance. Or it can be much more dramatic and far reaching—war, worldwide economic depression, or a natural disaster, for example.

Although no formal studies have been made of the phenomenon of the broken cycle, manufacturers and merchants have a theory about it. They believe that a broken cycle usually picks up where it has stopped once conditions return to normal or once the season that was cut short reopens. Widespread economic depressions also temporarily interrupt the normal progress of a fashion cycle. When there is widespread unemployment, fashion moves much more slowly, resuming its pace only with economic recovery and growth.

Wars also affect fashion. They cause shortages that force designers, manufacturers, retailers, and consumers to change fashions less freely or to restrict styles. People redirect their interests, and fashion must take a back seat.

Consumer Buying and the Fashion Cycle

Every fashion has both a consumer buying cycle and a consumer use cycle. The curve of the consumer buying cycle rises in direct relation to that of the consumer use cycle. But when the fashion reaches its peak, consumer buying tends to decline more rapidly than consumer use. Different segments of society respond to and tire of a fashion at different times. So different groups of consumers continue to wear fashions for varying lengths of time after they have ceased buying them. While each group is using and enjoying a fashion, the producers and retailers serving that group are already abandoning the style and marketing something newer. Their efforts in this direction are most profitable when they anticipate, rather than follow, the trend of consumer demand. Figure 1.9 illustrates the relationship between the consumer buying cycle and the consumer use cycle. Consumer buying is often halted prematurely. This happens because producers and sellers no longer wish to risk making and stocking an item they believe will soon decline in popularity. Instead, they concentrate their resources on new items with better prospects for longevity. This procedure is familiar to anyone who has tried to buy summer clothes in late August or skiwear in March.

The Intangibles of Fashion

Fashion itself is intangible. A style is tangible, made up of a definite silhouette and details of design. But fashion is shaped by such powerful intangibles as group acceptance, change, the social forces important during a certain era, and people's desire to relate to specific lifestyles.

Group Acceptance

The fig leaf, the first fashion creation, was widely accepted, and we have since come a long way. Basically, fashion is acceptance: group acceptance or approval is implied in any definition of fashion. Most people have a great wish to express themselves as individuals, but they also want to be part of a group and belong. However, acceptance need not be universal. A style may be adopted by one group while other segments of the population ignore it.

CONSUMER BUYING CYCLE VERSUS CONSUMER USE CYCLE

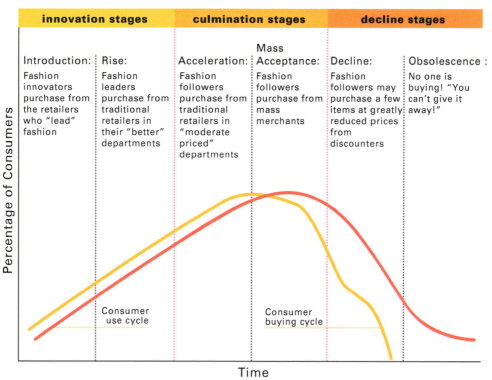

innovation stages		culmination stages		decline stages	
Introduction: Fashion innovators purchase from the retailers who "lead" fashion	**Rise:** Fashion leaders purchase from traditional retailers in their "better" departments	**Acceleration:** Fashion followers purchase from traditional retailers in "moderate priced" departments	**Mass Acceptance:** Fashion followers purchase from mass merchants	**Decline:** Fashion followers may purchase a few items at greatly reduced prices from discounters	**Obsolescence:** No one is buying! "You can't give it away!"

Percentage of Consumers

Consumer use cycle

Consumer buying cycle

Time

Figure 1.9 Consumer use of a fashion product follows a cycle similar to the buying cycle; however, the use cycle begins after the buying cycle and endures beyond the buying cycle's decline and obsolescence stages.

The way we dress is a personal signature. The dress or suit we wear is not just a confirmation of the old adage that "clothes make the man . . . or the woman," but rather an example of the fact that our need for acceptance is expressed largely in the way we dress. Acceptance also means that a fashion is considered appropriate to the occasion for which it is worn. Clothes considered appropriate for big-business boardrooms would not be considered acceptable for casual weekends.

If any of you should doubt the power of acceptance in fashion, try a simple experiment. Put on clothes that were worn ten or twenty years ago by family members or friends or that are totally different in style from what is considered the fashion. Then go out casually among your friends, acquaintances, or even strangers, and note their reactions toward you and then your feelings toward yourself. There will be quizzical looks, doubtful stares, and in some cases smirks and laughter. No one can really "belong" to a chosen group and at the same time choose to be completely "out" of present-day fashion. Such is the power of fashion acceptance.

Change

Fashion changes because ideas about politics, religion, leisure, democracy, success, and age change. This is particularly true when the society is no longer able to provide identity and maintain social order through custom or tradition. In the United States and across the globe, fashion is one means of providing a social bond.

Fashion is subject to change—both rapid and gradual. Modern communications play a major role in today's accelerated rate of fashion change. The mass media spreads fashion news across the face of the globe in hours, sometimes seconds. Even slight fashion changes are given faster and wider publicity than ever before. Fashion coverage of events around the world enables us to see not only what people are doing but also what they are wearing. Our morning newspapers, television shows, blogs, and websites show us what fashion leaders wore to a party the night before. Today, we even know what they are wearing at the moment with live postings via Twitter, Instagram, Facebook, and other social media networks.

LEVI'S: They Can Take a Little Dirt

You invent the blue jean. You maintain market leadership for over 140 years. The garment has become the universal symbol of youth and freedom. The brand is iconic.

So, how do you keep improving, especially in a world of fast fashion and fickle trends?

It's not easy, but innovation and social responsibility have been priorities in recent years for the denim giant. "How you make the garment is just as important as the garment itself," according to Michael Kobori, vice president of social and environmental sustainability for Levi Strauss.

For twenty years, Levi's has integrated sustainability and responsibility in a wide platform of initiatives, including workplace well-being, product innovation and design, how products are made, and work toward lowering the carbon footprint of manufacturing facilities. Some initiatives have worked better than others. For example, based on the belief that consumers would pay more for sustainable products, Levi's replaced

the iconic red label with the "green tag" on a line of eco-jeans, using fabric that was good for the planet but did not live up to consumer expectations of style or durability—and they didn't sell. Instead of paying a premium price for sustainable goods, consumers answered back loud and clear: they expect sustainability at the core of the product and at the center of how a global brand functions, not a sideline venture.

With refocus and assessment, Levi's learned that water is at the center of its business. It is a crucial resource in how cotton is grown, how the product is produced, and how the garment is cleaned and maintained by the consumer. So, the company addressed and improved water-consumption levels at every stage of the product cycle.

Levi's started by joining the Better Cotton Initiative, which helps reduce water and chemical use in cotton growth and production. Better Cotton has reduced water consumption significantly and increased profits for participating farmers. Better Cotton

currently accounts for about 9 percent of the world cotton supply.

Through manufacturing modifications named Water<Less, Levi's has reduced water usage by more than 2 billion liters since 2011. Through the "Care Tag for Our Consumer," Levi's stands to make an enormous impact in sustainability. And it's in the hands of the consumer. By washing jeans less—once every ten times the jeans are worn—washing in cold water, and line drying, water use for product care can be decreased by 77 percent and total energy use for the care of the product is reduced by 64 percent.

Doubling down on fast fashion trends of recent years, Levi's stands by its principle of making durable products that last. And they are building on that iconic status through promoting the resale of denim through their Authorized Vintage line. This program takes used Levi's denim clothing from consumers and resells it, getting twice the use and life out of a product without consuming any additional resources.

Levi's jeans, an iconic brand in the twenty-first century.

A promotional party for the new Water Levi's iconic double-stitch and red tag.

The pocket stitching is one of the oldest trademarks.

Another change that is affecting today's fashion world is that a growing number of environmentally conscious consumers are demanding eco-friendly products. The fashion industry is working hard to satisfy this need. With advances in technology, the industry is producing more "green," or sustainable, fibers and fabrics. Marketers are also affected by these changes and must rethink how to successfully target these types of consumers. According to a study from *Adweek*, researchers evaluated more than 200 million "green consumers" in the United States and separated these consumers into the following different groups:[5]

Alpha Ecos (43 million adults): Committed to green causes and saving the planet.

Eco-Centrics (34 million adults): Concerned about how environmental products benefit them personally.

Eco-Chics (57 million adults): Understand the cachet of being seen as "green." This younger generation uses social networking to show others just how green they are.

Economically Ecos (53 million adults): Less concerned about saving the planet—more concerned about saving money.

Eco-Moms (33 million moms of children under eighteen): Interested in cost-effective, socially responsible practices and products with an emphasis on kids.

With any fashion industry change, when consumers like what they see, they demand it from merchants, who in turn demand it from manufacturers.

The Futility of Forcing Change

Fashion expresses the spirit of the times, and in turn influences it. Fashion designers are successful or not, depending on their abilities to sense and anticipate changes—if not to initiate them. Changes can be initiated, but there are as many examples of failures as there are of successful changes. Efforts have been made from time to time to force changes in the course of fashion, but they usually fail. Fashion is a potent force that by definition requires support from the majority.

In the late 1980s, designers and retailers tried to repeat the 1960s with a change to very short skirts. The public disliked the radical change and refused to buy miniskirts when they were first introduced—as they did in the '60s. Today, however, women are seen wearing both miniskirts and long skirts.

Meeting the Demand for Change

After World War II, a new French designer, Christian Dior, caught and expressed the desire for a freer line and a more feminine garment in his first collection, which achieved instant fashion success. Using fabric with a lavishness that had been impossible in Europe or the United States during the war years, he created his "new look," with long, full skirts, fitted waistlines, and feminine curves.

Dior did not change the course of fashion; he quickened it—from a slow evolutionary course to a revolutionary one. He recognized and interpreted the need of women at that time to get out of stiff, short, narrow, unfeminine clothes and into soft, free, longer, feminine ones. Consumers wanted the change, and the lifting of the very limiting wartime restrictions made it possible to meet their demands.

A Mirror of the Times

Fashion is a nonverbal symbol. A study of the past and careful observation of the present make it apparent that fashions are social expressions that document the tastes and values of an era (see Figures 1.10 and 1.11), just as

Figure 1.10 The cast of *Seinfeld*, dressed at the height of 1990s fashion.

Figure 1.11 Reality TV stars Chip and Joanna Gaines, with relaxed, upscale style, provide a time-stamped picture of notable fashion trends and styles in the early twenty-first century.

the paintings, sculpture, and architecture of the times do. The extreme modesty of the Victorian era was reflected in bulky and concealing fashions. The sexual emancipation of the flappers in the 1920s was expressed in their flattened figures, short skirts, "sheer" hosiery (the first time the bare leg was exposed), and short hair. The ethnic influences and individualistic fashions of the 2010s are a true reflection of the current freedom of expression and lifestyle.

Social Class

Fashions mirror the times by reflecting the degree of rigidity in the class structure of an era. Although such ideas are difficult to imagine today, throughout much of history certain fashions were restricted to the members of specific defined social classes. In some early eras, royal declarations regulated both the type of apparel that could be worn by each group of citizens and how ornate it could

be. Class distinctions were thus emphasized. Certain fashions have also been used as indications of high social standing and material success. During the nineteenth century, the constricted waists of Western women and the bound feet of high-caste Chinese women were silent but obvious evidence that the male head of the household was wealthy.

Today, social classes are far more fluid and mobile than ever before. Because there is no universal way of life today, people are free to choose their own values and lifestyles—and their dress reflects that choice. Many fashions exist simultaneously, and we are all free to adopt the fashions of any social group. If we do not wish to join others in their fashion choices, we can create our own modes and standards of dress. The beatniks of the 1950s and the hippies of the 1960s had their typical fashions (see Figure 1.12), as did the bohemians of the 1920s and the liberated groups of the 1970s. In the 1980s, the punk rockers existed side by side with the yuppies. In

Figure 1.12 A modern homage celebrates the fortieth anniversary of hippie fashions from the late 1960s.

the 1990s, hip-hop fashion coexisted with Ralph Lauren's Polo Sport. In the 2000s, vintage has found a home alongside celebrity glamour.

Lifestyle

Fashions also mirror the times by reflecting the activities in which the people of an era participate. The importance of court-centered social activities in seventeenth- and eighteenth-century Europe was evident in men's and women's ornately styled apparel. Fashions became less colorful and more functional when a new working class was created by the Industrial Revolution.

Currently, our clothes vary according to lifestyle. More casual and active sportswear in wardrobes reflects our interest in active sports and leisure pastimes. The difference in the lifestyle of an urban, career-oriented woman and that of a suburban housewife is reflected in their choice of wardrobes.

Principles of Fashion

Diversification of fashion has added new dimensions to the interpretation of the principles of fashion. While the intangibles of fashion can be vague and sometimes difficult to predict and chart, certain fundamental principles of fashion are tangible and precise. For many decades these principles served as the solid foundation for fashion identification and forecasting. They still do, but today's student of fashion must recognize that in the current vibrant and changing atmosphere, the application of these principles becomes a more intricate and challenging task.

The five principles we will discuss are the foundations upon which the study of fashion is based.

1. **Consumers establish fashions by accepting or rejecting the styles offered**. The popular belief that designers create artistic designs with little regard for the acceptance of these designs by the public is quite false. No designer can be successful without the support and acceptance of the customer.

   A customer is a patron or potential purchaser of goods or services. Thus, a retail store's dress buyer is a customer of a dress manufacturer, and the dress manufacturer is a customer of a fabric producer. The consumer is the ultimate user: the person who uses the finished fashion garment.

Designers create hundreds of new styles each season, based on what they think may attract customers. From among those many styles, manufacturers choose what they think will be successful. They reject many more than they select. From the manufacturers' offerings, retailers choose styles they believe their customers will want. Consumers then make the vital choice. By accepting some styles and rejecting others, they—and only they—dictate what styles will become fashions.

2. **Fashions are not based on price. Just because something is expensive does not mean it will be successful**. Although new styles that may eventually become fashions are often introduced at high prices, this is happening less and less. What you pay for an item of apparel is not an indication of whether the item is considered fashionable.

   In the fashion diversity offered to consumers today, successful fashions are to be found at every price level. Upper-income consumers will accept fashions at very low prices, and consumers at the opposite end of the income scale will often splurge and buy a very expensive item—if it is in fashion.

3. **Fashions are evolutionary in nature; they are rarely revolutionary**. In these days of rapid cultural and national revolutions, it is hard to believe that a worldwide phenomenon such as fashion is evolutionary in nature—not revolutionary. To the casual observer, it appears as though fashion changes suddenly. Actually, fashion change comes about as a result of gradual movements from one season to the next.

   Throughout history, there have probably been only two real revolutions in fashion styles. One occurred during the twentieth century: the Dior "New Look" of 1947. The other was the abrupt change of styles brought about by the French Revolution, when the fashion changed overnight from elaborate full skirts, low-cut daring bodices, and ornate and glamorous fabrics to simple, drab costumes, in keeping with the political and moral upheaval.

   Consumers buy apparel and accessories to supplement and update the wardrobes they already own, some of which they purchased last year, some the year before, some the year before that, and so on. In most cases, consumers will buy only if the purchase complements their existing wardrobe and does not depart too radically from last year's purchases.

4. **No amount of sales promotion can change the direction in which fashions are moving**. Promotional efforts on the part of producers or retailers cannot dictate what consumers will buy, nor can they force people to buy what they do not want. The few times that fashion merchants have tried to promote a radical change in fashion, they have not been successful.

Also, promotional efforts cannot renew the life of a fading fashion unless the extent of change gives the fashion an altogether new appeal. This is why stores have markdown or clearance sales. When the sales of a particular style start slumping, store managers know they must clear out as much of that stock as possible, even at much lower prices, to make room for newer styles in which consumers have indicated interest.

Figure 1.13 This Dior Spring 2011 couture dress proves the concept that all fashions end in excess!

5. **All fashions end in excess**. This saying is sometimes attributed to Paul Poiret, a top 1920s Parisian designer. Eighteenth-century hoopskirts ballooned out to more than eight feet in width, which made moving from room to room a complicated matter. The French tried to accommodate these skirts by designing doors that could be opened to a width far beyond that of regular doors. They became known as "French doors" and can still be found in architecture today. Similarly, miniskirts of the 1960s became so short that the slightest movement caused a major problem in modesty. This same trend toward excess can be found in men's wear. Just think of the growth of the width of a tie. It will start as a thin string tie and become wider and wider until it becomes as wide as a bib!

Once the extreme in styling has been reached, a fashion is nearing its end. The attraction of the fashion wanes, and people begin to seek a different look—a new fashion (see Figure 1.13).

Summary and Review

In its narrow sense, fashion is the prevailing way a group of people at a particular time and place dress themselves. The fashion industries, which manufacture the materials and finished products of clothing, also produce related goods, including cosmetics, fragrances, and home fashions. Fashion designers attempt to determine what styles—characteristic appearances of garments and other fashion items—will appeal to their target group of consumers. The designs that are offered to the public are versions of a style that are distinguished by their silhouettes, details, textures, and colors.

Public acceptance of a fashion follows a course called the fashion cycle, which includes the following stages: introduction, rise, culmination, decline, and obsolescence. A fashion that reaches the culmination stage and then declines over a brief period of time is called a fad. A classic, alternatively, may not necessarily reach its peak of popularity very quickly, but its decline is gradual, and it never reaches the obsolescence stage.

Any fashion evolves according to the demands of its market. Neither pricing nor promotion by the producers can force consumers to embrace a new fashion. Usually changes evolve gradually, building up to an extreme and then reversing and moving toward the other extreme. The success of fashion merchandisers depends on their abilities to predict the changing tastes of their public with scientific accuracy and to use their artistic creativity to satisfy those tastes.

FOR REVIEW

1. What group ultimately decides whether a style will be "fashionable" or not? Explain your answer.
2. Apparel styles are often named for the periods in history in which they were introduced. Name three such styles and the historic period in which they originated.
3. Give two examples of "classics" that are in style today for each of the following groups: (a) men, (b) women, and (c) children.
4. Distinguish among (a) style, fashion, and design, and between (b) a classic and a fad.
5. Fashions go through a five-stage life cycle. Name and explain each stage.
6. In what respects does the consumer buying cycle differ from the consumer use cycle? How is such information useful to fashion merchants?
7. Can designers, manufacturers, or retailers force unwanted fashion on consumers? Explain your answer.
8. What are the five basic principles relating to fashion? What are the implications for fashion merchants?

FOR DISCUSSION

The following statements are derived from the text. Discuss the significance of each, giving examples of how each applies to merchandising fashion goods.

1. Men today are as influenced by and responsive to fashion as women.
2. Predicting the time span of a fashion cycle is impossible because each fashion moves at its own speed.
3. Because there is no universal way of life, people are free to choose their own values and lifestyles.

Trade Talk

Define or briefly explain the following terms:

adaptation
classic
culmination stage
decline stage
design
details
fad
fashion
fashion business
fashion cycle
fashion industries
fast fashion
high fashion
knockoff
marketing
mass or volume fashion
merchandising
obsolescence stage
rise stage
silhouette
style
style number
taste
texture
trend

2

The Environment of Fashion

Key Concepts

- **The four major factors affecting fashion**

- **How research is used by fashion producers and retailers to help them with market segmentation**

- **The five basic psychological factors that motivate human behavior—and how each affects fashion**

A cardinal rule in any business is "know your customer." This rule is especially true in the fashion business. Accurate facts about customers that are properly interpreted help designers, manufacturers, and retailers make major decisions about what to offer those customers. Guesswork and misinterpreted facts can lead to major business failures.

To satisfy the greatest number of customers and make them want to buy their products, every designer, manufacturer, and retailer must know the answers to the following questions:

- How many potential customers for your products and services are there in a given community?
- How old are these customers?
- How much are they willing to spend on your product?
- What level of service do they expect?
- Are they married or single, homeowners or renters?
- How many children do they have?
- What kind of work do they do?
- What is their annual income?
- What is more important to the customer—value or style? Prestige or price?
- How much do they have available to spend on "extras"?
- Do they like to shop early or late in the day? Weekdays or weekends?
- What motivates them to shop in a particular store?
- How do they spend their leisure time?

In other words: who are your customers?

One major source of information about the consumer market is the US Census Bureau. The bureau produces more than 3 billion separate statistics about the American people and the conditions that affect their lives and influence their actions. It helps businesspeople who are interested in translating the data and projections drawn from them into new product and profit opportunities.

Collectively, the conditions under which we live are called our **environment**. Just as the environment of one nation or society differs from that of another nation or society, so the environment of one neighborhood differs from that of another. In fashion merchandising, it is important to be aware of the conditions that affect a particular customer's environment and to know how the environment differs from one group to another.

The following four major environmental factors affect fashion interest and demand:

1. Market segmentation by geographics, demographics, psychographics, and behavior
2. The degree of economic development and well-being of a country or society
3. The sociological characteristics of the class structure
4. The psychological attitudes of consumers

Market Segmentation

Both manufacturers and retailers try to identify and select target markets for their goods. **Target markets** are specific groups of potential customers that a business is attempting to turn into regular customers. Businesses try to determine who their customers are, what those customers want, how much the customers are willing to pay for goods, where potential customers are located, and how many targeted customers exist. Today, geographic, demographic, psychographic, and behavioral research studies are a vital part of determining these important factors.

Most manufacturers and designers are concerned with national trends. Retailers, however, must consider the impact of statistics in their local areas as well as statistics from national studies. **Market segmentation** is the separation of the total consumer market into smaller groups. These are known as market segments. By identifying and studying each market segment, producers and retailers can target their goods and services to their special markets. Markets are divided or segmented in four major ways: by geographics, demographics, psychographics, and behavior.

Geographics

Geographics are population studies that focus on where people live. These studies organize data by region of the country, by county or city size, by population density, and by climate.

Demographics

Demographics are popul ation studies that divide broad groups of consumers into smaller, more homogeneous market segments. The variables covered in a demographic study include the following:

- Age
- Gender

- Family size
- Stages in family life cycle
- Income
- Occupation
- Education
- Religion
- Race and ethnicity or nationality

Psychographics

Psychographics are studies that develop more extensive and personal portraits of potential customers and their lifestyles. Psychographic studies more fully predict consumer purchase patterns and distinguish users of a product. The variables covered in a psychographic study include social class, values and lifestyle, and personality. Sometimes researchers request information about the actual product benefits desired by consumers. These studies help greatly in matching the image of a company and its product with the type of consumer using the product.

Many research firms combine geographic and demographic studies for retailers and manufacturers. One such firm, the Nielsen Corporation, produces the PRIZM system, which divides and then clusters the population of the United States into sixty-two market segments, or "clusters," based on postal zip codes, housing, and lifestyle choices.

In order to reach and keep profitable customers, you must know what drives their purchasing decisions. PRIZM combines demographics, consumer behavior, and geographic data to help fashion industry marketers identify and understand their customers and prospects.[1]

PRIZM tells you what people buy, but not why. To get closer to that information, many people turn to another widely used research system that applies demographics and psychographics: the VALS 2 system, which stands for Values-Attitudes-Lifestyles-Segmentation. This sorts customers into eight major categories based on two key concepts for understanding consumer behavior:

- **Innovators**: on the leading edge of change. Have the highest income and gravitate to luxury goods and services.
- **Thinkers**: motivated by ideals. Mature, responsible, well-educated professionals. Activities center on their homes and families. Have high incomes but are practical consumers.

- **Achievers**: motivated by achievement. Successful, work-oriented people who get satisfaction from jobs and families. Favor established products and services that show success to their peers.
- **Experiencers**: motivated by self-expression. Youngest of all the segments, with a median age of about twenty-five. Significant energy; exercise; social activities. Spend heavily on clothes, fast food, music, with emphasis on new products and services.
- **Believers**: motivated by ideals. Conservative, predictable, and favor established brands. Lives centered on family, church, and community. Modest incomes.
- **Strivers**: motivated by achievements. Lower social, economic, and psychological resources. Strive to emulate people they admire.
- **Makers**: motivated by self-expression. Practical people who value self-sufficiency. Focused on family. Appreciate practical and functional products.
- **Survivors**: consumer group with the lowest income. Relatively few resources and tend to be among the oldest of all segments, with a median age of sixty-one. Brand-loyal consumers.

The categories are arranged into a framework that puts consumers with the most resources on the top and those with the fewest on the bottom. It also arranges consumers into three groups horizontally: principle-oriented, status-oriented, and action-oriented. This system of market segmentation was developed by Arnold Mitchell in 1978 and was quickly embraced by advertising and marketing agencies as a framework to better understand psychographic segments.[2]

Behavior

In an attempt to gather even more insight into customer preferences, some retailers and manufacturers use behavioral research. These studies group consumers according to their opinions of specific products or services or their actual rate of use of these products or services. Behavioral studies help companies understand and predict the behavior of present and potential customers. If you segment your market by behavior, you might be able to identify the reasons for one group's refusal to buy your product. Once you have identified the reason, you may be able to change the product enough to satisfy their objections. A more recent extension of VALS, GeoVALS, uses psychographics to identify where customers live and further explain their behavioral trends.

DONNA KARAN

Donna Karan remade fashion in her own image. Now she's working to change our ideas about death and healing, encompassing new approaches to health and wellness practices and introducing her Urban Zen Collection.

The year 2010 marked the twenty-fifth anniversary of Karan's fashion label, which she originally started "to design modern clothes for modern people." Her goal was to create the kind of clothes that she and her friends needed, and Karan's now-iconic system of "seven easy pieces" offers busy women a wardrobe that could be mixed and matched to go anywhere.

In her new direction, the uniting principle is Karan's conviction that nontraditional health and wellness practices can enhance the lives of everyone from schoolchildren to cancer patients, and she is working hard to extend such techniques to a range of disciplines.

Karan began her fashion career in the 1960s as an assistant designer at Anne Klein, eventually promoted to associate designer in 1971. Upon Anne Klein's death in 1974, the brand was bought by Takihyo Corporation of Japan, and Karan became head designer. She eventually left Anne Klein in 1984 and, together with her husband Stephan Weiss and the Takihyo Corporation, started her own label, Donna Karan New York, which was followed by DKNY, DKNY for Men, DKNY Active, and other DKNY lines. It was while juggling business and family that Karan also got involved with charitable causes. "My first true philanthropic passion was when the AIDS epidemic broke out," she says. "I thought, there is an emergency here; how do you bring a community together? You get the retailers, the manufacturers and designers, and the consumers—and now you have a movement."

Karan went to work with Elizabeth Glaser's Pediatric AIDS Foundation and cofounded the fashion industry's Seventh on Sale events and the annual Super Saturday ovarian cancer research fundraiser in the Hamptons, both of which she continues to support. Donna Karan's goals for her foundations are ambitious. "My three major passions are preserving culture, improving health and well-being, and empowering children," she says, "and I see Urban Zen [Foundation] as being about past, present, and future: the wisdom of cultures of the past; the health care of today; and education and children, which is the future. Urban Zen is a center

Donna Karan with 2018 Stephen Weiss Apple Award Honorees; Joel Towers, Donna Karan, Iman Bowie, and Jimmy Nelson.

Plenty of designers cite the environment as a seasonal inspiration, but for Donna Karan, the landscape has been an ongoing motif. She channeled an intense femininity into nature-inspired wares with sinuous shapes. Here, her crinkled satin twill jacket over a stretch silk bias-cut slip dress.

Urban Zen Initiative cofounders Donna Karan (L) and Sonja Nuttall at the Urban Zen store in New York City.

Urban Zen Presents The Alchemist Collection.

where we create, collaborate, and communicate change of the minds who want to be catalysts for change."

In order to devote more time to her Urban Zen line and its foundation, Karan stepped down from Donna Karan International in June 2015. Since then, Karan has expanded Urban Zen into a full lifestyle brand, including apparel, accessories, and home décor.

To commemorate her late husband and business partner, Stephen Weiss, the Urban Zen Foundation honors humanitarians from many industries and interests with the Stephen Weiss Apple Awards. In 2018, the foundation honored Cosmetics CEO and model, Iman Bowie; photographer Jimmy Nelson; and Executive Dean of Parsons School of Design, Joel Towers. Past honorees include Hillary Rodham Clinton and Nadja Swarovski, among others. Three distinguished humanitarians have been honored each year since the award's inception in 2011.

The Economic Environment

The growth of fashion demand depends on a high level of economic development, which is reflected in consumer income and population characteristics, including technological advances.

Consumer Income

Consumer income can be measured in terms of personal income, disposable personal income, and discretionary income. Many people use the amount of personal income as an indicator of "arriving" in their particular social set. The more personal income they have, the more socially acceptable they consider themselves to be. We will also discuss how the purchasing power of the dollar affects consumer income later in this chapter.

Personal Income

The total, or gross, income received by the population as a whole is called **personal income**. It consists of wages, salaries, interest, dividends, and all other income for everyone in the country. Divide personal income by the number of people in the population and the result is **per capita personal income**.

Disposable Personal Income

The amount a person has left to spend or save after paying taxes is called **disposable personal income**. It is roughly equivalent to take-home pay and provides an approximation of the **purchasing power** of each consumer during any given year.

Disposable income per household and per capita varies according to age groups and gender. While household after-tax income starts to drop after age 49, individual after-tax income does not peak until ages 60 to 64, showing that consumers in the 50- to 64-year-old age bracket have the highest disposable income of any group.

Discretionary Income

The money that an individual or family can spend or save after buying necessities—food, clothing, shelter, and basic transportation—is called **discretionary income**. Of course, the distinction between "necessities" and "luxuries" or between "needs" and "wants" is a subjective one.

In the 2010 Annual Report of the White House Task Force on the Middle Class, various definitions, middle-class values, and aspirations were examined. The principle findings of the report are as follows:

> Middle-class families are defined by their aspirations more than their income. The report assumes that middle-class families aspire to home ownership, a car, a college education for their children, health and retirement security, and occasional family vacations. Families at a variety of income levels aspire to be middle class, and under certain circumstances can put together budgets that allow them to obtain all the items that are assumed to be part of a middle-class lifestyle.
>
> Estimates of a middle-class family budget for married-couple families with two school-age children range from about $51,000 to about $123,000.[3]

The lucky few are like consumer royalty, able to buy a wide variety of goods and services. Although marketers like to target these consumers, it may not be a wise long-term strategy. The super-rich have greater purchasing power, but they are declining in number. While middle-class households have less money, they still have overwhelming strength in numbers.

Purchasing Power of the Dollar

Even if the average income increases, it does not mean that people have an equivalent increase in purchasing power. The reason for this is that the value of the dollar—its purchasing power, or what it will buy—has steadily declined since 1950, which is illustrated in Figure 2.1.

A decline in the purchasing power of money is caused by inflation. *Webster's* defines inflation as a continuing rise in the general price level usually attributed to an increase in the volume of money and credit relative to available goods and services.[4] **Inflation**, therefore, is an economic situation in which demand exceeds supply. Scarcity of goods and services, in relation to demand, results in ever-increasing prices.

When income taxes increase, the purchasing power of the family income drops; a decrease in income taxes has the reverse effect. With an inflationary economy, the working time required to acquire the necessities of

PURCHASING POWER OF THE DOLLAR: 1950–2019

year	average*
1950	1.00
1960	1.23
1970	1.61
1980	3.42
1990	5.42
2000	7.15
2005	8.10
2010	9.05
2015	9.83
2019	10.65

*As measured by the Bureau of Labor Statistics consumer price index

Figure 2.1 According to the Bureau of Labor Statistics consumer price index, by 2019, prices were 965.39% higher than prices in 1950. In other words, what a consumer could buy for $1.00 in 1950 would cost about $10.65 in 2019.

life—basic food, clothing, transportation, and shelter—increases. The increase is not, however, uniform among all items.

A recession is one of several discrete phases in the overall business cycle. The beginning of a recession is known as a business cycle "peak," and the end of a recession is referred to as a business cycle "trough." The National Bureau of Economic Research (NBER) has a more precise definition:

> A **recession** is a significant decline in economic activity spread across the economy lasting more than a few months, normally visible in real GDP, real income, employment, industrial production, and wholesale retail sales. A recession begins just after the economy reaches a peak of activity and ends as the economy reaches its trough. Between trough and peak, the economy is in an expansion.[5]

Both inflation and recession affect consumers' buying patterns. Fashion merchants in particular must thoroughly understand the effects of inflation and recession when planning their inventory assortments and promotional activities. Manufacturers must also understand how consumers are affected by economic factors.

Population

The majority of the population of the United States has some discretionary income and thus can influence the course of fashion. Two factors relating to population, however, have an important bearing on the extent of fashion demand:

The size of the total population and the rate of its growth

The age mix of the population and its projection into the future

Size of Population

The size of the population relates to the extent of current fashion demand. The rate of population growth suggests what tomorrow's market may become. In 1920, the United States had a population of about 106 million. By 1950, that figure had reached 151 million, and by 1980 it was 227.6 million. In 2019, the population reached 330.7 million. By 2030, the US population is estimated to reach 355.1 million, and by 2060, it is expected to reach 404.5 million.[6]

Age Mix

The age mix and its projection into the future affect the characteristics of current fashion demand and suggest what they may be in the future. While the overall population continues to grow, the growth rate is not the same for all age groups or for both genders, as illustrated in Figure 2.2. Since each group has its own special fashion interests, needs, and reactions, changes in the age mix serve as vital clues to future fashion demand.

Because both men and women are living longer, the group over age sixty-five is steadily growing. People who are fifty years old and older account for more than one half of all discretionary spending power. This mature group becomes increasingly important in the fashion world as their earlier retirement—and in many cases, increased retirement incomes—allows them to spend many active years wherever and however they choose. They are healthier, better educated, and more active, and they will live longer. Their interests and discretionary purchases vary radically from those of their younger counterparts, offering a real challenge to businesses to meet the demands of the "new old." The demand of older consumers for items such as package travel tours, cosmetic aids, and apparel that suits their ages and retirement lifestyles will offer growth opportunities for marketers, especially in fashion.

CALLY CARBONE
Director of Creative Development, *twelveNYC*

MEET CALLY CARBONE, DIRECTOR OF CREATIVE DEVELOPMENT FOR *TWELVENYC*. *twelveNYC* produces a variety of promotional merchandise to help a company support its message and communication its program. As a director of a creative development team, Carbone collaborates with client partners to source and develop promotional, marketing-related, or private-label merchandise that is relevant to the client's brand story. She leads creative product development, develops client relations, and oversees and reviews the logistic process for each product design.

Communication and organization skills are essential, along with the tenacity to work through various challenges in the product development process. Because of the logistics involved in this profession, attention to detail is crucial. And knowledge of product construction and materials is vital.

Carbone earned a Bachelor of Science in fashion marketing and management from Stephens College, and a Master of Arts in fashion studies from Parsons School of Design. The business aspect of her degree in marketing and management has proven essential. She is called upon to produce multiple spec sheets each week, and the knowledge gained from product development coursework was crucial in understanding the process. In addition to being responsible for creating the physical merchandise, she also must communicate pricing and understand costs and margins. Retail math at its finest! Her graduate work in fashion studies influenced her perspectives on the global fashion industry and the end consumer's relationship with a branded item.

In her professional world, no two days are alike, an aspect of her position that she appreciates. There are many typical daily activities, such as following up with overseas factories first thing in the morning because of the global time difference; reviewing samples that arrive from the sample room; checking samples against the spec sheet and client expectations; creating custom pitches for client project requests; communicating pricing, production timeline, and delivery information to clients; brainstorming ideas for client projects; and supporting team members in their projects or associated work to mutual projects. Sometimes she visits client offices or schedules phone meetings to pitch new project concepts or discuss current project needs.

Networking is essential. As a core business of *twelveNYC* is developing cosmetic bags for promotional items for a number of cosmetic companies, Carbone is a member of CEW—Cosmetic Executive Women.

Carbone's advice to students interested in a career in product development is this: "Diversify your knowledge base; it truly is a mix of creativity and business. Promotional and private label merchandise is a unique product category that is not focused on a specific category. For example, on a daily basis my focus can switch from a water bottle, to a cosmetic case, to a portable cell phone charger, to socks, to stickers, and that could be in the morning alone! Having a desire to learn many subjects is key in researching new product details and having the confidence to communicate those to clients."

Cally Carbone's desk space. Her inspiration board shows trends and details, and never far away is the trusty Pantone fan deck!

AGE AND GENDER DISTRIBUTION OF THE U.S. POPULATION

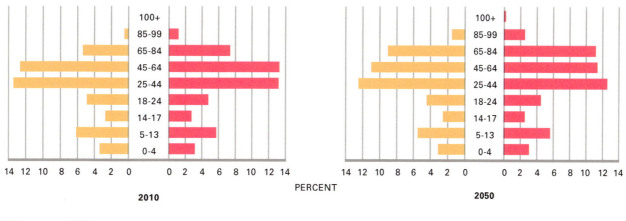

Male   Female

Figure 2.2 The aging of the population has several causes: healthier lifestyles and improved medical treatment have increased life expectancies, and with birthrates on the rise, there is a slow increase of the population in younger age groups.

The Sociological Environment

To understand fashion, one needs to understand the sociological environment in which fashion trends begin, grow, and fade away. Simply stated, changes in fashion are caused by changes in the attitudes of consumers, which in turn are influenced by changes in the social patterns of the times. The key sociological factors influencing fashion today are leisure time; ethnic influences; status of women; social and physical mobility; instant communications; and wars, disasters, and crises.

Leisure Time

One of the most precious possessions of the average US citizen today is leisure time, partly because it is also scarce. The demands of the workplace compete with the demands of family and home for much of people's waking hours, leaving less and less time for the pursuit of other activities, whether those activities be a fitness regimen, community work, entertainment, relaxation—or even shopping.

The ways in which people use their leisure time are as varied as people themselves. Some turn to active or spectator sports; others prefer to travel. Many seek self-improvement while growing numbers improve their standard of living with a second job. The increased importance of leisure time has brought changes to people's lives in many ways—in values, standards of living, and scope of activities. As a result, whole new markets have sprung up. Demand for larger and more versatile wardrobes for the many activities consumers can now explore and enjoy has mushroomed.

Casual Living

A look into the closets of the US population would probably reveal one feature that is much the same from coast to coast, in large cities and in small towns: most would contain an unusually large selection of casual clothes and sportswear. The market for casual apparel developed with the growth of the suburbs in the 1950s and led to "dress-down Fridays" at work in the 1990s. The choice as to what is suitable for an activity is still largely left to the individual, and into the 2000s and 2010s a shift in the direction of casual dress has begun a reverse trend as an interest in "dressing up" starts to grow again.

Active Sportswear

There is no doubt about it: the superstar of the fashion market in the 1970s, the 1980s, and the 1990s was sportswear. Its growth was phenomenal! While sports clothes have been around since the turn of the century, when they first appeared they were not particularly distinctive. Women's sport dresses for playing tennis or golf

Figure 2.3 Notice the modest dress exhibited by female tennis players of the 1930s.

Figure 2.4 Modern sportswear for women is much more body conscious, as seen in Belinda Benic's Nike ensemble.

were not much different from their regular streetwear, and men's outfits similarly varied little from business suits. By the 1920s, consumers began demanding apparel that was appropriate for active sports or simply for relaxing in the sunshine. But it is the emphasis on health and self in the past three decades that has caused the fantastic growth of the active sportswear market. Figures 2.3 and 2.4 show a comparison of early sportswear to more contemporary designs.

From 2000 through today, sports-minded people play tennis in specially designed tennis fashions. Golfers want special golf wear. Joggers want outfits only for jogging. And cyclists seem able to bike only in spandex biker shorts and high-tech helmets. Rollerbladers also want helmets, wrist and knee guards, and appropriate fashions. The same goes for ice skaters, skiers, runners, hang gliders, sky divers, yoga practitioners, and climbers. Health clubs, exercise classes, and workout gyms exploded in popularity in the 1980s, and a whole new and vast world of leotards, exercise suits, warm-up suits, and other self-improvement fashions and accessories was born. Whatever the activity, the specialized

fashions—from jogging suits to biker shorts—quickly followed and became *de rigueur*. Today, even those who do not participate in a particular sport beyond watching the pros on television feel the need to look the part!

Ethnic Influences

In recent years, minority groups in the United States, representing more than 30 percent of the nation's total population, have experienced vast population increases and sociological changes. The future holds even more change, as illustrated in Figure 2.5. In 2005, African Americans slipped from the largest minority group in the United States to the second largest. Hispanics now outnumber African Americans, and Asians continue to exhibit a rapid growth rate. This historic shift in the racial and ethnic composition of the US population will have many long-range implications. For example, the growth of the Hispanic and Asian populations has brought about an increased demand for clothing in smaller sizes because both men and women in these groups are typically smaller in stature than people whose ethnic heritage is Northern European.

U.S. POPULATION 1960 – 2050
SHARE OF TOTAL, BY RACIAL AND ETHNIC GROUPS

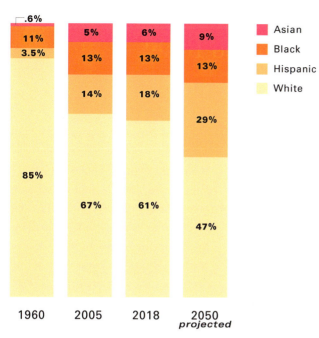

Legend:
- Asian
- Black
- Hispanic
- White

1960
- .6%
- 11%
- 3.5%
- 85%

2005
- 5%
- 13%
- 14%
- 67%

2018
- 6%
- 13%
- 18%
- 61%

2050 projected
- 9%
- 13%
- 29%
- 47%

Figure 2.5 Projections show the proportion of the non-Hispanic white majority shrinking, the Hispanic population replacing African Americans as the largest minority, and the percentage of Asian Americans increasing at a fast rate.

Figure 2.6 Temperly London Ready-to-Wear Spring/Summer 2020 collection shows significant Spanish and South American inspiration in styles, colors, and surface design.

Hispanics

In 2018, Hispanics made up 18.3 percent of the US population, and new Hispanic immigrants are expected to continue to settle in the US for the foreseeable future.[7] Projections show the Hispanic population will reach 20 percent of the population by 2020 and over 30 percent by 2050. Hispanic customers will be a large part of the shopping experience, and in fashion this has been evidenced with the success of fiery new colors and prints reminiscent of lush South American rain forests, as seen in Figure 2.6.[8]

African Americans

At 13.4 percent of the population in 2018, African Americans were the second largest minority in the United States.[9] They are better educated and hold higher-level jobs than they did in the past. With better education comes a stronger sense of oneself and one's heritage. Many black people show the pride they feel in their African heritage by wearing African styles, fabrics, and patterns. Other ethnic groups and fashion retailers have adopted these styles as well. Fashion companies have acknowledged the changes that have occurred among the African American population and have reflected these changes in the products they market and the models they use. Once thought of as a niche market, cosmetics are now widely available that emphasize the beauty of a full range of darker skin tones. African American men and women have become widely influential throughout mainstream fashion trends, music, and culture.

Asians

According to Census statistics, the Asian American population reached 5.6 percent of the total American population in 2018. Asian Americans are considered the second–fastest-growing minority group, following the Hispanic population.[10] But they are not one homogenous group. They come from more than a dozen countries and speak at least forty-one different languages!

THRIFT IS THE NEW BLACK: Thrift, Vintage, and Consignment Shopping Is on the Rise!

Do words like *trendy*, *hip*, and *cool* come to mind when describing a secondhand or thrift store? If not, you probably haven't been into a thrift store lately. Thrift stores, consignment stores, and secondhand stores are on the rise and growing in popularity across a broad spectrum of demographic groups. The phenomenon even has its own language; an item bought from a thrift or consignment store is *thrifted*.

The Great Recession of 2008 and the aftermath of a very slow recovery left many looking for strategies to make their fewer dollars go farther. Many families felt the blow of lowered income or job loss, inspiring creative ways to economize and tighten their belts. Millennials graduated from college into a bleak job market and looming student loans.

Thrift, consignment, and secondhand shopping became very appealing options, especially for furniture and clothing.

Inventory has not been a problem for the resale clothing market. Emptying out the closet of gently or never-worn clothes provides a tax-deductible donation to nonprofit stores like Goodwill, Savers, or any number of church or community-based organizations. Instead of donations, many choose the consignment route, selling clothing for cash or store credit to purchase additional clothing from the store. Online consignment and resale stores have blossomed since 2008. In the earliest phases of e-commerce, eBay showed consumers how the online consignment and auction platform can transform a local network of buyers and sellers into a global enterprise. But

the playing field has expanded, especially in the upscale categories.

InternetRetailer reported that top preowned consignment site TheReal-Real.com earned $500,000 in its launch year, 2011, increasing revenue to $15.1 million by 2012, and reached an estimated $500 million by 2018 with 9 million member subscribers. To complement their online presence, they opened a 12,000–square-foot space in Los Angeles to help those new to thrifting to touch and feel the product before making a purchase. The online luxury consignment reseller went public at $20 per share on June 28, 2019. After years of mass production and mass consumption, it appears that today's consumer is benefitting economically from the overabundance of useful, still-stylish merchandise.

Even as the economy continues to recover, thrift, consignment, and secondhand stores do not show signs of fading away. Quite the opposite is true, in fact. Thrift and consignment stores are one of the fastest-growing segments of retail business. According to the National Association of Retail and Thrift Shops (NARTS), reports more than 25,000 resale establishments in the United States.

According to consumer research firm America's Research Group (ARG), about 16 to 18 percent of Americans will shop at a thrift store during a given year, and about 12 to 15 percent will shop at a consignment or resale shop. Compare this to 11.4 percent of Americans shopping

Gently used children's clothing is a significant part of the clothing resale market.

Julie Wainwright, cofounder and chief executive officer of online designer consignment store The RealReal. Fashion items are sold at flash sales lasting seventy-two hours.

Thrift and consignment stores are a great place for the fashion adventurous or fashion curious to find affordable, fun fashions.

in factory outlet malls, 19.6 percent in apparel stores, and 21.3 percent in major department stores.

Thrift, resale, and consignments stores are not just finding traction with the thrifty. Irma Zandl, of Zandl Group, a consumer-tracking firm, reports that fashionable finds in secondhand stores help young consumers stand out and make a fashion statement. She explains to *USA Today*, "People today take pride in being individual and unique, in setting trends versus following them, and with so much sameness at the malls throughout the country, one way to achieve this originality is by buying retro and vintage items that are no longer in production." A surprising number of items found in resale and thrift shops are new or nearly new, allowing the fashion curious to take an affordable risk.

Thrift and consignment resale are also considered not only a great resource for the money-savvy, but for the planet-friendly shoppers, too. Buying resold goods helps limit the amount of textile goods going into landfill, while also reducing

A twist on thrifting is the concept of renting fashions. With Rent The Runway, members wear designer fashions for a while, then return them, receiving more fashions to try each month.

manufacturing demand, which in turn reduces the need for water, pesticides, and other pollutants required in the various manufacturing processes.

Thrift stores also provide fertile resources for do-it-yourselfers, interior designers, fashion up-cycling, costuming, and the growing cosplay phenomenon. And we can't forget the treasure hunters.

These are the top six online consignment sites, according to *US News*:

Threadup.com
TheRealReal.com
Poshmark.com
VestiaireCollective.com
Worthy.com
Kidizen.com

Asians in the United States are more geographically concentrated than African Americans or Latinos. The states that account for roughly half of the Asian population are California, New York, and Texas. In Hawaii, the nation's only majority-Asian state, Asians made up the highest proportion of the total population.[11]

The end of the Vietnam War and the influx of thousands of refugees from Cambodia and Vietnam brought additional traditions and costumes to be shared. This stimulated interest in traditional Eastern fashions and in the everyday comfort of the Chinese sandal and quilted jacket. Figure 2.7 shows an example of Asian influence in fashion.

Immigration from many Asian countries continues to rise. As of 2015, Chinese Americans were the largest Asian group, followed by Asian Indians, Filipinos, Vietnamese, Koreans, and Japanese.[12]

Figure 2.7 American designer Ralph Rucci demonstrates the ever-growing influence of Asian fashion in the RR331 Haute Couture Fall/Winter 2019/2020 collection.

Status of Women

In the early 1900s, the US woman was, in many ways, a nonperson. She could not vote, serve on a jury, earn a living at any but a few occupations, own property, or enter public places unescorted. She passed directly from her father's control to her husband's control, without rights or monies. In both households, she dressed to please the man and reflect his status.

Profound changes began to occur during the First World War and have accelerated ever since. The most dramatic advances have happened since the mid-1960s and the advent of the women's movement. Women's demands for equal opportunity, equal pay, and equal rights in every facet of life continue to bring about even more change. These changes have affected not only fashion but also the entire field of marketing.

Jobs and Money

The number of women who work outside the home has increased dramatically, nearly doubling since 1975. The number of women who work outside the home rises each year, despite the fact that women's salaries are still, on average, only about 82 percent of men's salaries.[13] In the age groupings of those thirty-five years and older, women have earnings that are roughly three-fourths as much as their male counterparts. Among younger workers, the earning differences between women and men are not as great. Women earn 89 percent as much as men among workers twenty-five to thirty-four years old and 95 percent as much among those sixteen to twenty-four years old. Both financial pressures and career satisfaction should keep the number of working women growing.[14] Figure 2.8 demonstrates the wage gap between men and women of different ethnic groups.

The dramatic increase in the number of working women has led to a surge in fashion interest because a woman who works is continuously exposed to fashion. It is everywhere around her as she meets people, shops during her lunch hour, or goes to and from home. As a member of the workforce, she now has the incentive, the opportunity, and the means to respond to fashion's appeal.

Finally, women in general today have more money of their own to spend as they see fit. Approximately four women in every six have incomes, earned and unearned, of their own. These women and their acceptance or

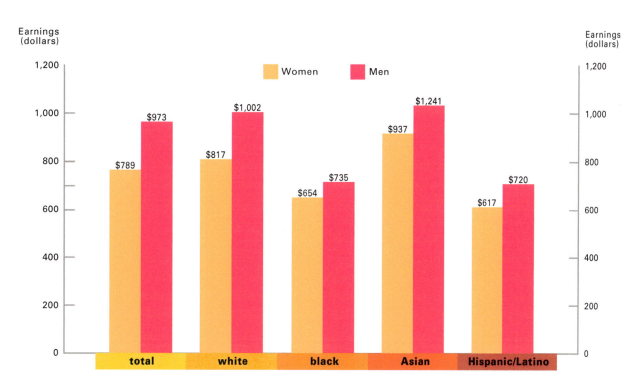

MEDIAN WEEKLY EARNINGS OF FULL-TIME WAGE & SALARY WAGES
(BY SEX, RACE, & HISPANIC OR LATINO ETHNICITY 2009 ANNUAL AVERAGES)

NOTE: Persons whose ethnicity is identified as Hispanic or Latino may be of any race.

Figure 2.8 According to the US Census Bureau, Asian women and men earn more than their white, black, and Hispanic counterparts.

rejection of offered styles have new importance in the fashion marketplace.

Education

Often the better educated a woman becomes, the more willing she is to learn new things. She is also more willing to try new fashions, which of course serves to accelerate fashion change. With more women today receiving more education than ever before, the repercussions on fashion are unmistakable. Today's educated women have had wider exposure than their mothers or grandmothers to other cultures and to people of different backgrounds. Consequently, they are worldlier, more discerning, more demanding, and more confident in their tastes and feelings for fashion.

Social Freedom

Perhaps the most marked change in the status of women since the early 1900s is the degree of social freedom they now enjoy. Young women today are free to apply for a job and to earn, spend, and save their own money. They are free to go unescorted to a restaurant, theater, or other public place. Women travel more frequently than they did in the past, and they travel to more distant locations at younger ages and often alone. Many own their own cars. If they can afford it, they may maintain an apartment or share one with others. It is difficult to imagine that the social freedoms and responsibilities that today's young women accept as normal were considered unfeminine or outrageous as recently as forty years ago.

Short skirts, popular in the 1920s, the early 1940s, the 1960s, and the 2000s, are commonly interpreted as a reflection of women's freedom. So, too, is the simplicity of the styles that prevailed in those periods: chemises, sacks, tents, shifts, other variations of loose-hanging dresses, and pants.

Different theories exist about why these changes came about. Some people believe that stiff, unyielding corsets went out with a stiff, unyielding moral code. Others believe that the changes had no particular social significance. They believe that women rejected inflexible corsets not because of a change in the moral code, but because the new materials were simply more comfortable. Similarly, pants may be viewed as an expression of women's freedom or merely as suitable garments for hopping in and out of the indispensable car.

Whatever the reasons, the lifestyles of US women and their opinions and attitudes about fashion have changed radically in the past fifty years. US women have gained hard-won freedoms in their social and business lives. They are just as definite about their freedom of choice in fashion. The thought of today's independent women accepting uncomfortable and constricting clothing or shoes just to follow the dictates of some fashion arbiter, as they did years ago, is ludicrous. Today's busy, active women, whether at home or at the office, have very carefully defined preferences for fashions that suit their own individual needs and comfort. Successful designers recognize these preferences and make sure their drawing boards reflect them.

Social Mobility

Almost all societies have classes, and individuals choose either to stand out from or to conform to their actual or aspired-to class. Sociologists have related fashion change to changes in **social mobility**, when an individual or group moves within a social hierarchy. There is also an effort to associate with a higher class by imitation.

The United States is sometimes called a classless society, but this is valid only in that there are no hereditary ranks, royalty, or untouchables. Classes do exist, but they are based largely upon occupation, income, residential location, education, or avocation, and their boundaries have become increasingly fluid. They range from the immensely wealthy (self-made millionaires or their descendants—the Vanderbilts, Whitneys, and Rockefellers, for example) at the top, through the very wealthy (mostly nouveau riche), through the many middle-income levels, and finally to the low-income and poverty levels. At the very bottom are the unemployed and the homeless.

Middle-Class Influence

Most fashion authorities agree that there is a direct relationship between the growth and strength of the middle class and the growth and strength of fashion demand.

As discussed earlier, the middle class has the highest physical, social, and financial mobility. Because it is the largest class, it has the majority vote in the adoption of fashions. Members of the middle class tend to be followers, not leaders, of fashion, but the strength of their following pumps money into the fashion industry. The persistence of their following often spurs fashion leaders to seek newer and different fashions of their own. They have both fashion interest and the money to indulge it. Despite fluctuations in the economy, this growth generally means a widespread increase in consumer buying power, which in turn generates increased fashion demand.

Physical Mobility

Physical mobility, like social mobility, encourages the demand for and response to fashion. One effect of travel is "cross-pollination" of cultures. After seeing how other people live, travelers bring home a desire to adopt or adapt some of what they observed and make it part of their environment.

Thus, Marco Polo brought gunpowder, silks, and spices from the Orient, introducing new products to medieval Europe. In the nineteenth century, travelers brought touches of Asian and African fashions to Western dress and home furnishings. In the twentieth century, Latin American and pre-Columbian influences were introduced into North America, dramatically changing the direction and emphasis of fashion in this country.

In the United States, people enjoy several kinds of physical mobility. For example, the daily routine for many people involves driving to work or to a shopping center, often in a different city. Among the broad range of influences they are exposed to during their daily trips are the fashions of others and the fashion offerings of retail distributors.

A second form of physical mobility popular among Americans is vacation travel. Whether travelers are going to a nearby lake or around the world, each trip exposes them to many different fashion influences and each trip itself demands special fashions. Living out of a suitcase for a few days or a few months requires clothes that are easy to pack, wrinkle-resistant, suitable for a variety of occasions, and easy to keep in order.

A third form of physical mobility is change of residence, which, like travel, exposes an individual to new contacts, new environments, and new fashion influences.

Faster Communications

Related to physical mobility is faster communications. Not many years ago, news of every sort traveled more slowly. This meant not only that life moved more slowly but also that fashions changed more slowly. It could take weeks or months for people in one section of the country to learn what was being worn in another part of the country. Fashion trends moved at a pace that was as leisurely as the news.

Our electronic age has changed all that. We now enjoy rapid communication in ever-increasing quantities and infinite varieties. By means of satellites, round-the-clock broadcasting, radio, Twitter, Facebook, iPhone applications, and blogs, we have the world at our fingertips. Thus, these have become important mediums for transmitting fashion information.

A significant shift began in 2009 when fashion bloggers, for the first time, were seated in the front row of fashion shows with the press. So influential, with significant numbers of followers, bloggers have launched lucrative careers and become celebrities in their own right (see Figure 2.9). Part model, part scribe, part stylist, and part marketer, fashion bloggers help translate the latest fashions into wearable outfits for legions of men and women. And by using social media, they do it at breakneck speed! No more waiting for the next issue of a favorite magazine—just log on and follow. Fast communication is becoming even faster and is essential for the ever-changing world of fashion.

War, Disaster, and Crises

War, widespread disaster, and crises shake people's lives and focus attention on ideas, events, and places that may be completely new. People develop a need for fashions that are compatible with the changes in their attitudes and environments.

Such changes took place in women's activities and in fashions as a result of the two world wars. The First World War brought women into the business world in significant

Figure 2.9 Fashion blogger Caro Daur and Internet celebrity Sistine Stallone walk the runway, wearing Dolce & Gabanna Spring/Summer 2018.

numbers and encouraged their desire for independence and suffrage. It gave them a reason to demand styles that allowed freer physical movement. The Second World War drew women into jobs traditionally thought of as masculine work, or work more suited to men, such as truck driving, motor repair, airplane repair, radio operators, test-piloting and transporting military aircraft, heavy factory work, and more, for which they previously had not been considered strong enough. Women worked in war plants on night shifts. Gas shortages and rationing required more walking, and often more layering to keep warm in colder temperatures, which influenced footwear, accessories, and outerwear. Other shortages related to textiles required women to keep clothing longer, remake old clothing, limit fullness and unnecessary embellishment, and, in general, learn ways to do more with less. This generated more interest and emphasis in areas of one's appearance such as hairstyling, cosmetics, hats, and gloves.

The Psychological Environment

The five basic psychological factors that influence fashion demand are boredom, curiosity, reaction to convention, need for self-assurance, and desire for companionship.[15] These factors motivate a large share of people's actions and reactions.

Boredom. People tend to become bored with fashions too long in use. Boredom leads to restlessness and a desire for change. In fashion, the desire for change expresses itself in a demand for something new and satisfyingly different from what one already has.

Curiosity. Curiosity causes interest in change for its own sake. Highly curious people like to experiment; they want to know what is around the next corner. There is curiosity in everyone, though some may respond to it less dramatically than others. Curiosity and the need to experiment keep fashion demand alive.

Reaction to convention. One of the most important psychological factors influencing fashion demand is the reaction to convention. People's reactions take one of two forms: rebellion against convention or adherence to it. Rebellion against convention is characteristic of young people. This involves more than boredom or curiosity; it is a positive rejection of what exists and

a search for something new. However, acceptance by the majority is an important part of the definition of fashion. The majority tends to adhere to convention, either within its own group or class or in general.

Need for self-assurance. The need for self-assurance or confidence is a human characteristic that gives impetus to fashion demand. Often the need to overcome feelings of inferiority or of disappointment can be satisfied through apparel. People who consider themselves to be fashionably dressed have an armor that gives them self-assurance. Those who know that their clothes are dated are at a psychological disadvantage.

Desire for companionship. The desire for companionship is fundamental in human beings. The instinct for survival of the species drives individuals to seek mates. Humans' innate gregariousness also encourages them to seek companions. Fashion plays its part in the search for all kinds of companionship. In its broader sense, companionship implies the formation of groups, which require conformity in dress as well as in other respects. Flamboyant or subdued, a person's mode of dress can be a bid for companionship as well as the symbol of acceptance within a particular group.

Summary and Review

Fashion marketers determine their customers' wants and needs by examining various market segments, identified by geographics, demographics, psychographics, and behavior. Each marketer identifies the group or groups within the general population that are its target customer. Determining the average customer's personal income helps marketers make pricing decisions and estimate sales, especially when population trends are matched with income figures. For example, businesses that target middle-age and retirement-age consumers know that their customers are increasing in number and that the average income for consumers in these age groups is also increasing. The teenage and young adult markets are a smaller portion of the population than they were earlier in the century, but they are an influential market segment, often spending their discretionary income on fashion merchandise. The growing value placed on leisure time and leisure-time activities has increased the market for casual clothing and active sportswear.

Marketers also track trends in the population of targeted ethnic groups. Changing patterns of immigration bring with them new influences from different parts of the world. The Hispanic market has become the largest ethnic minority in the United States in the twenty-first century, superseding the African American market in size. The Asian American market is the second-fastest-growing minority, following Hispanics. The non-Hispanic Caucasian population is expected to remain the majority, but by a reduced percentage.

The role of women in society changed dramatically in the twentieth century, and their increased freedom, better education, and growing presence in the labor force increased their average income and changed their buying habits.

Other social forces that affect business include greater mobility and more rapid communication, which bring individuals wider choices in their purchases. Political, economic, and natural upheavals also affect fashion marketing, often leading to trends that last beyond the crisis. As consumers become more knowledgeable about their growing choices in their buying behavior, marketers are paying more attention to psychographic factors as they attempt to identify and meet the demands of their target customers.

FOR REVIEW

1. Name the four major environmental influences on fashion interest and demand in any era.
2. Market segmentation is vitally important to producers and retailers of fashion merchandise. Explain why, giving at least two examples of how such information could be used by the fashion industry.
3. How does the size and age mix of a population affect current fashion demand? What does information about size and age mix today tell us about the future of fashion demand?
4. In what ways has increased availability of leisure time affected the fashion market?
5. How has the changing status of ethnic groups affected fashion interest and demand? Cite at least two examples.
6. How does a higher level of education affect fashion interest and demand?

7. What is social mobility? How does the degree of social mobility affect fashion interest and demand? Illustrate your answer with examples.
8. Upon what factors are classes in the United States usually based? Why is it more difficult to identify an individual's social class in this country than it is in other countries?
9. Describe three kinds of physical mobility that people in the United States enjoy today, explaining how each influences fashion demand.
10. Five basic psychological factors motivate much of human behavior. List them, explaining how each affects fashion interest and demand.

FOR DISCUSSION

1. Is discretionary income or disposable personal income the more significant figure to fashion producers and marketers? Why?
2. Discuss the similarities and differences between the GeoVALS and PRIZM 2 systems.
3. How has the status of women changed during the twentieth century? How have these changes affected fashion interest and demand?
4. How are the changes in technology and social media affecting fashion today?

Trade Talk

Define or briefly explain the following terms:

demographics
discretionary income
disposable personal income
environment
geographics
inflation
market segmentation
per capita personal income
personal income
psychographics
purchasing power
recession
social mobility
target market

3

The Movement of Fashion

Key Concepts

- The factors influencing the movement of fashion
- How to predict the movement of fashion
- The theories of fashion adoption
- How to identify fashion leaders and fashion followers

F ashion is, in many ways, like a river. A river is always in motion, continuously flowing—sometimes it is slow and gentle; other times it is rushed and turbulent. It is exciting and never the same. It affects those who ride its currents and those who rest on its shores. Its movements depend on the environment.

All of this is true of fashion, too. The constant movements of fashion depend on an environment made up of social, political, and economic factors. These movements, no matter how obvious or how slight, have both meaning and definite direction. There is a special excitement to interpreting these movements and estimating their speed and direction. Everyone involved in fashion, from the designer to the consumer, is caught up in the movement of fashion.

The excitement starts with the textile producers. Fully twelve to eighteen months before they offer their lines to manufacturers, the textile people must choose their designs, textures, and colors. From three to nine months before showing a line to buyers, apparel manufacturers begin deciding which styles they will produce and in which fabrics. Then, two to six months before the fashions will appear on the selling floor, the retail buyers make their selections from the manufacturers' lines. Finally, the excitement passes on to the consumers, as they select the garments that will be versatile, appropriate, and suitably priced for their individual needs and wants.

How can all these people be sure their choices are based on reliable predictions? Successful designers, manufacturers, buyers, and consumers have a good understanding of basic cycles, principles, and patterns that operate in the world of fashion. Their predictions are based on this understanding.

Factors Influencing Fashion Movement

The movement of fashion can be accelerated or retarded by a variety of factors. I will also discuss later in this chapter how recurring fashions affect this movement.

Accelerating Factors

There are general factors that speed up fashion cycles. These influences are themselves ever growing and accelerating in the twenty-first century as the pace of life becomes more all-encompassing. The accelerating factors are as follows:

- Widespread buying power
- Leisure time
- Increased education
- Improved status of women
- Technological advances
- Sales promotion
- Seasonal change

Widespread Buying Power

Widespread income means there are more people with the financial means to respond to a fashion change. The more consumers flock to a new fashion, the sooner it will reach its culmination. The more widespread the financial ability of consumers to turn to yet a newer fashion, the sooner the current fashion will plunge into obsolescence.

Leisure Time

In the past, the majority of the population worked long hours and had little leisure time, so they paid scant attention to fashion. More leisure time usually means people have more time to buy and enjoy fashion of many kinds. Since 1900, decreases in working hours and increases in paid vacations have encouraged more use of at-home wear, casual clothes, sports apparel, travel clothes, and different types of ordinary business dress. Increased purchases of these types of apparel give impetus to their fashion cycles.

One result of today's frantic pace has been the return to catalog buying and the emergence of other forms of nonstore retailing. Catalog buying originally evolved because people in farming societies lived far from stores and had little leisure time for shopping. Today's leisure time has allowed people to add new physical and mental activities to their lives, such as sports and hobbies, leaving little time for shopping once again. Realizing that their customers are using leisure time for other pursuits, retailers are bringing shopping into the consumers' homes with catalogs, cable TV shopping channels, and websites. Consumers can browse at any time of day, and with customer service telephone lines and computer connections available all day, every day, customers can place their orders whenever they wish.

Increased Education

The increasingly higher level of education in the United States helps to speed up fashion cycles in two ways. First, more people have broadened their horizons and have new interests and new wants. Second, more people are better educated and earn more money to satisfy those wants. These two factors provide significant impetus to the adoption of new fashions.

Improved Status of Women

In a society with few artificial social barriers, women with discretionary income can spend it as they choose. No law or custom in the United States prevents any woman from buying the newest and most prestigious styles in dresses, hats, or shoes if she can afford to do so. Sex discrimination in the job market has steadily decreased, and social acceptance of women who manage both homes and jobs has steadily increased. As a result, today's women have more discretionary income and are influencing the speed of fashion cycles by the way they spend it.

Technological Advances

Today we live in an "instant" world. The stunning advances in technology in almost every area have put us in immediate possession of facts, fantasies, and fashions. We see news as it happens around the world. Goods are sped to retail stores by land, air, and sea more rapidly than could have been dreamed of just a few decades ago.

You do not have to be at the catwalk shows at Lincoln Center in order to see New York fashion. Audiences in Tokyo, Paris, and Dubai watch the designer shows streamed live to their computers and mobile devices. More and more designers are live streaming their shows on the Web. You can now enjoy the feeling of being at the show—and in the front row![1] Technological advances combine to make goods available almost at the instant that the consumer is psychologically and financially ready to buy. Thus, the cycle of fashion becomes more accelerated.

Sales Promotion

The impact of sales promotion is felt everywhere in the fashion world. Magazines, television, newspapers, billboards, direct mail, the Internet, and mobile ads all

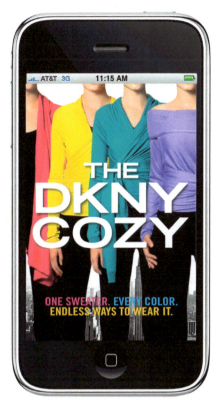

Figure 3.1 Brands now keep in touch with their customers via updates delivered straight to personal smartphones.

expose the public to a never-ending procession of new fashions. Figure 3.1 shows an example of how brands keep in touch with their customers via updates delivered straight to personal smartphones. While there is no way to force consumers to accept new fashions, nor any way to save a fashion if consumers reject it, sales promotion can greatly influence a fashion's success by telling people it exists.

Seasonal Change

Nothing is so consistent in bringing about change in fashions as the calendar. As the seasons change, so do consumer demands. After months of winter, people want to shed their heavy clothing for lightweight spring and summer fashions, which is natural in climates where there are radical seasonal changes, even though our homes, schools, cars, and places of business are kept at desired temperatures through central heating and air-conditioning. However, even in areas such as Florida and Hawaii, where the weather is constant year-round, people change their wardrobes with the seasons. Even if the twenty-first century brings complete climate control, people will never accept the boredom of a year-round wardrobe.

FASHION INFLUENCER, STYLE ICON

In 1959, as a young high school student in Willows, Wisconsin, she entered the fashion scene as a teen model. Throughout the next sixty years, this fashion influencer and style icon has been dressed by at least seventy-five the world's top designers—Vera Wang, Diane von Furstenberg, Zac Posen, Bob Mackie, Oscar de la Renta, Moschino, and Badgley Mischka to name just a few.

Her career includes working in over 200 professions—she traveled through outer space in 1965, became one of the first female surgeons in 1973, and became a top CEO in 1985. In 1992 she ran for President of the United States for the first time and has run in every election since. In 1962, she built a beautiful home in Malibu, which is now listed on Airbnb for her fans to enjoy a nice vacation stay.

Who is this marvelous woman? If you haven't already guessed, it's Barbie! According to Mattel, more than 100 dolls are sold every minute, with 58 million sold annually, and the Barbie brand has 99 percent brand awareness globally. The Barbie YouTube station has over 5 million subscribers, 14 million Facebook followers, 267,000 Twitter followers, and 1.2 million Instagram followers. She's a social media powerhouse!

At a time when most little girls played with "baby dolls," American inventor and co-founder of Mattel, Ruth Handler, named Barbara Millicent Roberts after her own daughter, and created her as a symbol of freedom and possibility for young girls who would one day make up the major wave of women in management and professional roles. "My whole philosophy of Barbie was that, through the doll, the little girl could be anything that she wanted to be. Barbie always represented the fact that women had choices."

The fashion designer behind the icon, Carol Spencer, celebrates her years at Mattel as Barbie's stylist,

Paris Fashion Week 2016 included a display at Musee des Arts "Barbie, Life of an Icon."

Promoted by Mattel as the most diverse doll on the market, t he company has added tall, petite and curvy body types to a new line more ethnically diverse dolls.

dresser, and designer in her memoire *Dressing Barbie*. From 1963 through 1999, the doyenne of the doll looked at current events in science, technology, politics, and world affairs and translated it into fashions and accessories that helped children—boys and girls alike—identify with their world.

In creating a modern wardrobe for Barbie and her ever-growing group of friends—Skipper, Ken, and Midge to name a few—Spencer inspired the work of future designers like Bob Mackie, Nicole Miller, Jeremy Scott and Jason Wu. Playing with Barbies inspired these young creatives, and possibly many others, to become designers themselves. To the Barbie-bashers who take issue with the dolls unreal proportions and privileged lifestyle, Spencer points out that her original proportions were modeled after popular paper doll cut-outs found in newspapers, and she defends Barbie as a springboard for the imagination—a blank slate that children can use to play and imagine whoever they want to be.

2019 marked the sixtieth anniversary of Barbie. Likewise, the CFDA Fashion Awards payed tribute to the fashion icon with the Board of Directors' Tribute. According to CFDA President and CEO Steven Kolb, "Barbie has had such a wide influence on American fashion and culture. Her story personally resonates with so many CFDA members that the board of directors decided to honor her with a special tribute."

For sixty years, children around the world played make-believe with the most glamorous clothes and chic accessories.

The Scarlett O'Hara Barbie is one of thousands of "limited edition" dolls developed to commemorate and celebrate a wide variety of cultural moments.

Because people are so accustomed to travel at all times of the year to all types of climates, the seasonal changes are accelerated and a kind of preseason testing occurs. Resort wear appears in retail stores in time for selection by the public for winter vacations in tropical areas. The late June appearance of the first fall fashions in leading stores makes it possible for the style-conscious to make their selections well in advance of the first cold wind. Consumer responses to these early offerings allow manufacturers and retailers alike to know what appeals.

Retarding Factors

Factors that retard the development of fashion cycles either discourage people from adopting incoming styles or encourage them to continue using styles that may be considered on the decline. Retarding factors include the opposites of the accelerating factors, for example, decreased buying power during recessionary periods. Major retarding factors are habit and custom, religion, sumptuary laws, and reductions in consumers' buying power.

Habit and Custom

By slowing down the acceptance of new styles and prolonging the life spans of those that are already accepted, habit and custom exert a braking effect on fashion movement. Habit slows the adoption of new skirt lengths, silhouettes, necklines, or colors whenever shoppers unconsciously select styles that do not differ perceptibly from those they already own. It is easy for an individual to let habit take over, and some consumers are more susceptible to this tendency than others. Their loyalty to an established style is less a matter of fashion judgment than a natural attraction to the more familiar.

Custom slows progress in the fashion cycle by permitting vestiges of past fashions, status symbols, taboos, or special needs to continue to appear in modern dress. Custom is responsible for such details as buttons on the sleeves of men's suits, vents in men's jackets, and the sharp creases down the fronts of men's trousers.

Religion

Historically, religious leaders have championed custom, and their ceremonial apparel has demonstrated their respect for the old ways. In the past, religious leaders tended to associate fashion with temptation and urged their followers to turn their backs on both. Religion today, however, exerts much less of a restraining influence on fashion. Examples of the new relaxation may be found in the modernization of women's dress in most religious orders and in the fact that most women no longer consider a hat obligatory when in a house of worship.

Sumptuary Laws

Sumptuary laws regulate what we can and cannot purchase. For example, sumptuary laws require that children's sleepwear be flame retardant. In the Middle Ages and Renaissance, sumptuary laws regulated extravagance and luxury in dress on religious or moral grounds. Height of headdress, length of train, width of sleeve, value and weight of material, and color of dress have all at times been restricted by law to specific classes. Such laws were aimed at keeping each class in its place in a rigidly stratified society.[2]

School uniforms in public schools were common before the 1960s, but they were largely abandoned in the free spiritedness of that decade. However, in the 1990s, when school violence and classroom disruption increased across the country, uniforms became popular once again. People in favor of uniforms argued that they would promote a sense of discipline and belonging and serve as a concrete and visual means of restoring order to the classroom.

Reductions in Consumers' Buying Power

Consumers' buying power has a powerful effect on the movement of fashion cycles. When buying power increases, fashion cycles often speed up. Decreased buying power, conversely, can retard the movement of fashion cycles. During economic recessions, with their resultant high unemployment, consumers' buying power is sharply reduced. Many people make do with clothes they have and buy only necessities. A similar caution is shown by consumers affected by strikes, inflation, high taxes, or changes in interest rates. All these factors have a slowing influence on fashion cycles. The poorer people are, the less impact they have on fashion's movements. They become bystanders in matters of fashion and, as a result, do not keep cycles moving. James Laver emphasized the importance of buying power when he said that nothing except poverty can make a style permanent.[3]

Recurring Fashions

In the study of fashion history, we see that styles reoccur, with adaptations that suit the times in which they reappear (see Figure 3.2). Occasionally, an entire look is reborn. For example, Yves Saint Laurent resurrected 1930s and 40s Hollywood glamour, for the generation of the 1970s, and for Spring 2020 the excess of the 1980s was on every runway, recalling the bold colors and voluminous proportions.[4]

Sometimes a single costume component or a minor detail that had exhausted its welcome stages a comeback, like the chandelier earring. At other times, a single article of clothing, like the sandals of the ancient Greeks, returns to popularity.

Figure 3.2 The "fannie pack" of the 1980s, now the "belted purse." A model wears a whimsical version of this recurring fashion trend in the Pyer Moss September 2019 runway show.

Research indicates that in the past, similar silhouettes and details of design in women's apparel have recurred with remarkable regularity. Despite widely held opinions to the contrary, the three basic silhouettes (bell-shaped, back fullness, and straight) always follow one another in a 100-year sequence. Each silhouette, with all its variations, dominates the fashion scene for a period of approximately thirty-five years. Having reached an excess in styling, it then declines in popularity and yields to the next silhouette in regular sequence.

Playing the Apparel Fashion Game

According to Madge Garland, a well-known English fashion authority, "every woman is born with a built-in hobby: the adornment of her person. The tricks she can play with it, the shapes she can make of it, the different portions she displays at various times, the coverings she uses or discards" all add up to fashion.[5]

Many clothing authorities read a clear message into the alternate exposure and covering of various parts of the body—sex. J. C. Flügel cited sexual attraction as the dominant motive for wearing clothes.[6]

Another expert, James Laver, explained fashion emphasis in terms of the sexuality of the body. "Fashion really began," he said, "with the discovery in the fifteenth century that clothes could be used as a compromise between exhibitionism and modesty."[7] He also suggested that those portions of the body no longer fashionable to expose are "sterilized" and are no longer regarded as sexually attractive. Those that are newly exposed are **erogenous**, or sexually stimulating. See Figure 3.3 for examples of shifting emphasis in fashion. Laver viewed fashion as pursuing the emphasis of ever-shifting erogenous zones, but never quite catching up with them. "If you really catch up," he warned, "you are immediately arrested for indecent exposure. If you almost catch up, you are celebrated as a leader of fashion."[8]

Pieces of the Game

The pieces with which the women's fashion game is played are the various parts of the female body: waist, shoulders, bosom, neckline, hips, derrière, legs, and feet, as well as the figure as a whole. Historically, as attention

Figure 3.3 With ever-shifting erogenous zones, only certain parts of the body can be exposed at a given time, as seen in (left) Giambattista Valli's miniskirt, accentuating the leg, and (right) Louis Vuitton's designs, covering the leg and accentuating the décolletage and bust.

to a part of the anatomy reaches a saturation point, the fashion spotlight shifts to some other portion.

Rules of the Game

In the game of emphasizing different parts of the female body at different times, as in any game, there are rules. The first and strongest rule is that fashion emphasis does not flit from one area to another! Rather, a particular area of the body is emphasized until every bit of excitement has been exhausted. At this point, fashion attention turns to another area. For example, when miniskirts of the 1960s could go no higher and still be legal, the fashion emphasis moved on.

The second rule of the fashion game is that only certain parts of the body can be exposed at any given time. There are dozens of examples throughout fashion history

that back up this theory: floor-length evening gowns with plunging necklines, high necklines with miniskirts, turtlenecks on sleeveless fashions.

A third rule of the fashion game is that, like fashion itself, fashion attention must always go forward.

Predicting the Movement of Fashion

Designing and selling fashion merchandise to consumers at a profit is what fashion merchandising is all about. To bring excitement and flair to their segment of merchandising, producers, designers, and retailers must have a well-defined plan and follow the movement of general fashion preferences.

The success of fashion merchandising depends on correctly predicting which new styles will be accepted by the majority of consumers. These are suggested steps in developing a fashion forecast:

1. Identify facts about past trends and forecasts.
2. Determine the causes of change in the past.
3. Investigate the difference between past forecasts and actual behavior.
4. Analyze the factors likely to affect trends in the future.
5. Apply forecasting tools and techniques, using accuracy and reliability.
6. Study the forecast continually to determine reasons for significant deviations from expected plans.
7. Revise the forecast when necessary.

With information on these points, projections—a prime requisite in successful fashion merchandising—become possible.

Identifying Trends

A fashion trend, as discussed in Chapter 1, is a direction in which fashion is moving. Designers, manufacturers, and merchants try to recognize each fashion trend to determine how widespread it is and whether it is moving toward or away from maximum fashion acceptance. They can then decide whether to actively promote the fashion to their target customers, wait, or abandon it.

For example, assume that wide-leg pants have developed as a fashion trend. At the introduction and rise stages, retailers will stock and promote more wide-leg pants. When customer response begins to level off, retailers will realize that a saturation point is being reached with this style and will begin introducing narrower pants into their stocks in larger and larger numbers. If the retailers have correctly predicted the downturn in customer demand for wide-leg pants, they will have fewer on hand when the downturn occurs. And while some customers may continue to wear the wide-leg style, they will not be buying new wide-leg pants and certainly not at regular prices. Firms like Tobe Reports and WGSN offer trend and forecasting services for fashion producers, focusing on factors such as consumer behavior, retail, marketing, and business strategy. Organizations such as Color Marketing Group, which is covered in Chapter 7, offer color forecasting trend reports and services.

Sources of Data

Modern fashion forecasters bear little resemblance to the mystical prognosticators of old. Their ability to predict the strength and direction of fashion trends among their customers has almost nothing to do with what is often called a "fashion sense." Nor does it depend on glances into the future through a cloudy crystal ball. Successful fashion forecasters depend on a most valuable commodity: information. Good, solid facts about the willingness of customers to accept certain goods are the basis of successful merchandising decisions.

Merchants can keep "instant" records on sales, inventories, new fashion testing, and a myriad of other contributing factors that aid the fashion merchandising process. In addition, wise merchants keep their eyes open to see what is being worn by their own customers as well as by the public as a whole. They are so familiar with their customers' lifestyles, economic status, educational levels, and social milieu that they can determine at just what point in a fashion's life cycle their customers will be ready to accept or reject it. Merchants turn to every available source for information that will help ensure success. They use their hard-earned sales experience but do not rely just on their own judgment; they rely on the judgment of others, too. From the producers of fashion—resident buying, merchandising, and developing offices—to special fashion groups, they learn about the buying habits of customers other than their own. Successful merchants look at the larger fashion picture to predict more ably just where their local scene fits in.

Interpreting Influential Factors

In fashion forecasting, all the data in the world can be collected by merchants, producers, or designers, but this is of little importance without interpretation. That is where the forecasters' knowledge of fashion and fashion principles comes into the picture. From collected data, they are able to identify certain patterns. Then they consider the factors that can accelerate or retard a fashion cycle among their target group of customers. Among these factors are current events, the appearance of prophetic styles, sales promotion efforts, and the standards of taste currently in vogue. A recent study revealed that 25 percent of consumers are willing to pay more to receive a personalized product or service and 22 percent of consumers are willing to share data in return for personalized products and services.[9] This trend is remaking designs in the following ways:

- Crowdsourcing: While definitions are controversial, generally this means using the many social possibilities of the Web to either create something or solve a problem. Examples could include open-source software and news aggregation sites such as Digg and Wikipedia.
- Mass customization: Brands like Levi's, NIKEiD, Timberland, Kenneth Cole, and Lori Coulter Swimwear are some of the companies that have used technology and factory production rather than traditional craftsmanship to produce a custom product at a popular price.
- Desktop manufacturing: Digital printers can create three-dimensional objects, such as eyeglasses, jewelry, and electronics, by fusing layers of plastic or metal.[10]

Current Events

The news of what is going on in the country or the world can have a long-term or short-term influence on consumers and affect their responses to a fashion. For example, in the mid-1980s, many newspapers, magazines, and TV shows were discussing opportunities for women at mid- and upper-management levels. Success in responsible positions in the business world demanded "dressing for success," and career-minded women responded by adopting the severely tailored business suit look. By their very appearance, these women indicated their determination to succeed in the still–male-dominated world of business. A reaction to this strictly tailored look occurred in the early 1990s, when women turned to a softer, less tailored look and many men abandoned the business suit "uniform" that had been the standard for generations. Today, men and women choose what fashion is right for them.

Prophetic Styles

Good fashion forecasters keep a sharp watch for what they call **prophetic styles**. These are particularly interesting new styles that are still in the introduction phase of their fashion cycle. Taken up enthusiastically by the socially prominent or by the flamboyantly young, these styles may gather momentum very rapidly or may prove to be nonstarters. Whatever their future course, the degree of acceptance of these very new styles gives forecasters a sense of which directions fashion may go.

Importance of Timing

Successful merchants must determine what their particular target group of customers is wearing now and what this group is most likely to be wearing one month or three months from now. The data these merchants collect enable them to identify each current fashion, who is wearing it, and what point it has reached in its fashion cycle.

Since merchants know at what point in a fashion's cycle their customers are most likely to be attracted, they can determine whether to stock a current fashion now, one month from now, or three months from now.

Theories of Fashion Adoption

Fashions are accepted by a few before the majority accepts them. An important step in fashion forecasting is isolating and identifying those fashion leaders and keeping track of their preferences. Once these are known, the fashion forecaster is better able to predict which styles are most likely to succeed as fashions, and how widely and who will accept each.

Three primary theories have been advanced to explain the "social contagion" or spread of fashion adoption: the downward-flow theory, or trickle-down theory; the horizontal-flow theory, or mass-market theory; and the upward-flow theory (see Figure 3.4). Each theory attempts to explain the course a fashion travels or is likely to travel, and each has its own claim to validity in reference to particular fashions or social environments.

Downward-Flow Theory

The oldest theory of fashion adoption is the **downward-flow theory** (or trickle-down theory). It maintains that to be identified as a true fashion, a style must first be adopted by people at the top of the social pyramid. The style then gradually wins acceptance at progressively lower social levels.

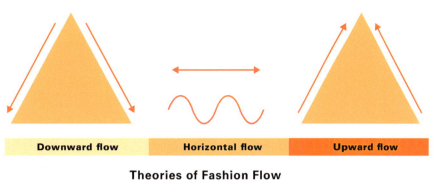

Theories of Fashion Flow

Figure 3.4 The three theories of fashion flow.

This theory assumes the existence of a social hierarchy in which lower-income people seek identification with more affluent people. At the same time, those at the top seek disassociation from those they consider socially inferior. The theory suggests that fashions are accepted by lower classes only if, and after, they are accepted by upper classes, and upper classes will reject a fashion once it has flowed to a lower social level.

Implications for Merchandising

To some extent, the downward-flow theory has validity. Some fashions may appear first among the socially prominent. Eager manufacturers then quickly mass produce lower-priced copies that many consumers can afford, and the wealthier consumers seek newer styles.

Because our social structure has radically changed, this theory has few adherents today. It can apply only when a society resembles a pyramid, with people of wealth and position at the apex and followers at successively lower levels. Our social structure, however, is more like a group of rolling hills than a pyramid. There are many social groups and many directions in which fashion can and does travel.

This altered pattern of fashion acceptance is also a result of the speed with which fashion news now travels. All social groups know about fashion innovation at practically the same time. Moreover, accelerated mass production and mass distribution of fashion goods have broadened acceptance of styles. They are available at lower prices and more quickly than ever before.

Industry Practice

For the reasons given previously, those who mass produce fashion goods today are less likely to wait cautiously for approval of newly introduced styles by affluent consumers. As soon as significant signs of an interesting new style appear, the producers are ready to offer adaptations or even copies to the public.

Horizontal-Flow Theory

A newer theory is the **horizontal-flow theory** (or mass-market theory) of fashion adoption. This theory claims that fashions move horizontally among groups on similar social levels rather than vertically from one level to another.

Implications for Merchandising

The theory of horizontal fashion movement has great significance for merchandising. It points out the fallacy of assuming that there is a single, homogeneous fashion public in this country. In reality, a number of distinctly different groups make up the fashion public. Each group has its own characteristics and its own fashion ideas and needs. The horizontal-flow theory recognizes that what wealthy society people are wearing today is not necessarily what middle-class suburbanites, college students, or office workers will either wear tomorrow or wait until tomorrow to accept. This theory acknowledges that there are separate markets in fashion goods as in any other type of merchandise.

WEDDINGS!
Big Business and Getting Bigger

WITH AN ESTIMATED 2.5 MILLION WEDDINGS EACH YEAR IN THE UNITED STATES ALONE, WEDDINGS ARE BIG BUSINESS. Annual revenues from weddings are estimated between $40 and $70 billion per year. According to a survey from The Knot, the average budget for the big event is $33,931, with an average price for the wedding gown at around $1,631.

So it is no surprise that wedding planning—the venue, the ceremony, the gown, and every last detail—is becoming a popular and sought-after career. Hollywood has glamorized the profession with star-studded films like *The Wedding Planner*, *Father of the Bride*, *27 Dresses*, and more. Television shows like *Martha Stewart*, *Say Yes to the Dress*, *Four Weddings*, and *Amazing Cakes*, just to name a few, give viewers an up-close look at a wide variety of weddings, from the most grandiose to the most humble, and everything in between.

Sandy Malone, professional wedding planner and owner of Sandy Malone Weddings and Events, shares tips for students interested in entering this profession. First, a degree in communications, public relations, or business will provide a substantial base for the demands of the profession. Communication skills—both oral and written—are essential. As each event operates almost like its own small business, the ability to organize, manage budgets, negotiate contracts, and work with vendors is essential. If the creative side of the event—the gown, the decorations, the favors, the venues—is appealing, a degree in fashion, fashion merchandising, or interior design with a strong focus on business also provides a good foundation.

Next, experience is a must. Do an internship, work for a hotel that holds large events and weddings, or help plan the weddings of friends and relatives for free. Build a portfolio of photographs and information to demonstrate your skills and abilities and post your experience by starting a blog or website. Work part-time at a bridal store, a florist, a wedding bakery, or any number of vendor businesses that serve the industry. Meet people, network, and let people know what you are interested in doing.

Finally, weddings are social events involving family and friends. While they are lovely, they are also personal events in the lives of the clients. Wedding planners have to be outgoing and gracious to the clients and their guests.

Malone's advice to those interested in wedding and event planning as a career is this: "Learn everything you can, say thank you a lot, and work hard."

Full-service bridal salons provide the dress and so much more for the bride and groom's special day.

Retailers who apply the horizontal-flow theory will watch their own customers closely rather than being guided solely by what more exclusive stores are selling. They will seek to identify the groups into which customers can be divided in terms of income, age, education, and lifestyle. Among their customers, they will look for the innovators and their style choices as well as the influentials and their selections. Charles King defined a **fashion innovator** as a person who is quicker than his or her associates to try out a new style. A **fashion influential** is a person whose advice is sought by associates. A fashion influential's adoption of a new style gives it prestige among a group. The two roles may or may not be played by the same individual within a specific group.

Industry Practice

A distinction can be drawn between the spread of fashion within the industry itself and its adoption by consumers. A vertical flow definitely operates within the industry. Furthermore, as any reader of *Women's Wear Daily* knows, the hottest news in the industry concerns what the top designers and the top producers are showing.

Moreover, the innovation process in the industry represents a great filtering system. From an almost infinite number of possibilities, manufacturers select a finite number of styles. From these, trade buyers select a small sampling. Finally, consumers choose from among retailers' selections, thereby endorsing certain ones as accepted fashions.

This process is quite different from the consumer reaction in the downward-flow theory. The difference lies in the fact that today the mass market does not await the approval of the "class" market before it adopts a fashion.

Upward-Flow Theory

The third theory that attempts to explain the process of fashion adoption is relatively new. It reflects the enormous social changes that have occurred in the past five decades. Because the process of fashion dissemination that evolved in the decades of the 1950s through the 2000s was the exact opposite of that which prevailed throughout much of recorded history, this theory has important implications for producers and retailers alike.

This theory of fashion adoption is called the upward-flow theory. It holds that the young—particularly those of low-income families and those in higher-income groups who adopt low-income lifestyles—are quicker than any social group to create or adopt new and different fashions. As its name implies, this theory is exactly the opposite of the downward-flow theory. The **upward-flow theory** holds that fashion adoption begins among the young members of lower-income groups and then moves upward into higher-income groups (see Figure 3.5).

The decades of the 1950s through today have outstanding examples of the upward-flow theory. In the 1950s, young people discovered Army/Navy surplus stores and were soon wearing khaki pants, caps, battle jackets, fatigues, and even ammunition belts. In the 1960s, led by the Hell's Angels, the motorcycle clubs

Figure 3.5 Once reserved only for the court or field, today sneakers are high fashion, showing up on the runways of Paris. Here, a model sports Chanel sneakers.

introduced the fashion world to black leather—in jackets, vests, and studded armbands. Soon the jet set was dressed in black leather long coats, skirts, and pants. Meanwhile, other young people were discovering bib overalls, railroad worker's caps, and all-purpose laborer's coveralls that were soon translated into jumpsuits. Peasant apparel, prairie looks, and styles and designs from various minority groups followed the same pattern. They began as part of a young and lower-income lifestyle and were then quickly adopted among older people with different lifestyles and incomes.

One of the more dramatic illustrations of this has been the T-shirt. In its short-sleeved version, it has long been worn by truckers, laborers, and farmworkers. In its long-sleeved version, it was the uniform of local bowling and softball teams. In the 1970s, the T-shirt became a message board and sprouted a brand-new fashion cottage industry. The ultimate T-shirt was the Chanel No. 5; first the perfume, then the T-shirt. Actually, the Chanel T-shirt was a logical application of a tenet long held by the late Coco Chanel, who believed that fashion came from the streets and was then adapted by the couture.

In the 1980s, sources of inspiration for fashion styles representing the upward-flow theory were everywhere, especially in the world of rock music. By following the fashion statements of rock-and-roll idols, America's youth were dressed in worn-out denim, metal, leather, lace, bangles, spandex, and glitter.

In the 1990s and the early 2000s, rap artists not only composed lyrics that spoke of "ghetto" life in street language but also introduced and popularized hip-hop clothing styles. In the 2010s vintage apparel became high fashion. Reusing and reviving older fashions may have been born out of economic necessity, but the trend has reached the red carpet and the runway.

Implications for Merchandising

For producers and retailers, this new direction of fashion flow implies radical changes in traditional methods of charting and forecasting fashion trends. No longer can producers and retailers look solely to name designers and socially prominent fashion leaders for ideas that will become tomorrow's best-selling fashions. They also must pay considerable attention to what young people favor, for the young have now become a large and an independent group that can exert considerable influence on fashion styling.

As a result, today fewer retailers and manufacturers attend European couture showings, once considered fashion's most important source of design inspiration. Now producers and retailers alike are more interested in ready-to-wear (prêt-à-porter) showings. Here they look for styles and design details that reflect trends with more fashion relevance for American youth.

Industry Practice

Apparently, fashion will never again flow in only one direction. Of course, customers will always exist for high fashion and for conservative fashion. But producers and retailers must now accept that they will be doing a considerable proportion of their business in fashions created or adopted first by the lower-income young and by those who choose to be allied with them.

Fashion Leaders

As different as they may be, the three theories of fashion flow share one common perspective: They recognize that there are both fashion leaders and fashion followers. People of social, political, and economic importance here and abroad are seen as leaders in the downward-flow theory. The horizontal-flow theory recognizes individuals whose personal prestige makes them leaders within their own circles, whether they are known elsewhere. Finally, the important fashion role played by young, lower-income groups is recognized in the upward-flow theory.

The theories of fashion adoption stress that the fashion leader is not the creator of the fashion, nor does merely wearing the fashion make a person a fashion leader. If a fashion parade is forming, fashion leaders may head it and even quicken its pace. They cannot, however, bring about a procession, nor can they reverse a procession.

Innovators and Influentials

Famous people are not necessarily fashion leaders, even if they do influence an individual style. Their influence usually is limited to only one striking style, one physical attribute, or one time. The true fashion leader is a person constantly seeking distinction and therefore likely to launch a succession of fashions rather than just one. People like Beau Brummel, who made a career of dressing fashionably, or the Duchess of Windsor, whose wardrobe

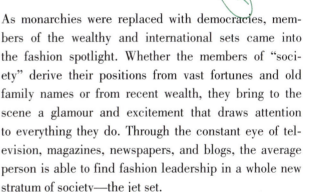

Figure 3.6 Singer Taylor Swift, walking the red carpet in a dress by Sachin & Babi and shoes by Charlotte Olympia, is an example of the young entertainer as a fashion leader.

was front-page fashion news for decades, influence fashion on a much broader scale. Or, in our modern era, there is an entertainer like Taylor Swift, whose look is admired and emulated by her young fans (see Figure 3.6).

What makes a person a fashion leader? Charles King made it clear that more than just daring to be different is required. In his analysis, a person eager for the new is merely an innovator or early buyer. To be a leader, one must be influential and sought after for advice within one's coterie.[11]

Royalty

In the past, fashion leadership was exclusively the province of royalty. New fashions were introduced in royal courts by such leaders as Empress Eugenie and Marie Antoinette. In the twentieth century, the Duchess of Windsor, although an American and a commoner by birth, was a fashion innovator and influential from the 1930s through the 1960s. When the King of England gave up his throne to marry "the woman he loved," style and fashion professionals throughout the world copied her elegance. The Sotheby auction in the late 1980s of the Duchess of Windsor's jewelry sparked new interest in her style, and designers are still showing copies of her jewelry.

Until Princess Diana and Sarah Ferguson married into the British royal family, few royal personages had qualified as fashion leaders. In 2015, Kate Middleton is continually seen on best-dressed lists and has become a fashion icon for the younger generation. Despite the belief held by some people that kings and queens wear crowns and ermine, the truth is that modern royalty has become a hardworking group whose daily lives are packed with so many activities that sensible and conservative dress is necessary for most occasions.

The Rich

As monarchies were replaced with democracies, members of the wealthy and international sets came into the fashion spotlight. Whether the members of "society" derive their positions from vast fortunes and old family names or from recent wealth, they bring to the scene a glamour and excitement that draws attention to everything they do. Through the constant eye of television, magazines, newspapers, and blogs, the average person is able to find fashion leadership in a whole new stratum of society—the jet set.

What these socialites are doing and what they are wearing are instantly served up to the general public by the media. As far as fashion is concerned, these people are not just in the news; they *are* the news. Any move they make is important enough to be immediately publicized. What they wear is of vital interest to the general public. The media tell us what the social leaders wear to dine in a chic restaurant, to attend a charity ball, or to go shopping. Because they are trendsetters, their choices are of prime interest to designers and to the world at large.

Of course, this inundation of news about what social leaders wear influences the public. The average person is affected because so many manufacturers and retailers

Figure 3.7 Kourtney and Kim Kardashian have used their wealth and fame to influence fashion, even launching their own K-Dash by Kardashian line through the QVC network.

TABLE 3.1 FASHION STYLES NAMED FOR THE FAMOUS

Trendsetters	Styles
Amelia Bloomer	Bloomers
Earl of Chesterfield	Chesterfield jacket
Dwight D. Eisenhower	Eisenhower jacket
Geraldine Ferraro	"Gerry cut" (hairstyle)
Mao Tse Tung	Mao jacket
Jawaharlal Nehru	Nehru jacket
Madame de Pompadour	Pompadour (hairstyle)
Nancy Reagan	"Reagan plastics" (costume jewelry), red
Duke of Wellington	Wellington boots
Earl of Cardigan	Cardigan sweater
Duke of Windsor	Windsor knot (tie)
Duke of Norfolk	Norfolk jacket
Nelson Mandela	Madiba smart (shirt)
The Beatles	Hairstyle

of fashion take their cues from these social leaders. Right or wrong, fashion merchants count on the fashion sense of these leaders. They know that the overwhelming exposure of these leaders in the media encourages people of ordinary means to imitate them—consciously or unconsciously. Pictured in Figure 3.7 are Kardashian sisters Kourtney and Kim, who have translated their wealth and fame into their own fashion products.

The Famous

Fashion today takes its impetus and influence from people in every possible walk of life. These people have one thing in common, however: They are famous. Because of some special talent, charisma, notoriety, or popularity, they are constantly mentioned and shown in the media. They may or may not appear in the society pages.

In this group can be found presidents and princesses, movie stars and religious leaders, sports figures and recording stars, and politicians and TV personalities. Because they are seen so frequently, the public has a good sense of their fashions and lifestyles and can imitate them to the extent of the public's means and desires. See Table 3.1 for a list of fashion styles named for the famous.

Athletes

Today, there is strong emphasis on sports. And what prominent sports figures wear is of great importance to the people who seek to imitate them. Television has increased the public acceptance of several sports. For

example, people have enjoyed going to baseball, football, or basketball games for years. But sports of a more individual nature, such as tennis and golf, were of minor interest. Now these sports are brought into the living rooms of an increasing number of viewers. As a result, fashions for participating in these sports have grown remarkably in importance (see Figure 3.8). Tennis is now a very popular participation sport and has given rise to an entire specialized fashion industry. Today, every aspiring tennis player has endless fashion styles, colors, and fabrics to choose from. A wide selection of fashion is also available for golf, jogging, running, swimming, skating, cycling, snorkeling, snowboarding, and other sports. The names of Michael Jordan, LeBron James, David Beckham, Tiger Woods, Serena Williams, and Sean White are known to most Americans.

Fashion Followers

Filling out forms for his daughter's college entrance application, a father wrote of his daughter's leadership qualities: "To tell the truth, my daughter is really not a

leader, but rather a loyal and devoted follower." The dean of the college admissions responded: "We are welcoming a freshman class of 100 students this year and are delighted to accept your daughter. You can't imagine how happy we are to have one follower among the 99 leaders!"

Most people want to be thought of as leaders, not followers. But there are many people who are followers, and good ones. In fact, followers are in the majority within any group. Without followers, the fashion industry would certainly collapse. Mass production and mass distribution can be possible and profitable only when large numbers of consumers accept the merchandise. Though they may say otherwise, luckily more people prefer to follow than to lead. The styles fashion leaders adopt may help manufacturers and retailers in determining what will be demanded by the majority of consumers in the near future. Only accurate predictions can ensure the continued success of the giant ready-to-wear business in this country, which depends for its success on mass production and distribution. While fashion leaders may stimulate and excite the fashion industry, fashion followers are the industry's lifeblood.

Reasons for Following Fashion

Theories about why people follow rather than lead in fashion are plentiful. Among the explanations are feelings of insecurity, admiration of others, lack of interest, and ambivalence about the new.

Feelings of Insecurity

A person about to face a difficult interview or attend the first meeting with a new group carefully selects new clothes. Often a person can hide feelings of inadequacy by wearing a style that others have already deemed appropriate.

Admiration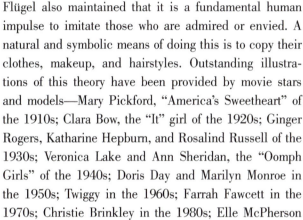

Flügel also maintained that it is a fundamental human impulse to imitate those who are admired or envied. A natural and symbolic means of doing this is to copy their clothes, makeup, and hairstyles. Outstanding illustrations of this theory have been provided by movie stars and models—Mary Pickford, "America's Sweetheart" of the 1910s; Clara Bow, the "It" girl of the 1920s; Ginger Rogers, Katharine Hepburn, and Rosalind Russell of the 1930s; Veronica Lake and Ann Sheridan, the "Oomph Girls" of the 1940s; Doris Day and Marilyn Monroe in the 1950s; Twiggy in the 1960s; Farrah Fawcett in the 1970s; Christie Brinkley in the 1980s; Elle McPherson and Cindy Crawford in the 1990s; Jennifer Lopez, Cameron Diaz, and Britney Spears at the beginning of the twenty-first century; and today the Kardashians, Beyoncé, Lady Gaga, and Taylor Swift. Their clothes and hairstyles were copied instantly among many different groups throughout this country and in many other parts of the world. On a different level, the young girl who copies the hairstyle of her best friend, older sister, or favorite aunt demonstrates the same principle, as do college students who model their appearance after that of a campus leader.

Lack of Interest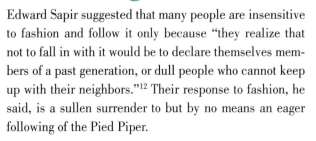

Edward Sapir suggested that many people are insensitive to fashion and follow it only because "they realize that not to fall in with it would be to declare themselves members of a past generation, or dull people who cannot keep up with their neighbors."[12] Their response to fashion, he said, is a sullen surrender to but by no means an eager following of the Pied Piper.

EXPRESS YOUR SOLE

The Rise of Sneaker Culture

Hype and promotion herald their release. Lines of teens and adults alike curl around the block in wait for up to five days for their launch. Websites, blogs, and podcasts are dedicated to them. Is it the latest action hero? A teen idol? The opening of a superhero movie? No, it's a shoe, or more precisely, a sneaker. Once for the exclusive use of game and sport, sneakers walked out into mainstream culture as the shoe of choice for comfort and style, revealing status and class, as well as making social and political statements. Considering sneakers works of art and technology, millions of enthusiast collectors are part of the growing "sneaker culture" experience.

Partially rooted in celebrity athlete endorsement, partially the product of an active, sporting culture, and partially a marker of hip-hop and other political and social subcultures, the rubber-soled, canvas, leather, or nylon-topped footwear is its own sort of personal and fashionable statement.

Sneakers date back to the 1830s, developed as part of a growing active society. Sneaker culture began some time later in the twentieth century as part of increased interest in sports and the celebrity athletes who played them. Converse Rubber Shoe Company kicked off this craze when it designed an elite shoe in the 1920s for professional basketball players. The company's own team, the Converse All Stars, wore the shoes, and star player Chuck Taylor sold the shoes at high school basketball clinics. With a few tweaks to the design, his name became part of the logo, and the iconic canvas high-top sneakers became known as "Chuck Taylors." The shoe of choice for professional and aspiring basketball players, their use extended to the Olympics and as a training shoe for Second World War soldiers. With significant business expansion after the war, the majority of professional basketball players wore Chuck Taylors by the 1960s.

But the sneaker was still an athletic shoe for use on the court or course, not to be worn to school, church, or work. As Tommy Ramone of punk band the Ramones points out, "It was punky and snotty to wear sneakers instead of shoes. Punky and snotty was very important to the Ramones." As a result, the sneaker, including the Converse, became the symbol of rebellion and antiestablishment sentiment. The utilitarian fabric structure became literally a canvas for artists and artistic

Palais 23 in Paris celebrates the thirtieth anniversary of Michael Jordan's eponymous Nike imprint.

Spike Lee accepts his Oscar for "Black Klansman" donning golden sneakers.

Dwayne Wade wearing sneakers by footwear designer Alejandro Ingelmo.

Lebron James' famous golden sneakers.

expression across a variety of groups and subcultures, from punk rockers of the 1970s to hip-hop culture. In fact, Run DMC celebrated the importance of the sneaker as essential urban fashion in the 1980s hit "My Adidas."

Technological breakthroughs and new fabrications for the sneaker after the 1960s resulted in increased comfort and enhanced performance. The fitness and running craze of the 1970s ushered in a variety of upstart brands. The simple canvas upper and rubber sole was supplanted with a wide variety of special designs, colors, and fabrications for a host of sports, and wearers could proudly show their belonging with the type of shoe they wore. Brands used the growing celebrity of professional athletes to sell more shoes. Basketball proved, once again, particularly useful to market shoes. An extremely popular sport from grade school through college, basketball engaged people from a wide spectrum of ages, social statuses, and economic backgrounds.

"It's Gotta Be the Shoe."

Celebrity endorsements presented brands unique opportunities to showcase and market new technologies. For example, combine the NikeAir technology with the skill and showmanship of Michael Jordan on the court in the 1980s and a dynasty is born. Three decades later, in 2019, Jordan Brand, a division of Nike, dominates the US basketball shoe market with a reported $3 billion in annual sales.

The North American sneaker industry is valued at $3.6 billion, with 85 percent of sneakers sold for fashion, compared to 15 percent for sport use. The top four brands are Nike/Jordan, with 62 percent of the market; the Skecher and Adidas brands, with 5 percent each; and Asics rounding out the top four brands with 4 percent.

Special-edition shoes, limited-edition shoes, and retro releases of iconic styles like NikeAir Jordan-1 have created an overwhelmingly lucrative aftermarket or resale market, valued at over $1 billion. Sneaker collectors, or "sneakerheads," are willing to pay premium prices, well over established retail, to get their sneaker of choice. For a style retailing for about $104 a pair in North America, a buyer might expect to pay upwards of two and half times retail or more in the resale marketplace. Resale markets include eBay, which alone accounts for about $450 million in sneaker sales annually. Resale also happens through sneaker boutiques and consignment stores and through sneaker conventions.

Sneakers Under Glass

An exhibit, "Out of the Box: The Rise of Sneaker Culture," laced together the history and culture of iconic "kicks." Sneakers from three centuries, beginning with a pair from 1830, were part of an exhibit originated by the Banta Shoe Museum in Canada, traveled to the Brooklyn Museum in New York as well as Toronto and Louisville through 2016.

According to Brooklyn Museum curator Elizabeth Semmelhack, "sneakerheads" are historians. "They are interested in the nuances of this history, they suck the information dry. They spend time with the artifacts. They read every label. I tell you, there is not a better museum audience than the sneakerheads."

One museum visitor pointed out that people designed these, made these, and used these shoes. They are not just shoes. They are part of the culture.

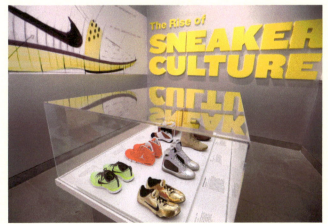

Brooklyn Museum hosts the exhibit "The Rise of Sneaker Culture," featuring the cultural history of the sneaker.

Ambivalence

Another theory holds that many people are ambivalent in their attitudes toward the new; they both want it and fear it. For most, it is easier to choose what is already familiar. Such individuals need time and exposure to new styles before they can accept them.

Varying Rates of Response

Individuals vary in the speed with which they respond to a new idea, especially when fashion change is radical and dramatic. Some fashion followers apparently need time to adjust to new ideas. Merchants exploit this point when they buy a few "window pieces" of styles too advanced for their own clientele and expose them in windows and fashion shows to allow customers time to get used to them. Only after a period of exposure to the new styles do the fashion followers accept them.

Fashion and Individuality

In the early part of the twenty-first century, a strange but understandable trend became apparent across the nation. People were striving, through their mode of dress, to declare individuality in the face of computer-age conformity.

People had watched strings of impersonal numbers become more a part of their lives—zip codes, bank and credit card account numbers, employee identification numbers, department store accounts, automobile registrations, Social Security numbers, and so on. An aversion to joining the masses—to becoming "just another number"—became prevalent. So while most people continued to go along with general fashion trends, some asserted their individuality. This was accomplished by distinctive touches each wearer added to an outfit. A freedom in dress, color and texture combinations, use of accessories, and hairstyles allowed people to assert their individuality without being out of step with the times.

We have all known people who at some point in their lives found a fashion that particularly pleased them. It might have been a certain style of dress, a certain shoe, or a hairstyle. Even in the face of continuing changes in fashion, the person continued to wear that style in which she or he felt right and attractive. Instead of slavishly adopting any one look, today's young person seeks to create an individual effect through the way he or she combines various fashion components. For instance, if a young woman thinks a denim skirt, an ankle-length woolen coat, and a heavy turtlenecked sweater represent her personality, they will likely be considered acceptable by others in her group. Having experienced such fashion freedom, young people may never conform again. Yet, despite individual differences in dress, young experimenters have in common a deep-rooted desire to dress differently from older generations. This is an assertion of individuality in the face of conformity.

Most social scientists, however, see this as a paradox—an endless conflict between the desire to conform and the desire to remain apart.

Designers and Self-Expression

Forward-looking designers recognize a consumer's desire for self-expression. Designers say that basic wardrobe components should be made available, but that consumers should be encouraged to combine them as they see fit. For instance, they advise women to wear pants or skirts, long or short, according to how they feel, not according to what past tradition has considered proper for an occasion. They suggest that men make the same choice among tailored suits, leisure wear, and slacks to find the styles that express their personalities.

Designer Kenneth Cole said, "Clothing is maybe the single greatest form of self-expression. Whether you're fashion-impaired or fashion-inspired, I urge everyone to take a few extra minutes every day to contemplate the message you're sending to the world."[13]

The Paradox of Conformity and Individuality

For decades, experts have tried to explain why people seek both conformity and individuality in fashion. One suggestion is that two opposing social tendencies are at war: the need for union and the need for isolation. The individual derives satisfaction from knowing that the way in which he or she expresses a fashion represents something special. At the same time, people gain support from seeing others favor the same style.

Retailers know that although some people like to lead and some like to follow in fashion, most people buy fashion to express their personality or to identify with a particular group. To belong, they follow fashion; to express their personalities, they find ways to individualize fashion.

Summary and Review

It is the nature of fashion to change, but the speed and direction of its changes are difficult to predict. Some factors that accelerate the pace of change are widespread buying power, increased leisure time, increased education, the improved status of women, technological advances that bring new and improved products to the market, sales promotion, and seasonal changes. However, the pace of change can be slowed by habit and custom, religious restrictions, sumptuary laws (laws placing limits or requirements on the construction of apparel), and reductions in consumers' buying power.

Some types of fashion merchandise change more slowly than other types. For example, men's fashions change more slowly than women's. Some fashion historians have tracked the basic shapes of apparel, particularly women's wear, and concluded that three basic silhouettes dominate fashion in turn, each for about thirty-five years, creating a cycle that lasts about 100 years. Other details of line, such as sleeve shape and skirt length, have similar cycles.

Fashion also focuses on different parts of the body at different times, accentuating the seductive appeal of each part in turn. For fashion merchandisers, success depends on the accuracy of predictions of trends and judging when and to what degree a fashion will be adopted by the producer's or retailer's target market. Inventory and sales records and a careful following of current events, the reception of new styles at the introductory stage of the fashion cycle, sales promotion, and current canons of taste help forecasters make accurate predictions.

Three theories attempt to explain the movement of fashion; they are the downward-flow, horizontal-flow, and upward-flow theories. The acceptance of a fashion depends on innovators, who are the first to wear it, and influentials, whose personal style is copied by others. On a broad scale, public figures are often innovators and influentials. The buying public watches the fashions of royalty, high society, athletes, entertainers, and other celebrities. On a smaller scale, individual communities have their own fashion innovators and influentials, but a fashion's acceptance ultimately depends on fashion followers. They are the people who spread a fashion and account for the number of sales. Each person adjusts his or her wardrobe to balance a sense of belonging to a group and being an individual.

FOR REVIEW

1. Describe the theory of fashion cycles and explain why it accelerated in the twentieth century.
2. According to leading fashion authorities, what are the three basic rules that govern the fashion game?
3. What basic resources are available to the fashion merchant to predict fashion?
4. Explain the term *prophetic style*.
5. Is the downward-flow theory of fashion adoption as valid today as it was in years past? Explain your answer.
6. How does the horizontal-flow theory of fashion adoption affect fashion merchants today? How are merchants today affected by the upward-flow theory?
7. Explain why rich people, famous people, and athletes are prime candidates for positions of fashion leadership.
8. Give four reasons why most people follow, rather than lead, in regard to fashion. Explain each.
9. How can fashion be used as a means of expressing individuality?

FOR DISCUSSION

1. Give at least one current example of each of several factors that are accelerating the forward movement of fashions today.
2. Certain factors tend to retard the development of fashion cycles by discouraging the adoption of newly introduced styles. List these factors and give at least one example of how each factor exerts a braking influence on fashion development.
3. Why do people today seek both conformity and individuality in fashion? How does this affect the fashion designer or manufacturer? The fashion retailer?

Trade Talk

Define or briefly explain the following terms:

downward-flow theory
erogenous
fashion influential
fashion innovator
horizontal-flow theory
prophetic styles
sumptuary laws
upward-flow theory

4

The Business of Fashion

Key Concepts

- **The four levels of the fashion business**

- **The three common forms of business ownership**

- **The roles of franchising and licensing**

- **The roles of the designer, the manufacturer, and the retailer in the fashion business**

Fashion is a business, affected by the same technological advances, investment patterns, and economic forces that affect other major businesses in the world. Fashion is not just limited to apparel, and it impacts our complete lifestyle as well as the products that we buy. Fashion influences the automobile, housing, and entertainment industries, and like these industries, it is shaped by the basic principles of business and economics.

What is business? Business is the activity of creating, producing, and marketing products or services. The primary objective of business is to make a profit. **Profit**, or net income, is the amount of money a business earns in excess of its expenses. Consequently, in the United States, business can be defined as the activity of creating, producing, and marketing products or services for a profit.

Economic Importance of the Fashion Business

The business of fashion contributes significantly to the economy of the world through the materials and services it purchases, the wages and taxes it pays, and the goods and services it produces. The fashion business is one of the largest employers in the country, despite the decline in employment since the industry boom in the early 1970s. The apparel industry in the United States employs 1.9 million people, including employees who work in textile mills, garment manufacturing, footwear manufacturing, piece goods, notions, clothing sales, and accessories sales.[1]

The growth and development of mass markets, mass-production methods, and mass distribution have contributed to the creation of new job opportunities in the fashion industry—not only in the production area, but in design and marketing as well. Young people are entering the fashion business in greater numbers each year and are having a marked effect on the business. Innovation and change have become increasingly important factors in the economic growth of the fashion business.

Scope of the Fashion Business

The fashion business is composed of numerous industries all working to keep consumers of fashion satisfied.

A special relationship exists among these industries that makes the fashion business different from other businesses. The four different levels of the fashion business—known as the primary, secondary, retail, and auxiliary levels—are composed of separate entities, but they also work interdependently to provide the market with the fashion merchandise that will satisfy consumers. Because of this unique relationship among the different industries, the fashion business is unusually exciting (see Figure 4.1).

The Primary Level

The **primary level** is composed of the growers and producers of the raw materials of fashion—the fiber, fabric, leather, and fur producers who function in the raw materials market. The earliest part of the planning function in color and texture takes place on the primary level. It is also the level of the fashion business that works the furthest in advance of the ultimate selling period of the goods. Up to two years' lead time is needed by primary-level companies before the goods will be available to the consumer. Primary-level goods may often be imports from Third World emerging nations, where textiles are usually the earliest form of industrialization.

The Secondary Level

The **secondary level** is composed of industries—manufacturers and contractors—that produce the semi-finished or finished fashion goods from the materials produced on the primary level. On the secondary level are the designers and manufacturers of women's, men's, and children's apparel and also legwear, bodywear, and underwear; accessories; cosmetics and fragrances; and home furnishings.

Manufacturers who function on the secondary level may be based in the United States or overseas. Fashion goods are produced in the Far East, the Caribbean, South America, and Europe. Secondary-level companies work from six months to one and a half years ahead of the time that goods are available to the consumer.

The Retail Level

The **retail level** is the ultimate distribution level. On this level are the different types of retailers who buy

THE LEVELS OF THE FASHION INDUSTRY

Primary level	Secondary level	Retail level		Consumers

Farms/Laboratories	Designers	Department Stores	Category Killers	
Fibers	Manufacturers	Specialty Stores	Wholesale Clubs	
Yarns	Contractors	Chain Stores	Flea Markets	
Greige Goods	Wholesalers	Mail Order/Catalogs	Mom & Pop Stores	
Converters	Vendors	Boutiques	Mass Merchants	
		Discount Stores	Superstores	
		Off-Price Stores	Internet	
		Factory Outlets		

Buying/Merchandising/Product
Development Offices
Fashion Forecasters
Specialists/Consultants
Trade Associations

Magazines
Newspapers
Advertising Agencies
Research Agencies

AUXILIARY LEVEL

Figure 4.1 The fashion industry operates collaboratively on four levels to serve the customer.

their goods from the secondary level and then supply them directly to the consumer. In many cases, the retail level works with both the primary and secondary levels to ensure a coordinated approach to consumer wants. The relationship among the primary, secondary, and retail levels is vertical. The further removed a level is from the consumer, the further in advance it must be planned. Retailers make initial purchases for resale to customers from three to six months before the customer buying season.

The Auxiliary Level

The **auxiliary level** is the only level that functions with all the other levels simultaneously. This level is composed of all the support services that are working constantly with primary producers, secondary manufacturers, and retailers to keep consumers aware of the fashion merchandise produced for ultimate consumption. On this level are all the advertising media—print, audio, and visual—and fashion consultants and researchers.

Diversity and Competition

The enormous variety and diversity that exist in the kinds and sizes of firms that operate on each level of the fashion industry make it an intriguing and competitive business. There are giant firms, both national and international, and small companies with regional or local distribution, doing business side by side as privately or publicly owned corporations, partnerships, or sole proprietorships. Fashion-producing companies may also be part of conglomerates, which also own, for example, entertainment companies, oil wells, professional sports teams, or consumer foods and products divisions.

Whether large or small, the different types of producers have one need in common—the need to understand what their ultimate customer will buy. Only through complete understanding and cooperation can the four levels of the fashion business be aware of new developments in fashion and apply them to satisfy the wants of their customers. This cooperation allows them to have the right merchandise at the right price, in the right place, at the right time, in the right quantities, and with the right sales promotion for their customers.

However, when you begin to try to sell a product or service in our economic system, chances are that someone else will be trying to sell something similar. No matter what the size of the firm involved, potential customers are free to buy where and what they please. Each company must compete with the others for those customers' business. A company can choose to compete in one of three ways: price, quality, or innovation.

RENT THE RUNWAY! A Closet in the "Cloud"

For decades, someone in need of formal attire could rent a tuxedo or a gown from a local formalwear rental shop. The selections were often limited but renting solved the problem of having to pay dearly for something to be worn only once for scores of prom dates, grooms, bridesmaids, fathers of the bride and groom, groomsmen, brides, and maybe even an Oscar nominee or two!

So, renting clothes is not necessarily a new idea. But the co-founders of Rent the Runway, Jenn Hyman and Jenny Fleiss, have put a new twist on this old idea. Since 2009, the online rental business has grown into a $1 billion business. With expanded offerings and online accessibility, clothing rentals are revolutionized.

Whether it's a special outfit for a big event, or a regular rotating wardrobe to venture into the latest fashions, Rent the Runway uses digital technology, the vast reach of the Internet, and the "share" economy to help solve the problem of a closet full of clothes and nothing to wear. Some time ago, the Internet changed the way we shop. Now, Rent the Runway fashion rental business is changing the way consumers think about shopping.

People normally wear about twenty percent of the clothes in their closets, leading to an average of eighty-one pounds of clothing waste per person every year. Rent the Runway strives to solve this problem by offering a "cloud" of fashions, from which clients can choose. Through a monthly subscription program, customers can rent for a single occasion, like a wedding or formal event. Or, they can update their wardrobe on a regular, rotating basis. Started in 2009, the service was immediately recognized as a ready solution for the one-off purchase—the bridesmaid dress or cocktail dress. But as the company has grown, it has become a viable long-term option, allowing customers to rent, wear for several days, and return. With shipping, mending, and dry cleaning included in the monthly subscription, for many it has become an alternative to shopping. In 2019, Rent the Runway was named the fifth most disruptive company, alongside the likes of Uber and its disruption of taxi services, and Airbnb and its disruption of the hotel business.

Co-Founder of Rent the Runway Jenn Hyman.

Co-Founder of Rent the Runway Jenny Fleiss.

The future of fashion is here.

Expand your closet.

In addition to eCommerce sales, members can also visit Rent the Runway store locations in San Francisco, CA, Santa Monica, CA, Chicago, IL, New York, NY, and Washington DC.

Rent the Runway inventories about 450,000 items. The operation is controlled by an intricate logistics process, which is managed entirely in-house in a 150,000 square foot facility. To manage cleaning and maintenance, they designed and built the nation's largest dry-cleaning facility, and work with over 500 designers—some well-known, and some starting out. This business model helps young designers get started, and the company works directly with selected designers to create custom items only available through Rent the Runway.

Fashions rent for about ten percent of the retail purchase price, and the inventory carries sizes 0–22 depending on the designer. Shoes, jewelry, handbags, and sunglasses are all available to fully finish an outfit, and recent additions to the service include children's wear, and home décor items such as throws, pillows, bedding, and more through a partnership with West Elm.

The average woman throws away eighty-two pounds of clothing per year. Rent the Runway promotes renting things that are only worn once, or a few times, as the sustainable answer. Other sustainability practices include patented shipping bags to reduce cardboard, responsible dry-cleaning practices, high-quality garments that last and sustain reuse, plastic recycling, and only faux fur—no real animal fur or feathers in their inventory.

Rent the Runway takes the mom-and-pop clothing rental model into the twenty-first century. Their business model is based on efficiency, infrastructure, data collection and interpretation to understand what drives customer trends, and emphasis on a personalized shopping experience.

Competition and Price

Selling blue jeans for less than your competition may bring you more business. However, you are taking in less money than your rival does on each pair sold, and you still have to cover the same cost and expenses. The hope is that your lower price will attract more customers, sell more jeans than your competition, and so allow you to come out with a good overall profit. Head-to-head competition like this tends to keep prices down, which is good for the buying public. At the same time, it allows a company to look forward to a promise of profits if it can sell more of its product or service than competitors do. Shopping sites, such as Gilt and Overstock.com originally went into business to offer unsold merchandise from makers of luxury apparel, home furnishings, and other high-end goods during an economic recessionary period. Through a membership-only sales program, and limited supply of over-produced goods, they fueled demand, forcing potential clients to buy goods immediately, or run the risk of items selling out at the discounted prices.[2] Through the use of these private-sale shopping sites, businesses increase their competitiveness.

Competition and Quality

Rather than sell your jeans for less than your competition, you may choose to compete for customers by offering higher-quality goods. Although you may charge more for your jeans, you offer a better fit, more durable fabric, or better styling. This possibility provides a practical incentive for businesses to maintain high standards and increases the choices available to consumers.

Competition and Innovation

Our economic system encourages not only variations in quality and price but also immense variety in the types of merchandise and services offered to the public. Changes in taste and new technology bring about innovation so that your jeans could be trimmed or untrimmed, designer made, or French cut. The economy and the competitive environment are constantly creating new business opportunities. The result is an astonishing diversity of businesses.

Government Regulation of Business

In the United States, the right of government to regulate business is granted by the US Constitution and by state constitutions. There are two basic categories of federal legislation that affect the fashion industry: laws that regulate competition, and labeling laws designed to protect consumers. Key federal laws that affect and regulate the fashion industry are shown in Table 4.1.

Forms of Business Ownership

Ownership of a fashion business—or of any business—may take many different legal forms, each carrying certain privileges and responsibilities. The three most common forms of business ownership are the sole proprietorship, the partnership, and the corporation. Corporations tend to be large-scale operations that account for the greatest share of the profits earned by US business. However, sole proprietorships are more numerous, accounting for almost 73 percent of all businesses.

Each form of ownership has a characteristic structure, legal status, size, and field to which it is best suited. Each has its own advantages and disadvantages and offers a distinctive working environment with its own risks and rewards (see Table 4.2).

Business Growth and Expansion

The news media is filled with reports of businesses buying and selling other businesses and seeking new methods to make themselves more efficient and competitive.

One of the most distinct changes in the fashion business has been the rise of corporate giants, which grew through mergers, acquisitions, and internal expansion. The growth of these giants has changed the methods of doing business and has led to the demise of old-time famous-name sole proprietorships, partnerships, and small companies that could no longer compete.

Growth and expansion are fundamental to today's business world. Corporate growth has become a major

TABLE 4.1 Key Federal Laws Affecting the Fashion Industry

Laws affecting competition	Purpose and provisions
Sherman Antitrust Act—1890	Outlawed monopolies and restraint of competition
Clayton Act—1914	Same purpose as Sherman Act but reinforced that act by defining some specific restraint—(e.g., price fixing)
Federal Trade Commission (FTC) Act—1914 (Wheeler–Lee Act of 1938 amended the FTC Act)	Established the FTC as a "policing" agency; developed the mechanics for policing unfair methods of competition (e.g., false claims, price discrimination, price fixing)
Robinson–Patman Act—1936	Designed to equalize competition between large and small retailers (i.e., to reduce the advantages that big retailers have over small retailers)—outgrowth of 1930s Depression and growth of big chain retailers in 1920s Examples of provision of law: 1. Outlawed price discrimination if both small and large retailers buy the same amount of goods 2. Outlawed inequitable and unjustified quantity discounts (e.g., discounts allowable if (a) available to all types of retailers and (b) related to actual savings that vendors could make from quantity cuttings or shipments) 3. Outlawed "phony" advertising allowance monies (i.e., advertising money must be used for advertising) 4. Outlawed discrimination in promotional allowances (monies for advertising, promotional display, etc.)—equal allowances must be given under same conditions to small and large retailers alike
Wool Products Labeling Act—1939; amended in 2006	Protects consumers from unrevealed presence of substitutes or mixtures; FTC responsible for enforcing law
Cellar–Kefauver—1950	Made it illegal to eliminate competition by creating a monopoly through the merger of two or more companies
Fur Products Labeling Act—1951; amended in 2000	Protects consumers and retailers against misbranding, false advertising, and false invoicing
Flammable Fabrics Act—1954; amended in 1972	Prohibits manufacture or sale of flammable fabrics, interior furnishings, and apparel; transferred responsibility to the Consumer Product Safety Commission
Textile Fiber Identification Act—1960; amended in 2000	Protects producers and consumers against false identification of fiber content
Fair Packaging and Labeling Act—1966	Regulates interstate and foreign commerce by prohibiting deceptive methods of packaging or labeling
Care Labeling of Textile Wearing Apparel Ruling—1972; amended in 1984, 1997	Requires that all apparel have labels attached that clearly inform consumers about care and maintenance of the article

TABLE 4.2 Advantages and Disadvantages of Each Form of Business Ownership

Form of ownership	Advantages	Disadvantages
Sole proprietorship (single owner)	Ability to keep all profits Simple to form and easiest to dissolve Ownership flexibility	Unlimited financial liability Limited capital Management deficiencies Lack of continuity
Partnership (a few owners)	Ease of formation Greater financial capacity than sole proprietorship Less red tape than corporation	Unlimited financial liability Interpersonal conflicts Lack of continuity if partner dies Harder to dissolve than sole proprietorship
Corporation ("Inc."; many owners)	Limited financial liability Specialized management skills Greater financial capacity than other forms of ownership Economies of larger-scale operation Easy to transfer ownership	Difficult and costly ownership form to establish and dissolve Tax disadvantage Legal restrictions Depersonalization

economic, political, and social issue. Growth and expansion can occur in a variety of ways—internal growth, mergers, and acquisitions. Many large corporations grow by more than one of these methods. For example, cosmetics giant Estée Lauder developed the Origins brand to appeal to a more environmentally conscience consumer market. The company also acquired several smaller companies that cater to a younger market, including Bobbi Brown and MAC.

Internal Growth

A company's ability to grow internally determines its ability to offer more services and broader assortments of merchandise and to increase profits. This is true because internal growth is real growth, in terms of creating new products and new jobs. Internal growth can be accomplished through horizontal means, vertical means, or both. When a company has **horizontal growth**, it expands its capabilities on the level at which it has been performing successfully. An apparel company could add new lines to diversify its product offerings; a retail store could open new branches. When a company has **vertical growth**, it expands its capabilities on levels other than its primary function (see Figure 4.2). An apparel company could begin to produce its own fabric or could retail its manufactured goods in stores that the apparel company owns.

Figure 4.2 A Ralph Lauren store, an example of vertical growth.

Mergers and Acquisitions

In a **merger** (or acquisition), one company is sold to another company, with the purchasing company usually remaining dominant. Companies merge to form a larger corporate organization for many reasons. They may wish to take advantage of a large corporation's greater purchasing power, or they may want to sell stock to obtain the financial resources needed for expansion. The desire to constantly increase sales is often able to be fulfilled only by a merger. At the retail level, for example, the acquisition of the May Department Stores Company by

Federated Department Stores extended the conglomerate's market. In 2007, Federated Department Stores then changed its name to Macy's, Inc.

Operating economies can often be achieved by combining companies. Many times duplicate facilities can be eliminated, and marketing, purchasing, and other operations can be consolidated. **Diversification**, the addition of various lines, products, or services to serve different markets, can also be a motive for a merger. For example, the acquisition of Banana Republic by Gap broadened Gap's market to reach customers for clothing at higher price points. Then Gap started Old Navy to reach even lower price points. Now the company covers three price points.

The Franchise

A growing business arrangement is the franchise. The **franchise** arrangement is a contract that gives an individual (or group of people) the right to own a business while benefiting from the expertise and reputation of an established firm. In return, the individual, known as the franchisee, pays the parent company, known as the franchisor, a set sum to purchase the franchise and royalties on goods or services sold. Franchises may be organized as sole proprietorships, partnerships, or corporations, although the form of business organization that the franchise must use may be designated in the franchise contract (see Figure 4.3).

In 2018, franchises generated $757.2 billion in retail sales in the United States.[3] The franchise arrangement is most widespread among fast-food restaurants, convenience stores, and automobile dealers, but franchises are found at many levels of the fashion business, especially in retailing.

The growth in the number of manufacturer-franchised shops is phenomenal. One of the outstanding examples of this is the very popular Athlete's Foot stores. Although we will learn much more about designer-name franchising when we cover the apparel industries, it is important to note that Ralph Lauren, Donna Karan, and Oscar de la Renta are all involved in designer-franchised boutiques and shops in major cities throughout the United States, Europe, and Asia.

Figure 4.3 Lululemon Athletica is a fast-growing franchise.

KATE MCCONNELL OF ASIATICA

MEET KATE MCCONNELL, DESIGNER AND PRODUCTION MANAGER FOR ASIATICA. Asiatica is a unique retail store located in Westwood, Kansas, a suburb in the Kansas City metro area. Operating since 1977, Asiatica features a wide variety of merchandise curated from Japanese art and culture, including antique and modern Japanese objects, and one-of-a-kind fashions made from vintage Japanese kimono fabrics, contemporary artisanal fabrics from Japan, and other luxurious textiles.

Unlike most retail stores, Asiatica is unique in that it also functions as an *atelier* and production facility for the collection of contemporary Asian-inspired fashions marketed through the store and through a nationwide program of trunk shows. McConnell manages a production team of six employees, and all of the cutting and sewing is performed on-site, producing about 1,000 garments and accessories each year. Knowledge of garment construction, design, fit, fabrics, and alteration is essential. Because of the one-of-a-kind nature of the products, very little technology is used in the process. For each collection that is produced, decisions on design, fabrication, and size selection are made, and then each garment is cut individually, and each pattern is drafted and graded by hand. As each collection is developed, the production work is managed through weekly and daily goals to be performed by the production team.

McConnell's lifelong experience in sewing and clothing construction eventually led her to earn her BFA in textile design at the University of Kansas. Since vintage textiles are central to the product design, textile history and knowledge of fabrics is essential, and all of this background provides a perfect combination of skills and experience. Creative inspiration also plays an important part of this process. To this end, McConnell is active in the regional arts community and researches design and garment construction ideas on an ongoing basis.

Asiatica's unique fashion line is promoted and sold through an extensive trunk show program. So, in addition to her production responsibilities, McConnell travels to twenty to twenty-five cities each year, working with clients across the nation. The ability to call upon a wide range of skills to meet each day's challenges is essential. In addition to technical and artistic skills, McConnell emphasizes the importance of organization and communication skills as part of excellent customer relations.

Her advice to students: "Study what you love and have strong interests in. Make yourself valuable to your employer. Be curious, eager, and do whatever needs to be done. Tell everyone you know what you would like to do. Be positive and courteous."

Vintage fabrics of all sizes are artfully cut and pieced together to create unique, one-of-a-kind Asiatica fashions and accessories.

Advantages

Franchising offers advantages to both the franchisee and the franchisor. The franchisee can get into business quickly, use proven operating methods, and benefit from training programs and mass purchasing offered by the franchisor. The franchisee is provided with a ready market that identifies with the store or brand name, thus assuring customer traffic. The franchisor has a great deal of control over its distribution network, limited liability, and less need for capital for expansion. Expansion is therefore more rapid than would be possible without the franchising arrangement. Royalty and franchise fees add to the profits of the parent company, and the personal interest and efforts of the franchisees as owner-managers help to assure the success of each venture.

Disadvantages

Franchising also has drawbacks for both parties. The franchisee may find profits small in relation to the time and work involved and often has limited flexibility at the local level. In addition, there is the risk of franchise arrangements organized merely to sell franchises, rather than for their long-range profitability to all parties involved. The franchisor may find profits so slim that it may want to own stores outright rather than franchise them. Attempts to buy back franchises often lead to troubled relations with the remaining franchises.

Licensing

Licensing is an increasingly popular method of expanding an already existing business. **Licensing** is a legal arrangement whereby firms are given permission to produce and market merchandise in the name of the licensor for a specific period of time. The licensor is then paid a percentage of the sales (usually at the wholesale price), called a **royalty fee**. The royalty fee usually ranges from 2 to 15 percent.

Licensing grew tremendously in the late 1970s through the 1990s. The United States and Canada have accounted for about 58 percent of worldwide retail sales to licensed merchandise. By 2018, retail sales of licensed merchandise worldwide totaled $280.30 billion. The United States and Canada compose the largest single market for licensed merchandise worldwide, valued at $162.68 billion.[4]

The first designer to license his name to a manufacturer was Christian Dior, who lent his name to a line of ties in 1950. Many of the best-known women's and men's apparel designers are licensing either the use of their original designs or just their names without a design for a wide variety of goods, from apparel to luggage. Many fashion labels—Ralph Lauren and Badgley Mischka, for example—also extend into home furnishings through licensing. Among the many American designers involved in licensing are Michael (Michael Kors), Bill Blass, Calvin Klein, Ralph Lauren, and Oscar de la Renta. Most customers are not aware that some of the fashion merchandise they buy is licensed. For example, to customers every Kenneth Cole product is made by Kenneth Cole. In fact, this licensor manufactures *no* merchandise in-house.

The licensing phenomenon is not limited to name designers. Manufacturers of athletic shoes expand their business enormously by licensing their logos and names to producers of active sportswear. Nike, Reebok, and Adidas have been particularly successful. Popular movies and TV shows, such as *Star Wars* and *Game of Thrones*, have spawned apparel and other products based on their themes or characters. Superhero characters from Marvel and DC are licensed. And cartoon characters, like Mickey Mouse, Dora the Explorer, Spider-Man, and Strawberry Shortcake are frequently licensed, as are most professional sports teams and many players or athletes.

The advantage of a licensing arrangement to a manufacturer is that the merchandise is identified with a highly recognizable name, which also generally connotes high quality. Of course, the manufacturer also runs the risk of the designer's popularity fading. However, many manufacturers produce licensed goods for several designers.

The recognition factor can be valuable to retailers in presenting their own fashion images. And to consumers, the designer name not only indicates a certain quality of merchandise but symbolizes status or achievement as well. Because of that built-in appeal, stores have stocked up on designer goods from socks to fragrances and jewelry.

The Designer's Role

There are unlimited opportunities in the field of design for those who have the special talents, both artistic and practical, that are needed to shape the consumer's world.

Designers are everywhere and they design everything—fashions, furnishings, housewares, and office equipment. Their tools range from pencils and sketchpads to computer programs.

In creating designs that will not only reflect consumer attitudes and needs but also give expression to artistic ideas, fashion designers are continually influenced and limited by many factors. Of particular importance are practical business considerations. All designs must be produced at a profit and within the firm's predetermined wholesale price range. Consequently, designers must consider the availability and cost of materials, the particular image that the firm wants to maintain, available production techniques, and labor costs. Great designers use their creativity to overcome all these limitations and to produce salable, exciting designs.

Types of Designers

Most designers can be classified in one of the following three categories:

1. **High-fashion, or "name," designers**: They are responsible for the full range of decisions of a fashion house, as well as for establishing the image and creating designs for the company. They design ready-to-wear lines as well as custom designs, and many license the use of their prestigious names to manufacturers of accessories, fragrances and cosmetics, and home fashions.
2. **Stylist-designers**: They work for manufacturers and adapt the designs of others, typically of name designers. Usually they create variations in less-expensive fabrics to appeal to a market for lower-priced merchandise at the late rise or early culmination stage of the fashion cycle.
3. **Freelance designers**: They sell sketches of their original designs or adaptations to manufacturers. Freelancers typically work out of design studios. They are not involved in the selection of fabrics and colors or in the business decisions that are required to manufacture the products based on their designs.

Sources of Design Inspiration

Where does the designer get ideas and inspiration for new fashion? The answer, of course, is everywhere! Through TV, the designer experiences all the wonders of the entertainment world. In films, the designer is exposed to the influences of all the arts and lifestyles throughout the world. Because consumers are exposed to movies through international distribution, films prime their audiences to accept new fashions inspired by the costumes. Museum exhibits, art shows, world happenings, expositions, theater, music, dance, and world travel are all sources of design inspiration to fashion designers. The fashions of the past are also a rich source of design inspiration.

While always alert to the new and exciting, fashion designers never lose sight of the recent past. They know that consumers need to anticipate something new each season. But they also recognize that whatever new style is introduced will have to take its place with what consumers already have in their wardrobes. No one starts with all new clothes each season. Rarely does a revolutionary new style succeed. Instead, it is the evolutionary new style that so often becomes the best-selling fashion.

The Manufacturer's Role

Manufacturers would agree with Dwight E. Robinson that "every market into which the consumer's fashion sense has insinuated itself is, by that very token, subject to [the] common, compelling need for unceasing change in the styling of its goods."[5]

Even in such mundane items as writing paper, the need for change has produced rainbows of pastels, brilliant deep shades, and the traditional white with dainty or bold prints. Similarly, in basics such as bedsheets or men's dress shirts, the once traditional white has yielded to a variety of colors, stripes, and prints. There is scarcely an industry serving consumers today in which the manufacturer's success does not depend, in part, on an ability to attune styling to fashion interest and demand. A current trend is to hire merchandisers who do market research for the manufacturer, specializing in identifying the correct customer and his or her needs and wants.

Types of Manufacturers

In general, manufacturers of fashion goods can be divided into five groups, differentiated by styling and price. One group is made up of designers or firms that produce innovative, high-fashion apparel that is very expensive.

Another group bridges the price range between custom designs and high-quality but less-expensive merchandise, hence the name *bridge market*. Some high-fashion designers also produce bridge lines. The next group is usually identified as the better market. Its price range is just below that of the bridge lines. A fourth group of firms sometimes produces originals, but usually turns out adaptations of styles that have survived the introduction stage and are in the rise stage of their fashion life cycle. This group of firms is usually identified as the moderate-priced market. A fifth group of manufacturers makes no attempt to offer new or unusual styling. Rather, these firms mass-produce close copies or adaptations of styles that have proved their acceptance in higher-priced markets. This group is usually identified as the budget market.

Fashion Influence

In the field of women's apparel, manufacturers are committed to producing several new lines a year. A **line** is an assortment of new designs with a designated period for delivery to the retailer. Some of these may be new in every sense of the word and others merely adaptations of currently popular styles. Producers hope that a few of the designs in a given line will prove to be "hot"—so precisely in step with demand that their sales will be profitably large.

For the most part, the fashion industries are made up of manufacturers whose abilities to anticipate the public's response to styles is excellent. Those who do badly in this respect, even for a single season, usually reap small sales and large losses. Unless they are unusually well financed, they quickly find themselves out of business. In the fashion industry, the survival of the fittest means the survival of those who give the most able assistance in the birth and growth of fashions that consumers will buy.

The Retailer's Role

Although retailers do not usually create fashion, they can encourage or retard its progress by the degree of accuracy with which they anticipate the demands of their customers. They seek out from manufacturers styles that they believe are most likely to win acceptance from these target groups.

Some large retailers work directly with manufacturers and firms at the primary level to develop styles for exclusive sale at their stores. Thus, retailers such as Gap and The Limited can stock only their own labels. Others, such as Macy's, sell private-label merchandise along with national brands (see Figure 4.4). (We will examine the practice of product development by retailers in more detail in Chapter 7.)

Figure 4.4 Brands that are limited in distribution or exclusive to certain stores, such as Tommy Hilfiger's sportswear to Macy's, are a growing trend in the industry.

PERSONALIZATION IS THE NEW BLACK

In what seems to many shoppers like a sea of merchandise where everything looks the same—same colors, same quality, same design—retailers at all merchandise levels find success by amping up their personalization efforts, and making their customers feel like their own unique, personal style or need is at the forefront of their shopping experience.

Shoppers want individualized service and products that help them express themselves and help them stand out from the crowd. According to a study by Deloitte, one in four customers are willing to pay more for a personalized product or service, and more retailers are using brick-and-mortar to help bring this to customers. Using data and technology, retailers curate an experience for the in-store shopper and provide them options based on that data to ensure that whatever they purchase is truly their own. And the personalization pays back! When products and services are more personalized, customers are happier. And happy customers like to post their product or experience on social media.

"Due to leaps forward in technology, the products for sale are able to be customized and personalized as well, often while you watch," explains Sterling Plenert, SVP and Sector Leader for Luxury Retail at Callison RTKL. "In-store fabrication facilities are becoming more common and allow everyone to be able to purchase one-of-a-kind products from their favorite brands. This kind of individualized experience is what is making brick-and-mortar retail more exciting than it has ever been. The smart retailer has learned how to keep the environment fresh so that it's new and engaging every visit . . . spaces that make the customer feel special and enhance the experience of making a purchase."

Some retailers are improving on existing products through personalized services:

- De Beers uses blockchain to authenticate its diamonds as conflict-free for shoppers.
- L'Oreal is using augmented reality (AR), artificial intelligence (AI) and facial recognition to go beyond simulating make-overs on a screen, adding skin health diagnostics to their capabilities.
- Burberry is empowering associates with data and iPads to provide sales associates access to shoppers' purchase histories in order to enable meaningful conversations with

Blockchain is an automated and safe way to send information digitally from one point to another.

customers.

- Dr. Scholl's kiosks offer on-the-spot scanning of the foot, noting the areas that receive the most pressure, and recommendation of the appropriate orthotic based on that specific data.
- Chanel sales associates change it up by going old school, and send hand-written, personal thank-you notes to customers.
- Retailers use former purchase data gleaned from loyalty programs or other data gathering sources to personalize targeted advertising based on prior purchases.
- Dresden lets in-store shoppers create their own pair of eyeglasses or sunglasses.
- Levi's Taylor Shops allow customers to personalize their Levi's purchases with stenciling, monograms, embroidery, distressing, and more.
- Enfagrow uses birth data to tailor messages and sales pushes to moms about products based on the growing baby's age and stage of development.

Now it's your turn! What ideas do you have about how to personalize products and services at the places you like to shop?

Personal selling techniques like sampling and thank you notes are a key part of Chanel's customer service and makes the shopping experience personal to the buyer.

Types of Retailers

There are many ways to classify retail firms. However, when firms are evaluated on the basis of their leadership positions, they tend to fall into three main categories.

First, there are firms that are considered "fashion leaders." They feature newly introduced styles that have only limited production and distribution. These styles, called "designer collections," are usually very expensive. Examples of these firms include Bergdorf Goodman, Neiman Marcus, and Nordstrom.

A second group, called "traditional retailers"—by far the largest in number—features fashions that have captured consumer interest in their introduction stage and are in the late rise or early culmination stages of their life cycles. These styles are from designer "bridge collections" or from "better" or "moderate" manufacturers. Since these styles are usually widely produced by this time, they are most often offered at more moderate prices. Examples of these firms include Macy's, Dillard's, and Bloomingdale's. The distinction between the traditional retailers and fashion leaders is somewhat blurred in that the fashion leaders may also carry "traditional" merchandise, and the traditional retailers may have designer departments.

A third group of retailers, often called "mass merchants," features widely accepted fashions that are well into the culmination phase of their life cycles. Since fashions at this stage of development are usually mass produced, mass merchants can and do offer fashions at moderate to low prices. Examples of these firms include JCPenney and Sears. At the low end of the mass market are the discounters, like the off-price Dress Barn, for example, which sells merchandise at discounted prices. Other examples include Walmart and Kmart.

Fashion Influence

Sometimes, because of their constant and intimate contact with their customers, retailers are so intuitive or creative that they lead their suppliers in anticipating the styles their customers will accept. Such retailers accelerate the introduction and progress of new fashions by persuading manufacturers to produce styles that answer an upcoming need or demand. Because of this ability, retailers are doing more and more product development for their own customers (see Figure 4.5).

Figure 4.5 Retailers have to stay just a step ahead of their target customers. Retailers need to have sufficient stock available when customers are ready to buy a new fashion, but need to avoid being overstocked when customers' interests shift to a new fashion.

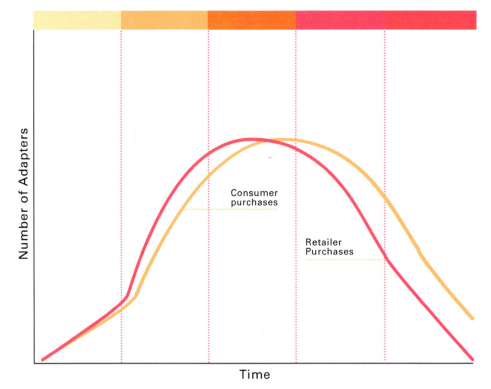

CONSUMER BUYING CYCLE versus RETAILER BUYING CYCLE

Number of Adapters

Consumer purchases

Retailer Purchases

Time

Summary and Review

The fashion industry is a major business sector in the United States and around the world. It employs people at four levels: (1) producers of materials, such as natural and manufactured textiles, leather, fur, and materials used in decorative trimmings; (2) manufacturers of apparel, accessories, cosmetics and fragrances, and home fashions; (3) fashion retailers; and (4) auxiliary services to the other three levels, including market research and forecasting and promotional services. Businesses at all four levels collaborate to capture their share of the market.

Companies compete with others at their level by offering advantages of price, quality, and innovation. The federal government regulates the production and sale of fashion goods to ensure safe, functional products for consumers and fair marketing practices among competitors.

Like other businesses, fashion businesses at all levels may be sole proprietorships, partnerships, or corporations. Fashion companies grow horizontally by getting into new markets or vertically by expanding into levels beyond the level of their original business. They may expand internally, acquire or merge with other companies, or franchise or license a part of their businesses. Continuing into the twenty-first century, licensing is an important part of virtually every major designer's business strategy, and businesses outside the fashion industry license their names and logos to apparel producers.

At all levels, fashion business executives must be able to predict the tastes of the consumers who wear and use their merchandise. Depending on the level, a company must anticipate consumer demand from six months to one year and a half in advance of the day a new fashion becomes available at retail.

FOR REVIEW

1. What is the primary objective of all businesses? Explain your answer.
2. Describe the four levels of the fashion business. Give examples.
3. How does the auxiliary level differ from the other levels?
4. Compare the advantages and disadvantages of a sole proprietorship and a partnership as a form of business for a fashion retailer.
5. Why do companies seek growth through mergers and acquisitions?
6. What are the practical obstacles that limit fashion designers? What additional factors must be considered in developing each fashion design?
7. List the three types of designers commonly serving the US fashion industry today. List the responsibilities of each.
8. If you were the president of a national chain of shoe stores, what are five laws and regulations that would affect how you do business? Which of these laws would not affect a small, privately owned bridal shop?
9. What is the difference between a license agreement and a franchise?
10. How is a licensed designer name an advantage to the manufacturer? To the consumer? To the retailer?

FOR DISCUSSION

1. What initial decisions need to be made by an individual or group of individuals who plan to form a company with regard to the form of ownership that will be most beneficial to all?
2. What does the statement "You're only as good as your last collection" mean in regard to fashion designers?

Trade Talk

Define or briefly explain the following terms:

auxiliary level
diversification
franchise
horizontal growth
licensing
line
merger
primary level
profit
retail level
royalty fee
secondary level
vertical growth

PART TWO

The Primary Level: The Materials of Fashion

In this part, you will examine the primary market suppliers—the growers and producers of the raw materials of fashion. You will begin to develop a basic vocabulary and a working knowledge of the following:

- The history, manufacture, and uses of natural, regenerated, and synthetic fibers and fabrics are explored in Chapter 5.
- The history, processing, and politics of manufacturing leathers and fur are explored in Chapter 6.

The earliest part of the planning function—in both color and texture—takes place on the primary level. It is also the level of the fashion business that works the furthest in advance of the ultimate selling period for the finished goods. Primary-level companies need up to two years' lead time before the goods will be available to the consumer. Goods at the primary level may often be imports from Third World emerging nations, where textiles are usually the earliest form of industrialization. The primary level is the foundation upon which the merchandisers and marketers of fashion products build their ideas and designs that will answer the needs and wants of the customer.

5

Textiles: Fibers and Fabrics

Key Concepts

- **The difference between a natural fiber, a regenerated fiber, and a synthetic fiber**

- **The major steps in the production of most fabrics**

- **The effect of imports on the US fiber and fabric industries**

- **The effects of new technology on textiles**

Fashion and the materials from which they are made are inseparable. Have you ever bought a fashion product simply because you loved the feel of it? Perhaps it was rough and coarse or silky and smooth. Maybe it was incredibly soft to the touch. If so, then you, like almost everyone else, have responded to a fabric rather than to the style or color of a fashion product.

The designer creating a style at the drawing board must consider the material best suited for the particular silhouette and details of design (see Figure 5.1). The manufacturer must then consider the various weights of material currently desired as well as the cost factors. Finally, the retailer must select fashions made of those materials considered appropriate and desirable by the target customers.

The material or fabric a garment is made of is so important that Christian Dior, the world-famous designer, once said of it: "Fabric not only expresses a designer's dream, but also stimulates his own ideas. It can be the beginning of an inspiration. Many a dress of mine is born of the fabric alone."[1]

Figure 5.1
Voluminous silk dress designed by Monique Lhuillier.

The enormous appeal of **fabric**—and the **fiber**s of which it is composed—lies in its many varied textures, finishes, uses, and colors. These are created, as we shall learn, by the fiber and fabric industries that work closely together to produce an end product, which is called fashion textiles.

The production of fiber and fabrics is the first step in the manufacture of clothing, accessories, and home fashions. As a result, textile fiber and textile fabric manufacturers are considered **primary suppliers**. The makers of **trimmings** are also at the primary level of the fashion business.

The Fiber Industry

A fiber—an extremely fine, hairlike strand almost invisible to the eye—is the smallest element of a fabric. It is also the starting point of a fabric. Fibers can be spun or twisted into continuous threads called **yarn**, and yarns can be knitted, woven, or bonded into fabrics. Although tiny, fibers have enormous influence on fashion. They are what give a fabric its color, weight, texture, and durability.

Fibers are from one of three categories: natural, regenerated, and synthetic. **Natural fibers** are found in nature—that is, they come from plant or animal sources. **Regenerated fibers** combine cotton linters and a natural cellulosic substance such as wood pulp from pine, spruce, hemlock trees, or bamboo, with caustic soda to create a fiber. **Synthetic fibers** are made in a chemist's laboratory from noncellulosic substances such as petroleum, coal, natural gas, air, and water, and these substances must be converted into fibers before they can be made into fabric. Because regenerated and synthetic fibers are produced in the laboratory, they are more plentiful than natural fibers. Currently, twenty-five regenerated and synthetic fibers are available. Regenerated fibers whose names you may recognize are rayon, acetate, triacetate, and lyocell. Synthetic fibers you might recognize are nylon, acrylic, spandex, and polyester.

History and Development

The use of natural fibers is ancient, whereas most of the regenerated and synthetic fibers have been invented in the past fifty years. Despite their relatively short life span, however, rapid advances have been made in the use of these fibers. In contrast, the natural fiber industry has developed much more slowly. In fact, many of the developments in natural fibers are actually advances made in the synthetic fiber industry that were transferred to the natural fiber industry.

The Development of Natural Fibers

The use of natural fibers predates written history. Prehistoric humans are known to have gathered **flax,** the fiber in linen, to make yarns for fabrics. There are four major natural fibers: cotton, silk, flax (linen), and wool. Two other minor natural fibers are ramie and hemp. In addition, there are many other natural fibers that are in short supply, and so limited to luxury items. See Table 5.1 for a list of natural luxury animal fibers.

Cotton, the most widely used of all the natural fibers, is the substance attached to the seed of a cotton plant (see Figure 5.2). Cotton fibers are composed primarily of cellulose, a carbohydrate that especially lends itself to the manufacture of fibrous and paper products. Cotton fibers absorb moisture quickly, dry quickly, and have a cooling effect that makes cotton a good fiber for hot or warm weather. Usually the fluffy cotton boll is white, but other growing methods have brought about naturally colored

TABLE 5.1 Natural Luxury Animal Fibers

Name	Source	Characteristics and uses
Alpaca	Member of the llama family found in the Andes Mountains in South America	Fine, hollow-core fleece; annual shearing yields 6–12 pounds of fibers; 22 natural shades; strongest, most resilient wool; scarce
Angora	Rabbit hair	Soft fibers, dyes well; sheds easily
Camel hair	Camel	Usually left in natural tones; used in coats, jackets, artists' brushes
Cashmere	Kashmir goat (60% found in China but also bred in United States)	Rare (1/100 of wool crop); sheared annually; one goat produces enough for one-quarter of a sweater
Goose down (often mixed with goose feathers to cut cost)	Goose	Most compressible insulation; lightweight warmth for jackets, vests, comforters, pillows, sleeping bags, feather beds
Llama	Llama, found in Andes Mountains of South America, United States, Canada, Australia, and New Zealand	Coarser, stronger than alpaca; used in utilitarian items such as sacks
Marabou	African marabou stork or turkey	Soft, fluffy material from feathers
Mohair	Angora goat, originally from Turkey, now from South Africa, Texas, and New Zealand	Twice-yearly shearing; 2.5 times as strong as wool; less allergenic than sheep's wool
Ostrich feathers	Ostrich	Used in high-fashion apparel, feather dusters
Pashmina	Mountain goats from Himalayas	Softer than cashmere-fiber
Qiviut	Musk ox down, from Canada and Alaska	Natural taupe color; soft, light, eight times warmer than sheep's wool; rare ($20–$25/oz)
Vicuna	Rare llama-like animal from Peru	World's finest natural fiber

Figure 5.2 This ad for Cotton USA highlights how much of our day-to-day fashion is made of cotton.

cotton. This type of cotton can be grown in many colors, thus eliminating the need for dyes. Long and extra-long cotton fibers (or staple) produce the finest fabrics. China leads the world in extra-fine cotton production, followed by the U.S. California produces eighty-eight percent of extra-fine cotton in the U.S.[2]

Wool is the fiber that forms the coat of sheep. Sheep produce one of the few replenishable natural commodities. Shear a sheep's coat time after time and it quickly grows a new one. An animal fiber, wool is composed mostly of protein. Wool fiber is a natural insulator and is used to make warm clothes. Wool fiber, in fact, has a natural crimp that is ideal for the production of bulky yarns that trap air to form insulating barriers against the cold. Wool absorbs moisture more slowly and dries more slowly than cotton. A lightweight summer wool has been developed to be machine washable.

Silk comes from a cocoon formed by a silkworm. The silkworm forces two fine streams of a thick liquid out of tiny openings in its head. These streams harden into filaments, or fibers, upon contact with the air. Silk, best known for its luxurious feel, is a breathable fabric that can be worn year-round. For many years, silk required dry cleaning, but much of today's silk is washable.

Flax, used to make linen, comes from the stem of a flax plant. Only after the flax fiber is spun into yarn and woven or knit into fabric is the product called linen. Flax is the strongest of the vegetable fibers (it is twice as strong as cotton), and like cotton, it absorbs moisture and dries quickly. These features make linen an excellent fabric for warm-weather apparel. However, even with new technology that makes linen less apt to wrinkle, it still has a tendency to become creased and is harder to iron than cotton. Most flax is imported from Europe, especially Belgium, Ireland, France, and the UK.

Ramie comes from a woody-leafed Asian plant grown mostly in China. It has been available in the United States only since 1979, when the United States and China reopened trade with each other. A linen-like fabric suitable for warm-weather apparel, ramie is also inexpensive.

Hemp is a fibrous plant, which was an agricultural staple in America for hundreds of years. A number of other natural fibers are used in apparel and home furnishings. They are relatively rare and thus expensive.

The Development of Regenerated and Synthetic Fibers

Regenerated and synthetic fibers have been improving the quality of our lives since rayon, the first regenerated fiber, went into production in 1910. Since then, many other regenerated and synthetic fibers have been introduced in literally thousands of new apparel, upholstery, and industrial applications (see Table 5.2).

Regenerated and synthetic fibers offer a variety of characteristics that are mostly unavailable in natural fibers. Each year, these fibers find new uses in our wardrobes, homes, hospitals, and workplaces. More and more, designers find synthetics and regenerated fibers beneficial—they are easier to produce, can be more precisely engineered, are often more durable, and while production does involve some carbon emissions, the environment impact is often lower in comparison to natural fibers, which require food, water, grazing land, pesticides, and produce significant animal waste.[3]

All regenerated and synthetic fibers start life as thick liquids. Fibers of continuous, indefinite lengths are produced by forcing the liquid through the tiny holes of a

TABLE 5.2 Regenerated and Synthetic Fibers

Date	Fiber	First commercial production	End use
1910	Rayon	The first regenerated fiber. The first commercial production of rayon fiber in the United States was by the American Viscose Company. Natural cellulose compounds (wood pulp) are combined with chemical compounds to create fiber. By using two different chemicals and manufacturing techniques, two basic types of rayon were developed: viscose rayon and cuprammonium rayon. Today, only viscose rayon is being produced in the United States.	Blouses, coats, dresses, jackets, lingerie, linings, millinery, rainwear, and nonwoven fabrics; nonapparel includes draperies, medical products
1924	Acetate	The first commercial production of acetate fiber in the United States was by the Celanese Corporation.	Lining fabric, lingerie, ribbons, and foundation garments
1938	Nylon	The first synthetic fiber. The first commercial production of nylon in the United States was by the E. I. DuPont de Nemours & Company, Inc. It is the second-most-used synthetic fiber in the United States, after polyester.	Wide range of products in apparel (blouses, hosiery, lingerie, underwear, raincoats, windbreakers); interior furnishings (bedspreads, curtains, upholstery); and industrial areas (sleeping bags, tents, luggage)
1950	Acrylic	The first commercial production of acrylic fiber in the United States was by E. I. DuPont de Nemours & Company, Inc.	Sweaters, blankets, carpeting, children's garments, socks; also outdoor products like awnings
1953	Polyester	The first commercial production of polyester fiber in the United States was by E. I. DuPont de Nemours & Company, Inc. Polyester is the most-used manufactured fiber in the United States.	Suits, skirts, career apparel, performance fabrics, curtains, and sheets; also includes fiberfill for pillows, sails, and tire cord
1954	Triacetate	The first commercial production of triacetate fiber in the United States was by the Celanese Corporation. Domestic triacetate production was discontinued in 1985.	Good for apparel that requires pleats or creases, such as dresses or skirts; also used in knitted sleepwear and robes
1959	Spandex	The first commercial production of spandex fiber in the United States was by E. I. DuPont de Nemours & Company, Inc. It is an elastomeric manufactured fiber (able to stretch at least 100 percent and snap back like natural rubber). Spandex is used in filament form.	Denim, undergarments, support products, ski pants, athletic apparel in which stretch is needed, and swimwear
1961	Olefin/ Polyolefin	The first commercial production of an olefin fiber manufactured in the United States was by Hercules Incorporated. A polypropylene-type olefin fiber followed; both are commercially produced.	Athletic clothing, specifically for running, cycling, diving, and surfing; also used in upholstery, industrial fabrics, and geotextiles
1993	Lyocell	The first commercial production of lyocell in the United States was by Courtaulds Fibers. The fabric was given the generic name lyocell in 1996. Environmentally friendly, lyocell is produced from the wood pulp of trees grown specifically for this purpose. It is specially processed using a solvent spinning technique in which the dissolving agent is recycled, reducing environmental effluents.	Blouses, dresses, pajamas, shirts, and coats
2002	Polylactide (PLA)	The first commercial production of PLA in the United States was by Cargill Dow Polymers. PLA is a plastic derived from natural plant sugars, bridging the gap between natural fibers and conventional synthetic fibers.	Primary uses include pillows, comforters, and mattress pads; also suitable for activewear and apparel

Source: Adapted from Fabric Link/Fabric University, http://www.fabriclink.com/Fabric University/Man-made Fibers, http://www.Fibersource.com, and http://www.fta.g ov.

Figure 5.3 Regenerated and synthetic fibers of varying lengths are produced by forcing thick liquids through the tiny holes of a device known as a spinnerette.

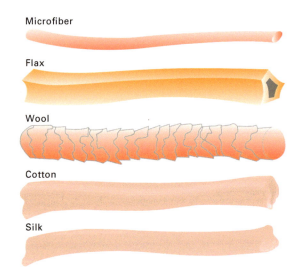

Figure 5.4 A microfiber compared with silk, cotton, wool, and flax.

mechanical device called a **spinnerette** (see Figure 5.3). This is similar to the way pasta dough is pushed through a pasta machine to make spaghetti.

Fibers are then cut into short lengths and spun into yarn, as is the case with natural fibers, or they are chemically processed into yarn directly. In the latter case, the production of fiber and yarn occurs simultaneously.

Generic Names for Regenerated and Synthetic Fibers

The Federal Trade Commission (FTC) has assigned **generic names**, or nontrademarked names, to twenty-five regenerated and synthetic fibers. Within any of these broad generic categories, fiber producers can modify the composition to produce a new fiber, called a variant. The variant is then given a brand name by the producer. There are hundreds of **brand names**, or trademarks, which are registered with the US Patent Office; only the manufacturer of a variant is allowed to use the registered name. For example, polyester is the generic name, and Dacron is the DuPont trademark for polyester (see Table 5.3).

The properties of these fibers greatly influence the behavior of the finished fabric made from them. Polyester, for example, is strong and wrinkle resistant, which contributes to its durability and washability. Once scorned as the dull material of inexpensive leisure suits, today's polyester has the subtle sheen of fine silk.

Microfibers

A major technological breakthrough occurred in 1989 with the first commercial production of microfiber in the United States by DuPont. A **microfiber** is a fiber that is two or three times smaller than a human hair—smaller than wool, cotton, or silk fibers (see Figure 5.4). Microfiber is the thinnest and finest of all synthetic fibers. It has a touch and texture similar to silk or cashmere but is wrinkle resistant and can usually be machine washed and dried. Today, microfiber is produced in a number of synthetic fibers—for example, nylon, acrylic, and polyester. Designers have used it widely in womenswear, menswear, activewear, outerwear, and home furnishings.

Organization and Operation of the Fiber Industry

Because of the differences in the origin and characteristics of fibers, each industry—the natural fiber industry and the manufactured fiber industry—is organized along different lines.

The Natural Fiber Industry

Cotton is produced in four major areas of the United States: the Southeast; the Mississippi Delta; the Texas-

TABLE 5.3 Generic Names and Trade Names of Regenerated Fibers Used in the United States

Generic name	Trade names
Acetate	Celanese, Chromspun, Estron, Microsafe
Acrylic	Acrilan, Bio Fresh, Bounce-Back, Creslan, Cystar, Cystar AF, Duraspun, Fi-lana, Pil-Trol, Sayelle, So-Lara, Smart Yarns, Wear-Dated, Wintuk
Aramid	Kevlar, Nomex
Lyocell	Lenzing Lyocell, Tencel
Modacrylic	SEF Plus
Nylon	A.C.E., Anso, Antron, Assurance, Avantige, Cantrece, Capima, Caplana, Caprolan, Captiva, Cordura, Creme de Captiva, Crepeset, DuraSoft, DyeNAMIX, Eclipse, Hardline, Hydrofil, Hytel, Matinesse, Microsupplex, No Shock, Power-Silk, Resistat, Shimmereen, Silkey Touch, Solution, Sportouch, Stainmaster, Stay Guard, Supplex, Tactel, Tru-Ballistic, Ultra Image, Ultra Touch, Ultron, Wear-Dated, Wellon, Wellstrand, WorryFree, Zefsprot, Zeftron
Olefin	Alpha, Essera, Impressa, Inova, Marvess, Patlon III, Polystrand, Spectra, Synera, Trace
Polyester	A.C.E., Ceylon, Comfort Fiber, Compet, Coolmax, Corebond, Dacronfi, ES.P, Fortrel, Hollofi, Kodaire, Kodel, KodOfill, KodOsoff, Pentron, Premafill Plump, Premafill Soft, Trevira, Trevira Finesse, Trevira Microness, Universe
PBI	PBI Logo
Rayon	Beau-Grip, Fibro, Galaxy
Spandex	Lycra
Sulfar	Ryton

Source: Adapted from www.fibersource.com/f-tutor/q-guide.htm and American Fiber Manufacturers Association (www.afma.org/afma/afma.html).

Oklahoma panhandle; and New Mexico, Arizona, and California. Nearly all cotton growers sell their product in local markets, either to mill representatives or, more typically, to wholesalers. The cotton wholesalers bargain at central markets in Memphis, New Orleans, Dallas, Houston, New York City, and Chicago.

The wool produced in the United States comes from relatively small sheep ranches in the Western states. Market centers, or wool warehouses, for wool trade are decentralized, mainly located near the growers throughout New Mexico, Texas, Utah, and South Dakota. Wool-marketing cooperatives help growers in remote areas attract commercial attention. The largest is Mid States Wool Growers Cooperative, with warehouses at the headquarters in Ohio and in Missouri.

Linen, silk, and ramie are not produced in any great quantities in the United States. As with hemp, these fibers are imported from foreign sources.

The natural fiber industry in the United States has been greatly affected by the advent of regenerated and synthetic fibers. The ability to tailor the regenerated and synthetic fibers to the demands of the ever-changing marketplace has forced the natural fiber industries to become more attuned to the needs of their customers. To compete, the natural fiber industries have become more aggressive about developing new uses for their products and promoting themselves. Cotton, usually a warm-weather fiber, is now promoted as a year-round fiber, largely through the use of heavier cotton fibers to make cotton sweaters. And wool, usually designed for cold-weather wear, is now being treated to make new lightweight fibers suitable for year-round wear. Through advanced technology and innovative chemical processing, many natural fibers are treated with special finishes to give them care-and-wear properties equal to those of regenerated and synthetic fibers.

ROTHY'S
A shoe made from a recycled plastic water bottle . . .

In 2015, Stephen Hawthornthwaite and Roth Martin launched a new shoe—between the eggplants and the Brussels sprouts at the grocery isle of San Francisco's Ferry Plaza Farmer's Market. Not a typical place to introduce a new shoe style? Well, Rothy's is not a typical shoe, and the creators are not typical shoe designers.

Stephen Hawthornthwaite, an investment banker, and Roth Martin, a gallery owner launched this product with the idea that women sought a polished work flat that combined style and comfort. To accomplish this with a totally sustainable platform—from materials to packaging—helped make the product much more relatable to eco-conscious consumers.

The shoes are constructed using proprietary 3-D technology that knits fibers made of recycled water bottles into a completely seamless shoe. Building on the same general technology that has been used to knit tubular shapes for decades, like socks and panty hose, this creates a product with virtually no waste. The stylish uppers, made from 100 percent recycled plastic water bottles, are washed, sterilized, chipped down to fragments, then fused into a yarn and knitted into a shoe shape. So far, Rothy's has repurposed over 12 million water bottles, and joins a growing number of brands using recycled plastic to make a wide array of products.

The uppers are just the beginning. The comfy insoles use recycled foam, the soles are made of carbon-free rubber. It's all joined by vegan adhesives and packaged in recycled biodegradable material. Can it get any better?! Yes it can! The moisture-wicking material fights against sweat and rain, and when they get dirty, just throw them in the washing machine. So far, Rothy's has filed thirty-one patents, with forty more pending in order to protect their brand and design.

Sustainability continues in their production model. Rothy's is building a responsive, make-to-demand model of manufacturing to avoid overproduction. And their styles, while not particularly edgy or fashion-forward, are stylish, sleek, flattering, and familiar—which means women will wear them and keep wearing them.

In 2018, Rothy's sold more than 1 million pairs of shoes, generating over $140 million in revenue, and has grown from nineteen employees in 2017 to over 450 by 2019. With one flagship brick-and-mortar store in San Francisco, most of their sales are generated through social media and word-of-mouth.

Right now, Rothy's come in three styles and dozens of color and pattern combinations, with plans to branch into children's styles and sizes, as well as offerings in the underserved women's market, sizes 12 and 13.

A stylish option for a work or casual flat, Rothy's come in three silhouettes for women, with plans to increase style and size offerings for both women and children.

Noted celebrities are spotted wearing Rothy's! Duchess of Sussex, Meghan is seen wearing them on her official visit to Australia with Prince Harry.

The Synthetic Fiber Industry

Obviously, climate and terrain have nothing to do with the production of a synthetic fiber. Chemical companies are extremely adaptable, requiring only supplies of raw chemicals, power, and labor. Chemical companies have built their factories in every part of the United States— up and down the East Coast, in the South, in the Midwest, and increasingly on the West Coast. Operations are located wherever companies have found raw materials or railroads and waterways for convenient shipment of those materials. Most of these factories are huge.

With synthetic fibers, the producing company can also serve as its own market. It purchases fibers from chemical companies, spins them into yarn, and knits or weaves the yarn into fabric. Burlington Industries and Swift Galey LLC are two of the giants that consolidate all operations, from spun yarn manufacture to finished fabric.

Fiber Development

The fierce competition among various producers of synthetic fibers is tied to the fact that in one season, a need may arise for fiber that is stretchable, offers warmth without weight, and is also wrinkle resistant. Armed with a list of customer preferences, competing laboratories go to work to develop new products to meet these preferences. It is no wonder that several of them come up with the same answer at the same time.

Under the Textile Fibers Products Identification Act of 1960, consumer products that use textile fibers are required to carry labels indicating the country where the fiber was processed or produced and the generic names and percentages of each fiber that is used, assuming that it is more than 5 percent, in order, by weight. Brand names or trademarks may also be used on the label, but the law does not require them.

Fiber Distribution

Producers of regenerated and synthetic fibers sell their fibers to fabric manufacturers in one of three ways:

1. As unbranded products, with no restrictions placed on their end use and no implied or required standards of performance claimed
2. As branded or trademarked fibers, with assurance to consumers that the quality of the fiber has been controlled by its producer, but not necessarily with assurance as to either implied or required standards of performance in the end product
3. Under a licensing agreement, whereby the use of the fiber trademark is permitted only to those manufacturers whose fabrics or other end products pass tests set up by the fiber producer for their specific end uses or applications

Merchandising and Marketing of the Fiber Industry

No matter how familiar producers and consumers may be with the qualities of each fiber, there is always the need to articulate and publicize information about the newest modifications and their application to fashion merchandise. To do this, producers of natural, regenerated and synthetic fibers make extensive use of advertising, publicity, and market research. They also extend various customer services to manufacturers, retailers, and consumers.

Usually, a producer of regenerated or synthetic fibers, such as DuPont or Monsanto, undertakes these activities on behalf of its own individual brands and companies. The National Council of Textile Organizations (NCTO), a domestic trade association representing the entire spectrum of the textile industry, provides a united voice of the US textile industry. Organized into four councils, NCTO represents fiber producers, yarn manufacturers, fabric makers, distributors, dyers, converters, printers, finishers, and other suppliers to the textile trade .[4]

So that they can better promote their new products (and themselves), the natural fiber industries also have organized trade associations that carry their message to the textile industry as well as to the customer (see Table 5.4).

Advertising and Publicity

As you might suspect, given their greater potential for competition, the synthetic fiber industries spend considerably more money on advertising than the natural fiber industries. They maintain a steady flow of advertising and publicity directed at both the trade and consumer markets. Sometimes an advertising campaign will promote an entire range of textile fibers; at other times, it will concentrate on only a single fiber (see Figure 5.5). Fiber companies give most of their advertising dollars to support the manufacturers who use their fibers.

Some natural fiber groups are putting more effort and money into campaigns to combat the growing domination of manufactured fibers. Because these campaigns are mainly handled by trade associations, they promote the

TABLE 5.4 Natural Fiber Trade Associations

Fiber	Organization
Cotton	Cotton Incorporated National Cotton Council, Supima
Linen	Masters of Linen (European)
Mohair	The Mohair Council of America
Silk	International Silk Association
Wool	America Wool Council, The Woolmark Company (Australian)

Source: Hemp Industries Association (http://www.thehia.org/).

fiber itself, not the products of an individual natural fiber producer. One of the most eye-catching campaigns is that of Cotton Incorporated. The ads and posters not only emphasize cotton's advantages as a fiber but also point to the cotton industry's importance in the economy and to cotton's ecological appeal.

Fiber sources also provide garment producers and retailers with various aids that facilitate mention of their fibers in consumer advertising, adding to the recognition already achieved by the fiber producer's name, trademark, slogan, or logo. For example, Woolmark encourages the use of its ball-of-yarn logo in producer and retailer advertising of all wool merchandise, as well as in displays.

Advertising undertaken by fiber producers in cooperation with fabric and garment manufacturers and retailers benefits the fiber industry in two ways. First, consumers begin to associate the fiber name with other names that are already familiar, such as the name of the fiber source or the name of the retail store selling the garment. This is particularly important in introducing a new regenerated

Figure 5.5 This Marks and Spencer ad promotes wool as luxurious and masculine.

or synthetic fiber. Second, fabric and garment producers, as well as retailers, are encouraged to use and promote the fiber because the fiber producer's share of advertising costs subsidizes its local or national advertising.

Research and Development

Producers of natural, regenerated, and synthetic fibers are constantly seeking ways to improve their products. Individual large synthetic fiber producers conduct research and development. The natural fiber producers, which tend to be small in size, often work through the trade group for a particular fiber.

Customer Services

All major producers of regenerated and synthetic fibers and many smaller firms offer a number of services to direct and secondary users of their products. Producers of natural fibers, working through their associations, also offer many such services. These include the following:

- Technical advice as well as know-how on weaving and knitting techniques
- Assistance to textile and garment producers and retailers in locating supplies
- Fabric libraries that include information about sources, prices, and delivery schedules (research in a fabric library saves precious time spent shopping the market for trend information)

- Fashion presentations and exhibits for the textile industry, retailers, garment manufacturers, the fashion press, and—occasionally—the public
- Extensive literature for manufacturers, retailers, educators, and consumers about fiber properties, use, and care
- Fashion experts who address groups of manufacturers, retailers, or consumers, staging fashion shows and demonstrations
- Educational films and audiovisual aids for use by the trade, schools, and consumer groups

Trends in the Fiber Industry

The most dramatic trend in the fiber industry is the increasing use of blends of natural and synthetic fibers. This trend will be discussed in more detail in the next section of this chapter, as will the second most widespread trend, the use of microfibers.

The fiber industry is fighting hard to overcome a major problem: the onslaught and rapid increase of imports into its domestic markets. Since regenerated and synthetic fibers account for more than 85 percent of fiber usage annually in the United States, it is obvious that this will be a continuing problem. The US fiber industry will have to fight harder than ever for its share of the international—and even the domestic—market. Added to this challenge is consumers' interest in sustainable products (see Figure 5.6).

Figure 5.6 Factory workers make garments in a factory in Colombo, Sri Lanka.

JILL MCDONALD
Jill McDonald Design

MEET JILL MCDONALD, OWNER AND CREATIVE DIRECTOR OF JILL MCDONALD DESIGN, a surface design and illustration studio specializing in developing art and surface design for the kids and baby market. With a style described as whimsical, fresh, fun, and unique, McDonald works with a variety of companies in many categories, including children's books, puzzles, wall art, fabric, and apparel, just to name a few. A small family business, Jill McDonald Design is staffed by Jill and her husband, so McDonald wears a lot of hats. In addition to generating the creative product, she also manages social media, which she emphasizes is so important these days. She manages the Jill McDonald Design blog, website updates, Instagram, and Facebook.

McDonald designs textiles and a variety of products for the children's market.

McDonald graduated from Rhode Island School of Design (RISD) in 1998 with a degree in textile design. She currently generates a strong mix of illustration work and surface design, and she credits RISD with having provided her with a wonderful platform to explore materials, think outside of the box, and trust her voice as an artist and designer.

After graduation, McDonald worked for Baby Gap as a print stylist, and after two years, returned to her hometown of Kansas City, Missouri, where she joined Hallmark Cards as an illustrator. In 2004, Jill opened her own studio. Her creative credits include illustrator of several children's books; fabric collections; wall art for Oopsy Daisy; and children's bedding collections for Target, Pottery Barn Kids, and the Land of Noz. In recent years, McDonald has developed her own line of products for babies and children, sold in a variety of outlets across America.

Although she starts most of her work by painting, she ultimately creates a digital file. Starting by hand allows her to give the art her unique, special touch. Then it is scanned to clean the art digitally in Photoshop so clients can easily manufacture and manipulate the art for whatever kind of product the art has been designed for. This also allows the art to be easily changed, altered, and manipulated as the specific product requires.

McDonald regularly exhibits at surface design trade shows each year, such as Surtex and Printsource in New York and Heimtextil in Frankfurt Germany. She takes the collection of work to these shows to sell or license. This is a great opportunity to meet with clients and connect with other print studios.

McDonald is organized in her approach to managing her time and work process. Each week she plans out a general idea of what needs to be accomplished. She checks email in the morning and then moves on to whatever is scheduled for the day. This varies from completing a commissioned project, making a new piece of art to add to the collection, or pulling together research. This helps keep her on track and accountable.

McDonald's advice to students interested in surface design or illustration as a possible career: "Work hard, have your own style (i.e. don't be a copycat) and keep pushing yourself. The market is constantly changing and so is what buyers are looking for. Having your own style is important but so is not getting in a rut and becoming a 'one trick pony.' To keep your art new and exciting, it needs to evolve which means always pushing past your comfort zone and not relying on what worked last time. Have fun with what you create. As I get older I realize more and more how lucky I am to get to do what I do. Many people don't like their jobs and loving what you do makes it not seem like work—which is great!"

Improvement in technology is also playing an important role in the fiber industries' abilities to service their customers more quickly and efficiently. In addition to facilitating communications, computers offer important linkages between the various industries and enable them to do such things as coordinate delivery schedules and provide bar coding.

To many observers, the regenerated and synthetic fiber story is just beginning, and the upcoming years promise to be even more exciting than the previous ones. Despite the economic challenges the United States has faced in recent years, textile productivity has continued to improve, and it appears as though a stronger industry is on the horizon. According to *Textile World*, US economic growth combined with slowdown in imports, rising overseas costs, a growing interest in reshoring, and strong capital spending by the mills on new machinery and equipment all add up to a stronger domestic textile industry.[5]

The Textile Fabric Industry

Midway between the fiber and the finished apparel, accessory, or home furnishing product is the fabric. **Textile fabric** is any material that is made by weaving, knitting, braiding, knotting, laminating, felting, or chemical bonding. It is the basic material from which most articles of apparel, accessories, and home fashions are made.

Americans use a lot of textile fabric. Each person consumes nearly eighty-six pounds of textile fabric annually. We use all types of fabrics for different purposes, including clothing, home furnishings, transportation, defense, recreation, health care, and space exploration.

The production of most fabrics begins with the creation of yarn from fibers. With the exception of felted fabric and a few other nonwoven fabrics, fibers cannot be made into fabrics without first spinning or twisting them into yarn. Yarns are then woven or knit into **greige goods**, or unfinished fabrics. (*Greige* is pronounced "gray.") Greige goods are converted into finished fabrics for consumer or industrial use.

Organization and Operation of the Textile Fabric Industry

For decades, there was no pattern of organization in the textile fabric industry. Some textile fabric companies were large corporations employing thousands of people, but many remained small operations with only a few dozen employees.

Imports overpowered the US textile industry in the late 1970s and 1980s. With industry investment of new plants and equipment from 2006 to 2017 equaling $22.8 billion, the US textile industry became more globally competitive. Producers have opened new fiber, yarn, and recycling facilities to convert textile and other waste to new textile uses and resins. With this increased pace of investment and innovation, foreign manufacturers now turn to the US for production.[6] The US textile industry is the second-largest textile exporter in the world. The industry primarily exports fiber, yarns, and fabrics. Textile exports in 2018 totaled $23.4 billion. The top five countries that import US fiber, yarn, and fabric are Mexico, Canada, China, Vietnam, and Honduras, with total exports equaling $19.72 billion in regenerated and synthetic fibers alone.[7]

Because commitments to specific weaves, colors, and finishes must be made six to eighteen months in advance, the textile fabric industry is extremely well informed about fashion and alert to new trends. Information about these trends comes from fashion designers, predictive services, fashion directors for fiber or yarn companies, and advance textile shows throughout the world. But, because they are geared to mass-production methods, most mills were reluctant to produce short experimental runs for individual designers. This is changing as new technology is developed.

The market centers for textile fabrics are not at the mills but in the fashion capital of the country: New York City. There, on the doorstep of the garment industry, every mill of importance has a salesroom. A fabric buyer or designer for a garment maker, or a retail store apparel buyer or fashion coordinator, has only to walk a block or two to obtain firsthand information on what the fabric market offers.

Merchandising and Marketing of the Textile Fabric Industry

Many designers let the fabric act as the creative impetus for their designs. Good designers respond to new fabrics and search for that special fabric that will drape in the way they want or that has just the color or texture they need. It is the job of the fabric industry to introduce designers to the particular fabric needed.

The textile industry works several seasons ahead. Fiber producers usually work two years ahead of a season. They must present their products this early to textile mills and converters so they will have enough lead time to plan their color and fabric lines. The fabric market presents its products a year ahead of a season. Their first presentation is to the manufacturers of apparel and accessories, after which they present their finished products to retail stores and the press—all ahead of season—so they can publicize upcoming trends.

Since the textile industry must work several seasons ahead of consumer demand, it must also take the lead in recognizing new fashion directions.

The Industry's Fashion Experts

To guide them in future planning, textile firms employ staffs of fashion experts. These experts work with textile designers to create fabrics in the weights, textures, colors, and patterns they anticipate consumers will want. Because most of the early decisions in both the fiber and the fabric market are based on color, the industry's fashion experts also work closely with specialized associations within the fashion industry that provide advanced research and trend information.

Most prominent among these groups are the ones that work exclusively with color, such as the Color Association of the United States, the Color Marketing Group, and Pantone. One of Pantone's partnerships includes Clariant International, one of the largest colorant and chemical companies in the world. The Pantone Fashion and Home Color System uses SMART colors, which are more environmentally friendly and help to shorten the color-development timeline.

Color forecasting services provide their clients with reports and newsletters, color swatches, palette predictions, and color-matching services—all geared to each of the apparel markets (men's, women's, and children's).

In addition to making decisions about color, the fabric industry must also consider fabrication and texture. If the trend is toward structured clothing, firm fabrication will be necessary, but when a soft, layered look is in, fabrication can be lightweight and soft. Since trends must be spotted so far in the future, the fashion experts play an important role as they work with fiber and fabric mills as well as designers and buyers.

Textile Trade Shows and Fairs

New trends are also introduced at trade shows and fairs held throughout the world (see Figures 5.7 and 5.8). Usually semiannual events, these shows are attended by designers, manufacturers, and retailers. Here are some of the important textile shows:

- China (Guangzhou) International Trade Fair for Home Textiles
- China International Trade Fair for Apparel Fabrics and Accessories
- Ideacomo (Ideas from Como), Como, Italy
- LA Textile in Los Angeles, California
- Pitti Filati (Pitti Yarns), Florence, Italy
- Premiere Vision (First Look), Paris, France
- Premiere Vision Review in New York
- Printsource in New York City
- Spinexpo, New York City
- Techtextil India
- Texworld USA in New York

Figure 5.7 (above) Australian wool on display at the Pitti Filati textile show in Florence, Italy.

Figure 5.8 Tables strewn with samples at the Los Angeles International Textile Show.

The failure to identify and act on a trend seen at a major textile show, for example, would mean that retailers and apparel manufacturers would be unable to supply the fashions that consumers want.

Advertising and Publicity

Unlike fiber producers, fabric manufacturers rarely advertise these days. But when they do, their advertising usually features the brand names of their products and frequently the names of specific apparel manufacturers that use their goods. Either with the cooperation of fiber sources or on their own, these fabric houses run advertisements in a wide variety of mass-circulation magazines and newspapers and share the cost of brand advertising run by retail stores. Their advertising generally makes consumers aware of new apparel styles, the fabrics of which they are made, and often the names of retail stores where they may be purchased.

Research and Development

Fabric producers, like fiber producers, now devote attention to exploring the market potential of their products and anticipating the needs of their customers. Success in the fashion industry depends on supplying customers with what they want. Swift changes are the rule in fashion. Anticipation of such changes requires close attention to the market and a scientific study of trends. Market research is used to identify changing lifestyles as well as geographic demands.

Many of the large fabric producers maintain product- and market-research divisions. Their experts work closely with both the trade and consumer markets in studying fabric performance characteristics. Many fabric producers provide garment manufacturers with sample runs of new fabrics for experimental purposes. The market researchers conduct consumer studies relating to the demand for or acceptance of finishes, blends, and other desired characteristics. Such studies also help fabric and garment producers to determine what consumers will want in the future, where and when they will want it, and in what quantities.

The Green Scene

The public is being asked to recycle waste, fly less frequently, and drive smaller cars. Being eco-friendly in the production of fibers and fabrics is at the forefront of customers' concerns, and textile manufacturers are responding to this need. Consumers collect plastic bottles, used clothing, and cotton and wool scraps, then turn them into first-quality fleece fabrics. For example, UK activewear brand RubyMoon, creates swimwear made from used fishing nets and plastic bottles taken from the ocean. By turning water pollution into garments, they have reduced their carbon footprint by forty-two percent. The brand also has a take-back program, offering trade-in discounts for new items with the return of old or used items."[8]

A variety of companies are taking on a greater interest in sustainability with recycling programs and policies. One example is Patagonia with the Worn Wear program. Worn Wear products are recycled Patagonia items. Some pieces have been used by customers, who receive store credit up to $100 for their trade in. Others are Patagonia seconds, which are functionally perfect, but may have a cosmetic flaw. Putting these items into use avoids both the landfill and the need to make new products.[9]

Other well-known companies that offer recycling programs include DuPont; Foss Manufacturing Company, Inc.; Polartec; Toray Industries, Inc.; and the Carpet America Recovery Effort (CARE).

There is also a crop of textiles with exceptional properties. Working hand-in-hand with Mother Nature, mills are developing some of the most comfortable, sanitary performance products using hemp, soy, and bamboo, which are good for moisture absorption and have antibacterial properties. While the original materials are considered more eco-friendly, it is important to note that some manufacturing processes may not be. The overall process and chemicals that are used must be evaluated to determine if the finished product really is "green."

Customer Services

Today's well-integrated and diversified fabric companies speak with great fashion authority. They also employ merchandising and marketing staffs whose expertise in fashion trends is available to apparel manufacturers, retailers, the fashion press, and frequently to consumers. Fashion staffs attend fashion forecasts. They conduct in-store sales training programs, address consumer groups, and stage fashion shows for the trade and press. They help retail stores arrange fashion shows and store-wide promotions featuring their products, and they assist buyers in locating merchandise made from their fabrics.

RECYCLED FASHION: Old Clothes, New Life

Did you ever wonder what happens to the souvenir t-shirt that you outgrew or the old curtains that used to hang in your room once you discard them? Donated clothing and home textiles average about twelve pounds per American each year, totaling about 3.8 billion pounds annually.

Many people assume that most of their castoffs are resold through thrift stores. The truth is, only about 10 to 20 percent actually serves as thrift store inventory. So what happens to the other 80 percent of donated clothing and home textiles?

The receiving charities resell salvaged but unsellable textile goods to secondhand clothing recyclers. These firms specialize in handling discarded textile goods, providing an estimated 15,000 to 20,000 jobs each year and generating revenue in excess of $700 million annually.

The process is highly efficient, and in just thirty to sixty days, textile goods are reused and recycled in one of three ways. First, 45 percent of donated goods are reused as clothing, exported from the United States as secondhand clothing. We might assume that this contributes to sustainability and provides goods for cultures facing economic strife, but the process is actually subject to a number of restrictions, such as import bans, requirements for fumigation, proof of sanitation documents, and pre-shipment inspections. Second, 30 percent of the goods are converted and reenter the market as wiping rags and other industrial and residential absorbents. Finally, 20 percent of donations return to the fiber stage, becoming insulation material for homes, carpet padding, and raw material for the automotive industry. Only about 5 percent of donated and discarded goods end up as landfill waste.

Worn or torn, all dry clothing and home textiles have another life through donation or recycling.

The Life Cycle of Secondhand Clothing

What happens to your donated or recycled used clothing?

On average, each American donates or recycles 12 pounds of apparel footwear, and household textiles. Here's what happens next...

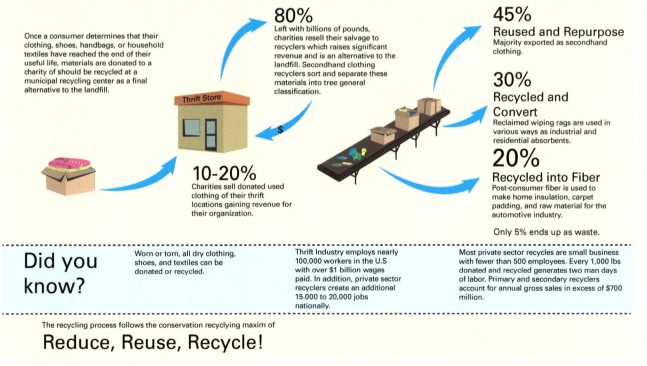

Once a consumer determines that their clothing, shoes, handbags, or household textiles have reached the end of their useful life, materials are donated to a charity of should be recycled at a municipal recycling center as a final alternative to the landfill.

80%
Left with billions of pounds, charities resell their salvage to recyclers which raises significant revenue and is an alternative to the landfill. Secondhand clothing recyclers sort and separate these materials into tree general classification.

Thrift Store

10-20%
Charities sell donated used clothing of their thrift locations gaining revenue for their organization.

45%
Reused and Repurpose
Majority exported as secondhand clothing.

30%
Recycled and Convert
Reclaimed wiping rags are used in various ways as industrial and residential absorbents.

20%
Recycled into Fiber
Post-consumer fiber is used to make home insulation, carpet padding, and raw material for the automotive industry.

Only 5% ends up as waste.

Did you know?

Worn or torn, all dry clothing, shoes, and textiles can be donated or recycled.

Thrift Industry employs nearly 100,000 workers in the U.S with over $1 billion wages paid. In addition, private sector recyclers create an additional 15.000 to 20,000 jobs nationally.

Most private sector recycles are small business with fewer than 500 employees. Every 1,000 lbs donated and recycled generates two man days of labor. Primary and secondary recyclers account for annual gross sales in excess of $700 million.

The recycling process follows the conservation recycling maxim of

Reduce, Reuse, Recycle!

The life cycle of recycled textiles.

Trends in the Textile Fabric Industry

A dramatic change in the mindset of the textile producers and marketing managers has broadened the product mix, quickened the response time required to meet customer demand, and made possible shorter runs of more innovative and fashionable fabrics. Currently, retailers, apparel manufacturers, and the fiber and fabric industries are working together to explore new and innovative ways to move textile products through the pipeline to the ultimate consumer more quickly and efficiently.

Fortunately, the consumption rate of textiles increases every year. Economists forecast that this trend will continue. The role of the textile fiber and fabric industries in the global economy has been an important one. Some of the major trends that affect both the fiber and fabric industries are the following:

- Innovations in high-tech fabrics
- Growing global competition
- Increased exports
- Greater diversification of products
- Increased government regulations
- New technology and equipment

Production of High-Tech Fabrics

We live in a high-tech age, when almost every new product is a result of combined effort and sophistication in research and development (see Figure 5.9). Fabric is no exception, as evidenced by the frequent introduction of new textiles endowed with some novel and valuable property, characteristic, or performance.

A fabric that has been constructed, finished, or processed in a way that gives it certain innovative, unusual, or hard-to-achieve qualities not normally available can be described as **high-tech fabric**.

Protective Uses of High-Tech Fabrics

Many common fabrics have been transformed into high-tech fabrics by coating or laminating them or by making them with innovative yarns such as Kevlar, Nomex, Spectra, and so on. These fabrics are engineered to be capable of **wicking**, or transporting moisture; have resistance to radiation, corrosive chemicals, and other stresses; and adjust to extreme weather changes.

A bright future is ahead for these specialized fabrics in a variety of situations, as follows:

- Activewear—Apparel for jogging, golfing, cycling, skating, sailing
- Rainwear—Raincoats, capes, hats (Figure 5.10)
- All-weather wear—Apparel for hunting, fishing, skiing, mountaineering, and so forth
- Swimwear—Bathing suits, bodysuits for diving, life vests
- Protective clothing—Garments to protect the wearer from hazardous waste; medical contamination; bullets or shrapnel; radiation; cutting or abrasion; electronic, computer, and pharmaceutical manufacture
- Heat- and fire-protection clothing—Occupational clothing for firefighters, blast furnace workers, car racers, tank crews
- Chemical protection clothing—Occupational clothing for chemical workers, workers at toxic waste sites and spills

Figure 5.9 Recycled polyester and Lycra spandex make up this beautiful white parka by Lundström.

Figure 5.10 A see-through raincoat protects much, but conceals little on the runway for designer Sonia Rykiel.

Figure 5.11 Hussein Chalayan is a designer at the forefront of the high-tech fabric movement, using microchip technology.

An outstanding example is a knit fabric blending Hydrofil, polyester, and Lycra spandex that moves moisture away from the body. It is used in cross-country ski tights, sports tops, cycling jerseys, jackets, face masks, and gloves. High-tech fabrics can help to keep an athlete's or worker's mind and body more comfortable, thus allowing the person to improve his or her performance or make that extra effort.

Other high-tech fabrics are seen in home furnishings. For example, KromaLon, an olefin fiber, is used to make carpets that are antimicrobial as well as stain and bleach resistant.

Use of High-Tech Fabrics and Materials in Apparel

Designers at all price points are incorporating a range of materials besides natural fibers—metallic threads, plastic, vinyl, rubber, and reflective material (see Figure 5.11). In one of his early collections, Alexander McQueen attracted a lot of attention when he cut out pieces of lace, backed them with latex, and splattered them on nude chiffon. The late Gianni Versace used clear vinyl extensively, as well as a chain-mail fabric that drapes easily. Helmut Lang adopted the reflecting strips commonly found on backpacks, running shoes, and firefighters' uniforms for reflective jeans. Frederic Molenac, designing for the Madame Gres collection, used Lycra with neoprene, a rubberlike fabric. And the list goes on. As the expanding field of textiles grows, more designers are finding inspiration and aesthetic value in high-tech fabrics and all kinds of materials.

Growing Global Competition

The major concern of the US textile industry is the competition of global markets. Although the domestic fiber and fabric industries produce a large amount of goods, the

United States still imports vast quantities of fiber, yarn, and fabric from around the world. Asia, and particularly China, has received large orders from US and European brands for years, but in the wake of China's increased domestic demand and rising energy and transportation costs worldwide, industry analysts predict opportunities for new players in global sourcing, which include African suppliers, Mauritius, and Turkey.[10] Another increase is in the Indian textile and apparel industry. The size of India's textile and apparel market was reported to be $108.5 billion in 2015 and is expected to reach $226 billion by 2023, growing at a rate of 8.7 per cent between 2009 and 2023.[11]

Increased Exports

Apparel import trade to the United States from regions including Guatemala, El Salvador, Honduras, Nicaragua, Costa Rica, and the Dominican Republic serves as a major export market for US-made fabrics and yarns. Textile exports rose from $7 billion in 2011, to $3.27 billion in 2018.[12]

India's reported overall textile exports $39.2 billion in 2018 and is expected to increase to $82.00 billion by 2021.[13]

With these shifts in the global market, the textile industry continues to focus on a number of corporate strategies, as follows:

- Increasing the focus on foreign markets and operations for apparel fabrics, since most studies indicate that the major growth in apparel markets will be outside the United States
- Developing overseas manufacturing operations, or exploring licensing in conjunction with foreign mills, to attain a stronger foothold on the international scene
- Devoting increased resources to market research
- Continuing technological advances

The industry is focusing more of its manufacturing and marketing activities abroad on fabrics for home furnishings, offices, hotels, military, and industrial end uses.

Greater Diversification of Products

The textile industry produces a more diversified range of fibers and fabrics than ever before. The specialization that once divided the industry into separate segments, each producing fabrics from a single type of fiber, has all but faded. To meet the needs of consumers, it is often necessary to blend two or more fibers into a yarn or to combine yarns of two fibers. Mills are learning to adjust their operations to any new fiber or combination of fibers.

Another bright spot for the domestic textile market is **geotextiles**, or manufactured permeable textiles that are currently used in reinforcing or stabilizing civil engineering projects. Two examples of industrial fabrics are Kevlar and Tyvek, which are used for diverse applications such as book covers and wrapping houses to prevent moisture penetration.

An example of an industrial protective coating is Teflon—yes, the coating used on nonstick frying pans—which is now being used to protect delicate fabrics. With fashion designers searching for new fabrics every day, can apparel applications for industrial and geotextiles be far behind?

Increased Government Regulation

One of the biggest impacts on the textile industry over the years has been the intervention of the federal government in every aspect of the industry: health and safety, noise levels and chemical pollution, consumer product liability, environmental impact, and hiring practices.

Until recently, federal regulation of the textile industry was mainly concerned with the fiber-content labeling of fabrics and products made of those fabrics. The law requires that most textile and wool products have a label listing the fiber content, the country of origin, and the identity of the manufacturer or business responsible for marketing or handling the item. In 1953, the Flammable Fabrics Act was passed, but it served to ban from the market only a few very ignitable fabrics and apparel made from them. The increasing strength and direction of the consumerism movement, however, resulted in more government regulation of the textile industry on both the federal and state levels.

In July 1972, two important changes in federal textile regulations took effect: the Federal Trade Commission's (FTC) rule on Care Labeling of Textile Wearing Apparel and the revision of the Flammable Fabrics Act. The FTC's care-labeling rule requires that all fabrics—piece goods as well as apparel and accessories made of fabric—be labeled to show the type of care they require. They indicate whether the fabric can be hand-washed or machine-washed or should be dry-cleaned. The symbols also indicate whether ironing is required, and if so, at what temperature. The manufacturer must sew a permanent label with these care symbols into each garment.

According to the Bureau of Consumer Protection, "recyclable" claims on labels and advertisements mean that the products can be collected, separated, or recovered—or reused in the manufacture or assembly of another product through an established recycling program.[14]

New Technology in Equipment

"New technology is totally revolutionizing the textile industry," says Jack Lenor Larsen, an eminent textiles designer in the home furnishings industry. The trend toward increased mechanization and automation is clearly apparent throughout the industry as it has changed from one that is labor intensive to one that is equipment intensive.

Over the years, the textile industry has experienced a number of technological developments—for example, the shuttleless loom and computer design of fabrics. In the mills, new machines combine higher production speeds with lower energy consumption. Automated weaving and knitting machines produce more with fewer operators.

The industry is also experimenting with new printing techniques. Digital printing on fabrics has yet to outstrip screen printing, but it is catching up fast with a push of innovative applications.[15] Rotary-screen printing is truly the technology of the twenty-first century and will replace flat-screen and roller printing techniques. Powerful computers will enable the industry to set the cost and price of fabrics before they are knitted or woven. Industry leaders need to be competitive in the global textile market. In addition, 3-D printing, or additive manufacturing, is a fast-growing area with innovative applications for textile design and development. Industry analysts forecast this market to reach $55.8 billion by 2027 for all product sectors, with significant applications for a variety of consumer products.[16]

Computer technology is playing a key role in quick response programs that improve communications among fiber, fabric, apparel, and retail businesses. Quick response shortens the time between the placement of orders by retailers and the delivery of goods. Bar codes have been established by the Fabric and Supplier Linkage Council so that vendors can label shipments with standard bar codes that purchasers can enter immediately into inventory records. This reduces inventory costs, warehouse time, forced markdowns, and stock outs.

Although new technology has the potential for creating job losses, it will ultimately help the industry by attracting bright, ambitious young workers and leaders who want to work in a progressive environment.

US textile plants are characterized by computer-run looms that feed a mile of yarn per minute, as well as completely automated yarn-spinning plants that can run twenty-four hours a day, seven days a week. Technological advances have long been introduced at the Bobbin Show, a three-day event held annually in the United States. Other major shows that focus on these areas are the International Machinery Show in Germany and the Japanese International Apparel Machinery Show.

Sustainability

Sustainability in the fashion industry is an increasingly covered topic. Clothing companies are responding to consumers' desire for greater transparency in how their clothes are made and are attempting to transform business operations to improve supply chain activities and reduce overall environmental impacts, as well as improve working conditions in factories. *Green Strategy*, a sustainability consulting firm based in Stockholm, Sweden, had identified a full range of initiatives that address not only fashion production, but also view consumer consumption as part of sustainability in fashion.

- On Demand and Custom Made—this includes made-to-order, DIY, tailor-made, and bespoke apparel, limiting production to items consumed on an as-needed basis. Instead of mass production of thousands of suits, sitting on the rack awaiting possible purchase, one suit is made for one customer at a time.
- Green and Clean—improving supply chains to reduce environmental impact and improve working conditions in factories.
- High Quality and Timeless Design—invest in well-made, well-designed clothing that remains fashionable from season to season, for many years.
- Fair and Ethical—attention to animal rights, fair compensation, and other fair and ethical treatment to the people involved in the design and production of fashions.

- Repair, Redesign and Upcycle—keep, mend, and remake clothing to extend use and wear.
- Rent, Lease and Swap.
- Secondhand and Vintage Apparel.

All of these methods of sustainability do not necessarily suit all people equally well because people have different needs and preferences. Some individuals prefer to experiment with and renew their wardrobes often. Using "Second hand and Vintage," "Repair, Redesign and Upcycle" and "Rent, Loan and Swap" strategies would possibly be of most interest. For those who prefer newly manufactured clothes without history and who have a consistent style, "On Demand" and "High quality and Timeless design" are likely to be most attractive sustainability options. Whether one prefers to renew their wardrobe often or more sporadically, "Green and Clean" and "Fair and Ethical" are important choices in sustainability when purchasing clothing.[17]

Summary and Review

Textiles begin with fibers, which may be natural (cotton, wool, flax, and silk), regenerated (made of cellulose, which is also the substance of natural plant fibers), or synthetic (combining chemicals in a laboratory). Variants of generic regenerated or synthetic fibers bear the trade name of the manufacturer. For example, Dacron is DuPont's brand of polyester.

The main market for fibers is the textile fabric industry, which weaves, knits, or otherwise turns fibers into greige goods. These goods are then finished by either the textile mill or converters, who add treatments such as dye, waterproofing, and fire-retarding and permanent-press finishes. Finishes added to natural fibers allow them to compete more effectively with manufactured fibers by taking on some of the properties that consumers demand in apparel and other textile products.

Textiles are sold primarily to manufacturers of apparel and home fashions, but marketing of fibers and textiles is directed at retailers and consumers, too, to build demand. US textile manufacturers compete with foreign imports through technological advances that speed production, minimize pollution, and improve the performance of fabrics in terms of colorfastness, insulation, and other desirable features. The textile industry will continue to build upon innovation to create faster, more sustainable, and more cost-effective processes, such as developments in printing technologies and computerized systems to expedite order fulfillment.

FOR REVIEW

1. What is the difference between a natural fiber, a regenerated fiber and a synthetic fiber? Give three examples of each and indicate the source of each natural fiber you name.
2. What has the natural fiber industry done to counteract the effects of synthetic fibers in the marketplace?
3. Trace the steps through which a new or newly modified synthetic fiber passes as it goes from conception to general availability.
4. Name and explain the three ways in which producers of regenerated or synthetic fibers usually sell their products to fabric manufacturers.
5. Describe the three major merchandising and marketing activities of natural and synthetic fiber producers.
6. Describe the major steps in the production of most fabrics.
7. What is the function of the textile converter? What are the advantages of dealing with a converter for a fabric mill and an apparel producer?
8. How do textile fabric producers keep informed about new fashion trends?
9. How have increased fiber, yarn, and fabric imports affected the US textile industry?
10. What are the provisions of the Flammable Fabrics Act of 1953 and the FTC's rule on Care Labeling of Textile Wearing Apparel of 1972?

FOR DISCUSSION

1. What is the role of trade associations in the marketing of fibers and textile fabrics?
2. When a major designer designed his collection for a mass merchandiser, he went directly to the textile mills with specifications for his fabrics in regard to width, pattern repeats, and so on. Can most designers do this? Why or why not?
3. Discuss the relationship of the designer and the manufacturer of fashion merchandise to the textile industry.

Trade Talk

Define or briefly explain the following terms:

brand names
cotton
fabrics
fiber
flax
generic names
geotextiles
greige goods
hemp
high-tech fabric
microfiber
natural fibers
primary suppliers
ramie
regenerated fibers
silk
spinnerette
synthetic fibers
textile fabric
trimmings
wicking
wool
yarn

Leather and Fur

Key Concepts

- The three major types of companies in the leather industry and their functions

- The nine different categories of leather and the special finishes used on leather

- The history and development of the fur industry in the United States

- The functions of the three major groups in the fur industry

- The steps in transforming fur pelts into finished garments

The most glamorous and sought-after textiles—leather and fur—are also the two oldest. Prehistoric people discovered that the animals they killed for food could serve another purpose, that of providing them with warmth and protection from the elements. Today, leather and fur are vital to the apparel, home furnishings, and automotive industries, contributing the raw materials for coats and jackets, handbags, shoes, gloves, and an ever-widening range of fashion products.

The leather industry is currently expanding its markets in ways that no one even dreamed of ten years ago. New processing methods have created leathers so thin and supple that designers can use them for everything from bikinis to shirts to evening wear—all available in an incredible array of colors.

Figure 6.1 Leather bomber jacket reinvented, paired with eveningwear, by Ralph Lauren.

After several years of decline because of environmental concerns over the use of scarce or rare animal **skins**, furs are making a comeback, especially with the young, first-time customer. Even amid controversy, the demand for furs continues to increase, at the very time when the fur industry is experimenting with new colors and styles.

The Leather Industry

Leather-making is a highly specialized and time-consuming operation. Because of the time involved, the leather industry must anticipate and predict trends far in advance of other textile suppliers. Leather producers typically decide what production method, textures, finishes, and colors they will use eight to sixteen months before a leather will reach apparel and accessory manufacturers. As a result, those in other fashion industries often look to the leather industry for leadership, particularly in terms of color and texture (see Figure 6.1).

Because leather is a by-product of the meatpacking industry, it is not as much of a target of animal rights activists as is the fur industry. Few animals are raised specifically for their **hides**. Most animals are raised to feed people, and their skins and hides, which have no food value, are then sold to the leather trade.

Categories of Leather

Almost all leather comes from cattle. But the hides and skins of many other animals from all parts of the world are also used in fashion apparel and accessories. There are nine major categories of leather, listed in Table 6.1.

The Equine Group

Horses provide a rugged leather. Some horsehide is tanned into cordovan leather, which makes extremely durable and sturdy shoe uppers. The hide is also used for leather jackets. But it is important to know that most of what is called "pony skin" is really stenciled calfskin, which is used because it is more pliable than real pony skin. Real top-quality pony skin comes from wild horses in Poland and Russia.[1]

TABLE 6.1 Nine Major Categories of Leather

Cattle group

Steer, cow, and bull hides, producing leather for:

- Shoe and slipper outsoles, insoles, uppers, linings, counters, welts, heels, etc.
- Traveling bags, suitcases, briefcases, luggage straps, etc.
- Gloves and garments
- Upholstery for automobiles, furniture, airplanes, buses, decoration
- Handbags, purses, wallets, waist belts, other personal leather goods
- Harnesses, saddles, bridles, skirting (for saddles), etc.
- Machinery belting, packings, washers, aprons, carders, combers, pickers, etc.
- Footballs, basketballs, volleyballs, and other sporting goods
- Laces, scabbards, holsters, etc.

Kips or kipskins (from large calves or undersized cattle), producing leather for:

- Shoe and slipper uppers and linings
- Handbags and other personal leather goods
- Gloves and garments
- Sweat bands for hats
- Rawhide and parchment
- Athletic helmets
- Bookbindings
- Handicrafts, etc.

Sheep and lamb group

- Wooled skins, hair skins (cabrettas), shearlings, producing leather for:
- Shoe and slipper uppers and linings
- Gloves and garments
- Chamois
- Handbags and other personal leather goods
- Moutons and shearlings (skins with wool on)
- Parchment
- Textile rollers
- Hats, hat sweat bands, millinery, and caps
- Bookbindings
- Piano actions
- Sporting goods (balls, gloves, etc.)

Pig and hog group

Pig, hog, boar, peccary, carpincho (a Brazilian rodent) skins, producing leather for:

- Gloves
- Innersoles, contours, etc.
- Fancy leather goods, luggage
- Saddlery and harnesses
- Shoe uppers
- Upholstery

Equine group

Horse, colt, ass, mule, and zebra hides, producing leather for:

- Shoe soles and uppers
- Luggage
- Gloves and garments
- Belts
- Aviators' clothing
- Sporting goods (baseball covers and mitts, etc.)

Buffalo group

Domesticated land and water buffalo (not American bison, whose hide is not tanned for leather), producing leather for:

- Shoe soles and uppers
- Handbags
- Fancy leather goods, luggage
- Buffing wheels

Deer group

Fallow deer, reindeer, elk, and caribou skins, producing leather for:

- Shoe uppers
- Gloves
- Clothing
- Piano actions
- Moccasins
- Mukluks
- Fancy leather goods

Goat and kid group

Skins producing leather for:

- Shoe and fancy uppers, linings
- Gloves and garments
- Fancy leather goods, handbags
- Bookbindings

Kangaroo and wallaby group

Skins producing very strong leather for:

- Shoe uppers, including track and basketball shoes

Exotic leathers

Hides from:

- Aquatic group—frog, seal, shark, walrus, and turtle
- Land group—camel, elephant, ostrich, and pangolin
- Reptile group—alligator, crocodile, lizard, and snake

Source: Leather Industries of America, *Dictionary of Leather Terminology*, 8th ed. (Washington, D.C.: Leather Industries of America).

SYNTHETIC LEATHER—IT MIGHT JUST BE YOUR CUP OF TEA!

Researchers from Iowa State University have developed a new form of synthetic leather made from a brew of kombucha tea. It is made with natural ingredients including vinegar, sugar, and cellulose fibers (taken from the tea). A symbiotic colony of bacteria and yeast (SCOBY) is added and the material grows on top of the liquid's surface. This cellulosic fiber has properties similar in look, feel, and function to leather and, once harvested and dried, the cellulosic fiber can be made into apparel, shoes, and handbags.

This material has been tested for use in cosmetics, foods, and biomedical tissue for wound dressing, but is new to the apparel industry. Researchers have successfully made prototype garments from the material. The product continues to be refined and improved. When it gets wet it tends to soften and becomes less durable. The current growth cycle takes three to four weeks, depending on environmental conditions, and research continues to shorten the growing cycle to make it more conducive to mass production.

Dr. Young-A Lee, who leads the Iowa State research team advises fashion students, "employees who work in the fashion industry need to be fully educated on the [environmental responsibility and sustainability] movement. The industry cannot shift things at one time. It is all about people in the industry. The key is changing their values to consider the betterment of people and the planet in a long run, instead of focusing on a consumer's short-coming interest." This "leather" is entirely sustainable, biodegradable, and natural, reducing contaminating chemicals present in the production of other synthetic materials.

Cellulosic fiber made from kombucha tea, vinegar, and sugar grows in a lab.

Prototype shoes made from the new kombucha tea fiber.

Harvested and dried cellulosic fiber.

The Exotic Leathers

Supplies of the so-called exotic leathers are diminishing worldwide, driving prices up sharply. There is some good news, however. From 1967 to 1987, the American alligator was listed as an endangered species. The alligator is now out of danger because of a policy called **sustainable use**. This refers to an environmental program that encourages landowners to preserve alligator eggs and habitats in return for the right to use a percentage of the grown animals. Louisiana leads the United States in the production of alligator skins. After rebuilding the population through research, management, and law enforcement, the wild harvest from 1972 through 2016 has produced over 1,000,000 wild skins. The 2016 wild harvest of 33,410 alligators was valued at $9.7 million. In 2016, farmer/ranchers sold 387,000 skins at a value of $74 million.[2] The United States is the only source of raw alligator hides, and half of all alligator tanneries are owned by major fashion houses in the United States or Europe. The main competitor of alligator hides is crocodile hides. To unfamiliar consumers, these two are almost identical. In more high-end stores, customers mistakenly identify alligator products as crocodile products.[3]

Leather Processing

Animal **pelts** are divided into three classes, each based on weight. Those that weigh fifteen pounds or less when shipped to the tannery are called skins. This class consists mostly of calves, goats, pigs, sheep, and deer. Those weighing from fifteen to twenty-five pounds, mostly from young horses and cattle, are referred to as **kips**. Those weighing more than twenty-five pounds, primarily cattle, oxen, buffalo, and horse skins, are called hides.

The process of transforming animal pelts into leather is known as **tanning**. The word is derived from a Latin word for oak bark, which was used in early treatments of animal skins. Tanning is the oldest known craft.

Three to six months are needed to tan hides for sole leather and saddlery. Less time is required for tanning kips and skins, but the processes are more numerous and require more expensive equipment and highly trained labor. The tanning process involves minerals, vegetable materials, oils, and chemicals, used alone or in combination. The choice of a tanning agent depends on the end use for which the leather is being prepared.

Tanning Methods

Mineral tanning uses chrome salts. Chrome tanning is now used to process nearly two-thirds of all leather produced in the United States. This is a fast method that takes hours rather than weeks. It produces leather for shoe uppers, garments, gloves, handbags, and other products. Chrome-tanned leather can be identified by the pale, blue-gray color in the center of the cut edge. Vegetable tanning uses the tannic acids that naturally occur in the bark, wood, or nuts of various trees and shrubs and in tea leaves. Vegetable tanning is used on cow, steer, horse, and buffalo hides. Vegetable-tanned leather can be identified by a dark center streak in the cut edge. Because it is so labor intensive, relatively little vegetable tanning is done in the United States.

Processing with oil is one of the oldest methods of turning raw animal skins into leather. A fish oil—usually that of codfish—is used. Oil tanning is used to produce chamois, doeskin, and buckskin—relatively soft and pliable leathers used in making gloves and jackets. The most widely used and quickest method of tanning relies primarily on the chemical formaldehyde. Because the processing turns the leather white, it can be easily dyed. Formaldehyde-tanned leather is washable. It is often used for gloves and children's shoe uppers. It is possible to combine tanning agents. A vegetable and mineral combination is used to "retan" work shoes and boots. Combinations of alum and formaldehyde or oil and chrome are common.

Finishing

The finishing process gives leather the desired thickness, moisture, color, and aesthetic appeal. Leather can now be dyed in nearly 500 different colors. Dyed leather is also sometimes finished with oils and fats to ensure softness, strength, or waterproofing. Special color effects include sponging, stenciling, spraying, or tie-dyeing. Other finishes include matte, luster or pearl, suede, patent, or metallic. It is important to note that suede is a finish, not a kind of leather.

Merchandising and Marketing

Because of the lead time needed to produce leather, the leather industry must stay abreast of fashion, and be several steps ahead of it. Months before other fashion industries commit themselves to colors and textures, leather producers have already made their decisions. They have started the search for the right dyes and treatments to meet expected future demand. As a result, the leather industry's forecasters are considered the best and most experienced in the fashion industry.

Fashion Information Services

Because they make their assessments of fashion trends so far in advance, others in the industry look to the leather industry for information. Like other fashion industries, the leather industry retains experts to disseminate information about trends and new products. They often produce booklets that forecast trends, describe new colors and textures, and generally promote the leather industry. Samples of important textures and looks are included.

Fashion experts also work directly with retailers, manufacturers, and the press to help crystallize their thinking about leather products. One-on-one meetings, seminars, and fashion presentations are used to educate the fashion industry and consumers about leather.

Despite all this activity, individual tanners are not known by name to the public. Nor is a fashion editor, in describing a leather garment, likely to mention its manufacturer. Leather producers are not named in retail stores or in leather manufacturers' advertising. Consumers who can name several fabric and fiber producers would have a difficult time naming any leather tanners.

Trade Associations and Trade Shows

For more than eighty years, Leather Industries of America (LIA) has served its members by providing environmental, technical, educational, statistical, and marketing services—all at the direction of its membership and to the benefit of the leather industry. Leather membership is available to any US business involved in the tanning, finishing, manufacturing, or selling of leather. General membership is available to foreign companies and those with an interest in the industry, including hide brokers, consultants, chemical suppliers, and equipment and leather product manufacturers. LIA provides the following:

- Government representation: Leather Industries of America's legal team works for congressional and regulatory action, which promotes the acceleration of leather exports and the elimination of protectionist trade restrictions.
- Environmental regulation: For more than two decades, it has been involved in the development and communication of fair and sensible environmental regulations affecting the tanning industry.
- Leather Research Laboratory: It provides valuable technical and consulting services through the state-of-the-art Leather Research Laboratory at the University of Cincinnati.[4]

Trade shows are another important source of information within the leather industry. Two years before the ultimate consumer sees finished leather products in retail stores, the leathers are introduced in several industry trade shows.

The Asia Pacific Leather Fair (APLF) (formerly known as the Hong Kong Leather Fair) began in 1984. Over the years, APLF has expanded its scope and currently organizes six premium events in Hong Kong, China, and India, covering a wide range of industry sectors.[5] There is also the Shoes and Leather Guangzhou, which is held in China in June, and the India International Leather Fair (IILF) held in February.

LINEAPPELLE, held in Milan, Italy, started in 1981, is the most important international exhibition dedicated to leather, accessories, components, synthetics, and models for footwear, leather goods, garments, and furniture. The exhibition is reserved exclusively for the operators of the leather sector and is held in February for Spring/Summer and in September for Fall/Winter. Events exhibiting more focused or "niche" offerings are held in New York and London.[6]

Research and Development

The leather industry retains and expands its markets by adapting its products to fashion's changing requirements. Before the Second World War, relatively few colors and types of leather were available in any one season, and each usually had a fashion life of several years. A major tannery today may turn out hundreds of leather colors and types each season, meanwhile preparing to produce more new colors and textures for the next season.

Trends in the Leather Industry

Until just a few decades ago, the leather industry concerned itself primarily with meeting consumer needs in relatively few fashion areas—mainly shoes, gloves, belts, handbags, luggage, and small leather goods. The use of leather for apparel was restricted largely to a few items of outerwear, such as jackets and coats. These were stiff, bulky, and primarily functional in appeal. Now designers offer colorful, supple leather vests, jeans, pants, blazers, anoraks, skirts, and suits of every description, in addition to jackets and coats (see Figure 6.2).

But the leather industry has changed. These changes are the result of three trends: enlarging market opportunities, increased competition from synthetics, and increased foreign trade.

Enlarging Markets

Improved methods of tanning are turning out better, more versatile leathers with improved fashion characteristics. In general, these improvements fall into three categories.

1. The new leathers are softer and more pliable. Tanners' abilities to split full-grain leather thinner and thinner create this new suppleness.
2. The new leathers can be dyed more successfully in a greater number of fashion colors.
3. Washable leather finishes and improved cleaning techniques have made it easier for consumers to care for leather garments.

Prada and Gucci are two upscale fashion companies built on leather. They continue to expand their offerings season after season. Other designers working with leather include Vakko, Donna Karan, Ralph Lauren, Escada, Michael Kors, and Calvin Klein.

Increased Competition from Synthetics

In the past few decades, the leather market has been eroded by synthetics. Leather heel lifts, which used to be commonplace, are now more often than not replaced with

Figure 6.2 Ralph Lauren pairs an elegant cocktail dress with southwestern-styled leathers.

plastic. Synthetics that look and feel like leather but are less susceptible to scratches and easier to maintain are used to make handbags and other small leather goods.

Because most synthetic leather products were not as attractive as leather, synthetics did not offer leather any real competition for a long time. However, imitation leathers and suedes that were true substitutes began to be marketed. The most important one, Ultrasuede, quickly became a fashion classic. Although a washable synthetic, Ultrasuede does not look fake or cheap, and it is used by high-fashion designers. Another artificial suede called Facile has improved suppleness. It is also widely used by high-fashion designers. Vinyl is widely used for shoes, handbags, and other accessories, and its appearance has improved over the years.

FAUX REAL

Worn as the whole garment, a detail, or an accessory, real or faux, fur provides a warmth, glamour, and luxury to fashionable garments like no other textile.

Through a concerted effort by the fur industry, real fur enjoyed an especially bright fashion moment in the Fall 2014 and 2015 collections, with over 70 percent of collections showing nips and bits of fur used in inventive and unexpected accents on fashions and accessories. However, in recent years, the fur industry faces challenges brought on by increased pressure from animal rights groups and more improved and innovative offerings from the faux fur producers.

In recent decades, the fur industry suffered setbacks and decline. Historically, fur demonstrated social rank and class and served as a true luxury item. Women seldom purchased furs for themselves, but received them as gifts from husbands or boyfriends, thus attaching a level of status. As early as the 1900s, technology enabled the development of faux fur, with increasing advancements in the types of fur, look, and feel through the first half of the twentieth century.

But market decline began in the wake of broader social and conservation movements in the twentieth century. Fronted by the Audubon Society in 1968, groups of conservation advocates picketed department store Saks Fifth Avenue, ordering the ban of fur of endangered species for fashion wear, and this expanded through the next decade to include protection of all animals. Faux fur makers gained momentum with this, and in the 1970s they launched advertising campaigns enlisting celebrity spokeswomen like Mary Tyler Moore and Doris Day portraying the real-fur industry as inhumane, undignified, and lacking true beauty. Fur eventually lost its luster as a luxury status item, and consumers considered the use of the fabric cruel and unnecessary in a modern, centrally heated world. Wearing fur was uncool.

In the 1990s, the message was reinforced by animal rights group PETA, which launched a campaign featuring top models Naomi Campbell and Cindy Crawford posing nude with the tag line, "I'd rather go naked than wear fur." Real-fur garments were portrayed as dowdy and old-fashioned. At this point, faux fur had surpassed the level of a cheap alternative, providing a viable substitute, and was often indistinguishable from the real thing. Technology for

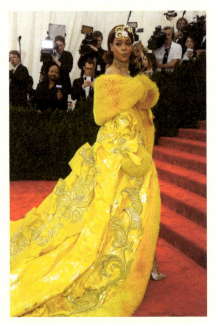

Rihanna arrives at the "China: Through the Looking Glass" Costume Institute Benefit Gala at the Metropolitan Modern multicolor and multitexture fur design. Museum of Art.

Modern fur designs appeal to a younger age group, with designs following street-wear and urban trends.

Gizele Oliveira poses wearing an Urban Outfitters coat.

beautiful faux fur had advanced, and manufacturers took advantage. Lush coats were donated to fashion houses for shows and accessories, and the use of faux fur became a signifier that the wearer was humane and possessed a modern, more sophisticated political and social point of view.

The fur industry continues to fight to remain relevant, using technological advances, reeducation, free samples for young designers to experiment with, and gifting garments to celebrities. The current fashion market accommodates luxury, and fur is still considered essential by many designers to produce exclusive, indulgent garments and accessories. Current marketing efforts spotlight fur as a sustainable product, and more environmentally sound than plastic-based synthetics used in faux fur. The fur industry worldwide is currently valued at $30 billion. And the customer base is young, with 55 percent of customers under the age of forty.

Each year beginning in 2008, the Fur Information Council of America (FICA) sponsors a student fur-design competition called REMIX with awards for women's and men's designs. Bright colors, lighter-weight pelts, and innovative surface and pile designs allow modern designers a wide range of ways to use fur.

Even with concerted marketing and educational efforts, the big news lately is that more and more designers are moving away from using fur. Many major retailers, including Macy's and Bloomingdale's, have stopped selling fur products. California passed a bill in October of 2019 banning the sale of fur state-wide and Los Angeles hosted its first Vegan Fashion Week. Other countries are also shifting in favor of fur-free fashions—the UK, Australia, Netherlands, and Norway have all banned fur farming.

More and more faux fur is showing up on the runways. But some designers remain faithful to the real thing! Fur remains one of the most controversial issues in the fashion world.

Street-wear spotted during the London Fashion Week February 2017.

Mendel multicolor fur.

Fur-embellished purse by Fendi.

Industry Growth Factors

Several factors point to overall industry growth. Foremost among these is the trend toward a classic and elegant fashion look with an emphasis on quality. When quality is desired, consumers want real leather, with all its mystique, and will not settle for substitutes. Another hopeful sign is the fact that the supply of raw hides is large enough to allow for growth in production. Actively supported by a federal export program, the industry's aggressive efforts to develop foreign markets ensure future growth for the industry, as do the industry's expanded research programs.

The Fur Industry

Long before prehistoric people learned how to plant crops, weave cloth, or build shelters, they figured out how to use fur. They spread it on the floor and used it as rugs. They used it to cover and create walls, thus bringing some warmth into otherwise cold and drafty caves.

By the Middle Ages, the wearing of fur announced one's wealth and status. Sable, marten, ermine, and fox were the favored furs of nobility. Italian cardinals wore ermine as a symbol of purity; English nobles wore it as a sign of power. Fur was also a valued commodity, something that was used in trading. For centuries in Northern Europe, furs were valued more than gold and silver. Fur was still as good as gold in 1900, when Chile banked chinchilla skins as security for a loan.

Fur is still big business in America, and men and women of all ages are buying it. Fur is found in designer boutiques, specialty retailers, sporting goods stores, and accessories shops, as well as the more traditional fur salons and department stores (see Figure 6.3).

History and Development

The search for a northwest passage that would shorten the route between Europe and the Orient led to the establishment of the fur trade in North America. The first posts were situated along the St. Lawrence and Hudson Rivers, but they soon dotted the continent. Early fur-trading posts played a role in establishing cities such as St. Louis, Chicago, Detroit, St. Paul, and Spokane.

Figure 6.3 A model wears a Ralph Lauren evening gown with a fur trapper-style hat and gloves. Accents, adornments, and accessories are a popular trend in fur.

The plentiful supply of furs helped the colonists in other ways. They were able to export furs and use the money to bring European necessities—and even some luxuries—to the New World. Furs were an important source of clothing and furnishings. For a while in the mid-eighteenth century, furs were virtually the currency of North America.

It is the beaver, however, that truly deserves a special place in North American history. The discovery of this fur led to a "fur rush" that rivaled the Gold Rush. Settlers pushed west in search of beaver fur, leaving behind communities with names like Beaver Creek, Beaver Falls, and Beaver Lake. Fortunes were made. John Jacob Astor was among the first to become a millionaire in the beaver trade. He dreamed of a beaver-fur empire stretching from New York to the Northwest Territory.

Fashions in furs do change, although they change less quickly than do other apparel styles because furs are expensive. While mink coats account for half of all furs sold today, fifty years ago a woman who wanted to look glamorous chose an ermine cape. Today, an ermine cape would be valuable only as a theatrical prop—and it could be picked up fairly cheaply in a secondhand store.

More than at any other time in the history of fur fashion, the current list of furs is long and varied (see Table 6.2). Mink is the overwhelming favorite among consumers. Sable is a distant second, followed by fox and beaver. A new category, called "sport" or "contemporary," includes such furs as raccoon, fox, beaver, coyote, muskrat, tanuki (Japanese raccoon), and nutria (a South American beaver-like animal).

Sometimes an interest in a fur comes about because fur manufacturers invent a finishing technique that makes a fur seem new. A renewed interest in raccoon can be traced to a technique that eliminated much of its bulkiness. In the 1940s, beaver was invariably sheared to look like a short fur; today it is sometimes left unplucked, giving it a totally new look.

Animal Rights Groups

For more than forty years, animal rights groups have protested the wearing of animal fur as cruel and inhumane. Some groups are opposed to trapping fur-bearing animals in the wild. Others also protest fur farming. Some groups, like **PETA** (People for the Ethical Treatment of Animals) and the Friends of Animals, have staged confrontations and demonstrations to get media attention. Still other groups, like the Animal Liberation Front, have raided mink and fox farms and let the animals loose. They also destroyed pedigree cards containing irreplaceable genetic data.[7]

The industry response has been strong on a number of fronts. It is working with the US and Canadian governments and the International Standards Organization to develop global humane trapping standards. Fur farmers are proposing legislation to make the crime of releasing fur-bearing animals a felony. Associations of American and Canadian fur farmers have also offered rewards for information leading to the arrest of fur raiders. Fur auction houses are offering farmers vandalism insurance.

The industry has done a great deal of consumer education to stress that today's farmed furs come from only nonendangered species.

Manufactured Furs

Manufactured, synthetic, or "fake" furs were long regarded as beneath the notice of serious designers and were limited to inexpensive garments. Technological developments in the 1980s and animal rights activism changed that. The new manufactured furs looked so good that fashion writers dropped the word *fake* and began calling them *faux* furs. (*Faux* is the French word for "false.")

Organization and Operation

The fur industry in the United States is divided into three groups, which also represent the three stages of fur production: the trappers, farmers, and ranchers who produce the pelts and sell them at auction; the fur-processing companies; and the manufacturers of fur products.

Pelt Production

The first step in the production of fur is to obtain the necessary pelts. A pelt is the skin of a fur-bearing animal.

Trappers are the primary source of wild-animal pelts, which must be taken only during the coldest season of the year to be of prime quality. As of 2017, 245 fur farms were in operation in twenty-two states. Wisconsin is the largest mink producing state at a rate of 972,000 pelts in 2018, followed by Utah, producing 708,000 pelts. The total number of mink pelts produced in 2018 was 3,100,000, compared to 3,365,700 in 1990. This is down 9 percent from 2017 figures. In 2018, the average price was $26.60, down from $36.10 in 2017 and from $57.70, as recently as 2013. The value of mink pelts was $82.6 million, down 33 percent from $123 million in 2017.[8]

The majority of furs come from farms or ranches, where fur-bearing animals are bred and raised strictly for their fur. Almost all mink, rabbit, fox, and—more recently—chinchilla, Persian lamb, and broadtail are ranched. **Fur farming** offers two important advantages. First, animals can be raised under controlled conditions. Second, they

TABLE 6.2 Selected Popular Furs and their Characteristics

Fur	Characteristics	What you should look for
Beaver	Sheared: Soft, plushy texture.	Silky texture. Well-matched pelts, evenly sheared.
	Natural: Long, lustrous guard hairs over thick underfur.	Lustrous sheen of guard hairs and thickness of underfur.
Calf	Short, sleek, flat hairs. Comes in many natural colors and patterns and may be dyed.	Lustrous, supple pelt with bright luster. Markings should be attractive.
Chinchilla	A short, dense, very silky fur. Originally from South America, but now wholly ranch raised.	Lustrous slate-blue top hair and dark underfur, although mutation colors are now available.
Coyote	A long-haired fur, often pale gray or tan in color. Durable and warm.	Long guard hair and thick, soft underfur.
Ermine	A fur with very silky white guard hairs and dense underfur.	Clear white color.
Fox	The widest range of natural mutation colors of any fur except mink; silver, blue, white, red, cross, beige, gray, and brown. Can also be dyed in a wide variety of colors.	Long, glossy guard hairs and thick soft underfur. Also clarity of color.
Lamb	American Processed: Pelts of fine wool sheep sheared to show the pattern near the skin. Naturally white but may be dyed.	Silky, lustrous moire pattern, not too curly.
	Broadtail: A natural (unsheared) flat moire pattern. Color may be natural browns, gray, black, or dyed in more exotic colors.	Silky texture and uniformity of pattern.
	Mongolian: Long, wavy, silky guard hair. May be natural off-white, bleached, or dyed in more exotic colors.	Silky texture, with wavy—not frizzy—hair.
	Mouton: Pelts are sheared, hairs are straightened for soft, water-repellent fur, generally dyed brown.	Uniformity of shearing.
	Shearling: Natural sheepskin (lamb pelt), with the leather side sueded and worn outside. The fur side (or inside) is often sheared.	Softness of leather side and even shearing.
	Persian lamb: From karkul sheep raised in Southwest Africa or central Asia. Traditionally black, brown, and gray, and new mutation colors available; also dyed.	Silky curls or ripples of fur and soft, light, pliable leather.
Lynx	Russian lynx is the softest and whitest of these long-haired furs, with the most subtle beige markings. Canadian lynx is next, while Montana lynx has stronger markings. Lynx cat or bobcat is reddish black fading to spotted white on longer belly hairs.	Creamy white tones and subtle markings.
Marten	See also *sable.*	Texture and clarity of color.
	American: Long silky guard hairs and dense underfur. Color ranges from blue-brown to dark brown.	
	Baum: Softer, silkier, and shinier than American marten.	
	Stone: The finest marten has soft, thick guard hairs and a bluish-brown cast with pale underfur.	

TABLE 6.2 Selected Popular Furs and their Characteristics (*continued*)

Fur	Characteristics	What you should look for
Mink	Soft and lightweight, with lustrous guard hairs and dense underfur.	Natural luster and clarity of color. Fur should be full and dense.
	Mutation: Most colors of any natural ranched fur, from white to grays, blues, and beiges.	
	Ranch: Color ranges from a true, rich brown to a deep brownish black.	
	Wild Pieced*: Generally brown in color. Color and pattern depend on pieces used. This is the least expensive mink.	Pattern and well-made seams.
Nutria	Similar to beaver, often sheared for a sporty, more lightweight feel. Popular for linings and trims. Often dyed in a variety of colors.	Clarity of color.
Rabbit	Generally long hair in a variety of natural colors, including fourteen natural mutation colors in ranch rabbit. May be sheared and grooved. Not very durable, shed easily.	Silky texture and uniformity.
Raccoon	Long silver, black-tipped guard hairs over woolly underfur. May also be plucked and sheared and dyed.	Silvery cast. Plenty of guard hair with heavy underfur.
Sable	Member of marten family. Russian sable has a silver cast; the most expensive. Crown sable is brown with a blue coat. Canadian golden sable, an amber tone, is less expensive.	Soft, deep fur in dark lustrous brown, with silky guard hairs.
Tanuki	Also called Japanese raccoon. Color is light amber brown with distinctive cross markings.	Clarity of color and dense, full texture.

*The same piecing technique can be used for almost any fur. The most common pieced furs are mink, sable, marten, fox, Persian lamb, raccoon, and beaver.

Source: Adapted from a number of sources, including the booklet *Choosing Fur* (Herndon, VA: Fur Council of Canada and the Fur Information Council of America), 4–5.

can be bred selectively. When wild mink roamed North America, they came in one color, a dark brown with reddish highlights. Today, many beautiful colors, some of which are trademarked and denote a manufacturer's private label, are available. Among the better-known names are Azurene, Lunaraine, Rovalia, Lutetia, Jasmin, Tourmaline, Cerulean, and the most recognizable name of all, Blackgama.[9]

Fur Auctions

Fur pelts are sold at auctions today, much as they were in the thirteenth century. Fur buyers and manufacturers bid on the pelts, which are sold in bundles. Buyers look for bundles that are matched in quality and color. This enables a manufacturer to make up a garment of uniform beauty.

Competition has increased among buyers to purchase a "top bundle"—that is, an unusually beautiful bundle that goes for an unusually high price. This, in turn, results in a much-touted coat—often costing $100,000 or more—that is made from the top bundle.

The auction trail is an international one, although except for England, Tokyo, and Beijing, each market sells indigenous furs. Fur buyers from the United States travel to Canada, Scandinavia, China, and Russia. To buy North American furs, fur buyers travel to auction houses in New York, Seattle, Toronto, and North Bay, Canada.

Fur Processing

After manufacturers of fur goods buy the pelts, they contract with fur-dressing and fur-dyeing firms to process them.

AUDREY CERVELLERO
Accessory Designer

MEET AUDREY CERVELLERO, FREELANCE HANDBAG AND ACCESSORY DESIGNER. Cervellero had not always planned on being a designer. With a BA in political science from Coastal Carolina University, she was headed to law school to study international law, but she could not silence her passion for fashion. It was the advice of a friend that changed her course: "You will likely be doing whatever it is you choose to do for over thirty years of your life, so at least enjoy it." Three years later, she graduated from Drexel University with an MS in fashion design. It was there that she learned the essential skills of turning an idea into a finished product—sketching, sewing, pattern design, line development, and a variety of CAD programs used in the industry. And, she emphasizes construction; it is not enough to create beautiful things, but a designer has to properly and clearly communicate instructions on how to make them to others.

As a freelance designer, Cervellero sees her responsibilities change significantly from one job to the next. Sometimes she might work in the client's headquarter offices, and sometimes she may work from home. While working from home might sound appealing, Cervellero shares specific advice for optimal productivity: It takes discipline. Get up, get dressed, and begin work by 8:30—no later than 9:00 a.m. Make a detailed list of the day's goals to be accomplished and work through them one by one. Take a lunch break and then back to work until 5:30 or 6:00 p.m. Refrain from taking personal calls or answering personal emails during the workday—it's too easy to get distracted.

Depending on the type of firm she works with, Cervellero's role and duties vary quite a bit. When working with an import company, she designs products from concept to completion, including working with private-label lines and multiple seasonal lines, overseeing full development and follow-up, managing design revisions, and negotiating prices with suppliers. For this type of project, travel for market research, to source materials, and to work with factories on the product development is essential. At the opposite end of the project spectrum, Cervellero might work with a large corporation where her role is to interpret and execute very specific design direction. Because of the variety, every project requires her to use a wide variety of skills—creative, organizational, and communication.

To Cervellero, the most important thing a designer can do for his or her career is to stay updated on current events. Know what is happening in politics, what's trending on social media, music, movies, and fine arts, as well as in the fashion industry. Shop, read magazines and newspapers, and network. Meet people who work in a variety of jobs and industries to help expand your world and your point of view. Cervellero also stresses the importance of knowing the customer—age, lifestyle, profession, income, hobbies. Learn to fully understand who is buying your product and be able to design with their needs in mind.

Cervellero's advice to students who are interested in a career in design: "You have to love it! There is a common misconception that being a designer is glamorous. While it has its special moments, the competition is fierce, the hours are long, the work is tedious, the pressure is high, and the sacrifice can be great. If you love the process and the craft, it is worth every second." She also advises those new to the industry: "Leave your ego at home! It is good to have confidence, but having an ego will likely stunt your growth. I have learned so much from others and, likewise, share my knowledge with many. Be patient. Take criticism gracefully."

The job of fur dressers is to make the pelts suitable for use in consumer products. The pelts are first softened by soaking and mechanical means. Then a flesher removes any unwanted substances from the inner surface of the skin. For less expensive furs, this is done by roller-type machines. At this point, the pelts are treated with solutions that tan the skin side into pliable leather. The fur side may be processed at the same time. This involves either plucking unwanted guard hairs or shearing the underfur to make the fur more lightweight. Although fur dressing has traditionally been a handcraft industry, modern technology is turning it into a more mechanical process.

After dressing, the pelts may go to a dyer. Fur dyes were once made from vegetable matter but are now mostly derived from chemical compounds. New dyes are constantly being developed, making it possible to dye fur more successfully and in more shades than ever before.

Fur Manufacturing

Most fur manufacturers are small, independently owned and operated shops, although a few big companies have emerged, largely as a result of the explosion in the number of fur products. New York City's fur district on Seventh Avenue between 23rd and 30th Streets is the main center for fur manufacturing. The production of fur garments lends itself neither to mass production nor to large-scale operations. Skill and judgment are required at every stage of manufacturing. Doing each step by hand lets a worker deal with each pelt's color, quality, and peculiarities. The following steps transform pelts into finished garments:

1. A design of the garment is sketched.
2. A paper pattern is made of the garment.
3. A canvas pattern is made.
4. The skins are cut in such a way as to conform to the designer's sketch, exhibit the fur to its best advantage, and minimize waste.
5. The cut skins are sewn together.
6. The skins are wetted and then stapled to a board to dry, a process that sets them permanently.
7. The garment sections are sewn together.
8. The garment is lined and finished.
9. The garment is inspected.

For some luxurious furs, the cutting operation becomes extremely complex. Short skins must be **let out** to a suitable length for garments. Letting out mink, for example, involves cutting each skin down the center of a dark vertical line of fur (the grotzen stripe). Each half-skin must then be cut at an angle into diagonal strips one-eighth to three-sixteenths of an inch wide. Then each tiny strip is re-sewn at an angle to the strips above and below it to make a long, narrow skin. The other half-skin is sewn in a similar manner.

The two halves are then joined, resulting in a longer, slimmer pelt that is more beautiful than the original. Considerable hand labor is required to do all of these operations. Ten miles of thread and more than 1,200 staples may be used in a single coat.

Generations of furriers have produced garments in much the same way as in ancient times. Recent innovations in processing, however, create lighter-weight, more supple pelts, enabling designers to use fur in much more creative applications.

Retail Distribution of Furs

There are approximately 1,100 retailers and 100 fur manufacturers in the United States. About 85 percent are small, family-run businesses that have been passed from generation to generation. In the global fur market, the United States ranks among the top countries for retail fur sales.[10] That said, the line between manufacturing and retailing is less clear in the fur industry than in most other industries. Retail fur merchants, for example, typically make up an assortment of garments to sell off the rack to customers, but they also maintain a supply of skins in their workrooms for custom work.

In retail stores, fur departments are either leased or consignment departments. Both operations permit a retail store to offer its customers a large selection without tying up a lot of capital in inventory.

A leased department is situated in the store but run by an independent company, such as BC International (it sells luxurious fur fashion in Bloomingdale's, Saks Fifth Avenue, and Macy's). It also pays a percentage of sales to the store as rent. The operator either owns or leases the stock. Lessees often run several similar departments in many stores and can, if necessary, move garments and skins from one location to another. Lessees, who are a unique kind of retailer, are usually well capitalized and have expert knowledge in both furs and retailing.

In consignment selling, a fur manufacturer supplies merchandise to a retail store, which has the option of returning unsold items. In effect, the manufacturer lends stock to a store. Consignment selling is influenced by the state of the economy. When interest rates are high, stores tend to buy less stock. Ritz is an example of a consignment seller.

Merchandising and Marketing

Fur traders, dressers, producers, and their labor unions all work through their various trade associations to encourage the demand for fur.

Trade Associations

Trade associations mount their own campaigns to promote furs, and they also work with retailers. FICA is the leading trade association, which represents fur retailers and manufacturers. It has placed ads in various fashion magazines to counter some of the animal rights arguments.

The North American Fur Auction is the largest fur auction house in North America and the largest wild fur auction house in the world. It is owned by North American Fur Producers Inc. which represents American Mink Council (AMC), Canada Mink Breeders Association (CBMA), Wild Fur Shippers Council (WFSC), and Canada Fox Breeders Association CFBA). The ranch mink association, formerly known as American Legend Cooperative, formed through the combination of two major mink-producing groups: Emba Mink Breeders Association and Great Lakes Mink Association. In 2018, this resulting organization was purchased by North American Fur Auction. The organization protects its trademarks from infringement and supplies labels with integrated security fibers woven into the label and other point-of-purchase materials to ensure retailers and consumers that garments and labels are not counterfeit.[11]

Trade associations not only monitor the industry but also help to educate consumers. Fur is a product that is most successfully purchased when the consumer has some specialized knowledge about what he or she is buying. Consumers need to know, for example, that the rarer the breed, the more expensive the fur. Another important factor in the quality of fur is whether the pelts are female or male. Most female skins are softer and lighter. Although there are exceptions, such as fitch, for which the male skins are preferred, a coat of female mink costs more than one of male mink.

International Fur Fairs

As the demand for fur increases and the world supply of fur pelts decreases, people are traveling farther than ever before to get the best buys. Designers, manufacturers, retailers, importers/exporters, wholesalers, and the media all attend one or more of the leading international fur fairs.

Labeling

The Fur Products Labeling Act of 1952 requires that all furs be labeled according to the following:

1. The English name of the animal
2. The Registered Identification Number (RN)
3. Its country of origin
4. The type of processing, including dyeing, to which the pelts have been subjected
5. Whether or not parts have been cut from a used garment or from the less desirable paw or tail sections

Years ago, such labeling would have been helpful, for example, to prevent a customer from buying a less expensive, dyed muskrat that was touted as the much rarer and more expensive Hudson seal. Such labeling is helpful in distinguishing one fur from another in an industry that, without intending to defraud, has learned to capitalize on fashion trends by treating less expensive furs to look like more expensive ones. And, with advancements in the development of faux fur, labeling prevents real fur being sold as faux fur or faux fur being mistaken for real fur.

Trends in the Fur Industry

As a general rule, the demand for furs is related to the economy. During the Depression, fur sales dropped off dramatically. After the Second World War, when the economy was expanding, fur sales boomed. In the early

1970s, conservationists' concerns about the diminishing wildlife species put a temporary damper on fur sales, but the industry rebounded in the 1980s. Mid-1987 saw the highest point, the $2 billion mark. But in the early 1990s, a combination of anti-fur activism and mild winters brought a rapid downturn in fur sales. Synthetic-fur sales rose rapidly. But then the record-breaking bad weather in the mid-1990s saw a renewed interest in real fur. From 2002 to 2006, the number of US mink farms fell by 16 percent, while average pelt production per farm rose 31 percent. The continued decline in 2007 came in spite of favorable weather conditions through the winter of 2007–2008. The decline instead has been attributed to growing concerns about the state of the economy and a decrease in discretionary spending.[12] However, even as the economy recovers, the fur industry continues to face challenges. Bans on the sale of fur garments is spreading, starting with the entire state of California in October of 2019, with a similar bill proposed in New York. Bloomingdale's and Macy's have joined a growing list of retailers getting out of the business of selling fur garments and accessories. And while quite a few designers continue to use fur in their collections, an ever growing number no longer use fur, including BCBG, Burberry, Michael Kors, Prada, Versace, Chanel, and many more.[13] In 2018, *InStyle* banned fur from its editorial content and no longer accepts fur advertising.[14]

The natural fur industry is fighting back with a message of biodegradability and sustainability, with an argument that synthetic fake furs are worn for a short time, discarded, and take decades to decompose, while a real fur is a luxury item, worn for years, passed down to one's children, and recycled into other decorative uses.[15] US retail fur sales come to about $1.4 billion of the $30 billion in global sales. The global leader in retail fur consumption is China, at $17 billion.[16] In recent years, fashion trends have moved to experimentation with color, texture, and increased use of fur details in small accessory items.[17]

Growth will be affected by the following four major trends:

1. Renewed fashion interest in furs
2. Foreign trade
3. Restrictive legislation that actually helps the industry
4. New channels of retail distribution

Renewed Fashion Interest

Once worn only by the rich or for formal occasions, furs are now bought and worn by many kinds of consumers for many occasions (see Figure 6.4). The average customer no longer buys one conservatively cut coat, either. Furs are now sporty and casual, elegant and classic, or faddish

Figure 6.4 Fur can be both elegant (left) and rock and roll (right).

and trendy—and with such choices, many customers have been persuaded to buy more than one. Even though designer Michael Kors has gone fur-free for future collections, he says:

"When you think about fashion today, we're certainly not living in era I think of edicts. . . . We're in a moment where fashion is more than ever up to the individual. I have a feeling that there will be many women who will mix it all up, that there will be customers we'll see who will wear faux fur, shearling, real fur, recycled. I don't think it's all or nothing."[18]

Foreign Trade

China has historically been one of the world's greatest markets for furs, and there is still increased interest for fur garments in the Far East. The United States also continues to produce innovative, high-style furs that are in great demand around the world.[19]

Restrictive Legislation

The Federal Trade Commission and the fur industry are constantly engaged in talks about fur labeling. Ironically, the most important recent legislation, which was intended to restrict the fur industry, has actually been helpful. The Endangered Species Act of 1973 forbade the sale of furs made from endangered species such as leopard, tiger, ocelot, cheetah, jaguar, vicuna, and a few types of wolf. Since women no longer have to worry about wearing an endangered species, many have returned to the fur market.

New Channels of Retail Distribution

Hotel, armory, and arena fur sales are held almost every fall and winter weekend in New York City and other large cities. Fur manufacturers can conduct these sales for a fraction of the cost in wages and rent that would be required if they were to maintain comparable facilities year-round. Even better, the average hotel ballroom, armory, or arena showroom is suitable for displaying thousands of coats, far more than the average fur salon can attractively exhibit. The sales appeal to customers, who like the hands-on approach and lower prices. The same customers who frequent weekend sales also can shop in manufacturer-leased discount and off-price stores.

Summary and Review

In the United States, the tanning of leather for clothing and footwear dates back to the precolonial Indian populations. The industry consists of three major types of businesses: regular tanneries, contract tanneries, and converters.

Most leather comes from cattle as an offshoot of the meatpacking industry, but leather is also produced from the pelts of eight other animal groups. Tanneries tend to specialize according to the end use of the leather. Tanning may involve one or more processes using minerals, vegetable materials, oils, and chemicals, alone or in combination, to achieve the desired color and textural finish.

Leather Industries of America (LIA), the industry's trade association, advises its members on fashion and technical issues and promotes the industry to its markets.

Fur has been used for warmth in clothing and shelter since prehistoric times. Fur trading, especially in beaver skins, was a major industry in the European colonization of America, and it remained so well into the nineteenth century. For much of the twentieth century, fur was considered a luxury fashion item for women, but in recent years, it has been used as a trim for various types of apparel. The efforts of animal rights activists, periods of economic downturn, and competition from imports and from faux furs have challenged the industry, but most recently, the industry has launched campaigns to educate the public about humane industry practices and natural fur as an environmentally responsible and sustainable choice.

The fur industry is made up of three groups: trappers, farmers, and ranchers; fur-processing companies, who buy furs at auctions; and manufacturers of fur products. Processing pelts and turning them into fashion products require skilled labor, although some mechanization has been introduced into the process. The distinction between levels in the fur industry is less precise than in other segments of the fashion industry. Because of the specialized knowledge and the financial investment required, furs are often sold to consumers by consignment or leased departments in retail stores, by mail order, or in manufacturers' shows in hotels or other large spaces.

FOR REVIEW

1. In what ways have technological advances in machinery and chemistry benefited the leather industry?
2. Name and describe the three major types of companies in the leather industry.
3. What are the nine major groups of fur-bearing animals?
4. What has Leather Industries of America done to broaden the leather market and soften the impact of competition from synthetics?
5. What factors point to growth for the leather industry?
6. Describe the history and development of the fur industry in the United States.
7. Into what three groups is the fur industry divided? Briefly describe the function of each.
8. What are the advantages of fur farming over trapping?
9. Outline the steps in transforming processed fur pelts into finished garments.
10. Differentiate between leased departments and consignment selling as these terms apply to retail distribution of fur garments. What major advantages does each have for retail merchants?

FOR DISCUSSION

1. Discuss the following statement from the text and its implications for leather merchandising: "The leather industry not only must stay abreast of fashion but also must be several steps ahead of it."
2. Discuss current trends in the leather industry that relate to enlarging markets, competition from synthetics, and increased foreign trade.
3. Discuss the pros and cons of trapping and raising animals for their fur. Explain your support or rejection of the arguments advanced by animal rights activists and by the fur industry.
4. Discuss current trends in the fur industry as they relate to fashion interest, increased foreign trade, new channels of retail distribution, low-cost imports, rising overhead, and lack of skilled workers and managers.

Trade Talk

Define or briefly explain the following terms:

fur farming
hides
kips
let out
pelt
PETA
skins
sustainable use
tanning

ELIZA   CORINNA

I-HUA   WANES

PART THREE

The Secondary Level: The Producers of Fashion

In this part, you will learn how the fashion apparel manufacturing business has changed from an industry of many small companies into an industry dominated by a growing group of giants. You will begin to develop a basic vocabulary and a working knowledge of the following:

- The six-stage process of developing and producing a line and the major industry practices of licensing, private label, specification buying, offshore production, factors, and chargebacks are discussed in Chapter 7.
- The history of the women's, men's, children's, and teens' apparel industries and the categories, size ranges, and price zones, as well as the roles of brand names and designer names, in the marketing process are explored in Chapter 8.
- The history, merchandising, and marketing of accessories are the subjects of Chapter 9.

The increased size of companies has influenced the way apparel is designed, manufactured, and merchandised. To understand these developments, you need to explore the aspects of apparel production, as well as the history and current activities of the producers of accessories.

7

Product Development

Key Concepts

- **The major advantages and disadvantages of the contractor system**

- **The six-stage process of developing and producing a line of apparel**

- **The major industry practices of licensing, brand extension, private label and specification buying, offshore production, CAD/CAM, PLM, use of factors, chargebacks, and SIC/NAICS codes**

- **The supply chain management movement and the mass customization theory and their effects on the product development chain**

- **How bar codes, scanners, and RFID are integral parts of supply chain management**

Apparel manufacturers seeking to serve today's world-class brands and retailers will need a continued uptick in their product development and design skills, an ability to innovate in both product and process, savvy risk management, and operational transparency.[1]

If new apparel and fashion-related products are not developed, sales and profits decline, technology and markets change, or innovation by other firms makes the original product obsolete. All of this points to the importance of product development for the continued success of a company.

Product development is the teaming of market and trend research, with the merchandising, design, and technical processes that develop a final product. Product development is used by both wholesale manufacturers, who develop products for signature brands, and retailers, who use it for private-label development at their own stores.

Whether making plain T-shirts or elaborate evening gowns, the men's, women's, and children's apparel industries in the United States have managed to settle into a basic cycle of design and production that repeats itself more or less unchanged from season to season. However, before an article of clothing reaches the retail store racks, a great deal of work and planning are involved. (There are similar cycles for accessories, cosmetics and fragrances, and home fashions; they will be discussed in Part Four.) This chapter will focus on the design and production of apparel for men, women, and children; Chapter 8 examines each area in detail.

What Is a Product Line, and Who Develops It?

Product lines of apparel are created and styled for wholesale presentation several times, or seasons, per year. In the fashion industries, a product line is referred to simply as a line. A line encompasses not only the individual item of apparel or accessories but also the entire season's production from that manufacturer as well. The term *line* is used for moderate- and popular-priced apparel. The term **collection** is used to describe an expensive line in the United States or in Europe. Lines are divided into **groups** of garments, linked by a common theme like color, fabric, or style. Each garment is known as a style number or number, such as 401 or 57.

It is important to note here that in the United States, designs cannot be copyrighted, as they are in France. Copying from creative designers is common throughout the fashion industry and is not considered piracy. At some firms, few if any designs are original; rather, they are copied **line-for-line** in a similar fabric, adapted from another designer in a cheaper fabric (knockoffs), or reworked from a previous season in a different color or fabric (**anchors**).

Designers typically work on three seasonal lines at a time. They monitor the sales of the current season's line, put the finishing touches on the next season's line, and begin to develop the new line for the following season. Clearly, this is a challenging undertaking.

We will now examine the roles played by the merchandiser, designer, and producer in the product development process.

Role of the Merchandiser

The merchandiser channels the creativity of the designer and design staff so that the six "rights" of merchandising can be successfully accomplished. These rights are the right merchandise, at the right price, at the right time, in the right place, in the right quantity, with the right promotion. To these rights must be added another—the right customer! Because this customer is so important, the merchandiser is given the responsibility to research who the "right" customer is.

Some people in the industry have described the merchandiser as the "glue" that holds the whole product development concept together. In fact, the merchandiser is the link among the design staff, production facilities, and sales staff. The merchandiser has to view the line from the design point of view and also has to be knowledgeable about production and sales efforts.

Role of the Designer

Designers can create by sketching, by drawing on a computer (**computer-aided design** [CAD]), or by draping cloth on a model. Although artistic excellence is the goal, designers must keep practical business considerations in mind. All designs must be produced at a profit and within the firm's wholesale price range. Consequently, designers must consider the availability and cost of materials, the cost of cutting and sewing the garment, and labor costs.

Role of the Producer

The fashion apparel industry consists of three types of producers: manufacturers, jobbers, and contractors. An **apparel manufacturer** performs all the operations required to produce apparel, from buying the fabric to selling and shipping the finished garments. An **apparel jobber** handles the designing, the planning, the purchasing, usually the cutting, the selling, and the shipping, but not the actual sewing operation. An **apparel contractor** is a producer whose sole function is to supply sewing services to the industry, where it is sometimes called an **outside shop**. Contractors that specialize in the production of one product are sometimes referred to as **item houses**. Increasingly, the term *manufacturer* is being used more loosely to describe any firm that handles any part of the cutting or sewing process, and the terms *jobber* and *contractor* are used less often.

Manufacturers

A manufacturer is a producer who handles all phases of a garment's production. Each line is planned by the company executives. After the staff produces the original design or buys an acceptable design from a freelance designer, the company purchases the fabric and trimmings needed. The cutting and sewing are usually done in the company's factories. On certain occasions, however, a manufacturer may use the services of a contractor if sales of an item exceed the capacity of the firm's sewing facilities and if shipping deadlines cannot otherwise be met. Finally, the company's sales force and traffic department handle the selling and shipping of the finished goods. One great advantage of this type of operation is that close quality control can be maintained. When producers contract out some part of their work, they cannot as effectively monitor its quality.

Apparel Jobbers

Apparel jobbers handle all phases of the production of a garment except for the actual sewing and sometimes the cutting. A jobber firm may employ a design staff to create various seasonal lines or may buy sketches from freelance designers. The jobber's staff buys the fabric and trimmings necessary to produce the styles in each line, makes up samples, and grades the patterns. In most cases, the staff also cuts the fabric for the various parts of each garment. Jobbers arrange with outside factories run by contractors to perform these manufacturing operations. The sales staff takes orders for garments in each line, and the shipping department fills store orders from the finished garments returned by the contractor.

Contractors

Contractors usually specialize in just one phase of the production of a garment: sewing. In some cases, contractors also perform the cutting operation from patterns submitted by a jobber or a manufacturer.

If a contractor is used, cut pieces of the garment are provided by the manufacturer. For an agreed price per garment, the article is sewn, finished, inspected, pressed, hung or packaged, and returned to the manufacturer for shipment to retail stores.

In the mass production of ready-to-wear, a single sewing-machine operator rarely makes a complete garment. Each operator sews only a certain section of the garment, such as a sleeve or a hem. This division of labor, called **section work** or **piecework**, makes it unnecessary for an operator to switch from one highly specialized machine to another or to make adjustments. Any change or adjustment in equipment takes time and increases labor costs. In the fashion trade, time lost in making such changes also causes delays in getting a style to consumers. Delays in production could mean the loss of timeliness and sales appeal before an article reaches market.

A contractor may arrange to work exclusively with one or more jobbers or manufacturers, reserving the right to work for others whenever the contractor's facilities are not fully employed. Such agreements are necessarily reciprocal. If a contractor agrees to give preference to a particular jobber's or manufacturer's work, the jobber or manufacturer gives preference to that contractor when placing sewing orders.

The advantages and disadvantages of the contractor system for the manufacturer are as follows:

Advantages
- Large amounts of capital are not required for investment in sewing equipment that may soon become obsolete.
- Difficulties in the hiring and training of suitable workers are minimized.

- The amount of capital necessary to meet regular payrolls is greatly reduced.
- By providing additional manufacturing facilities in periods of peak demand, contractors help speed up delivery of orders.
- It is unnecessary to keep one factory busy all year.

Disadvantages
- No individual has full responsibility for the finished product.
- Other manufacturers (jobbers) may use the same facilities and get preferential treatment because they place larger orders, offer repeat business, or even guarantee future business.
- The quality of the work and inspection tends to be uneven.

The Product Development Process

In a study published in the *Journal of Textile and Apparel Technology and Management*, the authors listed the following functions for an effective integrated system of product development:[2]

- Marketing
- Forecasting
- Merchandising
- Product line development
- Product design and specifications
- Material requisition planning
- Inventory control
- Costing
- Production planning and scheduling
- Sourcing and manufacturing
- Quality control
- Human resources
- Purchasing
- Logistics
- Warehouse inventory movement systems
- Finance
- Sales
- Field sales support
- Performance measurement
- External communication

Currently, many variations exist in the product development process, but we will discuss a simple six-stage process that covers the functions performed at every firm,

regardless of size. The major differences are the number of people involved and how they communicate and interact. The six-stage product development process is outlined as follows:

Stage 1: Planning a line
Stage 2: Creating the design concept
Stage 3: Developing the designs
Stage 4: Planning production
Stage 5: Production
Stage 6: Distributing the line

Stage 1: Planning a Line

The first step of the product development process involves the work of a designer or a product development team, working under the direction of a merchandiser. It is these people who are charged with creating a line. Their first task is research. They review information on trends, colors, fabrics, and other materials. Because they must keep in mind previous fashion successes or failures, past sales records are reviewed, as well as markdown reports. Some firms develop "trend boards" that contain visual or graphic representations of developments that are affecting their target customer (see Figure 7.1). All of this research helps designers or product development teams to formulate some idea of what the new line will contain.

Using all their merchandising and marketing skills, merchandisers or designers help to form and maintain a positive image in the marketplace for the manufacturer. It is this image that influences a specific consumer group to buy a particular line at the retail level.

In most cases, design has to be disciplined and directed so that the particular image of the manufacturer and the merchandise that is produced will continue to fit the needs and wants of a specific consumer group.

Stage 2: Creating the Design Concept

Next come designs for individual garments. Each one is sketched or developed in muslin. At this stage, the designer or design staff considers his or her work and weighs it on two points: first, on its own individual merit, and second, for its suitability in the line as a whole. Many designs are discarded at this point.

Price is also a critical factor in determining whether a design is deleted from a line. A cost analysis is often done at this stage, and designs that are too expensive to

Figure 7.1 Beach, sea, and sky are grouped together in color and texture on this inspiration board for the GEORGINE 2015 collection.

produce profitably at the desired price point are rejected (see Figures 7.2a and 7.2b).

Stage 3: Developing the Designs

Those designs that seem most likely to succeed are made up as finished sample garments. A patternmaker creates a production pattern in the garment size the company uses to produce its samples. From this pattern, one or more samples are cut. Finally, a designer's assistant who is also a seamstress sews the garment (see Figure 7.2c). This person is called a **sample hand**. Another option that is common in the industry is producing products off-shore by hired vendors.

Now the design is presented to various executives and managers of the company—people in sales, purchasing, production, and cost accounting. Both the cost of the fabric and the cost of producing the garment are carefully analyzed. Many designs are again discarded at this point, while others are sent back to the design department for

modification. A few are accepted. The accepted design is assigned a style number. At this point, it is officially part of a manufacturer's line.

Computer-Aided Design

Although the day has not yet arrived when designers will throw away their sketch pads and pencils, the advancements of **computer-aided design (CAD)** are giving designers the freedom to explore and manipulate their designs in relatively easy, quick, and inexpensive ways. A designer does not have to take a chance that he or she is having a sample made up in the best color. **CAD** is used to test various colors and color combinations, fabrics, and styles. **CAD** allows three-dimensional (3-D) contouring of objects on screen. Folds, creases, and textures are simulated so that **CAD**-generated garments drape and hang accurately. Once the design is set on the computer, the computer image is used to create a pattern that is complete with darts, seams, and tailor's markings.

(a)

(b)

(c)

Figure 7.2 We Are Handsome designs a swimwear collection. The inspiration and concept for the line is assembled, and the line is designed, developed, and prepared for production.

(d)

Because the computer can create the design in 3-D, the computer image can be rotated to see all sides of the garment. Many companies are thus reducing the number of costly sample garments that they produce. Instead of a physical sample, they use the computer image in the line development process to communicate design direction to suppliers and contractors, and in merchandising and sales presentations.

Linked CAD/CAM/CIM

CAD systems are continuing to expand with new technology and developments in the industry. In addition, CAD could be linked to **computer-aided manufacturing** (CAM) and **computer-integrated manufacturing**

(CIM) systems to provide information internally, to suppliers, and even to retailers across the country and across the world (see Figure 7.2d). Linked CAD/CAM/CIM technology and product lifecycle management (PLM) software will be discussed in more detail later in this chapter.

INNOVATION IN TEXTILE AND APPAREL DESIGN

Great new advancements in apparel technology and wearable gadgets are big news in the fashion world. With emphasis on sustainability, accessibility, and comfort, here is a list of some interesting new inventions.

New Textiles

Orange Fiber® is an Italian company that develops luxurious, silk-like fabric from the fiber of oranges and other citrus fruits. Salvatore Ferragamo used the product to make luxury scarves.

Algae Apparel was a finalist for the 2018 H&M Global Innovation Awards for its creation of a biodegradable textile and a range of eco-friendly dyes, all from algae. Algalife® produces a T-shirt using 2,100 less liters of water than a traditionally produced T-shirt, and also uses no chemicals, fertilizers, and generates a zero-CO_2 footprint.

Want to eliminate overstock and produce zero-waste garments? Unspun® developed a machine that makes jeans on demand, using 3D technology to capture the customer's measurements. Through a combination of digital customization and automated manufacturing, the goal of this company is to achieve zero cutting waste, zero inventory, and reduce global carbon emissions by 1 percent.

Evernu® has developed technology to recycle cotton from existing garments and uses 98 percent less water in the process. Levi's has recruited this firm to help improve its own sustainability practices.

Mobility and Accessibility

Aura Power Clothing, designed by Yves Behar, is a lightweight undergarment to help the aging and movement challenged people move around their homes and stay active and mobile for longer. The garment is aligned with natural muscular composition to support sitting and standing movement. It is powered by integrated electric muscles and sensors to provided added torso, hip, and leg strength. It is lightweight and can be worn discretely under regular apparel.

The Vigour Cardigan® by Dutch designer Pauline van Dongen, collects data through four stretch sensors embedded in the garment. The information is sent to an app and will help both wearer and medical providers understand activity and how to improve exercises for rehabilitation and greater mobility.

Parsons School of Design students created a line of apparel for people in wheelchairs who lead an active lifestyle. Izzy Camilleri continues to innovate a line of stylish and functional apparel for women who use wheelchairs.

Designer Izzy Camilleri holds a pair of jeans designed for women who use wheelchairs. Notice the specific design to provide comfort in the sitting position.

These garments designed by Izzy Camilleri integrate elegant fabrics, provide special fitting, comfort, and stylish details. Ten percent of the earnings are contributed to organizations that provide more mobile access.

Stage 4: Planning Production

This stage of the product development process begins with sourcing, or determining where the components of a garment (fabric, thread, linings, facings, buttons, trim, etc.) will be purchased and, in some cases, where the garments will be cut and sewn. It is now that the vital question of domestic or foreign manufacture must be decided. (The role of supply chain management in this decision is discussed later in this chapter.) Reservations for production must be made so that the garments will be available when needed. The fabric must be ordered, along with orders for the other components of the garment. Finally, each garment must be costed out, so that the selling price can be set. The samples are used to determine the cost of producing the garment. The money needed to finance production must be obtained. Only when all of these steps have been completed can actual production begin.

The samples, each with its style number, are then presented to retail buyers at the manufacturers' seasonal shows. Most manufacturers have set minimum orders for the quantity, number of styles, and/or dollar amount required to accept the retail buyer's order.

Because the manufacturer usually has not yet begun production when a line is shown to the buyers, it may be possible to fine-tune production to the buyers' orders. When a particular style receives a lot of attention from buyers, it is then scheduled for production. Items that generate little or no enthusiasm are dropped from the line.

Stage 5: Production

Cutting

One of the most important steps in the mass production of apparel is the cutting of the garment pieces. Once a garment is slated for production, it is **graded**, or sloped, to each of the various sizes in which it will be made. After a pattern has been graded to the various sizes, the pieces are laid out on a long piece of paper called a **marker**. The success of cutting depends on the accuracy with which each of the many layers of material are placed on top of one another. A **spreader**, or laying-up machine, carries the material along a guide on either side of the cutting table, spreading the material evenly from end to end. The marker is laid on top of these layers.

For many years, material was cut by hand, but the cutting process is now either computer-assisted or totally computerized. Computers are programmed to feed instructions to laser, blade, or high-speed water-jet machines that do the actual cutting.

Once the cutting is completed, the pieces of each pattern—the sleeves, collars, fronts, and backs—are tied into bundles according to their sizes. This process is called **bundling**, and it must be done by hand. The bundles are then moved to the manufacturers' sewing operators, who may be on the premises or in contractors' shops.

Sewing

Technology has dramatically changed the sewing stage of production. The industrial sewing machine sews much faster than a home sewing machine. Further, home sewing machines perform many functions, while industrial machines perform specialized functions. Some sew only seams, while others sew blind hems. Button machines sew on buttons. Computerized sewing machines that do embroidery can be set up to stitch whole patterns without a machine operator (see Figure 7.3). Robotic sewing equipment is currently under development.

Meanwhile, single-hand operations, in which one operator sews the entire garment, still exist. They are used for very high-priced garments that are produced in very small quantities. Today, most manufacturers use a combination of mass-production systems, including the popular modular manufacturing system, in which teams of seven to nine workers produce entire garments, passing them on to each other stage by stage, until the garment is complete. This system requires extensive cross-training

Figure 7.3 A worker at an embroidery plant in Bangladesh manually rethreads one of many industrial machines.

so each team member can learn all the tasks involved and perform them as the flow of work demands.

Finishing the Product

The sewn garment is still far from ready for the retail floor. Pants, for example, are sewn with the legs inside out. They must be turned right-side out. A label must be sewn in. Buttons and buttonholes may be added at this stage.

Some fabrics are washed at this stage to prevent shrinkage. Others have a wrinkle-resistant finish applied. Still others are dyed at this point, called garment-dyeing, which gives the manufacturer last-minute control of color.

The garment is then pressed and folded or hung on a hanger with a plastic bag over it. Some manufacturers also offer services that make their apparel **floor ready,** that is, with bar-coded price tickets attached, cartons labeled, and shipping documents attached. Of course, this adds to the cost, but many retailers find that this

portion of the supply chain management strategy makes up in speed for the cost. See "Stage 6: Distributing the Line."

Inspecting the Product

Garments are inspected many times during the production process. First, the fabric and the dye quality are checked. Cutting is checked for pattern matching and size specs, among other things. Sewing is also checked repeatedly along the way, for stitch length, seam type, buttonhole stitching, and hem stitching. In Figures 7.4 and 7.5, designers check garments at different points in the process for proper fit and quality construction. **Quality assurance,** or QA, which refers to the product meeting the standards established for it, includes the inspection of each ingredient of the garment: fabric, thread, buttons, snaps or zippers, hem tape, linings, shoulder pads, and so forth.

Figure 7.4 Jean Paul Gaultier adjusts his upcoming looks on a live model in his atelier ahead of their runway debut.

Figure 7.5 Designer Gilles Mendel inspects a J. Mendel resort pleated dress on a mannequin.

Stage 6: Distributing the Line

Once the line is completed, it still requires more work before the retailer can sell it. Sales tickets and bar codes must be added. These time-consuming tasks are frequently done by the manufacturer, except for the smallest stores. Then shipments must be consolidated and, finally, sent to retailers by truck, rail, air, or sea.

As the season progresses, manufacturers remain sensitive to retail sales. For example, when reorders come in, they recut only the garments that are most in demand—and therefore, the most profitable. Manufacturers may also recut "hot sellers" in different fabrics and colors to maximize the sales generated by high customer demand.

Specializing by Product

Apparel producers have typically been specialists, producing apparel for a particular gender and age, a particular size range, and a specific price range. A women's blouse manufacturer, for example, seldom makes dresses, and a dress manufacturer usually does not turn out dresses in both women's and junior sizes. A coat and suit manufacturer does not usually produce both expensive and popular-priced lines.

Historically, the US apparel industry has been divided into three major categories: women's, men's, and children's. These three categories are discussed in detail in Chapter 8. Despite a move toward greater diversification, producers and retailers still have to think and work like specialists. For instance, a producer must out of necessity choose an inexpensive fabric for a popular-priced line and a more expensive fabric for a better-priced line. Retail buyers still shop one group of producers for sportswear, another for coats, and still another for bridal wear—and this is not likely to change in the near future.

Brands and Labels

Five distinct kinds of brands or labels are used by the apparel industry:

1. National/designer brand
2. Private label
3. Retail store brand
4. Other brands
5. Nonbrands

Customers, of course, realize few of these distinctions. They think of them all as "brands" or "nonbrands." But to retailers and manufacturers, these distinctions are vital, heavily impacting their profits and offering differentiation in an era when customers complain of the "sameness" of many stores and the goods they offer.

National/Designer Brands

National brands are those that are owned by a manufacturer that advertises them nationally. Examples include Fruit of the Loom, Levi's, Reebok, Hanes, and Revlon. Some of the first apparel brands to gain national recognition were the Arrow Shirt Company and the B.V.D. Company, a maker of men's underwear, in the 1930s. National brands continued to grow in number over the next five decades, and the 1980s and 1990s saw a tremendous leap in sales for national brands. In part, this resulted from a huge increase in the number of national advertising campaigns directed at consumers. National brands benefit from broad recognition due to extensive advertising efforts and are sold in a wide variety of retail stores.

Designer labels carry the name of a designer; they have grown enormously in number and importance since the 1940s. Top US designer brands include names like Michael Kors, Marc Jacobs, Ralph Lauren, and Vera Wang, and hundreds more are working in the United States today. Many other designer names continue to be featured, although the original designer has left his or her namesake company, retired, or died. Examples include Anne Klein, Halston, and Bill Blass.

Designer labels are no longer limited to apparel. They are frequently found on accessories of every kind, on fragrances and cosmetics, and on home furnishings.

Private Labels

A **private label** is one that is owned by a retailer and found only in its stores. Examples of private-label apparel are Xhilaration at Target, Reba by Reba McEntire line sold by Dillard's, the Charter Club line sold by Macy's, and the Liz Claiborne line sold by JCPenney. These labels are sold alongside national/designer brands. The proportion of private labels to national and designer brands varies from retailer to retailer.

Retail Store Brand

A retail store brand is the name of a chain that is used as the exclusive label on most of the items in the store or catalog. Examples of retail store brands for apparel and accessories include Gap, The Limited, Ann Taylor, Victoria's Secret, Talbots, L.L. Bean, and Lands' End. Examples of store brands for home furnishings include Pier 1, Crate & Barrel, and Williams-Sonoma. Few, if any, national or designer brands are carried by these stores or catalogs.

Other Brands

This catchall category includes labels not in the preceding three categories, such as cartoon characters, like Disney's Mickey & Co. and Warner Brothers' Looney Tunes; sports teams, like the Chicago Bulls; colleges, like the University of California at Berkeley; and museums, like the Museum of Fine Arts—Chicago. These brands are often licensed.

Nonbrands

This is a label to which customers attach little or no importance. These labels are usually used by firms that manufacture low-priced goods and do little or no advertising to consumers. These labels are found in discount and off-price stores.

Industry Practices

Every industry has its own particular way of conducting business, and the apparel industry is no exception. Some of the practices discussed in this section developed as responses to specific industry problems. These practices were once considered "trends," but they are so well established now that they represent business as usual. The six major industry practices that we will discuss are manufacturers acting as retailers; licensing; brand extension; private-label and specification buying; offshore production; and the use of factors, chargebacks, and SIC/NAICS codes.

Manufacturers Acting as Retailers

An increasing number of clothing manufacturers are opening their own stores. Disappointed by the sales, service, and space allotted to them in retail stores and wanting to create the "right" atmosphere for their clothing, they are choosing to enter the retail business themselves. Of course, larger profits are also part of the attraction. The manufacturer can sell the product to consumers at full retail price, rather than at the wholesale price required by retail customers.

Designer Ralph Lauren was the first to take this step. Frustrated by the way department and specialty stores were selling his clothes, he opened the first Polo/Ralph Lauren shop on Rodeo Drive in Beverly Hills in 1971. Since then, he has built an empire of Polo/Ralph Lauren shops that stretches coast-to-coast in the United States and across the oceans to Europe and Asia. Eileen Fisher, Gucci, Marc Jacobs, and others have opened their own retail outlets.

But whether all manufacturers and designers will be successful retailers remains to be seen. A producer first has to compete for good retail talent, which can be expensive, as well as retail space in a prime location. The risks escalate if the manufacturer franchises, which many must do when they cannot personally oversee their retail empire.

Manufacturers' outlet stores, called "factory outlets," have also grown at a rapid rate. They allow manufacturers to dispose of poor sellers, overstocks, and "seconds" and still make more money on them than they could by selling them to discount retailers as "closeouts."

The opposite of manufacturers acting as retailers is retailers acting as manufacturers through the private-label programs of department stores and discounters and through the retail store brands of specialty chains like Gap and Talbots.

Licensing

Licensing, which was described in Chapter 4, experienced a boom in the United States in the 1980s and 1990s. This was largely the result of the emergence of an important new market segment—working women. As a group, these women are not quite in the income bracket to buy designer clothes, but designers have learned that they can capitalize on the market these women represent through licensing ventures.

The great appeal of licensing is that merchandise is identified with a highly recognizable name. The advantages for designers include the royalties they receive on the sale of each product (usually from 2 percent to 15 percent), greater exposure of their names, and little investment in product development and manufacturing.

KANANI MAHELONA
Technical and Creative
Design Consultant

Kanani Mahelona provides a variety of services as a consultant with textile-industry-related (apparel, furniture, automotive, etc.) clients to optimize their design and production processes through the analysis, selection, training, and implementation of current technologies in computer-aided design and manufacturing.

Kanani Mahelona in his studio.

Knowledge and application of design and production processes are critical. Topics include textile design, fashion illustration, technical sketching, manual and computerized patternmaking, grading, marker making, spreading, cutting, draping, industrial sewing/garment construction, fit analysis/engineering, textile science/printing, made-to-measure/mass customization, and CAD data conversion.

While still in high school, Mahelona worked for a womenswear designer at Stockton Manufacturing in Dallas, Texas, where he leaned the basics of industrial sewing, sample cutting, and storyboard design. He earned an associate of arts degree in both apparel design (creative) and pattern design (technical) from El Centro College in Dallas, focusing on patternmaking, draping, grading, textile science, and design development. During college and after, he worked as a first/sample patternmaker, assistant designer, designer, and production patternmaker in Dallas-area manufacturers, including Jay Jacks International, Jerell Inc., J. Ellis, Agatha Moon, MGM, and Malouf Co. In 1989, he joined Gerber Technology, a world leader in computerized apparel technology. There, he learned computerized patternmaking, grading, marker making, textile design, scanning, and 3-D virtual garment design. While working for Gerber Technology, he attended interior design studies at New York University.

After nearly twenty-five years with Gerber Technology, Mahelona saw a need in the industry for consulting, training, and implementation services and left to start his own textile technology consulting business. As the consulting business took off, he also started a textile design business in 2014.

With clients in many facets of the industry, workdays vary significantly from one day to the next. A week may begin with watercolor painting to develop a line of textile prints for a client, and the next day may involve working in Adobe Photoshop to turn the paintings into fabric repeats colorways. Some days require on-site visits to a client's manufacturing facility to observe the company's design and production process, followed up with several days to develop an optimization plan and then train employees to implement the plan. Sometimes Mahelona assists clients in a fitting session to determine pattern corrections, and then works with them on their computerized patternmaking system, executing the fit changes and optimizing the patterns for fit, material utilization, and cost effectiveness. He also conducts online trainings or provides technical support to clients via Skype, schedules new business, bills clients, and prepares status reports. Creative recharge is essential. Art museums and galleries, clothing/fabric/trim stores, bookstores and flea markets help him develop inspiration, stay aware of current trends, and keep those creative juices flowing.

Adobe Illustrator, Adobe Photoshop, and Gerber Technology's AccuMark software are vital. Microsoft Office programs are essential for creating client presentations, communicating with clients, scheduling, billing, and general business organization. Online collaboration programs such as Skype and TeamViewer allow client support from afar and in a timely manner.

Mahelona gives back to the fashion community through service and guidance to students and educators alike. He has served on the advisory boards and in other advisory roles at FIT, the Art Institutes, Baylor University, El Centro College, and Queens College. He frequently serves as a presenter for educational events hosted by FGI, the American Wool Council, the Cotton Council International, and industry trade shows around the world. Working with these groups allows him to learn the latest developments in the industry and develop an essential network of friends and colleagues.

Mahelona's advice to students interested in pursuing a career in creative or technical design is this: "Seek out and learn everything you can about patternmaking, draping, grading, garment construction, design, production, and marketing. Learn about technologies and trends. Find out the huge spectrum of possible careers in fashion and other textile-related industries—there are many possibilities available other than fashion design! Seek out mentors and network. Engage in conversation; and be a great listener. Ask lots of questions; take lots of notes. Stay inspired; and hone your creativity daily."

The disadvantages in licensing are few. When designers turn over control to a manufacturer as they do when they license a product, they may lose some quality control. A bigger problem is that a designer will move too far afield for his or her more exclusive customers, but considering the potential profits in licensing, this is unlikely to worry many designers.

A final note on the importance of a company's brand name: **Corporate licensing**, or the use of a company's name on related merchandise, is the fastest-growing segment of licensing today. The Nike "swoosh" is seen worldwide. Harley-Davidson and Disney characters have been licensed for T-shirts and children's wear; Dr. Scholl's has licensed its name, expanding from foot care to pillows; and Jeep has a line of sunglasses.

Brand Extensions

A common technique in consumer goods marketing is brand extension, which is a strategy in which a company uses a successful brand name to launch new or modified products. Brand extension saves the company the high cost of promoting a new name and creates instant brand recognition of the new product line. It is one way in which a company can diversify its product line.

In the apparel industries, a move into a related category of apparel is the easiest and cheapest way to diversify. A company that makes T-shirts may add a line of cotton sweatshirts, which are also sized small, medium, large, and extra large. A designer of men's suits may add coats.

A childrenswear manufacturer may add an infants' line. A woman's shoe manufacturer may add matching handbags.

The move to an unrelated line has traditionally been more difficult—and more costly. One of the first brand extensions by designers was expanding into fragrances and cosmetics.

Private Label and Specification Buying

The terms *private label* and *specification buying* may be used to describe the same items of merchandise, but the meanings are slightly different. If the retailer agrees, the manufacturer may design private-label merchandise for the retailer. The private labels of Macy's include Alfani, Charter Club, Style&Co, and Greg Norman for Tasso Elba. Alternatively, **specification buying** is a type of purchasing that is done to the store's standards rather than the manufacturer's. JCPenney and Gap are two examples of stores that make extensive use of specification buying. These retailers provide the standards and guidelines for the manufacture of clothes they order. Standards cover everything from the quality of materials and workmanship to styling and cost.

Specification buying has become so specialized that many stores now employ a **specification manager** or **product manager** who is trained in specification buying. While keeping an eye on industry and government standards, specification managers work closely with manufacturers to ensure that their products will be economically successful for both the retailer and the manufacturer.

As they grow more successful with specification buying, stores have begun to use it for their private-label lines. Initially intended as a way to keep production at home, a growing amount of private label is now purchased offshore. (See the following section and Chapter 10.)

Offshore Production

US manufacturers turn to **offshore production**, or the manufacture of US goods in foreign countries with inexpensive labor (see Figure 7.6). Offshore production is seen as a way to generally lower costs and, therefore, compete more effectively with low-cost imports. Some industry insiders view this practice as a threat to the health of American labor; others regard it as a necessity if US manufacturers are to remain competitive.

The American Apparel and Footwear Association (AAFA), the major trade association for apparel and footwear, commented that despite forty years of quotas and import tariffs, the industry has lost more than 1 million jobs in the United States—today, more than 97 percent of the apparel sold in the United States is imported. The "protections" appear to have done little to protect this industry. We now have to face the challenges of a quota-free world. We need to take a proactive approach by developing and promoting strong trading relationships with customers worldwide.

Although most companies no longer manufacture in the United States, they still employ hundreds of thousands of US workers in research and development, marketing, distribution and warehousing, and sourcing, as well as at the retail level. The American Apparel & Footwear Association cites that 92 percent of clothing, 53 percent of shoes and 68 percent of our home textiles is imported from China.[3]

Use of Factors

Apparel manufacturers and contractors need cash or credit to produce garments the season before they are sold. Some banks have been reluctant to lend money to apparel companies because of the high risks involved. So, an alternate system of financing has developed for the apparel industry. Called **factors**, these companies either purchase a manufacturer's accounts receivable or advance cash on the basis of the accounts receivable. Their interest rates are generally higher than those of a bank.

Another development is the use of credit insurance by firms that do not use factors. Credit insurance, used for decades in Europe, protects the insured company from losses as a result of a customer's bankruptcy or very late payment. Credit insurance is also useful for a US manufacturer with international business because it is cheaper than international letters of credit.

Figure 7.6
Textile workers in a factory in China.

Chargebacks

As retail chains have grown in size, their power over their suppliers has also increased. Apparel manufacturers are increasingly hit with demands for **chargebacks**, which are financial penalties imposed on manufacturers by retailers. The reasons for chargebacks include mistakes in purchase orders or ticketing. Sometimes retailers request chargebacks for partial or late shipments or even for poor-selling products. Chargebacks are also used for cooperative advertising. Naturally, chargebacks can cause financial problems for designers and manufacturers, especially small ones.

SIC/NAICS Codes

The change from the Standard Industrial Classification (SIC) codes to North American Industry Classification System (NAICS) is a reflection of globalization in the industry. SIC was originally developed in the 1930s to classify US establishments by "the type of activity in which they primarily engage and to create a database of comparable information that would describe the parts of the U.S. economy."[4] Over the years, the SIC was revised periodically to reflect the changes in the businesses that make up the US economy. The NAICS codes allow for a high level of comparability in business statistics among the North American countries, and they are also much simpler. Here are some examples of codes that are used in the industry today:

NAICS 313: Textile mills
NAICS 314: Textile product mills (nonapparel)
NAICS 315: Apparel manufacturing
NAICS 316: Leather and allied apparel manufacturing

These data are extremely useful among businesses in the fashion industry and are a good aide for decision making.

Advanced Technologies and Strategies

A number of advanced technologies and the strategies used to harness them have been implemented by the US apparel industry. These technologies have already had a profound impact on the profitability of the business and are poised to increase it further in the twenty-first century. They include the use of computer-integrated manufacturing, PLM, supply chain management, bar codes, scanners, radio-frequency identification (RFID), electronic data interchange (EDI), mass customization, and body scanning.

Computer-Integrated Manufacturing and Product Lifecycle Management

Stand-alone computerized equipment is now common in most manufacturers' plants. As discussed earlier in this chapter, this is known as CAM. It includes things such as programmable sewing machines, patternmaking machines, and cutting machines.

But the enormous power of the computer lies in its ability to be linked to other computers, so that the computers can direct the entire production process from design to finished garment. In CIM, computer-integrated manufacturing, and PLM, **product lifecycle management**, data from many computers within a manufacturing company are linked during all stages. Design, sourcing, sample-making, and shipping departments, as well as overseas factories, can view the same electronic files and see the status of any garment and its components at a moment's notice. For example, design, patternmaking, and grading are linked to cutting equipment as well as to computers that prepare costing reports and specification sheets. In some plants, these computers are even linked to stitching machines. The potential for cost savings is tremendous because repeated data entry is eliminated, along with entry errors.

These tools are essential for large apparel manufacturing and retail companies to streamline their operations and make better business decisions.

Supply Chain Management

A well-known business strategy that was used in the late 1990s was **quick response** (QR). QR shortened time frames from raw materials to design to production to finished product to the consumer. It was developed to give US manufacturers a powerful weapon against imports and foreign competitors, linking all parts of the supply pipeline directly to the nation's retailers. What it really means is a far closer association among manufacturer, supplier, retailer, and customer. It requires the

POWER SUIT INDEED!

It might seem old school, especially in a sportswear, dress-down, casual Friday culture, but the suit is the thing.

A well-tailored suit conveys an image to the world of power, confidence, and status. But what about how the suit affects the wearer?

A recent study shows that the suit not only changes the way others perceive the wearer, but it changes the way the wearer perceives him- or herself and the surrounding world. Wearing a suit can actually make the wearer become a more abstract thinker, deal more effectively with money, plan more efficiently, and deal with criticism more productively.

And, after some decline at the beginning of the century, suit sales are on the rise, showing steady increases each year in sales since 2009. The suit, combined with a casual no-tie modification, takes on a studied negligence approach to men's fashion and offers a polished yet relaxed feel to the business and social dress codes that have evolved.

So, even though suits are one segment of the growing menswear business, no doubt about it, they are here to stay.

David Beckham.

Jon Hamm.

(right from top)
Justin Timberlake.
Bradley Cooper.
Will Smith and son, Jaden.

development of trust and communication, and that goes all the way from the cash register to the apparel people and the textile suppliers. Simply put, it aims at delivering the right product at the right time.

A similar, and more recent, strategy is called **supply chain management** (SCM). Supply chain management has the same benefits of QR but takes it one step further. It allows companies to share forecasting, point-of-sale data, inventory information, and the supply and demand for materials or products.

Bar Codes, Scanners, and Radio Frequency Identification (RFID)

Bar coding, scanning, and RFID have become integral parts of SCM. Bar coding makes tracking merchandise—from fabric rolls to designer dresses—easier, faster, and more accurate. The **universal product code** (UPC) is one of a number of bar codes used for automatic identification of items scanned at retail cash registers. UPC is the symbol that has been most widely accepted by retailers and manufacturers. Bar codes are made up of a pattern of dark bars and white spaces of varying widths. A group of bars and spaces represents one character.

Scanners "read" the bar code. The UPC symbol does not contain the price of the merchandise; the price is added by the retailer to the store's computerized cash registers and can easily be changed.

Radio frequency identification (RFID) uses electronic tags for storing data. It involves a unique serial number that allows the tracking of products, cartons, containers, and individual items as they move through the supply chain. They hold more data than bar codes and can be read many times faster. This technology provides increased efficiency and accuracy of counting inventory.

Electronic Data Interchange (EDI)

Electronic data interchange (EDI) is the electronic exchange of machine-readable data in standard formats, linking computers from one company to another. It replaces a large number of paper forms that were the primary link between manufacturers and their retailer customers. These included forms like purchase orders, invoices, packing slips, shipping documents, and inventory forms.

Mass Customization

For the past eighty years, we have lived in a world where mass production was the model for products and services because standardized products meant lower costs. Every time a customer takes home a product with an attribute that he or she really does not want, it is a form of waste. In **mass customization**, the idea is to tailor the product to fit one particular customer—not one size fits all—and to supply thousands of individuals at mass prices, not custom-made prices.

Body Scanning

Within seconds, body scanners take a snapshot of the human form and produce a 3-D replica, with complete measurement data.[5] As technology continues to improve and become less costly, scanning of the entire body may become more common, resulting in a better fit for all customers.

Globalization

Globalization of the marketplace—finding both foreign competitors and foreign customers—has happened to a wide range of US manufacturing products, such as cars, televisions, electronics, steel, and computers. Starting in the 1970s, globalization occurred in the apparel industries and is still flourishing today. See Chapter 10 for further discussion on global sourcing and merchandising.

Sustainability

Fashion Revolution is a global initiative based in the UK and comprised of fashion industry professionals as well as other fashion enthusiasts from around the world. The goal of this organization is to achieve greater transparency in the fashion product supply chain. Based on a belief that the fashion industry values people, the environment, creativity, and profit equally, this group endeavors to radically change the way clothes are sourced, produced, and consumed to achieve a safe, clean, and fair industry.

Figure 7.7 People carry signs during a rally as part of the "Fashion Revolution Week."

Born from the April 24, 2013, Rana Plaza factory collapse, killing 1,138 people with many more injured, this anniversary marks the group's annual observance with Fashion Revolution Week and the social media campaign #whomademyclothes (See Figure 7.7). Since the launch of #whomademyclothes in 2015, the social media impact expands each year, with greater numbers of consumers wanting to know how their fashion products are produced. In 2018, there were 720 million impressions from the social media campaign, up 30 percent from the previous year.

According to Fashion Revolution, 3,838 fashion brands and retailers have responded to consumers by providing real information about suppliers, workers, and more. In reply, the #imadeyourclothes response campaign emerged, where brands posted images of actual apparel workers from around the world.

The Fashion Transparency Index reviews and ranks 150 of the largest global fashion and apparel brands and retailers, measuring how much information these firms disclose about their supply chain policies, practices, and social and environmental impact. In 2019, the top five highest scoring brands were Adidas, Reebok, and Patagonia, Esprit, and H&M. No major brand scored above 70 percent, however there are signs of improvement, as this represents a ten percent increase over 2018, and a 20 percent increase from 2017 scores.[6]

Here is a list of the ways Fashion Revolution encourages companies to build a greater commitment to transparency:

- Disclose your manufacturers and suppliers, right down to raw material level, in downloadable and accessible formats;
- Publish direct contact details for the company's sustainability, corporate responsibility or other relevant department so there is an open line of communication with your customers and stakeholders;
- Share more information about your purchasing practices and the steps brands are taking to be responsible business partners to your suppliers;
- Disclose more environmental data about the amount of carbon emissions, water consumption, pollution and waste created throughout your value chain;
- And finally, answer your customers' #WhoMadeMyClothes requests with practical information and data, not just policies and principles.[7]

Summary and Review

The men's, women's, and children's apparel industries develop and produce lines of apparel following a standard cycle. The six-stage process of developing and producing a line involves planning a line, creating the design concept, developing the designs, planning production, production, and distributing the line.

Types of producers include manufacturers, apparel jobbers, and contractors. Producers specialize by gender, age, and size categories, as well as by classification. While consumers generally do not know the differences, industry insiders distinguish among five major types of brands and labels: (1) national/designer brands, (2) private labels, (3) retail store brands, (4) other types of brands, and (5) nonbrands.

Major industry practices that directly affect profitability include licensing, brand extension, private-label and specification buying, offshore production, the use of factors, chargebacks, and SIC/NAICS codes.

Advanced technologies affecting product development of apparel include computer-integrated manufacturing, supply chain management, and the use of bar codes, scanners, radio-frequency identification, electronic data interchange, mass customization, and body-scanning computers.

Product development is also affected by globalization and the ongoing changes in our world. A large movement is sustainability, and consumers are demanding greater transparency from brands and manufacturers about exactly how their clothing and fashion goods are made.

FOR REVIEW

1. How does EDI differ from CIM?
2. How does a jobber differ from a manufacturer?
3. What are the major advantages of the contractor system? What is the key disadvantage?
4. What are the six stages of the product development process?
5. What is a chargeback?
6. What is the goal of supply chain management?
7. Why do most fashion producers sell directly to retail stores rather than through wholesalers?
8. What is the difference between a national brand and a private label?
9. What role do factors play in the fashion industry?
10. Discuss the major problems facing a manufacturer who is also a retailer.

FOR DISCUSSION

1. Compare and contrast the roles of the designer, the merchandiser, and the product manager in developing a line.
2. Give current examples of brand extensions in apparel, accessories, fragrances and cosmetics, and home furnishings.

Trade Talk

Define or briefly explain the following terms:

anchor
apparel contractor
apparel jobber
apparel manufacturer
bundling
chargebacks
collection
computer-aided design (CAD)
computer-aided manufacturing (CAM)
computer-integrated manufacturing (CIM)
corporate licensing
electronic data interchange (EDI)
factor
floor ready
graded
group
item house
line-for-line
marker
mass customization
offshore production
outside shop
piecework
private label
product development
product lifecycle management (PLM)
product manager
quality assurance (QA)
quick response (QR)
radio frequency identification (RFID)
sample hand
section work
specification buying
specification manager
spreader
supply chain management (SCM)
universal product code (UPC)

Fashion Apparel: Women's, Men's, Children's, and Teens'

Key Concepts

- Categories, size ranges, and price zones of women's, men's, children's, and teens' fashion apparel

- Roles of brand and designer names in the marketing of women's, men's, children's, and teens' fashion apparel

- Advertising and promotional activities in the marketing of women's, men's, children's, and teens' fashion apparel

Of necessity, the women's, men's, children's, and teens' fashion industry exists in a constant state of change, reacting on an ongoing basis to the consumer's tastes and styles, to an increasingly global economy, and to new technology. It is an industry that truly thrives on change and novelty.

Taken as a total entity, the women's, men's, children's, and teens' apparel industry is the largest and most recognized part of the fashion business. Although the history, development, and trends in the various apparel are similar in many ways, this chapter addresses each sector separately.

Women's Apparel

Organization and Operation

For many decades, the typical women's apparel company was a small, independently owned, and often family-run business. Unlike the automobile industry, no Ford or General Motors dominated the women's apparel industry. In the early 1970s, approximately 5,000 firms made women's dresses. The industry's power came from its collective size. Its 5,000 firms did $3 billion in business every year.

All this changed in the 1970s. An expanding economy led to increased demand for everything, including clothing. Many of the textile companies had grown into huge businesses, as had several major retailers. Pushed from both directions, the clothing manufacturers responded by merging to create large, publicly owned corporations.

Within a few years, it became obvious that many of the large corporations and conglomerates were not as successful as the smaller companies had been. The major problem was that the giants lacked the ability to respond quickly, a necessity in the fashion industry. Those that have survived and prospered have combined the advantages of large and small by creating divisions and subsidiaries that function independently within the larger structure.

Regardless of whether a company is part of a conglomerate or a family-owned shop, the way in which clothes are produced does not vary. The operation of the fashion apparel industry remains remarkably similar from business to business. The organization of the industry is currently undergoing changes, however. After years of specialization, the emergence of giant apparel producers has brought diversification. A number of the giants have divisions manufacturing womenswear, menswear, childrenswear, home fashions, and accessories.

Specialization by Product

Apparel producers have typically been specialists, producing apparel for a particular lifestyle, for a particular size range, and for a specific price range. Nowhere in the industry is this truer than in womenswear, the segment with the largest, most varied, and fastest-changing market. A woman's coat manufacturer, for example, seldom makes dresses, and a dress manufacturer does not make bathing suits. This is completely hidden from the customer by the growing practice of putting national brands and licensed designer names on a wide variety of merchandise—from evening gowns to bathing suits to shoes to perfume to sheets.

The Role of Designers

Designers, too, must balance diversification with specialization. From superstars to the new generation struggling to be recognized, all designers specialize to the extent that they are marketing their own artistic identity to a segment of the population that shares their vision.

As designers from the United States show in Paris and Milan, and European and Japanese designers show in New York, fashion-conscious consumers have a virtually limitless choice of looks they can adopt. There is the sustainable, casual style of Stella McCartney; the gentrified country elegance of Ralph Lauren; the vintage-inspired look of Marc Jacobs; the meeting of Asian and Western sensibilities in the designs of Issey Miyake; and the luxury and sumptuousness of Giorgio Armani and Oscar de la Renta. The established designers of upscale lines not only cater to the people who can afford their clothing but also lead the way for producers of more moderately priced fashion in interpreting trends in fashion and popular culture. Figures 8.1 and 8.2 show examples of design direction from Moschino and Nanette Lepore.

Figure 8.1 Design from Moschino.

Figure 8.2 Design from Nanette Lepore.

Categories in Women's Apparel

The following are the basic categories in women's apparel and the types of garments generally included in each. The categories of outerwear, suits, dresses, and blouses have been fixtures in the women's ready-to-wear industry from the beginning, and the category of sportswear and separates has been important since the 1940s. Jeans are considered a separate category by many manufacturers and retailers because of their unique position in Americans' wardrobes. The uniforms and aprons category fills a consumer need but does not set fashion trends. While the same is often true of the special needs category, designers like Izzy Camilleri and Stephanie Alves are bringing style as well as accessible function to the physically challenged consumer[1] (see Table 8.1).

Activewear

The "fitness craze" that emerged in the 1980s with workout programs on television and videotape intensified in the 1990s and is still very popular today in rental or subscription view-at-home fitness services such as DailyBurn. People flock to gyms and yoga studios to work out before and after work, and travelers maintain their exercise routines in health clubs that have become an essential hotel service. Running gained favor, and the New York and Boston marathons became national news. Women's sports received a boost in public attention with the formation of the Women's National Basketball Association and the Supreme Court ruling that universities accepting federal funding must offer equal athletic opportunities for male and female students.

TABLE 8.1 Basic Categories in Women's Apparel and the Types of Garments Included in Each Category

Category	Types of garments
Outerwear	Coats, rainwear, jackets
Dresses	One- or two-piece designs and ensembles (a dress with a jacket or coat)
Blouses	Dress and tailored
Suits	Jacket/skirt and jacket/pants combinations
Evening wear	Formal and prom gowns and other dressy apparel; this is often called "special occasion"
Bridal wear	Gowns and dresses for brides, attendants, and mothers of the bride and groom
Sportswear and separates	Town-and-country and spectator sportswear, such as pants, shorts, tops, sweaters, skirts, shirts, jackets, casual dresses, and jumpsuits
Activewear	Clothing for participatory sports and athletic activities such as swimwear, tennis dresses, running suits, cycling shorts, exercise apparel, and skiwear
Uniforms and aprons	Aprons, smocks, and a variety of uniforms
Maternity	Dresses, sportswear, evening clothes, suits, and blouses designed to accommodate the special needs of pregnant women
Innerwear	Brassieres, panties, shapewear, bodywear, sleepwear, and other intimate apparel
Special needs	Dresses, pants, skirts, sleepwear, hosiery, and other intimate apparel designed for ease of use by physically challenged women

All of these developments contributed to the growth of the market for comfortable and fashionable apparel for specific sports and exercise activities. This type of apparel is known in the industry as **activewear** (see Figure 8.3). Leading producers of activewear are the athletic shoe companies Nike, Reebok, and Adidas, all of which have developed lines of clothing. In the twenty-first century, their women's apparel divisions are given equal attention with the men's.

Formal Wear

Despite the growing casualness of everyday apparel, people all over the world still like to mark special occasions by wearing formal clothing. Elegant fabrics, trim, and silhouettes—worn with more elaborate jewelry, watches, and other accessories—mark most formal wear. This category is often called "after-5" or "special occasion." It is interesting to note that evening wear gets more media coverage than any other category, especially at the Academy Awards, the Tony Awards, the Grammy Awards, and similar events.

Designers like Elie Saab and Roberto Cavalli specialize in dressing Hollywood stars for opening nights

Figure 8.3 Megan Rapinoe of the US Women's National Team in the uniform sponsored by Nike. Nike continues to be a major player in the activewear business.

and award ceremonies. As a result, thousands of women across the country want similar looks for weddings, dances, and formal dinners.

Bridal Wear

Bridal wear has always been a category in which both brides and designers can make personal fashion statements. Designer runway shows in Paris traditionally conclude with the modeling of a bridal gown, and some designers, such as Vera Wang and Reem Acra, are known primarily for their work in this category. Weddings of movie stars, royalty, and other celebrities often inspire trends in bridal fashions, but the range of available styles runs from modern interpretations of Victorian designs to unadorned slip dresses (see Figure 8.4).

Maternity

Now that 80 percent of women stay on the job almost the entire nine months of their pregnancies, pregnant career women are an important submarket.

Destination Maternity Corporation is the world's leading maternity apparel omnichannel retailer, and owns the brands Motherhood Maternity®, A Pea in the Pod®, and Destination Maternity®.[2] In recent years, with greater use of stretch fabrics in clothing combined with more unstructured design, women integrate maternity fashions with more mainstream fashions (see Figure 8.5).

Size Ranges

Womenswear is produced in the following size ranges:

- Misses—Includes regular even-numbered sizes 4 to 20, tall sizes 12 to 20, and sometimes sizes as small as 0–2
- Juniors—Includes regular sizes 5 to 17 and petite sizes 1 to 15
- Petites—Includes misses' even-numbered sizes 2P to 16P and junior sizes 1P to 15P
- Women's and women's petites—Includes even-numbered sizes 12WP to 26WP, straight sizes 26 to 52, and XL to 5X

Major Price Zones

Within the wide range of prices, there are certain traditional **price zones**, or series of somewhat contiguous price lines, that appeal to specific target groups of

Figure 8.5 Meghan Markle, Duchess of Sussex, integrates "maternity-friendly" mainstream fashions to achieve a casual, stylish look during her pregnancy.

Figure 8.4 Kate Middleton's wedding dress, designed by Sarah Burton for Alexander McQueen, is sure to be an influence on bridal wear for years to come.

customers (see Figure 8.6). The women's **ready-to-wear** market has six major price zones. Listed from the most to least expensive, they are as follows:

1. Designer signature: The highest price zone includes lines by designers such as Ralph Lauren, Oscar de la Renta, Calvin Klein, and Jean Paul Gaultier.
2. Bridge: This zone is so named because it bridges the price ranges between designer and better prices. Bridge merchandise usually costs one-third to one-half of designer prices. Some designers who produce lines at the designer signature zone or at lower zones also have bridge lines. Examples include Tommy by Tommy Hilfiger, Donna Karan's DKNY, and Calvin Klein's CK.
3. Contemporary: This new zone is favored by young designers who want to enter the market with innovative, designer-quality lines but, at the same time, seek a broader market than that of the designer signature zone. By using less-expensive fabrics and locating in lower-rent spaces, they can offer their lines at lower prices. Labels in this zone include Vivienne Tam, Cynthia Rowley, and Laundry by Shelli Segal.
4. Better: Apparel in this zone is usually medium to high in price. Familiar labels include Liz Claiborne, Chaus, Nautica, Evan-Picone, and Jones New York. They appeal to a middle-class market, offering fashionable clothes at affordable prices.
5. Moderate: As the name suggests, this zone includes lines of nationally advertised makers, such as Guess, Esprit, Levi Strauss, and Jantzen, which have less prestige than lines with designer names but still appeal to middle-class consumers.
6. Budget: The lowest price zone is sometimes referred to as the "promotional" or "mass" market. It is primarily a mass market retailer private label, such as JCPenney's Arizona line of jeans, for example.

There is also a seventh price zone, the new high end, for the superrich. Some designers are trading up, offering special pieces in very limited quantities at astronomical prices. This range is **custom-made**, fitted specifically for the wearer, and aimed at people who crave exclusivity and have the means to afford it. Ralph Lauren calls his line of hand-tailored women's classic suits and sportswear in luxury fabrics the Purple Label Custom Collection. Carolina Herrera, Bill Blass, and Oscar de la Renta are also known for developing exclusive designs for special customers.

More recently, the industry has seen growth in what is called the **masstige** movement. This is when marquee designers apply their creativity to lower-priced apparel. It started in 2004 when designers like Karl Lagerfeld teamed up with fast-fashion giant H&M. Today there is the popularity of Target's tie-ups with designers such as Isaac Mizrahi, Lilly Pulitzer, Zac Posen, Alexander McQueen, and Rodarte. Vera Wang is another example, with her Simply Vera Wang line sold at Kohl's.[3]

Multiple Price Zones

Some producers offer merchandise in several price zones to capture a share of the business in each of several market segments. Manufacturer/retailer firms such as Gap cater to different price zone markets in each of their member store chains. Gap's stores have a somewhat overlapping price zone structure, with Banana Republic merchandise at its highest zones, Gap at the middle of its market, and Old Navy at its low end.

Designers also produce lines segmented by price zone. For example, Armani Exchange is the label of Armani's bridge collection, Giorgio Armani is the label of lines in the designer price zone, and Giorgio Armani Prive is the luxury collection. Ralph Lauren is another designer with lines in several different price zones. In order from most to least expensive, a partial list of his lines include Ralph Lauren Purple Label Collection, Ralph Lauren, RL, Polo Sport, Black Label, and Polo.

Figure 8.6 Guess stores cater mainly toward the middle-class consumer.

Private Labels

Traditional department and specialty stores can also compete in pricing by developing their own private labels. Much of this merchandise is priced in the better price zone, but the quality is comparable with that of designer signature or bridge apparel. Some of the same manufacturers who produce the name-brand merchandise that a store is selling at higher prices also make the store's private-label goods. Private-label merchandise is vigorously promoted to develop brand recognition, and some customers do not distinguish between private and national brands when they shop. (See Chapter 4.)

Merchandising and Marketing

Most fashion producers sell directly to retail stores rather than through intermediaries. The pace of fashion in all but a few staple items is much too fast to allow for the selling, reselling, or warehousing activities of wholesale distributors or jobbers.

As a result, women's apparel producers aim their sales promotion efforts at both retailers and consumers. Such efforts take the form of advertising, publicity, and sales promotion.

Fashion Shows, Press Weeks, and Trade Shows

The major public relations effort in womenswear goes into the presentations and fashion shows at which designers show their new collections for retailers, fashion reporters for the press, and the broadcast and Internet media. The shows provide the country's newspapers, magazines, radio, television, and Internet fashion editors and reporters an opportunity to examine the newest American designer collections, as well as those of leading European manufacturers (see Figure 8.7).

To coordinate shows of their new lines during market weeks, the manufacturers who lease permanent or temporary showroom space at the major regional markets in Los Angeles, Dallas, Miami, Atlanta, and Seattle depend on the services of the management of their market buildings. New York designers (including foreign designers with New York showrooms) are not housed at a single site. Together with IMG Fashion, designers showcase their designs at the biannual New York Fashion Week at Spring Studios in TriBeCa, as well as themed venues

Figure 8.7 The Chanel runway, a replica of a French rooftop, presents a dramatic backdrop and creates a sense of occasion for the buyers and members of the press waiting in the audience.

around the city during the seven-day event. IMG also sponsors an annual award show that attracts international press and broadcast coverage. The giant MAGIC show for womenswear is held semiannually in Las Vegas. Also in Las Vegas is the WomensWear in Nevada (WWIN) (formerly the Big and Tall Woman's Show or B.A.T.WOMAN) for plus and tall sizes, which has become an international hit. It specializes in the missy and plus-size markets with apparel and accessories. Other major international women's wear shows include those held semi-annually in Paris, London, Milan, Tokyo, and Hong Kong. These shows are discussed in more detail in Chapter 10.

Trunk Shows

Trunk shows are another excellent form of publicity for the women's apparel industry (see Figure 8.8). Trunk shows present a manufacturer's line to a retail store's sales staff and its customers. A representative of the company, sometimes a designer, typically mounts a fashion show of sample garments. After the show, the designer meets with customers to discuss the styles and their fashion relevance. The retail store's customers may review items they have seen and order them.

Everyone benefits from trunk shows. Customers see clothes as the designer planned them and coordinated them, and they experience some of the glamour of the fashion industry. The designer enjoys direct contact with customers, obtaining valuable input and feedback on the collection. The retailer enjoys the dramatic influx of customers who come to such personal appearances and

Figure 8.8 Guests attend the John Varvatos collection presentation and trunk show.

shows and any profits that result as clothes are ordered. The manufacturer tests the line on real customers to understand real consumers' needs *firsthand*! If customer response is enthusiastic, the designer achieves new status—and larger orders—from the retailer than otherwise expected.

Industry Trends

Throughout the coming decades, the US women's apparel industry and the US apparel industry overall will face dramatic changes. US designers have finally succeeded in rivaling designers from Paris and Milan as definers of high fashion. However, the US manufacturing industry faces what may be its toughest competitive challenge ever—the growth of a global clothing market out of which US manufacturers must carve their market share because a rise in imports has threatened the market they had enjoyed within the United States.

After decades of domination at home, the US wholesale market has been inundated with imports from countries with cheap labor. An increasing number of US manufacturers are using foreign labor, a process called global sourcing, in factories they own or lease in low-wage countries around the world. The US apparel industry is taking steps, however, to enable it to compete more effectively in an increasingly global marketplace. Some of its tactics include the following:

- Emergence of manufacturers as retailers
- Greater emphasis on licensing
- Increased offshore production
- Increased emphasis on supply chain management
- Use of computers and the Internet

Men's Apparel

Organization and Operation

The menswear industry traditionally has been divided into firms that make the following different kinds of clothing:

1. Tailored clothing—suits, overcoats, topcoats, sports coats, formal wear, and separate trousers
2. Furnishings—dress shirts, neckwear, sweaters, headwear, underwear, socks, suspenders, robes, and pajamas
3. Outerwear—raincoats, coats, jackets, and active sportswear
4. Work clothing—work shirts, work pants, overalls, and related items
5. Other—uniforms and miscellaneous items

The federal government uses these five classifications. Although it is not an official classification, sportswear (including active sportswear) has become a vital portion of the business and should be considered a menswear category.

Size and Location of Manufacturers

Menswear is growing, reaching $88.8 billion in the US apparel market in 2018.[4] Unlike women's apparel, the business has been dominated by large firms at the manufacturing level.

In recent years, Levi Strauss, PVH Corporation, and VF Corporation have been the largest manufacturers of men's and boys' wear. Because of diversification, mergers, and acquisitions by top menswear producers in the past few years, it has become more difficult to ascertain company size and production figures.

Designer Names

Currently, an entirely new world of menswear has emerged in which designer labels are promoted as heavily as well-established brand names used to be (see Figure 8.9). A designer who licenses his or her name in suits may also license men's jeans, shirts, jackets, sportswear, activewear, or ties. The manufacturer pays for the design or name of the designer in royalties based on gross sales. Royalties average from 5 to 7 percent on men's suits and 5 percent on men's sportswear, according to industry sources.

Figure 8.9 Kenneth Cole is a prominent designer in men's fashion.

Manufacturing companies that license name designers usually establish separate divisions and in many cases allocate separate manufacturing facilities for them. In licensing agreements, the extent of designer involvement varies; designers are not necessarily responsible for all the designs that bear their names. Some licensing agreements simply pay for the use of the designer's name, and the name designer has no design input at all.

The "name game" is big business in all segments of the menswear industry. While there are no hard figures on the amount of designer business alone at the wholesale level, the best market estimates for retail sales are more than $1 billion for all categories combined. One reason for the continuing popularity of designer names is that they are so easily promoted. Consumers associate them with prestige and fashion and recognize them when they see them. Designers have helped by becoming highly visible. Their names are household words, and their faces frequently appear in newspapers and magazines. They lend themselves to the fantasy of the customer who longs for wealth and excitement.

Designer names also get more exposure than brand names in stores because they often appear on many different kinds of goods displayed in several different departments. Designers often have their own boutiques within stores.

Market Segments

Most market segments are based on style differences, but some exist because they involve different production methods. The five main market segments in menswear are tailored clothing, sportswear, activewear, contemporary apparel, and bridge apparel.

Tailored Clothing

A **tailored suit** is structured, or three-dimensional, which gives it a shape even when it is not worn (see Figure 8.10). Until very recently, tailored clothing was graded according to the number of hand-tailoring operations required to make it. The grades were 1, 2, 4, 6, 41, and 61, with a grade 1 suit representing the lowest quality.

Figure 8.10 Well-tailored suit combined with a relaxed, studied negligence has become a trademark look for actor/director Bradley Cooper.

PETIT PLI—CHILDREN'S CLOTHING THAT GROWS WITH THE CHILD!

Ryan Yasin, designer and winner of the James Dyson Award for Innovation in Product Design.

Parenting comes with a whole host of challenges, but one of the most surprising is just how fast kids grow out of their clothes! Wouldn't it be great if clothes could "grow" with children?

Actually, this design challenge has been taken on by designers of children's fashions through the years, and brands have come up with some interesting ideas—great use of knits and fabrics with stretch, onesies that change length with double and triple rows of snaps, pants that lengthen through folding and cuffing methods, waistbands that expand and decrease through inside taping and buttoning mechanisms, ties versus buttons to easily adjust girth, or ruffles that come on or off depending on the desired length of skirts or sleeves. All of these, and more, are attempts to help extend the clothing wear, as well as the clothing dollar, for parents.

Designer Ryan Yasin experienced the same dilemma when purchasing a gift for his newborn nephew. While studying at the Royal College of Art in London, his sister in Denmark, had a little boy. Ryan bought some little clothes as a gift, but before the package arrived, the baby had already grown out of them!

This was his inspiration. "How can I solve this problem?'"

Yasin combined a few diverse perspectives to find an answer to this design dilemma. As a student at the Royal College of Art, an interest in Japanese design, and with an undergraduate degree in aeronautical engineering, he looked at this as much as an engineering challenge as a design challenge. He wanted to look at clothing as a dynamic product—changing, active, moving—rather than as a static or fixed item. His solution—origami!

The pleated design expands both in both width and length as a child's body grows, with expected wear for more than three years.

Designer and innovator Ryan Yasin showing a template of the folding design that creates the expanding pleats.

Origami pleats provide auxetic structure, which means that the pleats expand in both directions—widthwise and lengthwise—at the same time when stretched. This is how individual garments move in shape from one size to another, so how could this be accomplished in a single garment? The design process resulted in creating over 500 prototypes to find the right combination of fabric and technique, and the product is a single garment that can grow from size 9 months to 4-toddler—about seven children's sizes.

The concept of Petit Pli is built upon using materials sustainably. The design significantly reduces waste and CO2 emissions at the point of production, distribution, and after purchase. With expansion of up to seven sizes, parents are provided both convenience and cost savings.

Counter to "fast-fashion" consumer practices, Petit Pli hopes to build a culture of slow-fashion values in growing children. This idea is central to the company's mission. Yasin explains that "clothes are often the most intimate products we own, the respect for their value and for those that produce them has been lost. We throw our clothes away without even thinking about repairing them, with serious environmental consequences."

Comfort and wearability are key. The construction features concealed knee patches, adjustable waistband and wrists to avoid too-tight or too-big, pockets, silicone gripper waistband to keep clothes in place for active little bodies, and transfer labels to avoid scratchy labels.

Petit Pli garments are made of man-made, recycled fabrics and can be recycled at the end of their use, and the garments are manufactured in a plant that utilizing solar energy. Since winning the James Dyson Award in 2017, Yasin has added a few more accolades to his resume, including the Dezeen Award, the Red Dot Award, and the 2019 Global Challenge Award granted by the H&M Foundation.

Practical materials and functional, fun design for active little bodies!

Men's tailored clothing is produced in the following proportioned sizes, with the number ranges representing chest measurements:

- Short (36–44)
- Regular (35–46)
- Long (37–48)
- Extra long (38–50)
- Portly short (39–48)
- Large (46, 48, 50)

Suit Separates

The steady decline in structured and semi-structured tailored menswear has been offset by an increased demand for **suit separates**—sports jackets and trousers that are worn much as the tailored suit used to be. Tailored suits are now the business uniform only in large, sophisticated cities, and even there, only in some firms and industries and for some levels of management. Elsewhere, men often wear suit separates to work—or for almost any occasion except where formal wear is required.

Although an attempt was made in the 1960s to sell menswear consumers on the idea of coordinated sportswear—that is, jackets, vests, and pants that could be mixed and matched with one another—the idea never took hold. Suit separates today refer to sports jackets and trousers.

Suit separates are usually machine-made and, as a result, can be significantly lower-priced than tailored garments. When they are made for better-priced lines, they can also be expensive. Because each item is bought separately, the expensive alterations that manufacturers and retailers must often make on tailored clothes are avoided. One industry expert believes that men who buy separates are more fashion aware than those who need the reassurance of a preassembled look.

A trend in suits that has gain greater popularity in recent years is bespoke suits. These are crafted to the specific measurements of the client, with limited choices of cut, style, fabrication, and details.

Sportswear

Sportswear, or casual wear, runs the gamut from unconstructed jackets, knit and woven sports shirts, slacks, and leisure shorts to coordinated tops and bottoms (see Figure 8.11).

Figure 8.11 Cargo pants and sweaters dominate this contemporary menswear by Brunello Cucinelli.

Sportswear is unstructured or, at minimum, less structured than tailored clothing. Few if any hand-tailoring operations, for example, are required to make a sports jacket. Sportswear lacks padding, binding, and lining, and it takes its shape (if indeed it has any shape these days) from the person who is wearing it.

Activewear

As discussed, clothing worn during active sports participation as well as during leisure time is classified as activewear. The larger segment of this market is men who want to look as if they are doing something athletic, even when they are ambling to the store for the Sunday paper or flopping down in front of the television set to watch a ball game.

Contemporary Apparel

Contemporary menswear refers to a special type of styling that provides high quality and fashion. Contemporary menswear, which produces clothing in all categories, can often be distinguished by its use of bright colors (see Figure 8.12).

Bridge Apparel

Bridge apparel defines clothing that spans the style gap between young men's and men's collections and the price gap between contemporary and designer apparel. In broad terms, the bridge customer is one who has grown out of young men's clothing but cannot yet afford designer clothes. Bridge customers are usually between twenty-five and forty years of age and have sophistication and style.

Figure 8.12 Contemporary men's fashion from designer Garcia Madrid. More traditional styling and silhouettes, but with bold colors and prints, and fashion-forward proportions.

Merchandising and Marketing

Like the womenswear producers, menswear producers back their lines with advertising and publicity. Menswear fiber and textile producers sometimes promote their products. The largest percentage of promotion is done, however, by the menswear producers, who rely on agencies, freelancers, and less often, on an in-house department for advertising and publicity.

Industry Trends

The dynamics of population growth as well as lifestyle changes and developments in the economy are bringing about changes in all segments of the menswear industry. Some of the most noteworthy trends include a diversification of products on the part of producers, the automation of production processes, an increase in foreign production and sales, and a proliferation of specialty stores. Consumers are showing greater interest in style and are demanding quality in fabric and construction. All of these trends relate to the growing informality of US culture.

Children's, Tweens', and Teens' Apparel

Organization and Operation

The global childrenswear market is valued at $100,000 million in 2018, and is projected to reach $142,400 million by 2025.[5] Despite the prominence of giant companies such as Carter's, OshKosh B'Gosh, Gerber Childrenswear, and Health-Tex, most children's clothes are still made by small, family-owned businesses. Many adult apparel producers, including Levi Strauss, Patagonia, Old Navy, Gap, and Reebok, also operate children's

COMMUNICATING WITH THE CUSTOMER— A CAREER IN SOCIAL MEDIA

FOR THOSE INTERESTED IN PURSUING A PASSION FOR FASHION WITH A LOVE OF SOCIAL MEDIA, A SOCIAL MEDIA MANAGER MIGHT BE A CAREER AREA WORTH EXPLORING.

Pippa Bugg is a Social Media Manager for Oasis Fashion. She studied Fashion Public Relations and Journalism. She advises students interested in this career area to fully immerse themselves in the social media industry. The most interesting part of this industry to her is the opportunities for creativity. In this position, Pippa is responsible for social strategy, copywriting, content creation, influencer relationships, and tracking revenue and analytics.

Customer experience and satisfaction is a top priority for companies, and customers tend to base their preference for a product or brand based on meaningful and authentic experiences. At its core, social media management is about building personal relationships. Managed well, it can humanize a brand and help customers relate to it. As a result, companies and brands do not just rely on speedy checkout and easy navigation of a site to ensure customer satisfaction and loyalty—they are using social media more and more to build relationships and employ 360-degree communication with their customers. Social media is designed to share,

and sharing is a proven way to make a friend and build a relationship.

Used effectively, social media is more than free product promotion, or a way to respond to complaints; it offers real power to build customer connections and brand loyalty. Here are some important tools Social Media professionals use to reach customers:

Connect Communities. According to a report by Sprout Social, a social media marketing firm, customers

apparel divisions. Many adult apparel designers have also begun children's divisions.

Like adult clothing, childrenswear is divided into categories based on price, size, and type of merchandise. Children's clothes are produced in budget, moderate, better-priced, and designer price ranges. Most children's clothes bought by parents are in the budget and moderate price ranges, although better-priced and designer merchandise are common gift purchases by grandparents and other adults (see Figure 8.13).

Size Categories

A super-sophisticated marketplace makes sizing little customers more challenging than ever before. The industry debates whether the traditional size categories really reflect a child's age and maturity level. Across the country, retailers and manufacturers are questioning and reimagining the size standards, each with their own ideas of what would constitute the ideal size categories.[6]

believe in the power of social media to connect communities, and 76 percent of the respondents said they were more likely to buy from a brand they felt connected to on a social media platform than a competitor.

Customer Relationships. Developing a rich customer relationship through social media is more than just being entertaining and putting out content. It's also about listening. In what is referred to as "call-out culture," customers who use social media to complain want to be heard, and it's important for brands to listen. In 360-degree communication through social media, companies receive an abundance of feedback. The hope is that most of it is positive. But the negative feedback and comments are helpful too. This type of feedback provides a learning opportunity for the company. In a study on why consumers "call out" companies, 70 percent wanted to raise awareness of an issue among other consumers, 55 percent wanted an apology or a solution, 51 percent wanted to get the word out to a larger, traditional, or mainstream media audience, 38 percent wanted a refund, 19 percent hoped for a discount, and only 3 percent just wanted to complain.

Rapid Response. Responding quickly is the next step. Thirty-two percent of customers expect a response within thirty minutes, and 42 percent expect a response within an hour. Rapid response builds trust.

The human touch is essential. It is important to embrace personalization and authentic human connection. Things like staff photos, bios, and stories go a long distance in creating that human connection through social media and the customer.

Something Little Goes a Long Way! Look for ways to go the extra mile by treating customers with something fun, like a surprise discount, or an invitation to promotion just for active followers. Customers love a good deal, and when it feels exclusive and personal, it helps build trust and lasting connections.

Let Customers Tell the Story. Embracing user content is a way to tell customers that they matter and that the company values their point of view. According to Photoslurp, user-generated photos are five times more likely to generate sales and convert customers. By asking followers to share ideas about product, or post images of them with the product in use, brands gain greater insight about how people use the product and what they want from the company. When a follower's idea comes to life, then they feel more invested in the brand.

Results from the 2015–2016 National Health and Nutrition Examination Survey indicated that an estimated 18.5 percent of children and adolescents aged 2 to 19 years are obese.[7]

Some retailers and vendors do offer plus-size clothing, but the availability of attractive, flattering plus sizes is scarce.

Although the actual size range is the same, the preteen sizes for girls offer more sophisticated styling than the girls' sizes. Similarly, the young men's size category

Figure 8.13 Name-brand designers like Ralph Lauren offer distinct lines of high-quality childrenswear.

(also called prep, student, or teen) stresses sophisticated styling more than boys' sized apparel does (see Table 8.2).

Product Specialization

Childrenswear manufacturers typically specialize by product. One producer will make only girls' knits, while another makes only girls' dresses, and another makes only preteen sportswear. But unlike the producers of adult wear, childrenswear producers often make a single type of clothing in several size ranges. For example, a producer may make boys' sportswear in sizes 8 through 20, while a producer of girls' dresses may make a product in toddlers' through girls' sizes.

The same design and production methods that are used in the manufacturing of adult apparel are used in childrenswear, although they are often simplified. While children's garments require less fabric, they are usually more expensive to make because they require more labor.

The Role of Fashion in Children's, Tweens', and Teens' Wear

Even the most basic lines of children's clothing reflect attempts to make the clothes fashionable, and the demand for style, once primarily an urban phenomenon, is now felt in every area. The demand for stylish children's clothes, which has risen every year, has most recently culminated in designer clothing for children. Childrenswear, however, must still be viewed as a business that is a *fashionable* rather than a *fashion* business. The difference is that while the childrenswear industry produces fashionable clothing, the styles adapt men's and women's styles. They are not in themselves innovative, nor does new fashion start in childrenswear lines. The backpack is one recent exception.

Producers of children's clothing have typically operated on a one-line-per-season production schedule, and four lines—spring, summer, winter, and fall—are typical. Lines are not updated during a season. Once a line has been shown and accepted, that is all the manufacturer produces.

Increasingly, children look to their own peers and to the group just ahead of them, young adults, for pace-setting styles and trends. Successful childrenswear producers have learned that they, too, must look to the young adult fashion world for inspiration. This means watching fads as well as trends. Popular young adult fads and styles are increasingly being translated into childrenswear lines. The industry has also begun to use fashion forecasting specialists to enable manufacturers to incorporate new styles into their lines as soon as a trend is spotted.

TABLE 8.2 Size Ranges of Childrenswear

size category	age range	sizes
Infant's	Newborn–1 year	0–24 months (0–3 months, 6, 9, 12, 18, and 24 months)
Newborn, small, medium, large, extra-large	Toddler's	2–3 years
2T–4T	Children's	3–6 years
3–6X for girls	3–7 for boys	Girl's
7–14 years	7–16	Preteen
7–14 years	6–16 for girls	Boy's
6 or 7–14 or 15 years	8–20 (available in husky, regular, and slim)	Young men
8–20 years, concentrating on 14–20 years	8–20	

Merchandising and Marketing

Many of the features and activities of the childrenswear industry are similar, if not identical, to those of the women's and men's apparel industries. Sales promotion and advertising activities for childrenswear, however, are considerably more limited.

The few giants in the industry—Carter's, Health-Tex, and OshKosh B'Gosh—advertise aggressively to consumers. Smaller firms—the majority of firms producing budget and moderately priced childrenswear—leave most consumer advertising to retailers. Firms producing higher-priced, name-designer merchandise do a limited amount of consumer advertising. The high cost of this advertising is often shared with textile firms.

In general, the industry limits its advertising to the trade press. Specialized publications that are concerned with childrenswear include *Earnshaw's Infants' and Girls' and Boys' Wear Review*. Trade publications that report on adult fashions, such as *Women's Wear Daily*, also carry childrenswear advertising and news reports of interest to retailers on a regular basis. More and more companies are going on the Internet, often combining information about the company with a catalog.

Trade Shows

The LA Kids Market Los Angeles is held at the California Market Center in Los Angeles. It is the largest kids and maternity fashion and accessories showcase in the United States, with more than 800 brands from around the globe. The huge MAGIC International shows for men's, women's, and children's apparel and accessories are held in Las Vegas twice a year. Other popular childrenswear trade shows include the New York–based Children's Club trade show, produced by ENK International, and the annual KIDS at STYLEMAX event in Chicago.

Designer Labels

Children's designer-label clothing and accessories are highly visible in stores across the country. The appeal of these items seems to rise above income levels. Designer labels are available in stores geared to middle-income as well as high-income customers. Although designer wear for children has been around for a while—Izod introduced a boys' line in the late 1960s—the explosion in designer-label childrenswear took off in the late 1970s with the designer jean craze.

Well-known brand names in childrenswear include Carters, Gymboree, Little Me, Children's Place, Osh Kosh, Old Navy, and, of course, Guess and Gap. Because they have designer-name status, some childrenswear designers, following in the pioneering footsteps of Florence Eiseman and Ruth Scharf, have acquired celebrity status, such as Rachel Riley.

Several companies, including Esprit, Guess, Patagonia, and Ralph Lauren, have launched separate divisions of childrenswear. Other designers who offer children's lines include Gucci and Marc Jacobs (see Figure 8.14).

Licensing

Like designer labels, other kinds of licensed names provide a sense of fashion rightness, in addition to giving a garment or line instant identification in consumers' minds. As a result, as the childrenswear industry became more fashion conscious, manufacturers were quick to produce licensed goods. Today, in addition to designer names, the ever-popular cartoon and toy character licenses share the spotlight with a growing number of sports and corporate licenses.

Character Licensing

The first licensed cartoon character was Buster Brown, in 1904. Licensed cartoon and toy characters, long a staple with children, are still thriving today. Younger children especially enjoy wearing representations of their favorite characters and television shows. Widespread examples

Figure 8.14 The Marc Jacobs website has prominent page space devoted to the brand's apparel for children.

MARKETING TO TEENS—AN ELUSIVE BUT POWERFUL CONSUMER DEMOGRAPHIC!

What are the most important things in a teen's life, and what do they like to spend their money on?

This demographic cohort represents about $2.5 billion in consumer purchasing. Teens and tweens are a powerful, but often not-well-understood group of consumers. In a survey of 1000 Gen Z-ers, here's what researchers learned : Teens seek community, connectivity, recognition, and authenticity. These are some of the leading products and experiences they consume to help them achieve these goals:

THE SMARTPHONE REIGNS SUPREME!

Teens love their smartphones above all other technology. Ninety-five percent of teens surveyed have a smartphone or access to one on a regular basis. And, instead of Walmart, Macy's or Target, teens indicated a preference for Amazon as their

favorite shopping spot! So they're using those phones to make mobile purchases.

Eighty percent of teens prefer iPhone to an Android product.

INSTAGRAM!

Snapchat, Facebook, and Twitter are losing the battle to Instagram. Teens enjoy the superior design and greater social connectivity of the Instagram platform. Forty-eight percent of teens polled prefer Instagram, but teens

still use multiple social platforms to communicate and connect.

YOUTUBE!

In terms of streaming, more than 52 percent of teens polled favor YouTube, and more than 72 percent report visiting the site daily. What is it about YouTube that teens love? Access and interaction! Netflix, Spotify, and Hulu, as well as other streaming services, are static and the content moves one way. YouTube allows teens to upload, vlog, and create as well as consume entertaining content.

WATCHING SPORTS

In America, the top three most watched sports are football, soccer, and basketball, and this is the same with the teen cohort. One-third of teens polled chose football as their favorite sport to watch, but why? The answer: Fantasy Football leagues. Thirty-four percent of teens in the US participate in Fantasy Football leagues. It's safer to play than real football, it creates a multi-generational connection with other players who might be parents, relatives, or other teens, and each league can create its own rules and guidelines.

RUN, TEENS. RUN!

With more than sixty sports offered in US public high schools, more teens are participating in high school sports than ever. And running tops the list! Teens state that they participate for enjoyment, exercise, and to feel success and a sense of achievement.

CELEBRITIES

Teens have a higher "cool" factor for the celebs who keep it real. As 1.8 million teens battle mental health issues, a high number identify with Selena Gomez and her openness and transparency about handling her own mental health issues. Taylor Swift reaches teens with songs about relationships and heartbreaks.

BRANDS!

In general, boys spend more money on food, while girls spend more on clothes. The top ten apparel brands of US teens are Nike, followed by American Eagle, Adidas, Forever 21, Hollister, PacSun, Urban Outfitters, Lululemon (new to the list!), Victoria's Secret, and H&M. Vans shoes, owned by VF Corporation, have captured a growing market share among teens, but holds a firm second to Nike, declared as the favored shoe brand of the teen market. In the beauty sector, Ulta nudged Sephora out of first place as the preferred retail destination for cosmetics and other beauty products.

Taylor Swift and Selena Gomez are tops with teens, because these ladies keep it real!

are Paw Patrol, Disney characters, and Star Wars. Character licenses dominate in children's T-shirts, sweatshirts, and sleepwear and are also strong in accessories and sportswear.

Disney, a major studio that produces cartoons, has its own retail outlets, where the mix of apparel, accessories, and toys may help to extend the lives of the movie characters. Warner Brothers owns both Superman and Batman, perennial favorites with boys on sleepwear, underwear, and T-shirts. It made a licensing agreement with Spalding Sports Worldwide to put its Looney Tunes characters (Bugs Bunny, Daffy Duck, Road Runner, and Wile E. Coyote) on its leisure products line, including backpacks. Warner Brothers also oversees licensing arrangements for the Hanna-Barbera studio (whose characters include the Flintstones, Scooby-Doo, and Tom and Jerry) and The Wizarding World of Harry Potter.

Sports Licensing

Sports licensing is another prospering area of licensing. Sports figures and teams both have high visibility in the media and thus enjoy instant recognition among children and young adults. Areas with professional or school teams, college stores, airport shops, and stadium concessions increase the availability of licensed apparel at retail. Sports figures who have successfully put their names on sports equipment for years are now adding them to jogging and running suits, tennis clothes and accessories, as well as less-active casual and sportswear lines. And producers of athletic shoes, sweatshirts, and sports equipment feature their names and logos on active sportswear.

Industry Trends

Like women's apparel manufacturers, childrenswear producers are constantly on the lookout for ways to increase productivity and reduce—or at least minimize—costs while still maintaining quality. Computerized operations have become the norm for manufacturers. Even portions of the design process are now computerized in childrenswear, mostly because this helps producers respond more quickly to fashion trends in the industry.

E-commerce continues to thrive for suppliers, manufacturers, and retailers of childrenswear. E-commerce sites that attract the most traffic are already attached to a major retail brand, like the Disney Store (www.disneystore.com) and Warner Brothers (www.wbshop.com) for younger children and Abercrombie and Fitch (www.abercrombie.com) and Hot Topic (www.hottopic.com) for teens. Amazon.com is quickly becoming a favorite site of teen shoppers.

Specialty Retail Outlets

Increasing attention is being given to childrenswear by apparel retailers whose main lines are men's and women's clothing (see Figure 8.15). A related trend is the prominence of clothing in the merchandise mix of retail outlets carrying a broader array of children's goods. Even among clothing stores that have not opened freestanding children's outlets, distinctive stores-within-stores are now selling childrenswear exclusively. Carrying the trend to its logical conclusion, the infants' and toddlers' departments of the children's stores and stores-within-stores are being set up as separate outlets.

Figure 8.15 J.Crew's *Crewcuts* catalog for kids.

Separate Stores

Typical of this trend are Gap's GapKids and BabyGap. Begun in 1969 as a retailer of jeans for adults, Gap expanded into a private-label specialty store featuring casual wear for men and women. In 1986, the first GapKids store opened, offering Gap customers basic but fashionable childrenswear that catered to the same tastes as the adult lines. The BabyGap line began in 1990 and became a separate department within GapKids stores and departments, and in 1996, the first flagship freestanding BabyGap store opened in New York. Benetton is another producer/retailer that has developed a successful chain of childrenswear stores. Benetton 0–12 is packed with mini versions of the same stylish merchandise sold to adults.

Catalogs

Major catalog retailers such as Lands' End, J.Crew, and L.L. Bean have also increased their offerings for children in recent years. They offer specialized catalogs, such as J.Crew's *Crewcuts*. JCPenney has long had a separate catalog geared to kids. It also includes *JCPenney for Baby*, with furniture and accessories, and *JCPenney School Uniforms*. *Delia*'s, a catalog for girls and women aged ten to twenty-four, is another success story.

Resale of Childrenswear

Another important trend in the retailing of childrenswear is the growth of secondhand resale or consignment stores. For parents who are concerned about the price of their children's wardrobe basics, secondhand clothes received as hand-me-downs or purchased at garage sales or nursery school bazaars have always been a good source of clothing. Because children—especially infants and toddlers—so quickly outgrow their clothes, more budget-minded parents are using this kind of outlet.

Resale shops have emerged as a popular source of "lightly used" childrenswear. Franchise chains like the Children's Orchard, Kid to Kid, and Once Upon a Child have become prominent resale outlets and continue to grow.

Summary and Review

Womenswear is the largest segment of the fashion industry, and it sets the trends for other segments. In the twentieth and twenty-first centuries, merchandising of ready-to-wear apparel in the United States has been centered in the fashion district of New York City, with other major markets in Los Angeles, Dallas, and Atlanta. Mass production has depended on a unionized labor force.

The production of womenswear is segmented in several ways, and companies may specialize according to categories, such as activewear or bridal wear; sizes, including misses, junior, petite, women's, and half sizes; and price zones, ranging from designer signature to bridge to better and from contemporary to moderate and budget. Manufacturers and designers change their goods each selling season.

Merchandising and marketing activities include advertising; publicity; fashion shows, press weeks, and trade shows; trunk shows; and other promotion aids.

Five major industry trends include manufacturers acting as retailers, licensing, increased offshore production and imports, increased emphasis on the supply chain management strategy in the United States, and the widespread use of computers and the Internet.

Designer and brand names are part of the push to provide men with up-to-date fashion. While there will always be a market for classic or traditional men's clothes, industry forecasters predict that menswear will continue to be even more fashion oriented. The Europeanization of the American tailored clothing market has brought an appreciation of quality and fit. Comfort and convenience remain important to the average man, especially in casual wear and activewear.

While menswear changes more slowly than womenswear, the industry saw dramatic change and growth in the 1990s, as dress-down Fridays were adopted by most businesses in the United States. The activewear category also saw dramatic growth as firm, toned bodies became the goal of tens of thousands of men. As the Baby Boomers aged, more men turned to plastic surgery and cosmetics to hide the signs of aging.

The industry was quick to capitalize on the new interest in menswear, offering increasingly diverse products by using increased automation. Meanwhile, foreign production and imports continued to climb. Retailers jumped on the bandwagon, offering improved visual merchandising and increased advertising in newspapers, in magazines, and on the Internet.

The childrenswear market is segmented by gender and by size categories. The special features of infants' and toddlers' apparel must be taken into consideration by designers and manufacturers.

Designer labels, which are often licensed to manufacturers that specialize in children's products, are becoming increasingly important in this industry, as are character and sports licensing.

Established trends that bear watching are manufacturers offering multiple price lines and steady offshore production. Retail trends include establishing separate stores, the widespread use of catalogs, and establishing Internet sites.

Most experts are optimistic that the two prevalent trends—a move toward greater fashion in children's and teens' wear and another move toward buying better children's and teens' wear—are unlikely to reverse themselves in the coming years. This situation should serve to make this industry one of the more stable divisions in the fashion industry. The segment that has simply been called childrenswear can now rightly be called children's and teens' fashion.

FOR REVIEW

1. Name some specialized market segments served by apparel manufacturers.
2. List the traditional basic categories of women's apparel, giving types of garments in each category.
3. Into what size ranges is women's apparel traditionally divided?
4. List and describe the six major price zones into which women's apparel is divided. What are the major factors contributing to the wholesale price of garments?
5. Why do most fashion producers sell directly to retail stores rather than through wholesalers?
6. Discuss the merchandising activities of women's fashion producers today.
7. How does a manufacturer or designer benefit from attending a trunk show in a retail store?
8. Discuss the major problems facing a manufacturer who is also a retailer.
9. Discuss the development of sportswear and casual wear in the men's market and the influence they have had on the menswear industry as a whole.
10. Name the different segments into which the menswear industry is subdivided, on the basis of the type of product lines each produces. What specific products are produced by each segment?
11. How has the sizing of men's suits and dress shirts been simplified in recent years?
12. What is the role of trade shows in promoting men's fashions? Name and describe five trade shows that command national attention.
13. How have menswear producers tried to compensate for the rising cost of labor and the shortage of skilled workers in the United States?
14. Describe two menswear style trends that are likely to continue.
15. Name and briefly describe the seven size categories of childrenswear. What distinguishes girls' from pre-teen sizes and boys' from young men's sizes?
16. Explain the statement "Childrenswear . . . must still be viewed as a business that is *fashionable* rather than a *fashion* business." Do you agree with this statement? Explain your reasons.
17. How is consumer advertising handled by different types of firms in the childrenswear business?
18. What accounts for the popularity of character licensing in childrenswear?
19. What is the appeal of designer-label children's clothing?
20. What has been the attitude of US retailers and manufacturers toward the growth of imports in the childrenswear industry?
21. Describe the current trend toward specialty retail outlets for childrenswear.
22. Explain the popularity of resale shops for childrenswear.

FOR

1. Disc
   ardi

2. Wha
   desi
   to of
   cialt

3. Is th
   ing (
   dress
   monl
   you s

4. Wha
   Whic

5. Discu
   niqu
   the e

6. Discu
   drens
   work

7. Discu
   impac
   indus

8. What
   today
   clothi

9

Accessories

Key Concepts

- **Categories of accessories**
- **Merchandising and marketing of accessories**
- **Market segments in accessories**
- **Advertising and promotion of accessories**
- **Trends in the accessories industry**

The manufacturers of accessories must constantly forecast the changes in cycles of fashion so that their accessories are perfect for new fashions. This includes not only the changes in silhouette but also fabrications and color. The marketing of accessories gained an enormous boost with the entrance of well-known designers' names into the business. Today, the fame of the accessories designer is as important as the fame of the clothing designer; in many cases, it is the same famous name.

It is only through constant alertness to trends and degrees of customer acceptance that fashion accessory designers succeed. They must be prepared to design and produce styles that blend, follow or lead, and innovate. Personalized fashion and style sites like Polyvore and Pinterest, as well as numerous fashion bloggers, help consumers with wardrobe detail ideas by showing styles paired with fashionable accessories. The fashion accessories category includes footwear, handbags, gloves, hats, neckwear, eyewear, and jewelry.

Footwear

Footwear has always conjured up exciting, glamorous, and amusing times in history and literature. We read about gallant heroes in seven-league boots, princesses in glass slippers, Mercury with winged sandals, and, of course, the magic red shoes that took Dorothy from the Land of Oz back home to Kansas.

Feet, the base upon which our bodies stand, have been wrapped, covered, or left uncovered since the beginning of time. Primitive people wrapped their feet in fur, and later people strapped them into sandals. Chinese women bound their feet. Footwear often was—and still is—dictated by profession: Arctic trappers wear snowshoes, while ballet dancers wear *pointes*, or toe shoes; cowboys wear leather boots, and firefighters wear rubber boots.

Organization and Operation

Footwear production was once a major industry in New England, but many of that region's factories have downsized or closed. The largest shoe producer in the United States today is Nike, in Beaverton, Oregon. Nike actually does not own any of the manufacturing facilities that produce the shoes and apparel it sells. Rather, it acts more like a wholesaler and focuses on marketing its products. It designs, develops, and markets footwear and athletic apparel worldwide, and in 2019 had $39.12 billion in sales and $4.03 billion in profit.[1]

Imports are also a factor in dress shoes that are sold at higher price points. A long-standing reputation for quality craftsmanship and styling has contributed to the success of Italian manufacturers, such as Ferragamo, Prada, Gucci, and Diego Della Valle. Italy is the number-one producer of high-end designer shoes, with world-famous designs and quality craftsmanship. The bulk of less expensive imported shoes comes from Asia, mainly China. Other countries that export low-price shoes are Brazil, Portugal, and Spain.

Inventories, production problems, and capital investments in the shoe business are tremendous compared with those of other fashion-related industries. Thus, it is not surprising that giant companies dominate the industry. Among the fashion industries, only cosmetics has a higher percentage of production by giant companies.

Women's Shoes

Styles have run the fashion gamut from pointed to square toes, from high to flat heels, and from naked sandals to thigh-high boots. Typically—but not always—broad-toe shoes have low, chunky heels and narrow, pointed-toe shoes are more likely to have stiletto heels. The slim, elegant designs have been popular when apparel fashions have emphasized formality, and the heavier, more down-to-earth styles have been the rage in seasons when more casual clothing styles prevailed (see Figure 9.1).

Men's Shoes

Well-known US brand names for men's dress and casual shoes include Florsheim, Johnston & Murphy, Allen-Edmonds, and Alden. L.B. Evans has been making slippers and sandals in New England since 1804. At the high end of the market are Gokey boots and shoes, which are handmade in the United States to the customer's exact specifications; they are sold by Orvis through its catalog, stores and online.

US designer dress and dress/casual shoes are also predominately produced abroad. High-end imports from Europe include Clark's of England; Bally of Switzerland; and Ferragamo, Gucci, and Bruno Magli of Italy.

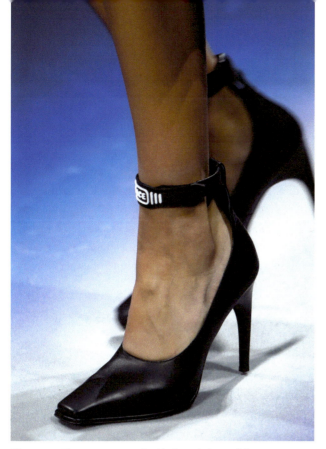

Figure 9.1 The square toe and athletic-style logo of these Versace pumps show signs of fashion trends moving to sportier, more casual styles.

Children's Shoes

From an early age, both boys and girls take a serious interest in their shoe wardrobes. Perhaps they are influenced by stories about shoes with magical powers, as in "Cinderella," "Puss in Boots," and "The 12 Dancing Princesses."

Shoes, especially everyday shoes, are subject to wear and tear, so even though they are outgrown as quickly as apparel, they are not as suitable for handing down or buying secondhand. Furthermore, a professionally fitted new pair of shoes is more likely to ensure health and comfort than used shoes. Children thus must be active participants in the purchasing decision. Having a deciding vote on the comfort of their shoes, children can easily make the next step to expressing opinions on appearances. Dressing in conformity with their peers and older children is an obvious way of showing that they fit into their social group.

As athletic shoes evolved from canvas sneakers, they became the preferred shoe for school wear. Children's preferences are influenced by practical features, such as Velcro fastenings; purely decorative features, such as L.A. Gear's briefly popular light-up shoe; and brand and

style identification, such as that provided by Nike's Air Jordans, Nike LeBron Zoom Soldier 9, Vans, and Adidas Superstar Primeknit.

Athletic Shoes

Sneakers, the original athletic shoe, were made possible by Charles Goodyear, who invented the vulcanizing process for rubber in the late 1800s. Keds were the first shoes to use this process, bonding rubber soles to canvas tops. In 1917, Converse, Inc., of North Framington, Massachusetts, introduced the All Star, which has sold more than 500 million pairs. From these humble beginnings a huge industry has grown—and shod the world.

Perhaps the most significant development in shoes since the 1980s—affecting men's, women's, and children's shoes—has been the proliferation of athletic footwear. Spurred by the trend toward more casual dressing, this separate category is now considered a mature market (see Figure 9.2).

Figure 9.2 One of many towering sneaker displays at the Nike store in Tokyo.

Athletic shoes have become even more specialized. Manufacturers make special shoes for virtually any sports activity—walking, running, climbing, aerobics, racquetball, biking, hiking, and golf. Most of the "super-specialty" shoes are carried in specialty sporting goods stores, while department stores and other general retailers stock a less specialized and more fashion-oriented range of athletic shoes.

Merchandising and Marketing

As with most fashion industries, New York City is the major US market center for shoes. It is there that most producers maintain permanent showrooms, and it is also home to the industry's trade shows. The Fashion Footwear Association of New York (FFANY), with a membership of 300 corporations and 800 brand names, stages the international footwear trade show New York Shoe Expo four times a year.

Some shoe manufacturers operate in the retail field through leased departments in retail stores. Because of the tremendous amount of capital required to stock a shoe department and the expertise needed to fit and sell shoes, many department and specialty stores lease their shoe departments to shoe manufacturers. Surveys by the National Federation of Retailers have repeatedly shown that shoe departments are among those most commonly leased by its member stores. One example is Finish Line, owned by J.D. Sports, branded athletic shoe departments, which operate athletic shoe departments in Macy's stores.

Industry Trends

US consumption of footwear reached 2.4 billion pairs in 2017, and the percentage of imports to the United States was at 98 percent. The footwear and apparel industry combined contributes $400.2 billion, and provides employment to 3.75 million Americans, according to the American Apparel and Footwear Association.[2]

Along with other categories of e-commerce, online footwear sales have experienced growth to about $15 billion in revenue. Amazon.com, which owns Zappos.com, Footlocker Retail Inc., and Nike Inc. hold the top three online sales positions.[3]

Whether in athletic or other footwear, there is a strong relationship between shoes and the clothes with which they are worn. Increased emphasis on fashion continues to be the major trend in the footwear industry. Shoe designers and manufacturers regularly attend the MICAM Milano in Italy, held twice yearly, or the Gallery Shoes International Trade Show for Shoes and Accessories, held in Dusseldorf, Germany. They also attend European apparel openings, as do shoe buyers from retail stores, gathering information on international trends in styling. More and more, apparel fashions influence both the styling and color of footwear. Skirt lengths, silhouette, pants, and sporty or dressy clothes are the fashion keys to women's shoe designs. It is therefore essential for retailers to coordinate shoes and apparel wherever and whenever they can.

Handbags

As fashion statements, handbags are used to dramatize, harmonize, or contrast with whatever else one is wearing. Styles vary from the most casual, used for sportswear, to the more formal, used for formal occasions. A handbag may be small or large, and its shape may be a pouch, or a tote, or draped or boxy. So important are handbags as fashion accessories that most women own a wardrobe of them. (See Figures 9.3a, 9.3b, and 9.3c.) Perhaps the most-copied, and declared the most popular handbag ever, is Chanel's Timeless or "2.55" diamond-quilted bag, with the shoulder strap that slides through golden chains.

Figure 9.3a (a) A fuchsia snakeskin makes Coach's Sabrina bag stand out.

Organization and Operation

Compared with other fashion industries, the US handbag industry is small. The number of domestic firms producing handbags diminishes each year, as imports made in Europe, South America, and Asia increase. Although US manufacturers' brand names are relatively unimportant in the handbag industry (except for certain classics such as Coach, Le Sportsac, and Dooney & Bourke), designer handbags have become popular. Famous names like Michael Kors, Ralph Lauren, and Marc Jacobs have entered licensing agreements with handbag manufacturers.

Several foreign manufacturers, such as Louis Vuitton, Hermès, Ferragamo, Bottega Veneta, and Gucci, have always enjoyed enormous status at the high end of the market, and the names of Chanel and, more recently, Prada are associated with distinctive styles of handbags.

Backpacks

Some of the larger manufacturers have recently diversified their lines, reaching out to men, who have flirted with the idea of carrying handbags since the 1960s. The backpack has gained favor with men who are on the go and do not have enough room in their pockets for everything they want to carry. Perhaps the backpack's acceptance is a carryover from its use as a school bookbag. For that purpose, it remains popular with boys and girls from kindergarten through college. Canvas is the most popular material, and names such as L.L. Bean, Lands' End, and JanSport carry status as well as school supplies. Meanwhile, smaller leather backpacks or Prada's nylon backpack have become a trendy handbag style among women.

Merchandising and Marketing

Few handbag manufacturers are large enough to advertise on a national basis in newspapers and television. The customer's impression of what is new and fashionable in handbags is mostly gleaned through store displays and advertising in magazines. Catalogs, home shopping networks, and Internet shopping sites are also increasingly popular ways of reaching customers.

Industry Trends

Faced with severe competition from foreign imports, many domestic handbag manufacturers have themselves become importers of foreign-made handbags. These importers employ US designers to create styles and then have the handbags made in countries with low wage scales.

The industry's trade organization, the Fashion Accessories Shipper's Association, Inc., was created by the former National Handbag Association. The organization supports the interests of importers as well as manufacturers of handbags and related accessories, including belts, small leather goods, gloves, and luggage.

The leather goods trade fair, Mipel, held in spring and autumn in Milan, attracts handbag buyers from all over the world.

Figure 9.3c (c) A simple red Kelly bag by Hermès is a long-lived classic.

Figure 9.3b (b) The quilted Chanel bag with gold chain is the most copied and most popular bag of the last one hundred years.

COLLEEN ATWOOD
Academy Award–Winning Designer Colleen Atwood

The description "living legend" has never been truer than for stage and screen costume designer Colleen Atwood. With twelve Academy Award nominations for Best Achievement in Costume Design, and four wins, for *Chicago* (2002), *Memoir of a Geisha* (2005), *Alice in Wonderland* (2010), and *Fantastic Beasts and Where to Find Them* (2016), Colleen Atwood is truly legendary in the world of filmmaking.

One of the most prolific designers in modern film, Atwood is credited as designer in over fifty films, as well as recipient of a Council of Fashion Designers of America (CFDA) award, a television Emmy, three BAFTA awards, and three Academy of Science Fiction, Fantasy & Horror Films. In addition to screen work, her resume includes work on a number of stage productions, including Sting's "Bring on the Night" world tour, and costumes for the 2005 and 2006 seasons of the Ringling Bros. Barnum & Bailey Circus.

Atwood began her fashion career in the 1970s after studying painting at the Cornish College of Arts in Seattle, Washington. She moved to New York in 1980 with $800 to her name and secured her first job sewing labels into the custom creations of Soho designers. From there, she landed a job as a production assistant on the film *Ragtime* (1981), and her career in film grew from that point.

Her creations range from contemporary to historical to fantastical, with a reputation for elaborate and highly skilled work. But her creative process begins with the character and the actor cast in the role and moves outward from there. Then, once she has formulated an

One of Atwood's favorite costume designs, for Johnny Depp in Tim Burton's 1990 fantasy film *Edward Scissorhands*.

Colleen Atwood, winner of the Academy Award for Best Costume Design in *Chicago*.

Colleen Atwood showcasing her line of handbags for Citizens of Humanity.

Meryl Streep as the witch in *Into the Woods*. Colleen Atwood received her eleventh Academy Award nomination for her costume designs for the film.

idea of what she wants, Atwood visits places she has discovered for materials, inspiration, and point of view. And she's not a fan of online shopping—she likes to touch and see things to really get inspired. Among her particular favorites she includes several of the little shops on Portobello Road in the Notting Hill neighborhood in London, and B&J Fabrics in New York.

One of the most prolific relationships in her design career has been her many collaborations with director Tim Burton, beginning with *Edward Scissorhands* (1990), which led her to create one of her most iconic costumes: Johnny Depp's scissors for hands. She embraces not only the creative role she has as a designer, but her technical one as well. She observes the actor's movements in the action of the scene and the best combination of fabrics to achieve the desired result, and she works with the technical stage team to determine things like chorography of wind movements, lighting, or other visual film effects. Costumes are part of the film narrative, helping the actor tell the story and play the character. It is creative, technical, and, according to Atwood, it doesn't just magically happen. It is hard work.

In her recent collaboration with Tim Burton, Atwood returns to the circus world and helps bring Disney's beloved *Dumbo* to life in the live-action revival of the animated classic. *Dumbo* is not only a fantasy circus film but also a period piece, so there was a great deal of

consideration to color and aging of the textiles as well as historical research into vintage circus costumes. She reported a total of over 2,000 costumes designed and manufactured for this film. This included period costumes for 500 to 600 extras, 120 circus performers, and the wardrobes for the principal cast. The 4:30 a.m. calls for hair, make-up, and wardrobe were typical to get the extras camera ready. A team of dressers had the cast prepared and dressed by 8:00 a.m.

The key to success for a cast this large was an organized system. Atwood explained the importance of a great team to execute the costumes for a major film production. "You have a lot of people working under you, so you have to be able to manage people, in a way that's wise and kind and inspirational for people, so that they enjoy doing what they do. It's really important that they love it, too. You have to share it. It's not just yours. That, as a designer, is a really important lesson." To Atwood, it's important to say, "Wow, you did a great job on that. That wasn't my idea, that was your idea, and that's really great."

Drawing upon years of working with beautiful materials from across the globe and an appreciation of the beauty and workmanship of leather objects, Atwood launched a line of handbags in with Citizens of Humanity featuring a variety of styles targeted to busy women who appreciate understated style and elegant versatility.

Gloves

Crude animal-skin coverings were the forerunners of mittens, which, in turn, evolved into gloves with individual fingers. Gloves are not new, though; leather gloves were discovered in the tombs of ancient Egyptians.

Gloves have enjoyed a long and varied history, at times even taking on symbolic value. To bring them luck, knights once wore their ladies' gloves on their armor as they went into battle. So long as women wore modest dress, men often cherished the gloves of their beloved as erotic objects. Gloves were once exchanged when property was being sold as a gesture of good faith. And in dueling days, one man would slap another across the face with his glove as an invitation to a duel. Gloves have also been used to denote rank or authority. Until the sixteenth century, only men of the clergy or of noble rank were allowed to wear them (see Figure 9.4).

Figure 9.4 Elbow-length black leather gloves by Chanel complete this opulent look.

For centuries, gloves were coordinated in styling, detail, and color with current apparel styles. To be specific, glove styles correlated to the currently popular sleeve length, especially in coats and suits.

Organization and Operation

The production of gloves varies, depending upon whether they are made of leather or fabric. Leather gloves are among the most difficult accessories to manufacture. Most leather gloves are made, at minimum, with hand-guided operations, and some are still made entirely by hand.

Leather gloves are typically made in small factories, since few machines and workers are required to run such a factory. Glove producers tend to specialize on one part, performing only one manufacturing operation, such as cutting or stitching. Other operations are farmed out to nearby plants, each of which, in turn, has its own specialty.

New York City was once the center of the glove-manufacturing industry. Today, glove manufacturers have turned to offshore production, and most gloves are made in China, the Caribbean, and the Philippines. Some specialist glove manufacturers in the United States are Totes Isotoner Corporation, which produces a line of leather gloves and the Isotoner line of fabric gloves. Other fashion glove makers in the United States are Fownes Brothers & Co., Inc. and LaCrasia.

Merchandising and Marketing

Compared with the dollars spent on consumer advertising for other accessories, the industry outlay for glove advertising is quite modest. Only a few large producers with nationally distributed brand names actively promote their products or offer even limited merchandising support services to retail stores.

Industry Trends

Sales of domestically produced leather gloves have suffered considerably from the competition of less expensive imports. To meet this challenge, the industry is trying to improve manufacturing procedures to reduce costs. Manufacturers have reduced the number of glove sizes, preferring to sell gloves in only small, medium, and large. Stretch fabric gloves, in which one size fits all, are made as well. In addition, improved materials are resulting from product research and development in the leather industry. These are expected to increase the market potential of domestically produced leather gloves. For example, many leather gloves today are hand-washable and come in a wide range of fashion colors.

The fabric glove industry is exploring innovative packaging techniques, such as packaging matching hats and gloves (or mittens) together, matching scarfs and gloves, or matching headbands and gloves for winter wear.

Millinery

According to an old saying, whatever is worn on the head is a sign of the mind beneath it. Because the head is one of the more vulnerable parts of the body, hats do have a protective function. But they are also a fashion accessory (see Figure 9.5).

Figure 9.5 A Marc Jacobs hat in dark, lustrous purple.

The man's hat of the nineteenth and twentieth centuries in Europe, which was derived from the medieval helmet, protected its wearer both physically and psychologically. The heavy crown kept the head safe from blows, and the brim shaded the face from strong sunlight and close scrutiny. In nineteenth-century America, the cowboy hat became an enduring national icon. Late in the century, the top hat was a status symbol of a special kind. This was the time of European immigration, and those who wanted to distinguish themselves from the immigrant peasants took care to wear hats.

After decades of prosperity and popularity, the men's **millinery**, or hat, industry began to collapse in the years following the Second World War. This was soon true for the women's millinery industry as well. Because of the more casual approach to dressing and the popularity of women's beehive and bouffant hairstyles, men's and women's hat sales hit bottom in 1960. During the free-wheeling 1960s and 1970s, a hat was worn only on the coldest days—strictly for warmth, not for fashion.

During that time, the millinery industry and its active trade association, the National Millinery Institute, researched, publicized, and campaigned in an extensive effort to reverse the trend, with little success. This was not surprising, since, as we have already learned, no amount of sales promotion can change the direction in which fashion is moving.

With the rise of hip-hop fashion and "ghetto fabulous" clothing styles, a new range of headwear, from streetwise Kangol hats, berets, and caps to elegant fedoras, has become must-haves among young fashion addicts. Many leading luxury houses, like Gucci, Louis Vuitton, and Burberry, are enjoying tremendous success with their logo-embellished newsboy caps, bucket hats, and fedoras.

Another factor was the featuring of flamboyant hats in designer shows, especially on the runways of Paris and Milan. Although these extreme styles are presented more as a display of the designer's imagination than as an attempt to introduce a trend, they remind fashion arbiters and consumers that hats can be a fun accessory and can make or break an outfit. Philip Treacy, a well-known British hat designer, has designed hats for the runway shows of Chanel, Valentino, and Versace. Treacy has also expanded into handbags. Well-known US millinery designers include Patricia Underwood, Eric Javits, and, at a lower price point, Betmar.

The third factor contributing to the increased popularity of hats is the awareness of the dangers of overexposure to the sun. Dermatologists recommend the wearing of hats for protection in all seasons. Straw and canvas hats with large bills or brims offer shade without undesired warmth. Hats are also available that are made of fabrics with SPF (sun protection factor). Baby hats that tie under the chin, or bonnets, have long been popular for infants; they are now widely used for toddlers as well. Along with the popular safari hat for men, hats with neck guards—once seen only in French Foreign Legion movies—have become popular in retirement communities across the country.

As with many fashion trends, the growing popularity of baseball caps as a fashion accessory started with young consumers. In this instance, boys and young men have worn them as a mark of support for their favorite teams. Soon the caps became promotional items for businesses, clubs, and other organizations. Designers took up the trend, putting their names and logos on this activewear accessory, often adding sequins, beading, or braid trims. Caps have proliferated, worn backward or forward, by men, women, and children.

The center of the women's millinery industry is in New York City in the West 30s, between Fifth and Sixth Avenues, with some smaller firms in Los Angeles and St. Louis. One-person millinery shops can be found in many cities, since millinery involves a great deal of handwork and is ideal for custom work.

Eyewear

Consumers have become increasingly aware of the need to protect their eyes from the sun's harmful ultraviolet (UV) rays. Even for children, sunglasses are now considered more than a cute, wearable toy.

At the same time, manufacturers of sunglasses have made a concerted effort to produce styles that are high fashion. Wraparound frames, clear frames, and lenses that are reflective or tinted different colors are some of the distinctive design features. Combine these factors with the high visibility of sunglasses on prominent celebrities and on MTV, and it is no wonder that sales of this category exploded (see Figure 9.6).

Dozens of styles are popular at the same time: aviators, "Jackie O" types, John Lennon grannies, "cat eyes,"

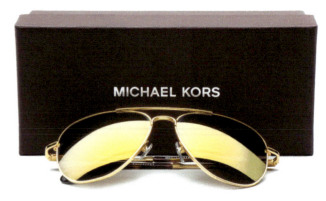

Figure 9.6 Michael Kors aviators, cast in 22-karat gold, make the world look a little bit brighter.

and "alien eyes." Riding the current wave of popularity are many designer names, among them Christian Dior, Gucci, Chanel, Kenneth Cole, and Calvin Klein.

In 2004, sunglasses maker Oakley released Thump, sunglasses embedded with a digital music player with $395 and $495 price tags. Too expensive and too goofy, said some, but Thump generated $20 million at Christmas alone. Then, in 2005, Oakley released Razrwire, a line of sunglasses that could be used as a hands-free phone. (Luxottica, a leader of luxury and sports eyewear with license brands including Burberry, Polo, and Ralph Lauren, bought Oakley in 2007.) More recent trends include retro, round, and colorful, echoing styles from the 1960s and 1970s.[4]

Designer frames for prescription eyeglasses are another important segment of the fashion eyewear category. Despite the popularity of contact lenses, optometrists now fit their customers to improve their looks as well as their vision. Aging Baby Boomers have spurred growth in the market for nonprescription reading glasses, or readers. The industry has responded with fashionable styles available at different price points. Designer eyeglasses are available from such famous names as Hugo Boss, Perry Ellis, Diane von Furstenberg, Tory Burch, Jimmy Choo, and Calvin Klein. Ecommerce innovator Warby Parker disrupted the eyewear industry in the early 2000s with affordable, fashionable styles at significantly lower prices than established brands. Marchon Eyewear is one of the largest manufacturers and distributors for many of these designer brands around the world. Lower-priced readers are available at drugstores.

Jewelry

A symbol of wealth and importance, jewelry was at certain times worn only by nobility. Laden with gold chains, their clothing adorned with gems, their fingers covered with rings, they carried on their persons the fortunes of their ruling houses. Medieval noblemen displayed elaborate heraldic emblems symbolizing their knighthood, and military men, another privileged class, used to make a great display of their decorations, which were once jewel encrusted. Jeweled tiaras were in vogue among the upper classes in the Napoleonic era because they simulated the laurel wreaths of antiquity.

Organization and Operation

Methods of making jewelry have changed little over time. Modern jewelers melt and shape metal, cut and carve stones, and string beads and shells much as jewelers have been doing for centuries. Jewelry designers have always used enamel, glass, ceramic, and natural mineral formations as their raw materials.

Based on the quality of their products, the jewelry industry in the United States can be divided into two primary groups: fine jewelry and costume or fashion jewelry. A third group, bridge jewelry, has gained popularity, as has a fourth group, ethnic jewelry.

Fine Jewelry

Only precious metals such as gold and platinum are used to make fine jewelry. **Sterling silver** is also considered a precious metal, although its intrinsic value is far less than that of gold or platinum. Too soft to be used alone, these precious metals are alloyed, or combined, with one or more other metals to make them hard enough to be fashioned into jewelry.

Platinum (which includes palladium, rhodium, and iridium) is the most expensive metal. It was first used for jewelry by Cartier and became a hallmark of the Art Deco movement of the 1920s and 1930s.

The gold content of jewelry is measured by weight in **karats**, which are abbreviated as "K." An item called solid gold actually has only 24 karats of gold—or 1/24 gold to 23/24 alloy. Less costly, 14K gold is popular in the United States, while 18K gold is popular in Europe, and 22K gold is popular in India. Gold-filled jewelry is made of an inexpensive base metal with a heavy layer of gold on top. White gold is a substitute for platinum; it is an alloy of gold and another metal, usually nickel. **Vermeil** (pronounced ver-MAY) is a composite of gold over sterling silver. The term sterling silver is used for jewelry (and flatware) with at least 92.5 parts of silver; the remaining 7.5 parts are usually copper. Not all sterling silver is equal; thicker items are generally more valuable than thin ones.

The stones used in fine jewelry are called gemstones to distinguish them from lower-quality stones that are used for industrial purposes. Gemstones, which always come from natural mineral formations, have traditionally been classified as either precious or semiprecious. Precious stones include diamonds, emeralds, rubies, and sapphires. Stones are measured by weight in a unit of measure called a **carat**, which equals 200 milligrams, or 1/142 of an ounce. Carats are subdivided into points; there are 100 points to a carat. Thus, a half-carat stone is a 50-point stone.

Diamonds are the hardest substance known and are in limited supply. From 250 tons of ore, only one carat of rough diamonds can be recovered, and only 20 percent of them are suitable for gemstones. Diamonds are found in South Africa, Siberia, Australia, and Arkansas. The world supply is dominated by the De Beers cartel of South Africa. De Beers has spent millions to promote the romance of diamonds with its ad slogan, "A diamond is forever."

Diamonds are usually cut into 58 facets, which are small, polished planes that are precisely placed to reflect the maximum amount of light. Traditional cuts or shapes of diamonds are round, emerald, marquise, pear, oval, and heart (see Figure 9.7). There is also a cut called the radiant cut, which was developed in 1976. It has about 70 facets and was originally developed to hide flaws.

Advanced technology has unleashed a crop of innovative cuts. Among them is the square-shaped context cut, which is not cleaved but based on the natural twelve-sided rough diamond crystal. Others include the circular spirit sun cut and the triple-brilliant Gabrielle cut, which has 105 facets (compared with the traditional amount of 58). They are available in a wide range of classic shapes.[5]

A solitaire is the mounting of a single gemstone; a diamond solitaire is the traditional engagement ring. A Tiffany setting refers to a four- or six-prong setting that flares out from the base to the top, with long slender prongs that hold the stone. A baguette is a rectangular-shaped small

EMERALD   OVAL   MARQUISE

ROUND   PEAR   HEART

Figure 9.7 Some classic shapes for diamond cuts.

stone used with a larger stone. A pave setting is one in which a number of small stones are set as closely together as possible, so that no metal shows between them, and they appear as an all-stone surface.

Real, or oriental, pearls are of animal origin but are still considered precious stones. Tahitian and South Sea pearls are the most expensive real pearls. Cultured pearls are pearls formed by an oyster around an irritant placed in the oyster's body by man. They are not considered precious stones, although they can be raised only in limited parts of the world's oceans. Freshwater pearls are nugget-shaped pearls that grow in lakes or rivers; they are more abundant and less expensive than real or cultured pearls.

Pearls are measured in millimeters around and in length. Size contributes to the value of pearls; large pearls are hard for oysters to grow and so are more expensive. Pearls cannot be cut or shaped like other gems. The more symmetrical the pearl, the more expensive it is. Pearls with irregular and asymmetrical shapes are called baroque pearls. The rarest—and most expensive—pearls are black; other natural tints are cream, a pinkish hue, or a bluish one.

The so-called semiprecious stones include a host of other natural stones that were once more costly and less rare than precious stones but are still quite beautiful. The Jewelers of America Association holds that the division of gems into precious and semiprecious is invalid because discoveries have added new varieties that are higher priced because of their rarity than the more well-known gems. For example, fine jade is more valuable than a lesser-quality emerald. Tanzanite, first discovered near Mount Kilimanjaro in 1967, is a deep purple gemstone that Tiffany & Co. has popularized. Although it is considered a semiprecious stone, it is being used by fine-jewelry designers in very expensive pieces.

Chemists have succeeded in creating synthetic stones that are chemically identical to real stones. Synthetic stones are now used in combination with 14-karat gold and sterling silver. The most popular of the synthetics is zirconia, which offers the dazzle of diamonds at a fraction of the cost. Other synthetic stones include synthetic spinel, which looks like emeralds or aquamarines, and synthetic corundum, which looks like amethysts.

Fine-jewelry production is still a handcraft industry. A lapidary, or stonecutter, transforms dull-looking stones in their natural states into gems by cutting, carving, and polishing them. Then the jeweler creates a setting for the stones to bring out their brilliance.

In the established fine-jewelry houses, as in haute couture houses, design, production, and retail sales typically take place under one roof—and one management team. Many fine-jewelry firms sell only the jewelry they create, much of which is custom designed for them. Names such as Cartier (a wholly owned subsidiary of Swiss Richemont Group), and Tiffany (owned by LVMH) have always been used to sell jewelry, but in the past, the designers who were in the employ of these companies were not well known. In the past few decades, however, individual designers have taken on new importance, and customers now look for jewelry designed by their favorite designers (see Figure 9.8).

Figure 9.8 Blinding pink sapphire-and-diamond clusters in this ring from "The Court of Jewels," a traveling collection of historical jewelry curated by Harry Winston.

Paloma Picasso and Elsa Peretti designs are sold at Tiffany & Co. Other leading independent designers with large followings include Barry Kieselstein-Cord, Robert Lee Morris, David Yurman, and Steven Lagos. As another example, Bergdorf Goodman's fine-jewelry department carries the work of thirty-five designers, including Alexander McQueen, Kimberly McDonald, Lanvin, and Stephen Webster.

Costume Jewelry

Costume jewelry, also referred to as fashion jewelry, is like mass-produced apparel. A wide range of materials—wood, glass, and base metals such as brass, aluminum, copper, tin, and lead—are used to make it. Base metals are sometimes coated with costlier precious metals such as gold, rhodium, or silver. The stones and simulated (fake) pearls used in costume jewelry are made from clay, glass, or plastic. While they are attractive and interesting in their surface appearance, they are less costly and lack the more desirable properties (durability, for one) of natural stones (see Figure 9.9).

Figure 9.9 Costume jewelry from Prada provides glamour at an affordable price.

The age of costume jewelry began with designer Coco Chanel. In the 1920s, she introduced long, large, and obviously fake strands of pearls to be worn with her clothes. This new accessory was called costume jewelry because it was meant to coordinate with one's costume. The pearls were called *simulated* in English and *faux*, which means "false," in French.

Chanel, it might be noted, not only helped to create an industry but also continued to wear her trademark pearls for the rest of her life. Today, simulated pearls—indeed, Chanel-style pearls—are a staple of the costume jewelry industry. Two first ladies also contributed to the popularity of pearls: Jackie Kennedy Onassis and Barbara Bush.

Mass-production methods are employed, in contrast to the handwork that exemplifies the making of fine jewelry. While a fine jeweler pounds and hand-shapes metal, manufacturers of costume jewelry cast metal by melting it and then pouring it into molds to harden. Designs are applied to the hardened metal surface by painting it with colored enamel or embossing it by machine. Electroplating is the name of a process that coats inexpensive base materials with a thin coat of silver or gold.

Large firms dominate the industry. Examples are the Monet Group and Carolee. The Jewelry Group, a division of Premier Brands Group Holdings, is a designer and marketer of branded and private-label costume jewelry, manufacturing and marketing the licensed jewelry collection for Givenchy, Judith Jack, and Napier.[6] While most large firms work with multiple price lines and many different materials, some companies do specialize. An example is Swarovski Jewelry US, which specializes in crystal jewelry.

Still, more than 90 percent of US jewelry producers are small, family-owned companies. Individuals with creative talent often open successful small retail or wholesale operations that cater to customers who are interested in individualized styling and trend-setting fashions. Such operations are an outgrowth of the handcraft movement of the 1960s and 1970s. Handmade jewelry had a major comeback at the beginning of the new millennium, which launched a rise of small, independent jewelry designers across the country. Today, online sites like Etsy also help promote individual jewelry designers.

Bridge Jewelry

Dramatic increases in the price of gold and silver in the early 1980s left jewelers seeking new ways to meet the public's demand for reasonably priced authentic jewelry. The solution was **bridge jewelry**, or jewelry that forms a bridge—in price, materials, and style—between fine and costume jewelry. Prices at retail range from about $100 to $2,500 for bridge jewelry. (Also see the discussion of bridge apparel in Chapter 8.)

The development of bridge jewelry led to increased use of sterling silver and its subsequent elevation to a precious metal. The boom in Native American jewelry in the early 1970s also helped to create interest in bridge jewelry. Many department stores and specialty stores created bridge departments to handle sterling silver and Native American jewelry, and when interest in it faded, they were open to other kinds of bridge jewelry that would help them keep the customer base they had developed.

Bridge jewelry departments at stores such as Bloomingdale's, Neiman Marcus, and Macy's now carry gold-filled, vermeil, sterling silver, and some 14-carat fashion jewelry set with semiprecious stones. Sterling silver jewelry continues to grow rapidly in popularity. Bridge designers include Zina and David Beck Bali. Judith Jack specializes in marcasite (crystallized mineral) jewelry, which attracts both costume and fine-jewelry customers.

Ethnic Jewelry

The category of ethnic jewelry includes pieces from all over the world at all price points, although some of these items are not made of intrinsically valuable materials, but rather of shells, stones, wood, or fabric. The artistry is so remarkable that these items can command a higher price than costume jewelry. As previously mentioned, Native American jewelry in silver and turquoise has been popular for decades. Two famous styles of silver necklaces, the squash blossom necklace and the liquid silver necklace, continue to be reinterpreted by modern Native American designers (see Figure 9.10).

Ralph Lauren popularized African jewelry for a widespread US audience with his 1997 collection that was inspired by the Masai of Kenya; it included arm cuffs, bead chokers, and hoop earrings. Similarly, traditional ethnic jewelry from India, made from 22K gold and decorated with ornate patterns and precious gemstones, became popular in the late 1990s after the growing popularity of colorful and fun Hindi Bollywood films with American audiences. Chinese-inspired jewelry made of jade, coral, and mother-of-pearl is perennially popular, as is the yin-yang symbol. Moroccan beads, the Egyptian

Figure 9.10 Navajo woman modeling turquoise pins and a squash blossom necklace made by Native Americans.

ankh, Guatemalan string figures, Greek worry beads, Caribbean shell necklaces, and Peruvian hammered copper earrings have fans worldwide.

Another category of ethnic jewelry involves wearing religious or spiritual symbols in necklaces, earrings, rings, or pins, such as the Jewish Star of David, the Christian cross, the Buddhist lotus blossom, the Native American eagle feather, and the New Age crystal. The famous Indian "Navratan Haar" ring is made of nine gems with astrological significance: a diamond in the center, circled by eight rainbow-colored stones: ruby, emerald, cinnamon, coral, cat's eye, blue and yellow sapphires, and pearl.

Designers must show sensitivity when adapting these powerful symbols into jewelry. A storm of protest arose when Madonna wore a cross as part of her on-stage costume during the early part of her career; it was interpreted by many as irreverent, even blasphemous.

Many people wear their so-called birthstone, to which folklore attributes good luck, according to their sign of the zodiac. In fact, the concept of the birthstone was introduced in the United States in 1912 by the predecessor of the Jewelers of America Association and is matched to calendar months rather than the zodiac.

Another interesting development in ethnic jewelry is the growing number of firms making licensed copies or reproductions of museum pieces of jewelry. Museums around the world, including the State Historical Museum of Moscow, the Vatican Library, and the Metropolitan Museum of Art in New York, are selling vast amounts of inexpensive reproductions of museum pieces in their stores and through catalogs. These pieces come from many different eras and many different cultures; what they have in common is that they have been preserved because of their beauty and power.

Watches

The useful, dependable wristwatch is a relative newcomer to the 500-year history of mechanical timepieces (see Figure 9.11). Nineteenth-century craftsmen made the pocket watch efficient—and a thing of beauty. In 1904, Louis-Joseph Cartier introduced the first modern wristwatch, the Santos-Dumont, named for a Brazilian aviator.

There are three basic types of watches made today: the mechanical, the self-winding, and the quartz movement. Mechanical watches are driven by a balance wheel and powered by a spring, which must be hand-wound. Automatic or self-winding watches wind themselves as the wearer moves a wrist. The quartz movement invented in the 1970s offers very accurate timekeeping at a low cost. Most quartz watches have removable batteries that last about one year.

Figure 9.11 This ad for Omega illustrates the idea of advanced technology in its operation and design.

Analog watches have faces with hands that sweep around the numbers "clockwise." Digital watches display the time in numbers, generally using a liquid crystal display (LCD). Extra features available in some watches include night-light buttons, calendars, moon-phase indicators, stopwatch (or chronograph) features, alarms, and chimes. Some watches also give the time in other countries or time zones. But watches have always been a fashion statement as well as a useful device.

The inexpensive Timex watch of the 1960s, which "took a licking but kept on ticking," broadened the market to include a huge number of people who could not afford even the mass-market watches of previous decades.

During the 1980s, Swatch made a splash in the market with its casual watches and has now spread its name and contemporary look into a number of other product categories, such as sportswear, sunglasses, and other accessories. The Swatch lines have become so popular that some retailers have created Swatch boutiques. As of 2015, Swatch was the number-one manufacturer of finished watches in the world.[7] Other well-known companies include Movado, Fossil, and Armitron.

Many companies later jumped onto the sports-watch bandwagon by adding resistance to water, wind, dust, shock, and magnetic fields. Chronograph watches that measure small fractions of a second have been best sellers; some are used to measure speeds, distances, and altitudes.

At the high end of the watch market are leading brands like Rolex, Omega, Patek Philippe, Audemars Piguet, and Cartier, all of which consistently introduce new models. Their watches can cost from $2,000 to $2.7 million.

At the other end of the market are children's watches. The Mickey Mouse watch for children was introduced in the 1930s. Timex makes watches for Disney, Joe Boxer, Nautica, and others. In 2001, Timex introduced TMXessories, a line aimed at tween and teen girls that included colorful, decorative watches disguised as bangle bracelets, rings, and pendant necklaces. Armitron is another maker of cartoon-character watches, such as Tweety, Bugs Bunny, Garfield, and Scooby-Doo. Mattel, the giant toy maker, has a line of Barbie watches.

But have cell phones and iPods made watches obsolete? With the advances in technology, the younger generation may have reduced interest in watches. Many retailers and manufacturers, however, believe the watch business is still thriving. Fashion, status, convenience— in 2018, the luxury watch market worldwide was $6.3 billion, with projections to reach $9.3 billion by 2025.[8]

DR. SARA MARCKETTI
Teacher, Researcher, and Historian

MEET DR. SARA MARCKETTI, PROFESSOR IN THE APPAREL, EVENTS, AND HOSPITALITY MANAGEMENT DEPARTMENT, AND DIRECTOR FOR CENTER FOR EXCELLENCE IN LEARNING AND TEACHING AT IOWA STATE UNIVERSITY.

Dr. Sara B. Marcketti.

What we wear, how we wear it, why we wear it, how it's made, and how we merchandise it have always interested Dr. Marcketti. It is these basic questions that eventually led her toward a career in researching and teaching fashion history. She earned an AB in art history and an MS in textiles, merchandising, and interiors from the University of Georgia. She combined both of these interests in a PhD in textiles and clothing at Iowa State University, where she researched how the fashion industry attempted to legally protect creative product designs against design piracy in the twentieth century. She has focused her education and interests toward a career in teaching and research, which she attributes to her own teachers and professors, as in them she could see wonderful role models in how to be a good teacher and a productive researcher, and how to engage with the larger community of scholars through active participation and networking.

As a university professor, Dr. Marcketti manages a wide range of responsibilities, including teaching, research, and directing graduate students toward their own research and advanced degrees, and it is the diversity of her work that she loves. Each semester holds different challenges. She might teach one or two classes, such as Survey of European and North American History, Twentieth-Century Fashion, or Creative Thinking and Problem Solving. Graduate students rely on her guidance as she reads drafts of their work and helps guide them through their own research and writing process. And in her role as Director of the Center for Excellence in Teaching and Learning, she guides faculty colleagues in the completion of a variety of work toward scholarship and research in the areas of improved teaching and learning. She dedicates one day a week to her own research and writing on a variety of research topics.

Teaching and research in a dynamic field like fashion studies requires keeping up with new research and networking. Two professional organizations, Costume Society of America and International Textile and Apparel Association, offer incredible resources for hearing about the latest scholarship in textiles, clothing, and history. Professional connections have also become friends, which makes work and life more enjoyable.

Dr. Marcketti's advice to students who might be interested in pursuing a career in teaching, higher education, or research is this: "I would encourage students to think about what interests them and to not get discouraged by failure. I didn't know what I wanted to do or become when I was in high school or even for most of my undergraduate degree. For me, the skills that I learned along the way, especially reading critically, persistence, and having a strong work ethic, help me every day."

GUCCI: Sustainability and Social Media

Gucci's sales growth in recent years is phenomenal—in 2017 sales grew by over 44 percent over the previous year, with revenues reaching $2.2 billion in 2018, up over 48 percent compared the same period during the prior year.

What is behind this? One reason is millennials. The brand appeals to their core values: personal satisfaction and purpose.

Traditionally, luxury brands have established themselves through two key elements: high-quality craftsmanship with superior quality and exclusivity. But millennials do not necessarily buy into these traditional selling points. Consumers in this generation crave purpose, authenticity, and passion. And they are attracted to companies that behave in a committed and ethical way. In short, luxury brands must embrace a higher purpose in order to win over millennial shoppers.

As issues like sustainability, transparency, and ethical manufacturing practices receive greater attention in the media, Gucci has responded with a progressive program, Gucci Equilibrium (http://equilibrium. gucci.com), which is an online communication platform outlining the brand's corporate social responsibility policies, environmental impact, employee satisfaction, and other innovations. This level of transparency and communication grants the Gucci brand the level of authenticity, transparency, and accountability that consumers now seek.

Gucci's parent company, Kering, has established detailed standards governing the procurement and production of leather throughout the supply chain. For more information on leather and tanning practices, visit www.equilibrium.gucci.com.

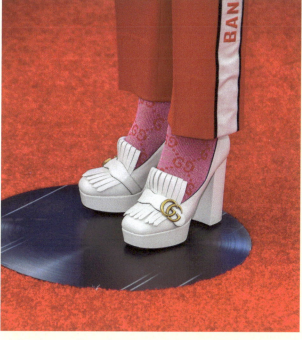

Bright colors, quality craftsmanship, and modern proportions, combined with supply chain transparency, appeal to millennial consumers.

Figure 9.12 New accessories lines debut at Moda Las Vegas and AccessoriesTheShow.

Merchandising and Marketing

Jewelry manufacturers present their new styles and, in the case of costume jewelry manufacturers, their new lines at semiannual shows sponsored by the Jewelers of America and the Jewelry Information Center. One of the largest trade shows is the AccessoriesTheShow held in New York in January and May. MAGIC Las Vegas in February and August host accessory and jewelry vendors as well as apparel and footwear for men, women, and children. Other major trade associations include the American Gem Society, the Diamond Council of America (DCA), and the Fashion Jewelry and Accessories Trade Association (FJATA).

Fine-jewelry manufacturers traditionally have concentrated on providing a wide range of basic pieces, most notably diamond rings and watches. They support their lines with a variety of services offered to stores. Some advertising assistance is offered, but this has not been common in a business where brand names have been relatively unknown. However, with the emergence of designer jewelry names, this is changing.

For all types of jewelry, but especially diamond rings, the Christmas holidays and Valentine's Day are especially busy. Birthdays and anniversaries provide a steady year-round business, while watches show a sales spurt around graduation time. The popularity of vintage clothing has led to a renewed interest in "estate pieces," or fine jewelry of earlier eras, still in the original settings.

Industry Trends

Today, all branches of the jewelry industry emphasize the production of designs that complement currently fashionable styles. For example, when turtlenecks are popular, jewelry companies make long chains and pendants that look graceful on high necklines. When sleeveless dresses are in fashion, bracelets become an important piece of jewelry. When French cuffs are in fashion, both men and women wear cufflinks. When prints are popular, jewelry styles become tailored, but when solid or somber colors are popular, jewelry often moves to center stage with more complex designs and bright colors.

Masculine and unisex designs in gold chains, earrings, rings, shirt studs, nose studs, and fashion/sports watches are popular. More men are also wearing colored gemstones.

To compete with costume jewelry, which has gained broad acceptance over the past few decades, fine-jewelry companies have begun to diversify. Some have broadened their lines by moving into bridge jewelry. Others have also diversified into complementary nonjewelry areas. Swank, for example, which for years has manufactured men's small jewelry items, now produces colognes, sunglasses, travel accessories, and a variety of men's gifts.

Other Accessories

There are many categories of accessories—and much variation within categories—from dress shoes to jellies, from briefcases to lunch boxes, from hard hats to snoods. Other ornaments, like ribbons, bows, feathers, and fabric flowers, come and go in popularity. The accessory maker needs to move quickly in and out of these trends. Other categories of accessories include umbrellas and hair ornaments.

Trends in the Fashion Accessories Industries

For accessory manufacturers, being supporters of apparel fashions does not necessarily mean being followers. In fact, accessory manufacturers must often be fashion leaders. In the fashion business, which always moves in the fast lane, accessory manufacturers must move in a faster lane than anyone else. They have to be able to adapt or change a style in mid-season if that is what is required to stay on top of current trends.

Market Weeks and Trade Shows

New accessory lines are shown during the five major fashion market weeks in New York so that merchants can buy a coordinated look. These include the following:

- Summer and January
- Transitional and March
- Fall and May
- Holiday and August
- Spring and November

In the United States, the MAGIC and WWDMAGIC shows held in Las Vegas in February and August are the largest trade shows for accessories. The International Fashion Jewelry and Accessory Show (IFJAG) takes place in Las Vegas and Orlando, Florida. Paris Première Classe, the Fashion Accessories Trade Show, is held in Paris in March and October. These shows are a reflection of the growing importance of accessories to retailers and consumers.

Summary and Review

Specific accessories wax and wane in popularity, but some accessories are always popular as most people do not consider themselves fully dressed until they have accessorized an outfit. In recent years, the business overall has boomed. Many people feel the accessory business, like many other fashion categories, has been given a boost by its association with designer names.

The benefits are mutual. At the haute couture shows of Paris and Milan, the clothing has become the designer's fashion statement, and accessories have generated the financial support—as well as supporting the look of the season—to allow designers to experiment. Made-to-order gowns and ensembles are individually produced by hand, whereas accessories can be machine-made in larger numbers and sold at higher margins. Similarly, American ready-to-wear designers literally display their names or logos on licensed accessories such as belts, scarfs, caps, handbags, and sunglasses. For the purveyors of fashion

as much as for the consumer, accessories support a complete, coordinated image. In addition, they are the source of a more attractive bottom line.

FOR REVIEW

1. Why have US shoe producers moved their factories offshore? How has this trend affected the footwear industry?
2. How do changes in lifestyles and activities affect the shoe industry? Give examples.
3. Describe the merchandising and marketing of handbags in the United States today.
4. What are the current trends in the millinery industry?
5. Why are shoe and fine jewelry departments often leased?
6. What three metals are considered precious? What is the difference between solid gold and 14-karat gold?
7. What are the major gemstones used in the production of jewelry?
8. Give several examples of how women's apparel fashions influence jewelry fashions.
9. What categories of merchandise are to be found in fashion accessory departments today? In outposts?

FOR DISCUSSION

1. How has the increasing informality of dress affected the accessories industries?
2. List each of the current important fashion accessory items and discuss why they are important to the total fashion look. At which stage of the fashion cycle is each item positioned? Give reasons for your answers.

Trade Talk

Define or briefly explain the following terms:

bridge jewelry

carat

costume jewelry

karat

millinery

sterling silver

vermeil

PART FOUR

The Retail Level:
The Markets for Fashion

In this part, you will examine the elements of fashion marketing and learn how markets operate to help manufacturers sell their products. You will begin to develop a basic vocabulary and a working knowledge of the following:

- Global sourcing, including its advantages and disadvantages for the US fashion industries, is discussed in Chapter 10.
- The history and development of fashion retailing in the United States is explored in Chapter 11.
- The many fashion services that work with all levels of the fashion industry, including magazines, newspapers, broadcast and TV, the Internet, and fashion reporting services, as well as trade associations are the subject of Chapter 12.

10

Global Sourcing and Merchandising

Key Concepts

- Meaning of the terms *market*, *market center*, *mart*, and *trade show* and the function of each in bringing fashion from producers to consumers in the United States and internationally

- Locations and activities of markets, marts, and trade shows

- Role of offshore production in product development

- International trading laws and agreements between the United States and its trading partners

- Domestic importing and exporting

Going shopping can be fun and exciting, whether going to the mall, or to a favorite website. Most of us make our purchases with great expectations, and sometimes the things we buy are perfect and other times they are just not right.

Regardless of the outcome, it is your money and you can spend it however you wish. However, this is not the case when you spend someone else's money, as is the case for store buyers. When buying for a store, you are using the company's money, which requires an exhausting amount of planning, organization, and hard work before you even go to market.

Market Terminology

Markets . . . market centers . . . marts—what are they? You will hear these terms used frequently and even interchangeably, which makes them that much harder to sort out.

Market

The word *market* has several meanings. We have already spoken of the market, or demand, for a specific product. In this chapter, the word takes on yet another meaning. A **market** is the place where goods are produced and sold at wholesale prices to store buyers. It is an important step in the pipeline that takes clothes and other fashion items from manufacturer to customer. Buyers attend markets, in effect, to choose the styles we will all be wearing within a few months.

Market Center

Actually, there is no one giant shopping mall that serves as a market for the entire US fashion industry. Instead, several **market centers**, or geographic locations, exist throughout the country and across the globe. A market center is a city where fashion is produced and sold at wholesale prices.

The first market center in the United States was New York City. For many people in and out of the fashion industry, New York City epitomizes the allure and excitement of the fashion world. But fashion has become regionalized, and while New York still markets much of the fashion in the United States, it no longer produces all of it. Los Angeles, Dallas, and Miami are all flourishing market centers.

Mart

A **mart** is a building or complex of buildings that houses a wholesale market, that is, an exhibition of fashions that are ready to be sold to retail stores. Most marts are owned and operated by independent investors, and some marts are operated by the cities themselves. A permanent, professional staff operates the mart, although a large number of temporary employees are hired for market weeks.

Like convention centers, marts consist almost entirely of exhibition space. Some space is rented out as full-time corporate showrooms, but in many marts, the space is rented only during market weeks. These marts often balance their income by sponsoring other shows and conventions.

New York City, despite the rise of regional marts, in many ways still reigns as the country's premiere market center. New York Fashion Week shows are held at Spring Studios in TriBeCa, with some designers presenting in edgy or thematic venues all around the city.

The oldest of marts is the Merchandise Mart in Chicago, which opened its doors in the early 1930s, making Chicago New York's only rival for years. Because the Merchandise Mart was centrally located, buyers from across the country found it convenient to meet in this huge building on the Chicago River several times a year to do their wholesale buying. The mart is still very much in use today for other goods, such as home furnishings, contract (office/institutional) furnishings, kitchen and bath, and gifts and decorative accessories.

Market Weeks

Buyers can and do travel to market centers and some marts at any time during the year to visit individual producers, but several times a year, they also gather for **market week**. Few buyers are willing to forego the glamour and excitement of market week. During market week, market centers and marts are filled with producers and designers, all of whom exhibit their new lines with as much style and panache as possible. The atmosphere is electrifying, heady with new, innovative ideas and the latest trends.

Trade Shows

In this chapter, you will also learn about **trade shows**, periodic exhibits that are scheduled throughout the year in regional market centers and some marts. Smaller than market weeks, trade shows are typically attended by buyers from one region of the country. Exceptions are a few huge trade shows, such as Magic, which attract buyers from all over the world.

The Development of Market Centers in the United States

As discussed, New York City was the first market center in the United States. When design and production clustered in New York, it followed that it would become a center for buying, too. The fact that New York was the most cosmopolitan and fashion conscious of US cities also helped. Even when travel was a strenuous undertaking, buyers at major stores tried to travel to New York twice a year. To service them, manufacturers set up showrooms near their factories in the garment district.

But for many, twice-a-year buying trips were not enough to service a store properly. And, many owners and buyers for small stores across the country could not afford to travel to New York. To handle accounts between New York buying trips and to help those who did not come to New York at all, manufacturers hired **sales representatives** who traveled to the stores and the buyers to show the lines.

Services of Market Centers and Marts

A market week is organized by manufacturers' associations, in cooperation with the market center or mart staff. It is the prime selling opportunity for market centers or mart staffs, fashion producers, and sales reps, all of whom devote themselves to making the visit as easy and convenient as possible for the buyers. Keeping buyers interested, comfortable, and happy encourages them to write orders.

Market weeks are scheduled several months before the clothes will be needed in the stores. Four or five market weeks are held each year for womenswear and childrenswear, three to five for menswear and boyswear, and two to five for shoes. Separate market weeks are held in many market centers or marts for accessories, infants' and childrenswear, lingerie, Western wear, sportswear, and bridal apparel.

Publicity

A market week is only as successful as the exhibitors it manages to attract, so most regional markets and marts mount an ongoing publicity program to draw interesting and exciting exhibitors. So the chemistry will be mutual, market centers and marts also do what they can to attract buyers. Flyers and brochures touting market weeks go out to stores and individual buyers several times a year. Buyers are also treated to buyers' breakfasts, luncheons, and cocktail parties throughout market week—all courtesy of the market center, mart, or a supporting organization.

The most popular form of publicity is the fashion shows that highlight every market week. The shows are hectic since they are so huge and so much is going on. They are also among the more extravagant and interesting fashion shows ever staged. Mostly this is because they are the work of many different designers, all of whom enter their most beautiful or interesting designs. To give some coherence to a market week fashion show, it is often organized around a theme, such as a particular color or, more often, an exciting new trend.

Information Services

A **buyer's directory** and calendar help buyers find their way to the vendors and the scheduled events they want to see. A steady flow of daily updates continues throughout the week to keep buyers abreast of breaking market week news. Most information is posted and updated on the show website or app.

Educational Services

An orientation program is typically scheduled for the first day, and consultants are on call throughout the week to discuss and deal with specific problems. Seminars and conferences are held to supply buyers with the latest information on fashion. Typical topics are new advances in fiber and fabrics, trends in fashion colors, the latest merchandising techniques, advertising and promotion ideas, and sales training hints.

CLAIRE MCCARDELL
and the American Look

Today, we take comfort, style, function, and performance in our fashions for granted. But a good deal of credit is owed to twentieth-century American fashion designer Claire McCardell. In many ways ahead of her time, her focus on comfort, separate pieces to be mixed and matched, innovation in fabric, and casual elegance became known as "The American Look," reflecting the lifestyles of American women through casual, sophisticated clothing with functional design and an accessible aesthetic.

Enduring hurdles and challenges early in her career, McCardell eventually triumphed in the 1940s and 1950s as a top creator and true innovator. After attending two years at Hood College in Maryland, McCardell transferred to Parsons School of Design and graduated in 1928. During the next few years, McCardell painted rosebuds on lampshades, worked as a model and sketcher, and eventually landed a job as a knitwear designer for a reported $45 per week, only to be fired eight months later. Henry H. Geiss, owner of Townley Frocks, hired McCardell initially as a model and sketcher, beginning her long association with the firm. Her big break came in 1931 when just weeks before the spring showing, the designer for Townley drowned in a swimming accident and the owner turned to McCardell to produce a collection.

Her success continued with Townley owing to experimentation, originality, and groundbreaking innovations. Although she trained in Paris in the 1920s and was an ardent admirer of Madeleine Vionnet, an element of her innovation was in her refusal to follow French fashion at a time when other designers clung to it. In 1938, McCardell introduced the "monastic dress," a loose, simple dress, cut on the bias, falling from the shoulder, to be worn belted or unbelted. The loose cut and versatility revolutionized the dress business, accelerating the success of more casual clothes, but it sent Townley Frocks, and its owner, into a tailspin. The simplicity of design left the firm open to

Claire McCardell in her studio.

copyists, reportedly causing Geiss to close the doors and shut down Townley Frocks.

McCardell went on to work for tastemaker Hattie Carnegie, but the simplicity of her aesthetic failed to suit the more elaborate tastes of Carnegie's clientele, so she left the firm after a year and a half. Meanwhile in 1940, Henry Geiss reopened Townley Frocks with new business partner Adolph I. Klein. On the lookout for a head designer for the new Townley enterprise, the story goes that Geiss and Klein happened to share an elevator with McCardell, who, upon expressing best wishes on the new venture, was offered a job on the spot. Klein, reportedly a shrewd and forward-thinking Seventh Avenue salesman, saw shifts in the industry and recognized McCardell's potential. Later, Klein remarked on this spur-of-the-moment decision, "In this business, you have to be exciting or basic. I figured [Townley was] too small to be basic, so we had to be exciting."

And excitement it was! McCardell's name was included on the label—one of the first American designers to achieve this recognition. In 1941, the United States entered the Second World War, and

Pantung loincloth (L) swimsuit designed by Claire McCardell, pictured with "Hug Me Tights" (R) swimsuit designed by Joset Walker.

Easy, casual, and stylish.

the simplicity, elegance, and economy of McCardell's design vision was ripe for the imminent cultural shifts. Women realized changing roles, and restrictions imposed by shortages and government regulations, known as L-85, urged creativity and innovation. Unexpected fabrics like denim, butcher's linen, and pillow ticking made their way stylishly into McCardell's fashion collections. Flattering but simple wrap designs called "popover" dresses eliminated the use of any sort of zipper or metal closure, which were in short supply, and became a signature element. Leather shortages inspired ballerina slippers and coordinate fabric shoes. McCardell's emphasis on dresses and sportswear, or "play clothes," contrasted the stiff, masculine look of wartime fashions. Forward-thinking, even prophetic, three years before Dior launched what the fashion press exalted and dubbed "The New Look," McCardell predicted and showed rounded shoulders and longer, fuller skirts.

Recognition and accolades followed. McCardell's designs were successful in the marketplace. In 1942, McCardell's popover design earned an American Fashion Critics' Award citation for her innovation working within wartime restrictions. Townley reported record sales in 1943. And in 1944 and 1956, McCardell received the coveted Coty Award. It is also reported that at some point during the Second World War, McCardell designed the women's uniform for the Red Cross Motor Corps. In 1945, Lord & Taylor store director and McCardell supporter Dorothy Shaver launched a promotion entitled "The American Look," featuring Claire McCardell designs. President Harry S. Truman presented McCardell with the Women's National Press Club Award in 1950, and with this, she became the first fashion designer to be voted one of America's Women of Achievement. Her innovation and achievement earned her a cover on *Time* magazine May 2, 1955. And in 1990, *Life* magazine named her one of the 100 most important Americans of the twentieth century.

In the postwar era, women's demands for a casual way of life expanded and McCardell's designs continued to push the boundaries of chic comfort and modern style. She continued to design and create up to her untimely death at the age of fifty-three, in 1958.

Her legacy is renewed in recent retrospectives and research of her life and work.

The New York Market

As a market, New York belongs in a category by itself, not only because it is the city with the most resources to offer the fashion world but also, as mentioned earlier, because it has no central mart building. While Spring Studios in TriBeCa has provided a central location in recent years for fashion week shows, designers show in unique, thematic locations all over the city.

Trading Area and Economic Impact

The New York market is made up of literally thousands of showrooms that line the streets of the garment district, or Fashion Center. The garment district is located between Fifth and Ninth Avenues from Thirty-Fourth to Forty-Second Streets. Generally, similar-quality apparel is grouped together. In the women's wholesale market, for example, the couture or higher-priced lines are situated primarily along Seventh Avenue in elegant showrooms. Moderate-priced lines and sportswear firms are housed around the corner on Broadway. Obviously, time and coordination are required to shop the New York market—as is a comfortable pair of shoes.

The lack of a central mart is a minor drawback compared with what many buyers consider the glory of shopping this *crème de la crème* of markets. Whatever is new will be seen here first. New York, most industry people agree, is the most dynamic and creative market center. Any buyers servicing stores of any size must come to New York to do so, regardless of the other markets they add to their schedule.

New York offers a wide range of shopping. Every kind of fashion can be found in every price range. Men's, women's, and children's clothing, accessories, intimate apparel, and cosmetics are located within the garment district. Textile and fiber companies and home furnishings producers maintain showrooms in or near the garment district. Most local manufacturers feel that they must maintain a New York showroom, and many regional manufacturers sponsor one as well, if only during market weeks.

In 1993, Seventh on Sixth was created to organize, centralize, and modernize the American collections, as well as to provide a platform for American designers to become important players in the global fashion business. Originally, New York Fashion Week was under the auspices of the Council of Fashion Designers of America (CFDA) and organized by the CFDA's offshoot known as Seventh on Sixth. In 2001, the former Seventh on Sixth was acquired by International Management Group (IMG), a sports management and marketing agency. Today, as the producers of Mercedes-Benz Fashion Week in New York and Mercedes-Benz Fashion Week Swim in Miami, IMG has an incredible outreach to thousands of buyers, retailers, and members of the national and international press. It also produces a variety of international fashion shows, including Mercedes-Benz Fashion Week in Berlin and Moscow, and Lakmé Fashion Week in Mumbai, among others.

Advantages of the New York Market

Buyers who come to New York can shop not only the market but also the department stores and boutiques for which the city is known. New York is home to the flagship stores of Macy's, Bloomingdale's, Barneys, Bergdorf Goodman, and Saks Fifth Avenue. There is also a high concentration of national and international flagship designer stores. Areas like the Upper East Side, Soho, and the meatpacking district are brimming with elegant flagship boutiques like Saint Laurent, Alexander Wang, and Prada. As New York is one of the fashion capitals of the world, practically every important international fashion house has a flagship store there.

New York City is also the hub of the fashion network. Many national organizations have headquarters there and stand ready to provide assistance and support services to buyers. Even on a personal level, the networking possibilities are good. Local New York buyers attend market weeks, as do buyers from all over the country. Buyers who can attend only a few market weeks each year generally head for New York.

The Regional Market Centers

Each market center has its own unique flavor, as does each city, and buyers look forward to the varied experiences they will have at different markets. Many small retailers attend New York market weeks less often than they once did, relying instead on regional market centers closer to home. Travel costs are lower, less time is spent away from the stores, and for many, the atmosphere feels more personal. As regional markets become more sophisticated, thus drawing more exhibitors, New York loses even more of its allure. If regional markets can meet their needs, buyers ask, then why struggle through what many consider to be a grueling week in New York? Some retailers have cut out New York entirely, while others have reduced the number of trips they make and fill in with trips to regional markets in Los Angeles, Dallas, or Miami. They can visit them year-round or during special market weeks.

The Los Angeles Market

Much of the look and style of California's markets revolve around its casual lifestyle, which it seems to sell almost as much as it sells its clothing. California leads the nation in retail apparel sales, and Los Angeles is the nation's largest apparel manufacturing center, employing 61,546 workers.[1] In addition, 75 percent of high-end denim that is sold worldwide is produced in Southern California, making it the largest domestic market for denim.[2]

Since the 1930s, when California introduced pants for women, the West Coast has been the source of many important trends in sportswear. Los Angeles is home to some of the country's largest sportswear manufacturers, Guess, L.A. Gear, and Speedo. Other Los Angeles successes are Bisou Bisou, Moschino, Laundry by Shelli Segal, Richard Tyler, St. John's Knits, and Rampage. Bob Mackie, who designs for Hollywood stars and is frequently seen on television home shopping shows, is also based in Los Angeles. Surf-fashion firms include companies such as Hurley, Billabong, and Blake Kuwahara's Kata Eyewear.

Apparel design, production, and distribution are spread out along the entire West Coast, but the heaviest concentrations remain in Los Angeles.[3] The California Market Center, the nation's largest apparel mart, located in downtown Los Angeles, has permanent and temporary exhibition space not merely for California's lines, but for New York and Dallas lines as well, along with a growing number of foreign producers (see Figure 10.1). The California Market Center is open year-round and offers five market weeks and a variety of specialty trade shows, such as LA Textile, LA Majors for large department stores chains, and online outlets, and Label Array showcasing footwear, apparel, accessories, beauty, gift and home wares.

Figure 10.1 An information table welcomes visitors to the LA Fashion Market.

The Dallas Market

The mood at Dallas market weeks is southwestern, as people will find handcrafted clothes, or clothes that look handcrafted, with bright, vibrant colors. Once a center for budget garments, Dallas has become an important production and market center. Dallas-produced fashions are shown alongside fashions from New York, California, and around the world. Designers Antthony Mark Hankins and Victor Costa, the firm Jerrell, and jewelry designers Elizabeth Showers, and Dian Malouf are based in Dallas.

The Dallas Market Center is comprised of four buildings containing more than 5 million square feet of exhibit and showroom space. The buildings in the center include the Trade Mart, the World Trade Center, the International Trade Plaza, and Market Hall. Fashion Center Dallas, located in the upper floors of the World Trade Center showcase fashions for women, children, men, swim, intimate apparel, bridal, prom, special occasion, footwear, and westernwear.[4]

The Miami Market

The Miami market weeks have a highly international—mostly Latino and Caribbean—flavor. Colors and styles are lively. The Miami market is also known for an outstanding selection of childrenswear.

Greater Miami has become one of the most dynamic, cosmopolitan, and international fashion-producing centers in the country. Drawn by the temperate climate and quality labor force, many apparel designers and manufacturers now call South Florida home. Retailers find that

Miami-produced clothing is well made, reasonably priced, and perfect for the semitropical weather that prevails in the Sun Belt. In Miami, three strong selling seasons—cruise wear, spring, and summer—are available year-round. In addition to cruise and resort wear, Miami design and production center around budget and moderate-priced sportswear, swimwear, and children's clothing. Miami-based designers of better-priced daytime and evening wear are also becoming known for their work.

The Miami International Merchandise Mart, opened in 1968, serves this area. Some exhibitors maintain permanent showrooms, but most show only during market week. Buyers from Latin America and the Caribbean account for much of the mart's business.

Trade Shows in the United States

Trade shows, which are held in market centers throughout the year, are sponsored by **trade associations**—professional organizations of manufacturers and sales representatives. A few of these events are major extravaganzas that attract buyers from across the country and even from abroad. Magic International, held twice a year at the Las Vegas Convention Center, has the atmosphere of an apparel mart market week minus the permanent facilities.

The typical US trade show, however, is much smaller than a mart show and lasts two to four days. Regional trade shows are held in hotels and motels, civic centers, and small exhibition halls. Specialized trade shows cover areas of fashion that may otherwise get lost at major market weeks. The Big and Tall Associates (BATA) is part of the Chicago Collective, showing suits and outerwear for big and tall men, for example, and the Surf Expo Florida Show features surf equipment and surf-inspired sportswear.

These small trade shows show every sign of being able to hold their own against the proliferation of marts and market weeks. Trade shows are especially popular with small retailers and exhibitors because they are typically less expensive than market weeks for both groups of participants to attend. Small retailers like to deal with sales reps who are personally familiar with their needs and can cater to them at these smaller exhibits. Buyers from boutiques find that trade shows are their best outlet for the kind of unique and unusual merchandise they seek. Trade shows are known for displaying the work of unusual or small designers who do not ordinarily exhibit at the major marts.

The disadvantage of trade shows is that the exhibitors are limited in number. Buyers have difficulty doing across-the-board buying that is easily accomplished during market weeks at major marts. Trade shows also cannot feature the ongoing service that marts do as they are increasingly open year-round.

Foreign Fashion Markets

For several centuries, the foreign fashion market consisted entirely of French designers' high fashions. In the 1960s, the ready-to-wear market emerged first in Italy and then in France. Today, cultural and economic changes and a renewed interest in nationalism and ethnicity have combined to encourage the development of fashion markets worldwide. US buyers no longer travel exclusively to France and Italy; they journey to fashion markets all over the globe.

Foreign fashion markets are designed to show off the fashion industries around the world. In the leading foreign markets, clothing is typically designed and presented on two different levels. First in prestige and cost are the **haute couture** (pronounced "oat-koo-TUR") clothes (see Figures 10.2a and 10.2b). A French expression originally meaning "fine sewing," haute couture is today synonymous with high fashion. These original designs, which use luxury fabrics and are known for their exquisite detailing, are of necessity expensive and thus are made in very limited numbers. With prices that start in the thousands of dollars for a single garment, haute couture design is affordable to only a small group of wealthy women.

The next layer of fashion design is called **prêt-à-porter**. A French term meaning "ready-to-wear," prêt-à-porter is produced in far larger numbers than haute couture. Like haute couture, it is introduced in foreign fashion markets at semiannual shows where design collections are revealed to the fashion world. Haute couture and designer prêt-à-porter provide the inspiration for the inexpensive mass-market designs that dominate the fashion market.

Figures 10.2a and 10.2b Drama and spectacle on the runway featuring Jean Paul Gaultier's couture creations.

France

France first emerged as a fashion showcase during the reign of Louis XIV (1643–1715), who was often called the Sun King, partly because of his lavish lifestyle. The elaborate clothing worn by his court was widely copied by royalty and the wealthy throughout Europe. The splendor of his court at Versailles created a market for beautiful fabrics, tapestries, and lace. Textile production in Lyons and lace works in Alençon were established to meet these needs. Paris, already an important city and located only a few miles from Versailles, became the fashion capital. Paris is still considered the cradle of the fashion world. New fashion is born there. After it is seen there, it is adopted and adapted by others around the world.

Paris Couture

France has been the center of haute couture since 1858, when the house of Charles Frederick Worth, generally regarded as the father of Parisian couture, opened its doors. Beginning about 1907, Paul Poiret became the second great fashion legend of Paris. Poiret was the first to stage fashion shows and to branch out into the related fields of perfume, accessories, fabric design, and interior decoration.

A **couture house** is an apparel firm for which a designer creates original designs and styles. The proprietor or designer of a couture house is known as a **couturier** if male, or a **couturière** if female. Most Paris couture houses are known by the names of their founders—Yves Saint Laurent, Givenchy, and Chanel, for example. The name may survive even after the original designer's retirement or death, but the signature style changes with his or her successor. In recent years, rapid changes of personnel and licensing of designer names has blurred the identity of the fashion houses and focused attention on individual designers. For example, Virginie Viard designs for Chanel.

In 1868, an elite couture trade association, called the Chambre Syndicale de la Couture Parisienne, came into being. Membership in the Chambre Syndicale (pronounced "shahmbrah seen-dee-KAHL") was by invitation only and was restricted to couture houses that agreed to abide by its strict rules. In 1973, Fédération Française de la Couture, du Prêt-à-Porter des Couturiers et des Createurs de Mode was established. La Fédération is the executive organ of all the trade associations (or Chambre Syndicales) of each fashion division. Haute couture, ready-to-wear, and menswear each have their own Chambre Syndicale. You can look up fashion show schedules and general information on the federation's website at www.modeaparis.com.[5]

Couture Shows The Parisian couture house trade shows are held twice yearly: The spring/summer collections are shown in late January, and the fall/winter ones in late July. These shows have evolved into a promotional outlet for the couturiers. The sales of haute couture clothing have steadily declined in recent years as prices have risen and customers have turned to the designer ready-to-wear lines. To survive, couture houses have expanded into other, more lucrative activities, such as the development of ready-to-wear collections and the establishment of boutiques, and the ever-present (and profitable) licensing arrangements.

Couturiers' Ready-to-Wear Most couturiers' ready-to-wear clothes are sold to department and specialty stores, which often set aside special areas or departments to display these prestigious items.

The exclusivity and cost of producing haute couture lines, in combination with declining craftsmanship skills among designers and atelier staff, have changed the Parisian fashion climate. The ready-to-wear business has completely eclipsed haute couture on the French prestige designer market. Today, many famous fashion houses, like Balenciaga, Chloé, Louis Vuitton, and Yves Saint Laurent, produce only ready-to-wear lines.

Couture Boutiques The French word for "shop," or **boutique**, has come to mean, more specifically, a shop that carries exclusive merchandise. In the past, many couturiers installed boutiques on the first floor or a lower floor of their design houses. Most famous fashion labels also have their own flagship ready-to-wear stores in key cities around the world. Goods sold in these shops are usually designed by the couture house staff and are sometimes even made in the couture workrooms. All bear the famous label.

Licensing Agreements The most lucrative business activities for couturiers are the numerous licensing arrangements they establish to sell their accessories and ready-to-wear lines and also a variety of goods produced by others on their behalf. The most popular prestige licenses include perfume, shoes, handbags, sunglasses, and watches.

French Ready-to-Wear

To meet the needs of ready-to-wear designers, the Chambre Syndicale created an autonomous section for designers who work exclusively in ready-to-wear, designating them **créateurs** to distinguish them from couturiers. Among the créateurs are such important names as Karl Lagerfeld, Sonia Rykiel, Christian Lacroix, and Jean Paul Gaultier.

Although their prestige is great, the couturiers and créateurs represent only a small part of the French fashion industry in terms of numbers and revenue. The remaining 1,200 companies are mass producers of ready-to-wear.

Prêt-à-Porter Trade Shows The French ready-to-wear producers present their collections at two market shows a year. The first, for the fall/winter collections, is held in March, and the second in October, for the spring/summer collections. Actually, two large trade shows take place simultaneously. The runway shows, sponsored by the Chambre Syndicale for the prêt-à-porter designers, take place at Carousel du Louvre. At the other, sponsored by the Fédération, the mass-market prêt-à-porter collections are exhibited at the Porte de Versailles Exhibition Center. This trade show, known as the Prêt-à-Porter Paris, brings together more than 14,000 exhibitors, with 75 percent from outside France. With each succeeding show, the press pays more attention and provides more coverage of this end of the French fashion business.[6]

Italy

Italy is France's most serious rival in the international fashion industry. In certain areas, such as knitwear and accessories, Italian design is considered superior to the French. Italy has long been recognized as a leader in men's apparel, knitwear, leather accessories, and textiles.

A centuries-old tradition of quality craftsmanship and a close relationship between designers and manufacturers are common features of Italy's otherwise disparate fashion houses.

Italian Couture

Italy has long had couture houses named for the famous designers who head them—Valentino and Giorgio Armani. Its designers are members of Italy's couture trade group (a counterpart to the Chambre Syndicale), known as the Camera Nazionale della Moda Italiana. The Camera Moda organizes the biannual ready-to-wear fashion week runway shows that take place in Milan each year in February and September. You can look up schedule and general information at the association's website at www.cameramoda.com.

Unlike French couture houses, however, Italian couture designers are not all located in a single city. Although Milan is the largest fashion center, couture designers may be found in Rome, Florence, and other Italian cities.

Like their Parisian counterparts, many Italian couture houses have set up boutiques for the sale of exclusive accessories and limited lines of apparel. The designs are usually those of the couture house staff, and the apparel and accessories are sometimes made in the couture workrooms. All items offered in boutiques bear the couture house label.

Italian couture designers also have established licensing agreements with foreign producers. Some design and produce uniforms for employees of business firms, most notably airlines and car rental agencies. Some accept commissions to create fashion products ranging from perfume to menswear to home furnishings.

Italian Ready-to-Wear

Italy began to develop both its women's and men's ready-to-wear industries along with its couture fashions. As a result, it started exporting earlier than France, and today its economy relies heavily on its exporting program. The textile, apparel, footwear, and leather goods industries account for approximately one fifth of Italy's **exports**. Much of this exported merchandise is in the medium- to high-price range, especially in knitwear and accessories.

Designers Innovative Italian ready-to-wear designers make their shows as exciting as the Paris ready-to-wear shows have become. Giorgio Armani and Versace are considered the standard-bearers for two very different definitions of Italian design. Versace is noted for brightly colored prints, and Armani for classic elegance combined with comfortable styling. Other well-known Italian ready-to-wear designers are equally protective of their reputations for distinctive, recognizable signature styles. Among the leading designers are Dolce & Gabbana, Gianfranco Ferré, Krizia, Missoni, and Miuccia Prada. Ferragamo and Gucci are major names in shoes and accessories, and Fendi is a major name in fur.

Trade Shows and Market Centers

Until the late 1960s, the most important Italian ready-to-wear shows were staged at the elegant Pitti and Strossi palaces in Florence. Milan grew as a fashion center in the 1970s, and many designers began to show there, in addition to or instead of Florence.

In addition to the ready-to-wear shows, Italy hosts a number of shows featuring the categories of apparel, accessories, and textiles for which Italian designers and manufacturers are internationally renowned. Trade shows are held in the regions where the respective industries are centralized. One of Italy's largest textile trade fairs is the Pitti Immagine Filati, held in Florence. This trade show features the latest in yarns and knit fabrics. Leather shoes, handbags, gloves, and small leather goods are one major segment of Italy's fashion industry. Other accessories that are world famous are knitted hats, scarfs, and gloves and silk scarfs and ties. Italy's fashion industry employs approximately 363,000 people and is reported to account for 1.3 percent of the nation's GDP.[7]

Great Britain

For many years, London's Savile Row was for menswear what Paris has been for women's apparel—the fountainhead of fashion inspiration. Savile Row is a wonderful place where each suit is handcrafted for its new owner.

British Couture

Although Britain has never supported a couture industry the way that France and Italy have, it does offer famous design schools, such as the Royal College of Art, the London College of Fashion, and Central St. Martins. St. Martins alumni include internationally famous names like John Galliano, Alexander McQueen, Hussein Chalayan, Julien MacDonald, Stella McCartney, and Suzanne Clements and Inacio Ribeiro (Clements Ribeiro). In addition to their own lines, these designers have or have had designer posts at leading French fashion houses. Other recent graduates of these schools, both British and foreign, are bringing design back to London. Philip Treacy is a five-time winner of the British Fashion Council's Accessory Designer of the Year award for his striking hats.

British Ready-to-Wear

Ready-to-wear was a minor industry in Britain until after the Second World War. The fact that it entered a period of expansion after the war is largely due to the efforts of the government. According to one English fashion authority, the government became "the fairy godmother" responsible for "the survival of [British] couture and the rapid development of [Britain's] large and excellent ready-to-wear trade."[8]

Vivienne Westwood is a talent who has sparked and shocked the London fashion scene with her unorthodox clothes and lifestyle since the mid-1970s. She continues to be an innovator and leader of the avant-garde pack.

Trade Shows

There was a period in the late 1980s and early 1990s in which the British runway shows and trade shows were dormant. However, today, they are a required stop on the European fashion circuit. British and foreign designers are showing, and British and foreign audiences are looking.

Other European Countries

For leadership in Europe, the fashion industry definitely focuses on France, Italy, and Britain. Other countries do attract international interest, however. In the 1990s and the 2000s, the Belgian town Antwerp became somewhat of a high-fashion mecca. Antwerp natives, like Dries Van Noten, Ann Demeulemeester, Martin Margiela, Veronique Branquinho, A.F. Vandevorst, and Raf Simons, have achieved great success with their innovative and creative clothes. Although all these designers show and have their business headquarters in Paris, some of them still live in Antwerp. Other European countries that have a presence on the global fashion market are Ireland, with its traditional garments and fine linen, and Spain, with its swimwear, lingerie, and bridal fashion trade shows.

Germany and Scandinavia

Until the mid-1980s, most US fashion buyers skipped Germany on their European buying trips. The country was still divided into East and West, and few West German designers were well known outside Europe. But a new wave of high-fashion women's designers is changing this. Two apparel firms, Escada and Mondi, are noteworthy successes with their high-fashion lines. Designers Hugo Boss and Wolfgang Joop have also developed international followings.

Although Germany's fashion industry is relatively small, its international trade fairs have become a major source of fashion inspiration for new fabric and designs (see Figure 10.3). The Igedo produces the CPD womenswear and menswear fashion shows twice a year in Düsseldorf. Interestingly, this company has exported the fashion trade show through joint ventures with exhibition producers in Hong Kong, London, and Beijing. For textiles, the major international show is Heimtextil in Frankfurt.

Each of the four Scandinavian countries—Norway, Sweden, Denmark, and Finland—has its own fashion industries and specialties. However, even though each country has its roster of designers, the styles tend to be alike, with emphasis on simple silhouettes and sturdy materials like wool, leather, and linen.

Leather apparel, primarily in menswear, is a popular Swedish product. Both Sweden and Norway are among the important suppliers of mink and other furs to countries around the world. Birger Christensen and Saga are leading furriers.

Scandinavia also offers some interesting textile designs. The best known, internationally, are the work of Finland's Marimekko.

Excellent jewelry in all price ranges is available in Scandinavia. The area has long been known for its clean-cut designs in gold and silver. Some well-known Swedish-born, contemporary designers include expatriates Lars Nilsson and Richard Bengtsson.

Figure 10.3 Visitors talk at a brand stand at the Premium trade show in Berlin, Germany.

Canada

The development of a group of new and innovative designers has given the Canadian fashion industry a growing sense of confidence that has paid off in real growth. The fashion industry is the fifth-largest employer in Canada and gets larger every year. It has two important centers: The largest is Montreal in Quebec, and the second is Toronto in Ontario. Especially the Montreal fashion scene is gaining more international notoriety for its creativity and independence.

Most Canadian apparel manufacturing is located in Montreal, but every province has a stake in the industry, and shows in each province bring local goods to the attention of other Canadians and buyers from the United States and around the world. Montreal and Toronto each have their own fashion week twice a year, where local men's and womenswear designers showcase their new collections in runway shows. Other women's apparel and accessories shows include METRO in Vancouver, TRENDS Apparel Show in Edmonton, and Toronto's Mode Accessories show. Childrenswear markets take place in Vancouver and Alberta. Alberta, Montreal, Vancouver, and Toronto all host gift shows.

The Americas and the Caribbean Basin

By the mid-1970s, the Central and South American market could be added to the growing list of international fashion markets. The fashion world began visiting market centers in Bogotá (Colombia), Buenos Aires (Argentina), Rio de Janeiro (Brazil), and São Paulo (Brazil).

For buyers and producers from the United States and Canada, the signing of the **North American Free Trade Agreement** (NAFTA) in 1994 brought new possibilities in the Mexican market. Replaced in 2019 by the **United States-Mexico-Canada Agreement** (USMCA), this trade arrangement supports balanced reciprocal trade between the three North American countries. Central and South America and the Caribbean countries began to press for inclusion in this trading pact.

From the perspective of Mexico and the Central and South American governments, the fashion industry has come to be seen as a means of increasing their gross national product and their status in the world marketplace. Mexico ranks third in terms of imports to the United States.[9]

The combination of Central America and the West Indies have also suffered from the economic downturn, but the Dominican Republic and Honduras remain as major suppliers in the apparel and textile industries.[10]

Fashion Products

The fashion industry in the Americas and the Caribbean Basin offers fashion on three levels. First, several countries have developed their own high-fashion, or couture, industries, many of which are ripe for **import** to the United States and Europe. The second level revolves around the development of fashion products that reflect each country's national heritage of crafts. With a renewed interest in ethnicity throughout the world, such products are welcome. Lastly, Central America, South America, Mexico, and the West Indies are important "offshore" sources of products made to North American manufacturers' specifications.

Trade Shows in the Americas and the Caribbean Basin

The single most important market center in South America is São Paulo, Brazil. At the turn of the millennium, the emergence of designer talents like Alexandre Herchcovitch, Rosa Chá, and Icarius de Menezes coincided with a major Brazilian boom in fashion in general. When superstar models like Gisele Bündchen appeared in these designers' shows, it attracted enough attention to put São Paulo fashion week on the map. Since then, São Paulo fashion week has been steadily growing in importance, and it may become one of the most attended and publicized fashion events in the world. Other important international fairs featuring textiles and textile products as well as fashion accessories are held in Bogotá, Colombia; Lima, Peru; San Salvador, El Salvador; and Santiago, Chile.

These shows offer not only an opportunity for buyers from North America and elsewhere but also a place for US textile producers to be seen by potential customers in the region.

Asia and Oceania

The United States imports more apparel from Asia than from any other area in the world. The major portion of these imports has been low-priced, high-volume merchandise, but hardly any of the apparel had qualified as "designer merchandise" in the past. However, this is changing with innovative styles offered by design-oriented Asian stylists. Buyers have used certain countries in Asia as a market in which to have fashions they saw in the European fashion centers copied and adapted. A fashion buyer needs to know which areas in Asia are best equipped to handle specific types of manufacturing. Japan and Hong Kong were once the two major contract or copyist countries. But Japan has upgraded its fashion image so that today it is a producer of outstanding high-styled, high-priced fashion apparel. Hong Kong is working to develop the apparel industry of China and promoting Chinese goods in its international trade fairs. In addition, recent patterns show that Vietnam and India may take over as leaders if costs get higher in China.

Oceania, which is made up of Australia and New Zealand, is connected to Asia economically. These markets are small in the industry and produce only a few apparel lines for export. However, Australia remains the world's top producer of wool fiber and fabric.[11]

Japan

Japan, long known for its export of silks and pearls, has moved most apparel production out of Japan, to lower-cost countries like Thailand, China, and the Philippines. Many Japanese designer boutiques in Tokyo—Japan's fashion center—have their own design staffs who create exciting new looks. Because of their ability to produce fashion goods quickly, the Tokyo fashion scene is often six months to one year ahead of other fashion centers.

Japanese Ready-to-Wear In the 1970s, as Western dress had finally won acceptance in Japan, a group of highly original Japanese designers—Hanae Mori, Kenzō Takada, Issey Miyake, and Kansai Yamamoto—emerged. They first worked in Paris, where their lines were design sensations that rivaled the French prêt-à-porter designers. For over a decade, in fact, these daring designers were thought of as French rather than Japanese. Some of them still show in Paris.

Japanese Designers In the early 1980s, a mostly new wave of avant-garde designers—Rei Kawakubo of Comme des Garçons, Yohji Yamamoto, and Mitsuhiro Matsuda—stormed the US fashion scene (see Figure 10.4).

Figure 10.4 Models display creations of Japanese designers Hiroyuki Horihata and Makiko Sekiguchi during the matohu 2015 spring/summer collection at Tokyo Fashion Week.

In the 1990s, the latest generation of Japanese designers, catering to a domestic market, have, like their British contemporaries, focused on retro pop-cultural influences such as hippie beads and T-shirts and 1970s punk.

More recently, Japanese designers like Hiroyuki Horihata and Makiko Sekiguchi, Takeshi Osumi, and Yoshio Kubo have come on to the scene with ingenious designs that incorporate over the top themes, gimmicks, and an eclectic mix of styles.[12]

China

In 2000, the United States entered a trade agreement with China that gave China normal trader status. This paved the way for the country's entry into the WTO (World Trade Organization). Since then, China's growth in the apparel industry has been clear—today the United States imports more goods from China than from any other country in the world.

Among the products that China exports, one of the most sought after is silk. Although it is the world's largest silk producer, China is just beginning to acquire the modern technology needed for quality weaving, printing, and dyeing. As the Chinese have been more proficient in these finishing processes, they have exported more finished silk fabrics and apparel products. Cotton and polyester production, once big exports, now barely meet China's domestic needs. Inexpensive plastic shoes are another major export. Leather and fur are also important exports. Several trade shows in Beijing and Shanghai have been instituted by Western-owned exhibition producers to promote Chinese leather to the international market.

Hong Kong In July 1997, Hong Kong rejoined mainland China after 156 years as a British Crown colony. The world held its collective breath, waiting to see what would become of this quintessentially market-driven world trading center when it came under Communist rule. The agreement between Britain and China calls for the governing of Hong Kong as a special administrative region for fifty years, and local businesses are reassuring their international customers that Hong Kong will continue to offer all the advantages they have enjoyed, plus more. In addition to the political change, Hong Kong has experienced a move in its economy from manufacturing to trade and service industries.

The Hong Kong Trade Development Council sponsors an international fashion week semiannually as well as several smaller shows. UBM Asia, a trade show producer based in Hong Kong, produces the All China Leather Exhibition in Shanghai and the APLF-Materials Manufacturing and Technology Fair in Hong Kong—the premier events of their kind—and the Cosmoprof Asia beauty fair.

India

India's centuries-old textile industry continues to make it a major force in the Asian textile market, and recently the industry has seen its potential to surpass China as a leader in the industry. India also has its own rapidly expanding fashion industry, with a variety of homegrown designers. Most set up their businesses at the end of the 1990s in response to India's growing upper class and its appetite for global styles. Mumbai has had its own Lakmé India Fashion Week since 1999, which draws tremendous attention and is produced by IMG—the same event-marketing conglomerate that runs the Mercedes-Benz Fashion Week. Manish Arora, Rohit Bal, Ritu Beri, Naeem Kahn, and Raghavendra Rathore are among the more well-known designers from India.

India is also the home of the largest handloom industry in the world, and cotton and silk are the strongest growth areas of the Indian textile industry. In 2018, India was the world's largest organic cotton producer,[13] ranking top in overall cotton production, along with China and the United States.[14] It is the only country in the world that produces all four silk varieties: mulberry, tussah, eriand, and muga. Its textile industry alone employs more than 40 million workers .[15]

The India Trade Promotion Organization (ITPO) conducts promotions and fashion events with major retailers and assists US and European designers in developing sourcing contacts in India.

Other Asian Countries

Indonesia, Thailand, Malaysia, Sri Lanka, Vietnam, and the Philippines are regarded by many Americans in the apparel industry as sites of offshore production, but that is only part of the story. As these developing countries become more industrialized and the standard of living improves, their own industries and markets are taking their place in the global economy. Thailand, for example, has for many years been a producer of fine printed

CAROLINE BARTEK
Creative Director for Cintas Uniforms

Caroline Bartek.

AS A CREATIVE DIRECTOR IN IMAGE APPAREL DESIGN AT CINTAS, CAROLINE BARTEK WORKS WITH THE WORLD'S LARGEST, MOST RECOGNIZABLE BRANDS TO BRING THEIR BRAND VISION TO LIFE THROUGH THE UNIFORMS OF THEIR EMPLOYEES. This is an industry focused on visible, functionally designed apparel that works as hard as the employees do. Whether it is a flight attendant, nurse, housekeeper, package delivery driver, or chef, everyone needs an identifiable, durable uniform. That is where every day begins for Bartek, with the question, "How do I design a uniform program of garments for my clients that are consistently branded, comfortable, durable and instill company pride and brand recognition?"

As creative director, Bartek establishes the product strategy and development for all apparel design projects for her clients, and she oversees the quality of creative work. She describes her role as sales-oriented with a strong emphasis on presentation skills. Organization, problem solving, working in teams, and verbal and written communication skills are imperative, as a creative director works cross-functionally. The ability to work as a team is a critical part of the apparel industry, integrating and coordinating the efforts of design, technical design, product development, global supply chain, merchandising, marketing, visual merchandising, and sales.

Bartek graduated from Dominican University in Chicago in 2003 with two Bachelors of Arts degrees, one in fashion design and one in fashion merchandising. The design courses allowed Bartek to develop her visual talents through various art forms, while the merchandising courses fostered analytical thinking. In 2015, she completed a Master of Fine Arts degree in fashion merchandising at the Academy of Art University, San Francisco. She attributes education as a critical part of her preparedness as a creative director, equipping her with the ability to oversee the entire creative process, from presale presentations of design concepts through the complete product development process. Her academic training allowed her to develop a "holistic vision" for her clients, and without those educational opportunities, she insists that she would not be where she is today.

Bartek started with Cintas as an assistant designer after she graduated from Dominican, and she moved up through the ranks. She eventually became the company's youngest creative director at the age of twenty-nine. Bartek attributes this achievement to hard work and having the ability to see the big picture and all of its moving parts. She found a niche segment of the apparel business and strived to become a subject-matter expert. She asked questions, listened to and learned from peers, developed relationships, and made friends across all aspects of the business.

A typical workday? No two are ever alike, according to Bartek. She keeps a daily to-do list and regularly checks email to keep up on the latest information regarding ongoing projects. The day often requires conference calls, meetings, and project tasks, such as sketches, illustrations, and merchandise lists. When on the road, the day begins with presentation preparations, steaming presentation samples, preparing presentation materials, and rehearsing the presentation. Every day is filled with wearing many hats, problem solving and meeting deadlines with a keen sense of urgency.

Bartek's advice to students who are interested in a career in the apparel industry: "It's all about attitude. Companies hire the right culture fit, the right personality, because the skills can be taught and talent can be cultivated. Be prepared to learn something new every day and plan on working your way up. As you progress and learn, there are opportunities for you to move up. Hard work and perseverance will pay off in the end.

"Seek mentors and advocates. Craft your own path to success and be grateful for opportunities. Job shadow, volunteer, intern, research and read about companies that interest you.

"The fashion industry has many facets. Keep an open mind. I never knew when I was growing up that there were designers of uniforms. But I was born to do what I do every single day at Cintas. We help get the world's workforce get ready for their workday."

---

silk and cotton. As discussed earlier, Vietnam has also increased its production capabilities, and as of 2018 ranked eighth in textile exports and fourth and clothing exports globally.[16]

Singapore has many of the advantages of Hong Kong—an easily accessible location, a multinational population, and expertise in international trade. It is Hong Kong's chief rival as a center for trade shows.

Korea, with a design history similar to Japan's, has some exciting young designers creating for the Korean fashion-conscious market. Much of the production of ready-to-wear in Korea is still contract work. But because of the fashion design movement among young Koreans, this is beginning to change.

Oceania

Australia is not a large producer in the textile and apparel industries, but it is known for wool. In 2012, Australia produced more than 360,000 metric tons of wool, most of which is exported to China.[17] Australia is also credited with the origin of UGG boots, which became a major trend in the United States in the 2000s.

New Zealand is similar to Australia in that it imports more than it exports. Their retail market operates approximately a season behind Europe and the United States. Due to this, local importers are able to purchase end-of-season surplus goods and sell them at the start of the season in New Zealand.[18]

Importing by Retailers

The fashion industry is very much a part of the global economy, so much so that those who work in the business invented a term to describe the process of shopping for and purchasing imported goods: **global sourcing**. When a firm in a country, such as the United States, buys foreign goods, it imports them. The country that furnishes the goods, such as Italy, exports them. Most countries are both importers and exporters, although, as we shall see, they do not necessarily do each activity in equal amounts.

Retailers are the primary importers of foreign goods in the fashion industry, although manufacturers also seek global sourcing. Retailers like imports for several reasons: their uniqueness, cost, and the variety they add to their stock. They constantly seek merchandise that will make their stores stand out in special and unique ways that will set them apart from the competition. Foreign merchandise often fits that bill.

Anyone who intends to buy goods from a foreign country needs to have a thorough knowledge of its local laws and regulations, particularly the laws that regulate exporting and importing, the efficiency of the transportation system, and the availability and skill of the labor force. The buyer must be well versed on the tax system and exchange rates. He or she must understand local and national customs and must be well informed about the current political and economic climate. Finally, the buyer must be up-to-date on US import-export regulations, including any pending legislation, and must know all this for any country in which he or she intends to do business. This is why importing is best done by someone with access to good suppliers and extensive experience in dealing with foreign manufacturers and import regulations.

To gain entry to foreign fashion markets, as well as to cover them extensively, US buyers rely on the help and experience of intermediaries. These specialists help US buyers shop in the international markets successfully. Foreign-made goods can be purchased at and by the following:

- Foreign fashion markets
- Store-owned foreign buying offices
- **Commissionaires** or independent agents
- Import fairs held in the United States
- Importers

American Buyers' Visits to International Fashion Markets

Buyers like and need to travel to foreign fashion markets so they can observe new trends firsthand and buy goods suited to their customers. By personally shopping in international markets, often during market weeks, US buyers can be sure they are obtaining goods that will sell at home. They are also able to soak up the cultural and social climates of the countries to which they travel, which, in turn, helps them translate what is new and exciting to their customers.

Store-Owned Foreign Buying Offices

Some stores—those that are large enough to do so or whose image is very special—maintain company-owned foreign buying offices. Buyers who work in these offices support and advise store buyers by surveying the market for new trends, supervising purchases, and following up on deliveries. Because they are an extension of the store, buyers in foreign buying offices are often authorized to make purchases just as store buyers are when they shop in foreign and domestic markets.

If the purchase is part of a new trend, stores need the goods when they are still new and customers are still eager to buy them. If it is part of a foreign theme promotion, goods must be delivered while the promotion is in progress. Delivery—especially timely delivery—has been a major problem with imported goods.

Stores generally locate their buying offices in major fashion capitals such as Paris, Milan, London, Hong Kong, Beijing, and Tokyo, from which their buyers can travel to smaller markets around the world. Saks Fifth Avenue, Neiman Marcus, and Macy's all maintain store-owned foreign buying offices, as do the large general-merchandise chains such as Sears, JCPenney, and Walmart.

Foreign Commissionaires or Agents

In contrast to store-owned foreign buying offices are commissionaires, or foreign-owned independent agents. Commissionaires, whose offices are also located in key buying cities, tend to be smaller than store-owned offices. Commissionaires also represent both retailers and manufacturers.

Apart from these differences, however, they provide many of the same services as store-owned foreign buying offices. They often have specialized buyers, or market representatives, who work closely with clients, keeping them abreast of what is generally available and helping them locate specific goods. As is the case with store-owned buying offices, a substantial part of the staff's time is spent following up on purchases to make sure they are delivered when they are needed.

Unlike store buyers, who are authorized to purchase on the store's behalf, commissionaires do not purchase unless they have been authorized to do so. Commissionaires are paid on a fee basis. Usually, they take a percentage of the **first cost**, or wholesale price, in the country of origin.

Foreign Import Fairs in the United States

Another way to buy foreign goods is to attend one or more of the foreign import fairs that are now regularly held in the United States. Many foreign countries participate in such shows or stage their own fashion fairs in the United States. The New York Prêt, a semiannual event in New York City, is one of the largest and most prestigious of these US-based shows.

These foreign import fairs increase the size and depth of the import market by giving buyers of small- and intermediate-size stores who would not ordinarily tap into the foreign market a chance to do so. To provide their customers with imported merchandise, these buyers need not maintain foreign representatives or shop in the foreign markets, neither of which would be cost-effective for their operations.

Importing by US Businesses

Last but hardly least in a market that relies increasingly on foreign goods is US buyers' purchase from US-owned importing firms. Import firms shop in the international markets to purchase their own "lines," which they put together and display to retailers. US manufacturers, initially upset about the growth of direct importing done by retailers, have increasingly turned to offshore sources for the same reasons that retailers do: price advantage, exclusivity, and workmanship. Like retailers, they often cite high domestic labor costs as a primary reason for resorting to imports. But labor costs must be viewed in light of the other considerations if a manufacturer is to maintain control of its brands' images. For example, a sportswear manufacturer may combine fine-quality knitwear produced overseas with domestically produced skirts or pants to create a line of separates.

Product Development: Specification and Private-Label Buying

In addition to importing unique or distinctive goods, many retail operations use product development to set their assortment apart from those of their competitors. They may rely on domestic manufacturers or foreign sources for specification and private-label buying.

These two terms may be used to describe the same items of merchandise, but the meanings are slightly different. If the retailer agrees, the manufacturer may design private-label merchandise for the retailer. On the other hand, specification buying is a type of purchasing that is done to the store's rather than the manufacturer's standards. Retailers provide the standards and guidelines for the manufacture of clothes they order (see Figure 10.5).

Figure 10.5 Workers check manufactured apparel for quality assurance.

International Trading Laws

In the global economy, trade is truly international, not merely a set of bilateral agreements between pairs of nations. (A bilateral agreement is one in which two countries reach their own separate agreement.) The trade relationship between any two nations affects the relationship of each party with its other trading partners as well. International trade laws have therefore developed out of need.

Counterfeit, Black Market, and Gray Market Goods

Three illegal practices that plague both importers and exporters are the importing of counterfeit, black market, and gray market goods. Counterfeit goods, like counterfeit currency, are inferior imitations passed off as the genuine article. Luxury goods and designer brands are the chief objects of counterfeiters. The sale of counterfeit goods at "bargain" prices devalues the real brand and deprives legitimate businesses of their fairly earned profits. US Customs officials are authorized to seize imported counterfeit goods.

Another problem for manufacturers is **bootleg goods**. Many of these goods are not cheap rip-offs; rather, they cannot be distinguished from the real ones. They are being made by the same manufacturers that make the real ones, but who are selling some goods to the black market.

Gray market goods are those that were not intended for sale in the country in which they are being sold; for example, an expensive Swiss watch is sold at a remarkably low price in the United States, but it does not have a warranty valid in the United States. The unfortunate customer usually does not realize this until repairs are needed.

The North American Free Trade Agreement (NAFTA) renegotiated into the United States-Mexico-Canada Agreement (USMCA) and Dominican Republic-Central American Free Trade Agreement (CAFTA-DR)

The North American Free Trade Agreement (NAFTA) went into effect in January 1994, eliminating quotas and tariffs for goods shipped among the United States and Canada and Mexico. In November 2018, this agreement was renegotiated and renamed the United States-Mexico-Canada Agreement (USMCA), promising to strengthen existing North American trade practices and supply chains. For the textiles and apparel sectors, this enhanced agreement means to open up new opportunities for exports of U.S. yarns, fabrics, and apparel. The enhanced benefits of this agreement to the U.S. economy remain to be seen, however, once fully enacted, this agreement proposes to balance trade in a way that supports high-paying jobs for American workers, while growing the North American economies.[19] Free-trade agreements between China, Canada, and Mexico complicate issues further.

The **Dominican Republic-Central American Free Trade Agreement** (CAFTA-DR), which was passed in July 2005, eliminated most trade barriers between the United States and Costa Rica, the Dominican Republic, El Salvador, Guatemala, Honduras, and Nicaragua. Combined, the countries in the CAFTA-DR represent the 18th largest trading partner to the U.S.[20] In 2005, quotas were fully lifted on all apparel and textile imports for the countries in the WTO.[21]

Penetration of the US Market by Foreign Investors

Direct investment in US properties and businesses is extremely attractive to foreigners. Since so many textile and apparel items are imported into the United States, foreign investors have long been interested in buying into US textile and apparel manufacturing companies. Only recently have they succeeded in doing so. Foreign investors, mostly from Europe and Asia, have taken three routes to ownership: joint ventures, total ownership, and licensing.

For example, L'Oréal of France purchased three important US cosmetic labels: Maybelline, Redken, and Helena Rubinstein. While the purchasing of manufacturers is a relatively new form of foreign investment, many retail operations have been foreign owned for some time, and there is even more activity in this sector than in manufacturing. Other foreign retailing successes are Laura Ashley, which is British owned;

United Colors of Benetton, which is Italian owned; Zara, which is Spanish owned; and H&M, which is Swedish.

New York's Madison Avenue, Chicago's Michigan Avenue, and Los Angeles's Rodeo Drive are lined with the boutiques of Italian designers such as Valentino, Armani, Ungaro, Dolce & Gabbana, Missoni, and Prada. Their presence in the United States is just a part of their global retailing strategy.

Licensing

Actually, investment by foreign manufacturers in the fashion industry is not entirely new. Licensing arrangements, which often involve ownership of domestic companies, were initiated more than twenty-five years ago by companies such as Christian Dior, Pierre Cardin, and Hubert de Givenchy. Today, the European presence is widespread. For example, Donna Karan's and Marc Jacobs's collections are financed by the French LVMH Moët Hennessy-Louis Vuitton family.

Penetration of Foreign Markets by US Companies

To counterbalance foreign investment, US businesses have been interested in investing in foreign countries, where US management is often welcomed because US know-how and standards for high quality are much-respected commodities. US investment in foreign countries also helps the balance of trade.

Licensing

Just as foreign manufacturers first penetrated the US retail market with licensed products, so too have US companies been able to license products abroad. Character licenses such as Mickey Mouse, Superman, and Dora the Explorer have been great successes abroad, as have sports licenses and brand names, such as Nike, and designer names, such as Calvin Klein, Donna Karan, and Ralph Lauren.

Many companies are now switching from licensing to importing strategies to establish and strengthen brand identity. As international distribution continues to develop, US manufacturers are finding that a mix of locally licensed products and US–manufactured apparel is the most effective way to sell locally.

Joint Ownership

While the United States permits total ownership by foreign investors, most other countries only allow foreign investors to be partners or joint owners. Among the US companies that are joint owners in foreign manufacturing firms is Blue Bell, producer of Wrangler jeans in Asia, Italy, and Spain.

US Exporting

Because the "Made in the U.S.A." label is desirable all over the world, the United States can export its fashion products around the globe. Increased US exports, in fact, are seen by many industry experts as the solution to the US trade deficit. The United States does not need to keep out foreign competitors as much as it needs to sell and promote its products abroad.

By the mid-1990s, US fashion producers had begun to see exporting as a solution to another challenge as well. With the domestic market saturated with their goods, they turned to other countries as a source of growth. The US industry's reputation for quality and trendsetting styles continues to grow. US exports of textiles and apparel in 2018 reached $30.1 billion, including $6.7 billion in cotton, wool, and fine animal hair, $4.4 billion in yarns, $9.1 billion in fabrics, $3.8 billion in home furnishings and carpeting, and $6.1 billion in apparel.[22]

Although US designer fashions are available in upscale department stores around the globe, a common strategy is to establish a presence in a new foreign market with a freestanding "signature store," or boutique. The ability to monitor consumer reaction to the designer's merchandise allows for rapid adjustment to local tastes and preferences, just as is true at home. In 1998, the late Bud Kohnheim, predicted that "by the end of the century, the term 'going global' will have lost its meaning. Foreign sales will just be another part of every firm's account list."[23] He was right!

THE UNITED NATIONS: Putting the Brakes on Fast Fashion #SolveDifferent

Fashion as an industry survives on following the latest trends, but to a growing number of consumers, the only trend that really matters is that consumption patterns are altered to ensure the survival of the planet.

In March 2019, the United Nations launched the UN Alliance on Sustainable Fashion to encourage the private sector, governments, and non-governmental organizations to create an industry-wide push to reduce the fashion industry's negative social, economic, and environmental impact, and help the industry to turn itself into the driver for the implementation of its own goals and initiatives for improvement.

Here are a few fashion facts that prompted the United Nations to look at clothing production and consumption from a global perspective:

- The clothing and textile industry contributes $2.4 billion to global manufacturing.
- It employs 75 million people worldwide, mostly women.
- It is responsible for 8–10 percent of the world's greenhouse gas emissions and originates up to 20 percent of industrial wastewater

pollution. This is more than all international flights and maritime shipping generates!

- It takes about 2,000 gallons of water to make a single pair of jeans.
- Textile dyeing is the second largest water pollutant globally.
- Washing clothes releases half a million tons of microfibers into the ocean annually.
- Provides consumers with so much fashion product that $500 billion of value is lost every year due to clothing underutilization and lack of recycling.
- From 2000 to 2014, clothing production doubled, with the average consumer purchasing up to 60 percent more garments during this same period.

Here are some companies who have taken up the challenge and found ways to be innovative, creative, and sustainable in their fashion development and design efforts:

- Founded by Javier Goyeneche in 2012, Ecoalf collects ocean plastics from 33 ports and turns the trash into shoes, clothing, and bags.

Model wears a jacket by Ecoalf—fabric for shoes, clothing, and bags created from recycled ocean plastics.

- Amsterdam company, GumDrop, estimates that 3.3 million pounds of gum ends up on Amsterdam's paths each year. So, they have developed a new kind of rubber, called Gum-tec. In collaboration with I Amsterdam marketing group, and Explicit fashion company, this recycled rubber is used to make shoes! It takes about 2.2 pounds of gum to make four pairs of sneakers!

Nudi Jeans store in Germany, offering free repair, to help extend the life, and use, of jeans.

- Tonle, a fashion company in Cambodia, uses surplus fabric from mass clothing manufacturers to create zero-waste fashion collections. The company reports using 97 percent in the clothing, and anything left over is made into paper.
- Based in the Netherlands, designers Yoni van Oorsouw and Manon van Hoeckel scour thrift stores and donation sorting facilities for blankets and curtains to remake into coats and jackets.

- Indosole, a company based in San Francisco and Bali, turns discarded tires into shoes, sandals, and flip-flops.
- Swiss firm, Freitag, upcycles tarps, seat belts, and bicycle innertubes to make bags and backpacks.
- Patagonia, Novel Supply, Mud Jeans, Nudie Jeans, and others have developed "turn back" programs, allowing customers to receive discounts or free merchandise for turning in old clothes for new ones.

- New York-based Queen of Raw connects designers with dead stock from factories, brands, and retailers, helping find use to more than $120 billion worth of unused fabric sitting in warehouses, waiting to be burned or buried.

The United Nations invites interested consumers to join the debate and discussion on social media using #SolveDifferent to share stories and see what others are doing to a ensure sustainable future for the planet.

Trends in Global Fashion Sourcing and Merchandising

The fashion industry survives through change. International fashion markets are working furiously to remain viable in a highly competitive global market. Fashion is increasingly becoming a global business. At the present moment, there are international fashion weeks in Australia, Brazil, New Zealand, Canada, India, Colombia, Mexico, Iceland, Hong Kong, Thailand, Japan, China, and South Africa.

The expense of attending markets and trade shows has had an impact on buyers and exhibitors at home and abroad. Economic globalization has made fashion capitals like Paris, Milan, and New York showplaces for designers from all over the world, not just from the home country. Retail buying trips to the national and international market centers have become the province of senior staff, who must make decisions for more departments or store units. Designers and other vendors carefully weigh the costs and benefits of several less elaborate exhibitions against fewer more lavish ones.

Another aspect of globalization is that developing countries are now becoming major players in the fashion industries, primarily as sources of materials and production, but also as importers and exporters of finished goods.

The increased worldwide use of computers and the Internet for buying, especially the basics, has had a great impact. Social media also provides buyers, press, and consumers with instant information. Some argue that all this product information has made the consumer's attention span for trends shorter. Photos of collections are now available so quickly that the clothes look old by the time they hit the stores.

Summary and Review

A market is a meeting place of buyers and sellers. Retail buyers of fashion goods go to market several times a year during market weeks, at the market centers of New York, Los Angeles, and Miami, and regional marts in other cities, including Atlanta, Chicago, Dallas, and Denver. With the exception of New York, where an entire district serves as a marketplace, markets are located in large convention centers with exhibition halls called marts. In addition to visiting the manufacturers' sales representatives in their showrooms or multiline sales representatives in temporary exhibition spaces, the buyers may attend trade shows and seminars sponsored by trade organizations.

In Europe, market weeks are semiannual. Designers' haute couture (custom designs) and ready-to-wear collections are shown in the market centers of Paris, Milan, and London. Numerous trade shows for apparel, accessories, and textiles are presented in other cities.

In Canada, market weeks and trade shows take place more frequently. Quebec is the province with the largest fashion industry, but all the provinces have apparel manufacturers, and market weeks and trade shows are held in major cities across the country.

The Americas and the Caribbean Basin are developing as centers for the production of wool and wool products, leather goods, and costume jewelry. Australia is also a big supplier of wool.

Japan's fashion designers and producers operate on an international scale, with showings, boutiques, and manufacturing facilities at home and abroad. The largest international market for fashion goods is in Asia, with increasing production development in India and Vietnam. Apparel businesses in these areas are using their manufacturing and marketing expertise to develop the silk, leather, and fur industries on the Chinese mainland. Singapore is also emerging as an important market center. The fashion industry is truly operating in a global economy.

Through imports, offshore production, and exports, the US textile and apparel industry is a major player in the global economy. Importing is a major source of merchandise for retailers, who rely on visits to foreign markets, store-owned foreign buying offices, commissionaires, import fairs, and US import firms. Apparel manufacturers are also purchasers of foreign products, especially fabrics and other materials and trimmings. Retailers may develop products bearing their private label by having their designs produced by foreign manufacturers.

US apparel manufacturers have turned to offshore sources for all or part of the production of their goods. To improve the unfavorable balance of trade that has resulted from this extensive import activity, the government has imposed quotas and tariffs on selected goods from countries whose products have a competitive advantage. The United States participates in multinational agreements such as those of the World Trade Organization and in separate trade agreements with individual countries or groups of countries.

US and foreign businesses mutually penetrate one another's markets through licensing arrangements, investments in manufacturing, and establishment of retail outlets. Export of US–made fashion goods is a growing aspect of the country's role in the global economy.

FOR REVIEW

1. What criteria must be met for an area to be considered a market center?
2. What support services for buyers are offered by the marts during and between market weeks?
3. What distinguishes New York City as the major fashion market center in the United States?
4. Describe the distinctive characteristics of the three regional market centers.
5. What business activities have the Paris couture houses undertaken to offset the decline in sales of haute couture clothing?
6. Name the fashion products for which Italy and Britain, respectively, are considered leaders.
7. What advantages do imports give retailers?
8. Name the five ways foreign-made fashion merchandise can be purchased.
9. What are the two important functions of foreign import shows in the United States?
10. What are the concerns that arise when retailers do specification buying of private-label merchandise?
11. What forms do US investing in foreign countries' fashion industries take?

FOR DISCUSSION

1. Discuss the importance of Asia to producers and retailers of fashion goods. What are some current emerging global markets?
2. The reputation of Paris as a prime source of fashion inspiration began to develop several centuries ago as the result of many interrelating factors. Identify those factors and discuss their importance in the development of any major fashion design center.
3. As a fashion consumer, do you advocate protectionism or free trade? What major items of your current wardrobe would you have been unable to purchase if broad protective legislation prohibiting imports had been in place?
4. What are the advantages of using a store-owned foreign buying office? A commissionaire?

Trade Talk

Define or briefly explain the following terms:

bootleg goods

boutique

buyer's directory

commissionaire

couture house

couturier/couturière

créateurs

Dominican Republic-Central American Free Trade Agreement (CAFTA-DR)

export

first cost

global sourcing

gray market goods

haute couture

import

market

market center

market week

mart

North American Free Trade Agreement (NAFTA)

prêt-à-porter

sales representatives

trade associations

trade shows

United States-Mexico-Canada Agreement (USMCA)

11

Fashion Retailing

Key Concepts

- History and development of fashion retailing in the United States

- Discussion of e-commerce and retail merchandising in the digital world

- Organization of department, specialty, and discount stores

- Discussion of sole proprietorships, chains, leased departments, and franchises

- Operation of off-price retailers, factory outlets, category killers, and boutiques/showcase stores

- Operation of nonstore retailers, including direct sellers, catalog retailers, TV home shopping, and Internet shopping sites

- Social media in retail promotion

- Trends in retail patterns (multichannel/omni-channel)

History and Development of Fashion Retailing

Since the earliest days of civilization, people have swapped, traded, and sold goods with each other. Trade centers evolved, primarily out of convenience—such as bazaars, markets, and fairs—where buyers or customers could come to a single location to compare and shop for a wide variety of needed and desired goods. In the Orient and eastern Mediterranean, bazaars and marketplaces still operate on the sites they have occupied for centuries. Not until the mid-1800s and the opening of the first department store—Bon Marche in Paris—did modern merchandising as we know it begin to develop. Even then, it developed differently in the United States from the way it did in Europe. In this chapter, we will explore the development of retailing in the United States.

Retailing is the business of buying and selling goods to those who will use them: the ultimate consumer. Fashion retailing involves the business of buying and selling—or merchandising—apparel, accessories, and home fashions. It is the way fashion products are moved from the designer or manufacturer to the customer.

Retailing is a vital industry in the United Stated today, and in many ways the heart of the fashion industry. It is the most challenging part of the fashion business, existing as it does in a constant state of change. Retailers must, for example, be among the first to spot and act on new trends. They must be attuned to their customers' needs and desires to a degree that is required in few other businesses. Retailers must react to a constantly changing and often unsettling economic climate.

The way customers consume retail merchandise is changing too. While consumers still gather around a marketplace to see and compare and buy, the digital or electronic marketplace is becoming a more and more important part of that marketplace. The first secure online purchase occurred November 8, 1994, a CD of Sting's *The Summoner's Tale* for $12.49, plus shipping.[1] This simple and rather unremarkable transaction ushered in what is now regarded by many as the era of **e-commerce**. This electronic platform of shopping is rapidly restructuring how customers learn about, shop for, and ultimately purchase a wide variety of consumer products. According to the US Census Bureau, US retail generated $1,380.5 billion by the end of the third quarter of 2019. Of that, $154.5 billion was generated through e-commerce, representing 11.2 percent of total retail sales.[2] This represents a 16.9 percent growth in online sales from the same period in 2018. In fact, from 2010 to 2019, online sales increased annually from between 14 to 17 percent each year.[3] Forecasts show continued increase in e-commerce, with sales predicted to reach over $740 billion by 2023.[4]

That first e-commerce transaction in 1994 inspired a continuum of growth and change in how customers relate to and interact with digital technology in the purchasing process. Brands and retailers initially ambled through challenges such as how to develop engaging and easy-to-navigate websites, and how to ensure secure shopping sites. In more recent times, brands and retailers must address increasingly complex issues that speed by with the latest technology—app development, social media, and fashion bloggers. The Internet has truly made retail a global enterprise, no longer limiting customers to the offerings of a single store location in their neighborhood, town, or city.

Even in this era of ever-increasing e-commerce, though, the lion's share of retail—nearly 90 percent— still occurs through traditional venues: department stores, specialty stores, boutiques, and an array of shopping venues that we will discuss in this chapter.

An extraordinary amount of planning and effort goes into the merchandising of fashion products. For people who are not in the fashion business, the process of merchandising fashion products can look easy. Fashion moves from concept to customer, that is, from designer to manufacturer to retailer to you—the customer! The most intricate part lies in the merchandising and retailing of the goods. As mentioned previously, an old adage among fashion retailers is called the five Rs, and stands for choosing the following:

- The right merchandise
- At the right price
- In the right place
- At the right time
- In the right quantities

If any one of these Rs is incorrect, it will collapse the remaining Rs. Think of it as smoothly juggling five balls at once. A merchandiser must keep them all in the air at the same time: constantly moving, never touching. The timing must be flawless. If one ball slips, they will all fall. It looks easy but is difficult to do!

Traditional Types of Fashion Retailers

As the frontier turned into towns and cities, peddlers became sales representatives and general stores and mail-order businesses evolved into something entirely different from their ancestors.

Retailers today usually can be classified into one of two broad categories—general and specialized—depending on the kinds of merchandise they carry. In each of these categories are many different kinds of retail operations: department stores, specialty stores, chain operations, discount stores, and leased departments, to name a few. Almost all retail stores offer some form of mail-order, telephone, or e-commerce. More recently, there are retailers who are exclusively online, like Zappos.com and Blue Fly. We will discuss Internet shopping sites later in this chapter. Some stores have grown into giant operations, but many others are still small, independently owned and operated businesses.

The retail scene is dominated by **general merchandise retailers**, such as Walmart, Costco, JCPenney, and Target. These retailers typically sell many kinds of merchandise in addition to clothing. They try to appeal to a broad range of customers. Most general merchandisers very broadly target their merchandise to several price ranges, and only a few limit themselves to narrow price ranges.

Specialty retailers, in contrast, offer limited lines of related merchandise targeted to a more specific customer. They define their customers by age, size, or shared tastes. Their customers are more homogeneous than those of general merchandisers. Examples are Crate & Barrel, Tiffany's, and Talbots.

The differences between types of retailers are not as clearly defined as they used to be. It has, for example, become increasingly difficult to distinguish a department store from a chain operation, a discounter from an off-pricer, a franchiser from a chain. In this section, we will look at three traditional types of fashion retailers: department stores, specialty stores, and discount stores.

Department Stores

The **department store** is the type of general retailer most familiar to the buying public. Many are even tourist landmarks. Few people, for example, visit New York without seeing Macy's or Bloomingdale's. In London, Harrods is a big tourist attraction, as is Printemps in Paris.

Department stores reigned as kings of retailers well into the 1960s, when there was only about four square feet of retail space per person in the United States. They had long dominated downtowns with main stores called flagships. In the 1960s and 1970s, department stores anchored malls. But in the turbulent 1980s, department stores failed all across the country, victims of overexpansion, mergers and acquisitions, and increased competition. Retail space is now occupied by many different types of stores.

Before getting into the ways in which stores are changing, let us look at how various kinds of traditional retailers operate and merchandise themselves. As general merchandisers, department stores typically serve a larger portion of the community than other stores and often offer a variety of quality and price ranges. A department store usually offers a category of apparel at several price points, each in a different part of the store.

Department stores have also traditionally enjoyed a certain prestige that often extends even beyond the communities they serve. They are usually actively involved in their communities. A department store, for example, will eagerly stage a fashion show for a local charity, knowing that such activities create goodwill and enhance the store's overall reputation.

Organization for Buying and Merchandising

Department stores are organized into special areas, or departments, such as sportswear, dresses, men's clothing, and furniture, as shown in Figure 11.1. Generally, buyers purchase for their departments, although in very large department stores, even the departments may be departmentalized, with individual buyers purchasing only part of the stock for a department. In some sportswear departments, for example, one buyer may purchase tops, while another buys bottoms.

Entertainment Values

The weaving of entertainment into modern retailing is reshaping the shopping experience. Entertainment values in retailing are defined in a number of ways. The most traditional way is by offering a compelling, frequently changing, merchandise assortment. Many retailers think

FASHION BLOGGERS

Once the domain of just the elite and select few who fit into a very limited set of size and height requirements, and who paid their dues and worked their way up the fashion ranks, fashion modeling, styling, opinion, and reporting is now held tightly in the hand of the fashion blogger!

Part model, part scribe, part trend-setter, part designer, part photographer, part influencer—fashion bloggers have harnessed the power of social media to get their own ideas about fashion and beauty out to an astounding number of enthusiastic followers. Here are a few top bloggers and how they use social media to reach their audiences with their own unique fashion perspectives.

MODESTMIRA Instagram—59K followers

Based in Manchester, England, Amira shows her followers how to dress modestly and stylishly. http://modestmira.blogspot.com

GABIFRESH Instagram—680K followers

Based in Detroit, Michigan, Gabrielle Gregg started blogging about 2007, but things really took off when a photo of her showing off her curves in a striped bikini went viral in 2012. She launched Premme, a plus-size apparel line, with Nicolette Mason in 2017. http://gabifresh.com

THE BLONDE SALAD Instagram – 10.4M followers

Italian-based blogger Chiara Ferragni and her fashion blog The Blonde Salad is the stuff of blogging legend. She turned her blog into a high-end brand and business employing twenty staff. She's moved from a blog in 2009 to what some describe as a digital empire, turning blogging into designing, netting an estimated $20 million in 2016 through her footwear and accessories line. https://www.theblondesalad.com/en-US

Through her blog Blonde Salad, blogger-celebrity Chiara Ferragni sponsors Pantene products as a "Pantene Global Ambassador."

GAL MEETS GLAM Instagram—1.2M followers

Based in South Carolina, Julia Engle started her fashion and lifestyle blog in 2011. Mixing upscale, casual, feminine, and traditional, she has parlayed her style and popularity into promotions with brands like Coach, Club Monaco, and Tory Burch. https://galmeetsglam.com/category/style/julias-style/

GabiFresh blogger, Gabrielle Gregg, attending a "WhoWhatWear Presents" promotional event.

MANREPELLER Instagram—2.1M followers

Not even the shortest list of top fashion bloggers would be complete without including Leandra Medine and her fashion blog MANREPELLER. Witty, funny, and sharply observant writing on fashion, lifestyle, and popular culture sets Medine apart. Her fashion brand collaborations include Topshop and Outdoor Voices, and in 2016 she launched her own line of shoes, MR. *https://www.manrepeller.com*

Julia Engel of Gal Meets Glam speaks onstage at Vionic Hosts Spring Style Secrets With Elle And Gal Meets Glam At Lord & Taylor Fifth Avenue.

Figure 11.1 The traditional department store "look" features separate, departmentalized classifications.

of their stores as theaters that provide entertainment. The walls are the stage, the fixtures are the sets, and the merchandise is the star. Other popular entertainment strategies include providing video walls, interactive Internet sites, store visits by celebrities, designer trunk shows, sponsoring charity fundraisers, and so on.

Contrary to the rumors that the department store is a dinosaur, many department stores are fighting back by adding entertainment value. One way that department stores have built relationships with their customers is through award and loyalty programs. These programs reward high-spending customers with bonuses and make members feel as if they are part of a VIP club. The stores will arrange events that range from meet-the-designer product launches to luncheons and cocktail parties. Neiman Marcus, for example, hosts lunches for its InCircle program that has featured guests, many from the world of entertainment, such as singers, TV personalities, and famous designers.

Specialty Stores

A specialty store carries a limited line of merchandise, whether it is clothing, accessories, or furniture. Examples of specialty stores include shoe stores, jewelry stores, bridal boutiques, and maternity-wear stores (see Figure 11.2). As noted, specialty merchandisers tend to target a more specific customer than do general merchandisers. They may offer a single line—just shoes, for example. Or they may offer related limited lines, for example, children's apparel, shoes, and other accessories. Or they may offer a subspecialty, like just athletic shoes or even socks.

Another variation of the specialty store is the private-label retailer, which sells only what it manufactures itself. Gap, Ann Taylor, and Brooks Brothers are leading examples.

Figure 11.2 Bridal boutiques are specialty stores, offering a wide variety of styles and accessories for the bride and members of the wedding party.

Organization for Buying and Merchandising

In small specialty stores, the buying and merchandising are done by the owner or a store manager, sometimes with the assistance of a small staff. Large multidepartment specialty stores are organized along the lines of department stores, with buyers purchasing merchandise for their own departments. Multiunit specialty stores belonging to chain organizations are set up in a unique way that is described under chain organizations, discussed later in this chapter.

Entertainment Values

Entertainment is a natural activity for specialty stores. In addition to exciting visual merchandising, many specialty stores now offer related entertainment. Niketown began the trend with its video wall, and then expanded to a town square with a staffed counter, banks of video monitors, and information about local and national sports teams. Gaylan's Trading Company, now owned by Dick's Sporting Goods, Inc., offers indoor and outdoor climbing walls, and an in-line skating area.

Discount Stores

The discount business got its start after the Second World War, when servicemen and servicewomen came home with a well-thought-out agenda for their lives: get married, establish a home, and start a family. Within a few years, with the help of the GI Bill, which funded both education and mortgages, they had managed to achieve at least one of their wishes. Millions of new houses were built in "new" suburban towns. The next step was to furnish them.

A **discount store** today is any retail operation that sells goods at less than full retail prices. Discounters are called discount stores, mass merchandisers, promotional department stores, and off-pricers. Discounters may be either general or specialty merchandisers, selling everything from cosmetics, accessories, and apparel, to health and beauty aids, to major appliances.

Organization for Buying and Merchandising

Early discounters searched the marketplace for closeout and special-price promotions. Their inventories consisted almost entirely of this type of goods. Today, discounters specialize in low-end open-market goods or special lines made exclusively for them. Most conventional retail operations do not want their buyers to purchase goods that will be sold to discounters, but this has not stopped manufacturers from making special lines for discounters. Some designers and manufacturers use discount outlets to sell their overstocks or slow-moving items.

Forms of Ownership

There are four types of ownership commonly found in US retailing today: sole proprietors, chain organizations, leased departments, and franchises. Partnerships, once a popular form of retail ownership (Sears and Roebuck, Montgomery Ward, Abraham and Straus, and so on), are seldom found today because of liability issues and tax considerations. Owners use many different formats, including the traditional department store, specialty store, or discount store, or the newer off-price, factory outlet, or category killer formats.

Sole Proprietors

Sole proprietors, or owners, are the entrepreneurs who shaped US retailing. Many of the retailing greats— JCPenney, John Wanamaker, Adam Gimbel, and Isaac and Mary Ann Magnin—began as sole proprietors with a great idea and went on to found great retailing empires.

More than 90 percent of all US retailers own and operate a single store. Sole proprietors usually have small stores because of the huge amount of capital required to support an adequate inventory for a large business. These so-called **mom-and-pop stores** are usually single stores, managed by the owner with a few assistants. They are most frequently specialty stores because department stores require more space and inventory. If the owner prospers and expands to more than four stores, he or she is said to have a chain.

Chain Organizations

A **chain organization** is a group of centrally owned stores—four or more, according to the Bureau of the Census definition—each of which handles similar goods and merchandise. A chain organization may be local, regional, or national, although it is the national chains

SHELLIE JEFFREY: COSTUME DESIGNER

If you think that great career opportunities in clothing and design are only to be found in New York, or Los Angeles, then think again!

Shellie Jeffrey, Costume Designer.

MEET SHELLIE REASY JEFFREY, COSTUME DESIGNER AND COSTUME SHOP MANAGER FOR WORLDS OF FUN THEME PARK LOCATED IN KANSAS CITY, MISSOURI. DUBBED "The Sparkle Factory," Shellie and her team develop over 1,500 creative, theatrical costumes each year for a cast of dancers and singers, a gang of goblins, and a frolic of winter fairies.

The Sparkle Factory houses a team of professional sewers called "Stitchers," and apprentice sewers lovingly referred to as the "Littles" who are learning the specific sewing and fitting skills required of an experienced costumer. "With the very specialized kind of sewing and costume production that we do, we hope we are building the Littles program enough to have seasoned Stitchers well into the future," Shellie explains. The team also includes "dressers" who assist performers with hair, makeup, costume changes, and who maintain and store the costumes from show to show. "Laundry attendants" clean, mend, store, and distribute the work attire worn by park employees.

Worlds of Fun is part of the Cedar Fair Entertainment Corporation, comprised of ten theme and water parks throughout the US, and the Worlds of Fun Sparkle Factory designs and produces costumes for their fellow parks, too. "Theme parks aren't just a summer business anymore," Shellie explains. "In the fall, during October, we produce 'Halloween Haunt.' We warm up the chill of the holiday season with 'WinterFest.' And we celebrate 'Grand Carnivale' during the middle of the summer. Our team provides the costumes for these special seasonal events to our sister parks, in addition to what our shop produces for Worlds of Fun."

Building a costume and managing a shop this size is multifaceted. The elaborate garment is just the beginning, requiring both creative and technical expertise to

Live entertainers performing in the summer Grand Carnivale celebration, dressed in elaborate costumes. A team of dressers provide hair and make-up, as well as maintenance and storage of the costumes.

Family-friendly ghouls and goblins come alive each October during the annual HALLOWEEN HAUNT celebration.

execute. Computer skills and the ability to think outside the box to source different materials or accessories are essential. Wigs, shoes, makeup, and accessories along with a management system to keep items in order and well-maintained require a great deal of detail, planning and organizational skills. And it all requires teamwork. When talking about her work, Shellie is very quick to acknowledge that she accomplishes none of this all by herself. Collaboration, teamwork, delegation, and open communication are essential to efficient operations and a creative, upbeat environment. Shellie credits her success to having a creative mind, a varied skill set, and the ability to keep learning new things with each new challenge. "Start with 'yes!' Then find a way to make it happen!" That's Shellie's motto.

A typical day in this world—well, there does not appear to be such a thing! Each day takes shape by whichever deadline is lurking around the next corner. One day might require Internet research to source elements for the latest costume project, the next day may require brushing up on the technical requirements of industrial laundry equipment. And not all of the work is inside the costume shop. Shellie and her team regularly take time to attend the shows and check out the live entertainment to check costumes, hair, and makeup in action on stage. When dressing a show at another park is underway, Shellie and her team travel and spend a week or two in the field, getting the actors fitted, dressed, and staged.

Shellie earned her Associate of Applied Science in Fashion Design and Merchandising at Metropolitan Community College-Penn Valley in Kansas City, Missouri. Upon graduation, she landed a job as Assistant Costume Designer at Worlds of Fun. Building on this experience, she started a custom design business, providing eveningwear for pageant contestants, and specialty costumes for local entertainers. Unique fabric and new challenges inspired constant learning and spurred her to hone her craft and develop new skills. Her reputation for skilled sewing and creativity eventually attracted custom bridal work, which became a specialty. In 2012, Shellie returned to Worlds of Fun to supervise the sewing room and was named head Costume Designer in 2017 upon the retirement of the longtime head of the department.

Her advice to students who want to pursue work in costume design is to get as much experience as possible—get involved in school theatrical productions, work in community theater, and never turn down an opportunity to learn something new. Get a wide variety of experience and learn about textiles. Dry cleaning, alterations, fabric and craft stores, and bridal work are all great places to learn and build skills.

that have had the largest impact on retailing. They also may be general or specialty merchandisers, and depending upon the kinds of stores they are, they will target their customer broadly or narrowly. A chain organization can be a mass merchandiser known for its low prices, a department store known for high-quality mid-priced goods, or a specialty merchandiser selling exclusive designs at high prices. Apparel chains may focus on a special size, age, or income group.

The oldest and best-known chain organizations are JCPenney and Sears, which *Stores* magazine categorizes as department stores. Other chains include Walmart and Target, which are categorized as discount stores. Prestigious specialty chains are Talbots and Brooks Brothers. Aeropostale is a juniors' specialty chain. Chico's is an example of a women's apparel specialty chain.

Organization for Buying and Merchandising

Most chain stores are departmentalized, but not in the same way as department stores. Chain-store buyers are typically assigned to buy a specific category or classification of apparel within a department instead of buying all categories for a department the way a department store buyer does. This practice is referred to as **category buying or classification buying**. Buyers in department stores, in contrast, are said to be responsible for **departmental buying**.

A departmental buyer in a sportswear department, for example, would buy swimwear, tops, jeans, sweaters, and slacks. A chain-store buyer who bought in the sportswear department might buy only swimsuits or only swimwear accessories. Category buying is necessary because huge quantities of goods are needed to stock the individual stores of a chain operation. Some chain operations have merchandise units numbering in the hundreds of thousands.

In addition to centralized buying and merchandising, most chains also have a system of central distribution. Merchandise is distributed to the units from a central warehouse or from regional distribution centers. Computer systems keep track of stock so that it can be reordered as needed; they also keep buyers informed of what is selling.

Leased Departments

Leased departments, which were first discussed in Chapter 4, are sections of a retail store that are owned and operated by outside organizations. The outside organization usually owns the department's stock, merchandises and staffs the department, and pays for its own advertising. It is, in turn, required to abide by the host store's policies and regulations. In return for the leasing arrangement, the outside organization pays the store a percentage of its sales as rent.

Leased departments work best where some specialized knowledge is required. Jewelry, fur, and shoe departments are often leased, as are beauty salons. Another example is JCPenney, which has a leased agreement with Sephora.

Department stores, chains, and discount organizations will lease both service and merchandise departments, while specialty stores usually restrict leased operations to services, such as jewelry or shoe repair or leather and suede cleaning.

Franchises

Franchises established themselves as a viable form of retailing when shops featuring fast food, bath linens, cookware, fabrics, unfinished furniture, electronics, and computers were successfully franchised. In a franchise agreement, the franchisee (owner-operator) pays a fee plus a royalty on all sales for the right to operate a store with an established name in an exclusive trading area. The franchiser (parent company) provides merchandise and assistance in organizing and merchandising, plus training. Firms as diverse as United Colors of Benetton and Gymboree have adopted this form of ownership. Athletic footwear, tennis apparel, and men's sportswear have all produced lucrative and popular franchises. The Athlete's Foot, for example, which sells athletic footwear and activewear, has 530 locations world-wide.[5]

The latest trend is for designers to get in the act. Examples of successful worldwide franchises by designers are Ralph Lauren's Polo Shops, Calvin Klein shops, and Yves Saint Laurent's Rive Gauche shops.

Industry experts see no signs that franchising will slow its pace, and many feel that this form of retailing will continue to grow.

Other Types of Fashion Retailers

In addition to the traditional retail formats discussed previously, a new group of businesses has evolved throughout the past forty years that adapts some of the attributes of the traditional retailers with some new ideas.

Types of retail formats popular today include off-price retailers, factory outlet stores, convenience stores, category killers, catalog showrooms, boutique/showcase stores, and nonstore retailers. Many overlap with existing traditional formats. Many are chains. We will focus on those that are most important to apparel, accessories, and home furnishings.

Off-Price Retailers

One area that is experiencing strong growth is **off-price retailing**, the selling of brand-name and designer merchandise at lower-than-normal retail prices when they are at the late rise or early peak in the fashion cycle. In contrast, regular discounters sell merchandise in the late peak and decline stages of the fashion cycle.

Off-price retailers attribute part of their success to the fact that they provide an invaluable service to manufacturers and price-conscious customers. Because manufacturers must commit to fabric houses so far in advance (up to eighteen months before garments will be in the stores), they risk not having enough orders to use the fabric they have ordered. Off-pricers have in effect helped to smooth out the cyclical and often financially disastrous course of apparel manufacturing. Customers, in turn, benefit from being able to buy garments very similar to those that are being sold in exclusive stores for less than they would pay in those stores (see Figures 11.3a and 11.3b).

Off-pricers managed to capture an important share of the brand-name market. The success of brand names such as Donna Karan, Bill Blass, and Calvin Klein meant that designers no longer had to give department stores exclusives, and they were soon selling their products to off-pricers. More recently, however, many designers have begun to sell their overstocks in their own stores. This has put severe pressure on off-pricers like Loehmann's and Syms to get enough inventory.

One other disadvantage seems to be built into off-price retailing: Off-price retailers get the goods later than regular-priced retailers. While a department store puts designer spring and summer clothing on the selling floor during the winter, the off-pricer does not get the same merchandise until several months later. As a result, the off-pricer has a shorter selling season than the regular-price retailer.

Factory Outlet Stores

Factory outlet stores, a discount operation run by a manufacturer—or increasingly these days, by a designer—are another booming area of discount retailing. Factory outlets have grown at a furious pace over the past few decades. There are entire communities—such as Freeport, Maine; Manchester, Vermont; and Secaucus, New Jersey—that are devoted almost exclusively to the selling of factory outlet goods. The draw in Freeport was the presence of L.L. Bean, an established force in mail-order retailing that expanded its factory store outlet

Figure 11.3 (a) One of Neiman Marcus's Last Call discount stores and (b) inside, overstocks and canceled orders are unloaded to shoppers looking for a bargain.

throughout the 1980s from a small outpost to a huge, multibuilding operation.

Like off-price discounters, factory outlets offer certain advantages to manufacturers and customers. Most important is the fact that they provide manufacturers and designers with a backup channel of distribution, which improves inventory control. Canceled orders and overstocks can be funneled into discount stores, which, if run correctly, also can be enormous image enhancers. Not to be underestimated is the possibility of strong profits. An outlet buys merchandise from the parent company for 30 percent off the regular wholesale prices and sells it for the same markup percentage as regular-priced retailers.

While designers and brand-name manufacturers use their outlets for overstocks and canceled orders, large manufacturers, such as Kayser-Roth and Carter, are careful to use their outlets only for closeouts and seconds. The latter are unwilling to risk offending department stores and other major customers with more direct competition. But now, even the department stores have opened outlet stores: Saks Fifth Avenue has Saks Off Fifth, while Nordstrom has Nordstrom Rack.

Category Killers

Superstores or category specialists carry one type of goods that they are able to offer in great amounts at low prices because of volume buying. They so dominate a market that they drive out or "kill" smaller specialty stores, and so are known as **category killers**. They offer a narrow but deep assortment of goods in stores of more than 8,000 square feet. Because of their buying power, they can get not only rock-bottom prices but also excellent terms and an assured supply of scarce goods.

Examples of category killers include Bed Bath & Beyond, Home Depot, Barnes & Noble, and Babies 'R' Us. Typically these are huge freestanding stores, often called big boxes. They are rarely located in malls. They carry thousands of related products at low prices, which they think offset no-frills service and decor.

Boutiques/Showcase Stores

Although boutiques originated as small shops with French couture houses, they really came to life as small, individually owned shops in the antiestablishment 1960s. The first freestanding boutiques opened in London and quickly spread to the United States. Their appeal lies in their potential for individuality. These stores are often owned and operated by highly creative people who are eager to promote their own fashion enthusiasms. Their target customers are like-minded souls who share their unique attitudes about dressing.

Some boutique owners design their own merchandise; others buy and sell other people's designs. Boutiques are one of the few outlets for avant-garde merchandise that is too risky for department and specialty stores to carry.

A trend in boutiques has been for designers to open their own shops. The French designers were the first to experiment with freestanding boutiques in the United States, but US designers soon followed suit. Among the French who have opened successful boutiques in the United States are Pierre Cardin, Valentino, Yves Saint Laurent, and Givenchy. Italian designers and manufacturers such as Armani, Gucci, and Ferragamo were quick to follow. Successful British firms that pioneered boutique selling on both sides of the Atlantic were Laura Ashley and Liberty of London. Designers of other nationalities have also followed this trend (see Figure 11.4).

Many US designers are expanding by opening showcase stores. A **showcase store** is a manufacturer's or designer's store that sells merchandise at the introductory and early rise stages of the fashion cycle. In addition to generating income, showcase stores are testing grounds for new products. Ralph Lauren, Donna Karan, Calvin Klein, Tommy Hilfiger, Anna Sui, and Esprit operate showcase stores in addition to factory outlets. As fewer well-known designers rush to open showcase stores, there is little doubt that this form of retailing will continue to grow.

Figure 11.4 Foreign designers open boutiques in the United States, such as Carlos Miele of Brazil in Manhattan, New York.

Nonstore Retailers

Nonstore retailing today is composed of four major formats: direct selling, catalog retailers, TV home shopping, and Internet shopping sites. As omni-channel retail continues to evolve, the lines between these individual types have blurred. Store-based retailers are looking to expand their customer base through catalogs and electronic options. For example, leading catalogers such as Lillian Vernon and Spiegel have established a major presence on the Internet, as have retailers such as JCPenney and Gap, which have giant online virtual storefronts.

Direct Selling

Direct selling, which used to be known as direct-to-the-home selling, is still a major force in the United States. According to the Direct Selling Association, in 2018 direct selling sales reached $35.4 billion dollars, an increase of 1.3 percent from 2017 reported sales.[6] Almost all people who work in direct sales in the United States are independent, part-time salespeople who buy merchandise from a large firm and distribute it by selling it to customers in their territories. The Carlisle Collection and Etcetera, Inc. are examples of top direct sales fashion companies, offering one-on-one stylings and consultations.[7]

Catalog Retailers

Catalog retailing, or mail-order retailing, as it was traditionally called, has been popular in the United States since the 1880s. But by 1982, the explosive growth of mail-order retailers had reached such proportions that *Time* magazine ran a cover story on it. The evolution of air delivery and computerized distribution played a vital role in increasing direct-mail and catalog sales. Other boosts to mail-order selling included providing customers with toll-free 800 numbers, fax, and website information for placing orders; the ability to use credit cards to pay for merchandise; and discount key codes. Companies became able to target their customers in very specific ways: **Versioning**, which is the ability to tailor different versions of a catalog to different customer segments, allows catalog marketers to focus on consumers by age, income, geographic region, lifestyle, and interests.

A few big problems plague catalog retailers, including the steadily increasing cost of paper, a general movement for companies to become more "green," and the growth of Internet shopping and e-commerce.

However, as the dynamics of omni-channel marketing and e-commerce emerge, catalogs are proving, once again, to be an important part of the multichannel marketing mix. Utilizing web traffic customer data allows for improved targeting and measurement capabilities through versioning, and the most relevant parts or pages of a catalog can be sent to a customer instead of the whole publication.

Retailers have learned the value of high-quality content marketing through this channel. **Magalogs**, which are catalogs that have editorial content, not just advertising, prove to be an excellent way to build emotion and personality around a brand. For example, The J. Peterman Company catalog weaves captivating, romantic stories into the product descriptions; Williams Sonoma includes recipes alongside the products needed to prepare them. IKEA serves as inspirational source books for interior design and lifestyle ideas.

TV Home Shopping

One of the most talked-about developments in retailing has been the growth of home TV shopping, a form of retailing that takes the catalog sales techniques one step further. The potential of television as a direct-mail sales tool has long been recognized; witness the late-night gadget demonstrations and the ubiquitous storm-window advertisements.

Not until the advent of cable television, however, with its lower production standards and costs, was it feasible to produce infomercials and to set up home shopping services that sell an array of goods. The cable TV infomercial, with its enthusiastic host and wildly appreciative audience, has been used to sell a large variety of goods, from Adam Levine and Katy Perry for ProActiv to Christie Brinkley and Chuck Norris for the Total Gym.

In 1977, Home Shopping Network (HSN) Inc. was the pioneer in the TV home shopping business. Today, Qurate Retail, Inc. is comprised of seven leading retail brands which include HSN and QVC, two of the top-rated video shopping networks. Other Qurate holdings include Zulily, Ballard Designs, Frontgate, Garnet Hill, and Grandin Road.[8] On the air twenty-four hours a day, seven days a week, HSN is the world's most widely distributed TV shopping network. It also has an e-commerce site and apps for the iPad and mobile phones. HSN reaches at least 4.5 million customers in the US, sells

1,290 brands, and showcases more than 630 products on air each week. Its fashion and accessories area includes collections from designers, models, and athletes like Betsey Johnson, Steve Madden, Sheryl Crow, Vanessa Williams, and Jessica Simpson.[9]

QVC and has grown significantly since it was founded in 1986. It offers on-screen demonstrations of merchandise that ranges from simple cookware to enormous amounts of apparel and accessories, especially jewelry. It also offers a wide array of home furnishings, tabletop goods, and gift items. QVC has separate weekly shows for gold jewelry, silver jewelry, simulated-diamond jewelry, men's jewelry, and watches. Los Angeles designer Bob Mackie has made many appearances on QVC, selling out their stock of his scarves and tops. Isaac Mizrahi is another example of effectively combining selling and entertainment. QVC also operates sales through its website; mobile phone applications; and operates QVC Local, a 45-foot motorcraft coach that takes the show on the road (see Figure 11.5).[10]

ShopHQ, formerly EVINE, is a multichannel electronic retailer. This shopping network reaches 87 million homes in the United States through cable and satellite television. It too offers an extensive array of products, including apparel and accessories from Burberry, Celine Dion Collection, Fendi, and Marc Jacobs.[11]

With flat-screen TVs and new advances in technology, customers get a better view of the products, enticing them to place even more orders.

Internet Shopping Sites

As of 2018, online sales of apparel, footwear, and accessories in the United States reached $102.2 billion, with projections to reach $145.8 billion by 2023.[12] And, Cyber Monday 2019 (the Monday after Thanksgiving) surpassed $9.4 billion in sales across all digital platforms, up 19.7% from Cyber Monday 2018.[13]

Key reasons for growth of apparel, accessories, and footwear online are the variety of sites available, liberal shipping policies, a larger customer base, easy search options for customers, and prevalent customer reviews (see Figure 11.6). High-speed broadband allows users to navigate quickly, and some sites give customers the opportunity to zoom in and see multiple views of products.

Multichannel retailers are companies that offer product through a variety of platforms: catalog, online,

Figure 11.5 A long-time favorite of QVC shoppers, designer Isaac Mizrahi.

Figure 11.6 Gucci's platform for the iPad lets customers easily shop for high-end timepieces wherever they might be.

and brick-and mortar stores. By no coincidence, the e-commerce players that have been the most successful are the online channels of apparel retail giants. In 2018, Macy's topped the list of e-commerce apparel sales, reporting revenue in this category of $3.88 billion, followed by Amazon.com, Gap.com, Nordstrom.com, and Kohls.com rounding out the top five.[14]

Omni-Channel Retail

While online shopping has been with us for over twenty years, rapid advances and proliferation of digital technology in recent years have impacted e-commerce in new ways. Since more portable access to the Internet through smartphones and tablets has developed, new ways of shopping have developed. **Omni-channel** retail is the seamless use of multiple shopping platforms in the decision and purchase process. It is becoming less and less a battle of brick-and-mortar versus online shopping and more of a seamless blend of the two platforms. Here is an example: A woman receives a catalog in the mail for one of her favorite stores—J.Jill. As she looks through the pages, a few items interest her. While she is watching television later that evening, she uses her iPad tablet to check the J.Jill website for customer reviews on several of the items and to consult the online sizing chart. She considers placing an order online, but since there is a J.Jill near where she works, she decides to visit the store during her lunch hour to see what the fabrics are like, and maybe try on a few things. Once in the store, she realizes that several of the color choices are only available online. The sales associate offers her free shipping to the store for later pick-up if she would like to use the store computer kiosk to place an order. As she is placing the order on the computer in the store, she uses her smartphone to pull up a J.Jill 30-percent-off coupon. Notice how many different shopping platforms and devices our customer used to make this one purchase—catalog, iPad tablet, brick-and-mortar store, computer, and smartphone.

Typically, omni-channel retailers are not start-ups. They are well capitalized with physical brick-and-mortar space, as well as a solid online presence, striving to meet consumers wherever they already are spending their time. And more and more, retailers are promoting their product across many online channels at once, in different ways, to maximize consumer reach, benefitting from the unique qualities of each social media platform.[15]

Mobile Devices

Mobile devices include smartphones, tablets, and laptops. As this technology has improved with longer battery life, and becomes increasingly more portable with compact size and increased connectivity, more and more consumers rely on their devises to buy, research, or track online purchases, inspiring a new sub-genre of e-commerce, referred to as **m-commerce**. By the end of 2019, a reported 2 billion people made purchases from a mobile device, and a whopping 95 percent of shoppers researched purchases from their mobile device prior to completing their purchase. About one-fourth of all e-commerce sales is generated on a mobile device, with annual spending exceeding $35 billion, and this trend is expected to continue to grow into the future.[16]

Social Media

With 72 percent of adults engaged in one or more forms of social media, retailers are effectively using these communication platforms to connect with customers. Moving beyond advertisements and discount opportunities, social media opens up two-way communication between retailer and customer, enabling valuable and timely feedback. According to a survey by Pew Research Center, the most used form of social media is YouTube, followed by Facebook, Instagram, and finally Snapchat. For 18–24 year-olds, Snapchat and Instagram are the most popular venues, Facebook is the most popular platform of 25–29 year-olds, while its overall use tends to be common among all age groups, and Facebook has the most daily users, with over half of survey respondents reporting visiting the site multiple times each day.[17]

Flash-Sale, Upscale Resale, and Rental Websites

A product of the Great Recession, **flash-sale** websites emerged in about 2007, offering deep discounts on merchandise for short periods of time. The strategy helped create a sense of urgency around the purchase, as well as effectively generating sales in a slow economy. Access to these deals required joining a members-only site. Following the early excitement around this form of shopping, the format leveled out in recent years. With the power and reach of social media platforms, flash-sales can be used effectively by established retailers to create interest and buzz around new products. These fast-paced promotions involve a limited inventory offered for a very short period of time, offering an extraordinary deal to the consumer.

Upscale resale websites such as Rebag, The RealReal, Tradesy, Poshmark, and ThreadUp, offer consumers the chance to find a deal on pre-owned fashion goods. This category of retail is on the rise. Valued at $24 billion in 2018, the resale sector is expected to reach $51 billion by 2023. This segment of retail meets consumers preferences for variety, unique product, value, and sustainability, with younger consumers adopting this segment two-and-a-half-times faster than other age groups. [18]

Fashion rental websites such as Rent the Runway, Dress & Go, Glam Corner, and Style Lend are proving to be one solution to the trend of using clothes for shorter periods of time and using fashion to create a unique personal style. This sector is expected to reach $1.86 billion by 2023. While renting clothing for one-time use or special occasions has been practiced for decades, online access and subscription services have opened this sector up to a broader audience. [19]

Viral Fashion Videos

Another by-product of the digital revolution in retail marketing is the ability to show-and-tell about products through the video format. While film and video advertising have been around for decades, online formats such as YouTube allow the consumer to watch, rewatch, and share through social media outlets. Brands can educate on process and craftsmanship, while entertaining the consumer with a multimedia production.

Mergers and Acquisitions

Until the 1930s, most department stores in the United States were independently owned. Most, in fact, were owned by the families whose names they bore, such as Marshall Field, John Wanamaker, Gimbel Bros., and J. L. Hudson. By the 1980s, most of these long-established stores had changed hands, and with these changes in ownership came new images and sometimes even new names.

So much change has occurred in the retail business recently that you need a scorecard to track the remaining players. Consolidations, changes in distribution channels, bankruptcies, altered buying organizations, and foreign investments have all caused retail as we knew it to change (see Figure 11.7).

Figure 11.7 Bal Harbour Shops—a luxury upscale mall featuring designer goods.

Trends

Changing Retail Patterns

Retail operations must not only constantly respond to change in their environments but also must change themselves if they are to survive. Figure 11.8 shows that the environment of this store interior is designed to reach

Figure 11.8 The environment of this Ralph Lauren store is designed to reach out to the customer.

out to the customer is an upscale and inviting manner. One theory, suggested by Malcolm P. McNair, retailing authority and professor emeritus at the Harvard Business School, describes the way in which retail organizations naturally change or evolve.

According to McNair's theory, called the Wheel of Retailing, most retail organizations begin life as lower-priced distributors. They offer strictly functional facilities, limited assortments, and minimal customer services. As time elapses, the successful businesses need to grow to survive, so they begin to trade up in an effort to broaden their customer profile. Facilities are modernized. Store decor becomes more attractive. Assortments become more varied and of higher quality. Promotional efforts are initiated or increased, and some customer services are introduced.

The process of trading up, however, involves considerable capital investment in the physical plant, equipment, and stock. Operating expenses spiral. As a result, retailers are forced to charge higher prices to cover the increased cost of doing business. To justify the higher prices, they also begin to stock more expensive merchandise.

According to McNair's theory, as retailers move out of the low-priced end of the market into the moderate-to-high-priced field, they create a vacuum at the bottom of the retailing structure. The vacuum does not exist for long, however. Enterprising new retailers move quickly to fill the vacated and temporarily uncompetitive low-priced area to meet the demands of customers who either need or prefer to patronize low-priced retailers. This pattern keeps repeating itself as successful retailers trade up and new ones move into the vacuum. This theory also applies to catalog companies—Spiegel is one example of a firm that moved upscale.

Even those who move up must still constantly cope with the ever-changing nature of the fashion business.

SOCIAL MEDIA AND HOW PEOPLE *REALLY* SHOP!

By most accounts, social media first emerged around 1997, and since that time designers and brands have continuously strived to harness its power. In the constantly evolving array of social media platforms, designers can now engage their customers and tell their story in a variety of ways.

Twitter can spread news like wildfire! This is a great format for a designer or brand to gain a huge number of followers, quickly let their customers know about new products and projects, and read what is being said about them. The trending topics and hashtag features allow Twitter users to easily see what others are talking about. The "retweet" feature for the most bold and newsworthy posts increases brand awareness and consumer engagement.

For browsers, Pinterest is the platform of choice. Brands and designers can create a variety of boards focusing on different categories of the product offerings – like "denim," "weekend," and "accessories." According to one study, fashion accounts for 45 percent of Pinterest searches and pins, and consumers are 10 percent more likely to make a purchase when directed by Pinterest than from any other social media platform.

For the authentic, personal, "behind-the-scenes" of it all, Snap-chat is the go-to! The platform boasts over 150 million global active users a day, with 60 percent in the 18-to-34 age category. This platform is favored for its captivating video format, far less static than the text and images used in most other platforms. Subscribers can choose from hundreds of designers to follow and get regularly updated content on fashion shows, ongoing teases about new product lines, and a general feel of the day-to-day things that go on behind the scenes in a big fashion brand.

YouTube is the second largest search engine and the third most visited site after Google and Facebook. On mobile devices alone, YouTube reaches more 18- to 49-year-olds than any single broadcast or cable TV network. The platform has launched in over ninety countries and available in eighty different languages. Vloggers and how-to fashionistas have found a home on YouTube for some time. But as the YouTube reach continues to expand, fashion designers and brands can now effectively advertise on any video that reaches their target audience with pre-roll, mid-roll, and post-roll ads.

The imaging power of Instagram is a natural fit for fashion designers and brands. With 1 billion active users, the potential consumer reach is enormous. The "see more" feature adds to this power. Through swipe technology, viewers can be taken directly to a Web site where they can buy the item viewed moments earlier in the

Instagram and Snapchat are favored social media sites for Gen Z and Millennial consumers.

For online consumers of all ages, Amazon is the top shopping choice.

Instagram post. This literally drops the item right into the palm of their hand—and all the consumer has to do is buy it.

Fashion marketing is ever evolving and changing, and social media is proving to be an essential part of the communication mix for any successful designer or brand.

The ability to touch and try-on items before buying them is far less of a concern to Millennials and Gen Z shoppers. What matters most to these younger shoppers? Brand coverage, social media preference, and lifestyle identification. And these younger consumers are influencing how the older generations shop – parents and grandparents value the input of their Gen Z children.

A recent study looked at social media and the omni-channel shopping experience, in an attempt to understand the modern consumer. In this study, researchers surveyed 3,000 consumers, looking at where they shop online, why they shop where they do, and shifting online shopping challenges.

Where Do Consumers Shop Online?

- Gen Z shoppers spend 2-3 times more on social channels than the average consumer.
- Both Millennials and Gen Z spend the majority of their shopping dollar on products they find on Instagram and Snapchat. Gen Z spends very little on products found on Facebook (11.8%).
- All U.S. consumer across all generations do shop across all the channels.

Why U.S. Consumers Shop Where They Shop

- The top three buying destinations for consumers are Amazon, branded ecommerce websites, and brick-and-mortar stores.
- Gen Z consumers rely more on product recommendations, seeing ads on social media twice as much as the average consumer.
- Convenience, price, and free shipping were the top three reasons US consumers across all generations chose to buy at a branded website. Brand reputation and loyalty rewards came in fourth and fifth.
- Convenience and price were the clear winners among all those surveyed for shopping at Amazon.
- The ability to touch and try on was the main reason for shopping brick-and-mortar, however twice as many Baby Boomers cited this reason, compared to Gen Z shoppers.

Shifting Online Shopping Challenges

- Historically, the biggest impediment to online shopping has been not being able to try an item before buying, and the long process of entering purchase and shipping information ranked high as one of the most annoying aspects of shopping online.
- For Gen Z shoppers, this is shifting. Findings indicated that wait time shipping costs were seen as the main impediments to a positive online shopping experience.
- Site security concerns rank about the same in importance for younger and older consumers alike.

Although mergers have taken their toll on department stores, causing some old, established stores to close their doors, some good has been served. Without mergers, many of the established department stores would not have survived the onslaught of competition from chains and discounters. In fact, mergers generally occur for one of two reasons: a need to reorganize for greater efficiency and a need to expand.

Merging for Efficiency

In the early 1980s, chain organizations, with their centralized buying, had developed a competitive edge over department stores, even though department stores had tried to keep up by expanding the number of branch stores. The department stores soon realized that the real way to meet the competition was to develop more streamlined, efficient internal organizations. This was often achieved by merging one or more internal divisions to create a parent organization large enough to sponsor centralized buying, shipping, and merchandising.

Summary and Review

The history of fashion retailing in the United States is an interesting one. From general stores and peddlers to the earliest mail-order sellers, all early retailers sought customer satisfaction. Today's retailers seek the same goals through a variety of formats.

Three traditional retailing formats were the department store, the specialty store, and the discount store. Other formats include off-price retailers, factory outlet stores, category killers, and boutiques and showcase stores. All of these formats can be owned in one of four ways: sole proprietors, chain organizations, leased departments, or franchises.

Four types of nonstore retailing are popular today: direct selling, catalog or mail-order selling, TV home shopping, and Internet sites. Through the emergence of multichannel and omni-channel retail, the consumer now uses multiple ways to research products and make purchases.

Mergers and acquisitions have changed the face of retailing as we knew it and will probably continue to do so. Malcolm McNair's theory of how retailers evolve and change proposes that most retailers begin as lower-priced distributors and then move upscale. This creates an opportunity for new retailers to fill the lower-priced niche. McNair calls this the Wheel of Retailing.

FOR REVIEW

1. Name and briefly explain the characteristics and importance of three early forms of retail distribution in the United States.
2. How is the buying function handled by a department store?
3. What is a specialty store? How are buying and merchandising handled in a specialty store?
4. What is a chain organization? How are buying and merchandising handled in chain operations?
5. How do successful discounters make a profit?
6. What is a leased department, and how does it operate? Name the departments in a retail store that are frequently leased.
7. What is a category killer?
8. What stage or stages of the fashion cycle would most likely be emphasized by a specialty store, a department store, a discount store, or a social media post?

9. What is the difference between home TV shopping and shopping on the Internet?
10. Compare the differences between multichannel and omni-channel retail.
11. According to Malcolm P. McNair, how do retail organizations typically evolve?

FOR DISCUSSION

1. Compare and contrast the organization for buying and merchandising among prestigious chain organizations, department stores, and large specialty stores; discounters and off-price mass merchandisers; and franchises and leased departments. Give examples of different types of retailers in your community.
2. What examples in your community can you cite that support McNair's theory of trading up by retailers?

Trade Talk

Define or briefly explain the following terms:

category buying or classification buying
category killer
chain organization
department store
departmental buying
discount store
e-commerce
factory outlet store
flash-sale
general merchandise retailer
leased departments
m-commerce
magalogs
mom-and-pop stores
multichannel
off-price retailing
omni-channel
showcase stores
versioning

12

So You Want to Be in Fashion? Fashion Auxiliary Services

Key Concepts

- **Information provided to fashion producers and retailers by fashion consultants and research agencies; trade associations and trade shows; and buying, merchandising, and product development offices**

- **Differences among advertising, publicity, and public relations**

- **Services provided to fashion merchandisers by media such as trade and consumer publications, broadcast media, and the Internet and social media**

- **Overview of store design and visual merchandising services**

When exploring career opportunities in the fashion industry, fashion design, buying, and retail merchandising might seem like the most obvious options. We know the names of famous designers, and see people working in these professions every time we walk into a store.

Bringing you and your fellow consumers the styles you want to wear is so huge and all-encompassing a task that the fashion industry requires many support, or auxiliary, services which also offer exciting and rewarding career opportunities. These services have either been created specifically to serve the fashion industry, as in the case of buying, merchandising, and product development organizations, or their function has been tailored to the fashion industry's specific needs, as in the case of advertising and public relations agencies, fashion magazines, and the variety of consultants and marketing groups.

Fashion Auxiliary Services Offered by the Media

The media offers three broad categories of fashion auxiliary services: advertising, publicity, and public relations. **Advertising**, which appears in everything from magazines and newspapers to radio, television, and on the Internet, is space and time for which an advertiser pays. **Publicity** is the free and voluntary mention of a firm, product, or person in the media. Its purpose is to inform or enhance public interest about something specific. **Public relations**, a broader term than *publicity*, is also a free and voluntary mention, but it is designed to enhance a long-term goal, such as the shaping of a company's public image. All three efforts are important elements of the remaining auxiliary services.

One difference between advertising and publicity/public relations is the amount of control a manufacturer or retailer can exercise over each. Since advertising is purchased, a great deal of control can be exercised over its execution. Public relations and publicity can be carefully developed and well presented to the media, but there is no guarantee that the material and information supplied will be used well—or at all.

Some media—like newspapers and magazines—are moving away from print and transitioning to digital formats. Regardless of the form it may be in the future, it will continue to be a vital part of communications for the fashion industry.

Fashion Magazines

Fashion magazines, which combine advertising, publicity, and public relations, came into existence about 150 years ago in the form of a single publication called *Godey's Lady's Book*. Prior to that, women discussed the newest fashions with one another but had no authoritative source from which they could learn what was new and exciting. The magazine's first editor, Sarah Josepha Hale, is now best remembered for her early feminism, especially her struggle to help women win acceptance in professions, but her influence on fashion was equally important. *Godey's Lady's Book* reported on the latest styles and was the forerunner of today's fashion magazines, such as *Vogue*, *Harper's Bazaar*, *Glamour*, and *Seventeen* (for young women) (see Figure 12.1). Several other magazines have also established themselves as fashion arbiters, most notably *Elle*, which competes with *Glamour*, *Marie Claire*, and *Nylon*, which specializes in avant-garde fashion. In the mid- to late 1990s, new important lifestyle magazines appeared on the scene. The success to emerge from these offerings is *InStyle*, a monthly glossy that married celebrity and style editorial by covering fashion trends among celebrities and rigorously reporting on red-carpet ceremony dressing. *InStyle* was launched in 1994 and quickly became hugely successful. In 2020, its circulation was 1.7 million copies.[1] Magazines that appeal to specific ethnic markets include *Essence* and *Ebony*, for African Americans, and the bilingual *Latina* for Hispanics. Even more specialized are magazines such as *Brides*, which reports on wedding fashions, and *More*, which caters to women over the age of forty.

Figure 12.1 Well over a century after its first publication, *Vogue* continues to exert tremendous influence over the fashion world.

Gentlemen's Quarterly (*GQ*) is the largest circulating men's fashion magazine. *Esquire*, which covers topics beyond fashion, is still widely regarded as an authority on the latest trends in menswear. Other men's magazines that cover fashion in addition to other topics like health and sports include *Playboy*, *Men's Journal*, *Outside*, *FHM*, and *Maxim*. Some men's magazines, like *Maxim* and *FHM*, also have their own biannual men's fashion magazine editions, which tend to be considerably more upscale than their parent magazines.

The "shelter magazines" are devoted to home fashions. Among the better known are *Elle Decor*, *Architectural Digest*, *House Beautiful*, *Martha Stewart Living*, *Wallpaper**, *domino*, and *Surface*.

Fashions that appear in magazine articles are accompanied by an **editorial credit**, a unique form of publicity that names the manufacturer and lists retail stores where the clothes may be purchased. Editorial credit benefits even stores that are not listed because, if they have seen a magazine in advance, they can often stock the fashions. For advertisers whose merchandise is featured and credited in the editorial pages of a magazine, this publicity reinforces the paid advertising message.

General Consumer Publications

General-interest consumer publications also play a role in disseminating fashion news to the public. Practically every newspaper reports on fashion, and some, such as the *New York Times*, the *Los Angeles Times*, the *Chicago Tribune*, and the *Washington Post*, devote regular weekly sections to apparel and home fashion design. Their fashion editors cover fashion openings, press weeks, and trade shows around the world. In *Paper*, *Time Out*, *City*, and other magazines that deal with pop culture, fashion gets extensive coverage. *Time*, *Newsweek*, and *People* provide occasional but important fashion coverage, as do the traditional women's magazines such as *Good Housekeeping* and *Ladies' Home Journal*. *Cosmopolitan*, whose primary market is young singles, has a circulation of 2.6 million. Other women's magazines that are geared to women who are not full-time homemakers also carry fashion news for their market segments. Among the most influential are *O, The Oprah Magazine*; *Ms.*; and *Working Mother*, which covers career fashions. *Seventeen* and *Teen Vogue* are designed for young teenagers. Women's sports magazines, such as *Self*, *Shape*, *Fitness*, and *Sports*

Illustrated Women/Sport, include articles that cater to the fashion interests of female athletes and sports fans.

The New Yorker, *Vanity Fair*, *Harper's*, and the *Atlantic Monthly* occasionally bring fashion news to their urbane, sophisticated audiences.

Spanish-language versions of *People*, *Playboy*, *Cosmopolitan*, *Harper's Bazaar*, *Elle*, and *Marie Claire* are also in the market. The Spanish version of *Reader's Digest*, called *Selecciones*, is widely circulated. The publicity departments of most stores across the United States usually have no difficulty getting their messages across in local newspapers, since apparel stores are a major source of advertising revenue for newspapers.

Trade Publications

One of the most important aids to the merchandising of fashion are **trade publications**. Unlike the fashion magazines, trade newspapers and magazines are published just for the industry. Many discourage subscriptions from people outside their field; few are available at newsstands, except in fashion markets and marts.

These publications announce new technical developments, analyze fashion trends, report on current business conditions, and generally help all who work in the fashion industry keep up-to-date on a staggering number of new products, techniques, and markets. Even government regulations are covered, as are personnel changes and classified ads for jobs.

The best-known fashion trade publication is *Women's Wear Daily*, often referred to as the bible of the industry. It is one of the oldest publications of its kind, having first been published in 1910. *Women's Wear Daily* (commonly known as *WWD*), covers every aspect of the fashion industry from fiber and fabric to apparel, from day-to-day developments to new directions and trends. Each daily Web and weekly print issue highlights a different segment of the fashion industry. In 2008, *WWD* started including coverage of men's fashion, retail, and related industries in its pages. Special *WWD/Global* issues are published, providing an overview of the major international markets that prepare readers for the upcoming spring and fall fashion weeks.

Footwear News and *Accessories* cover their specialties as intensely as *WWD* covers the women's market. The youth market is covered in *Earnshaw's*. Department store and specialty store management and merchandising executives read *Stores* and *Chain Store Age*. The fiber and fabric professionals read *Textile World*.

The Broadcast Media

Fashion merchandisers have a choice of standard broadcast mediums: television, cable television, and radio. Or, they may choose the newest medium—the Internet and social media. Unlike the print media, the broadcast media are time- rather than space-oriented. Radio and television stations sell three levels of commercials in descending order of cost: network, spot, and local.

Broadcast media focused on children have received a good deal of critical attention over the years. Many new children's channels were launched, and the kids' market seemed like a place of golden opportunity for advertisers. However, the climate slowed down at the turn of the millennium and the children's channels that turned a profit were the already established and relatively inexpensive giants like Cartoon Network and Nickelodeon. The legendary *Sesame Street* left public television and moved to cable mainstay HBO in 2015. And Internet streaming services such as Netflix, Amazon, and DisneyNOW now provide their subscription-based services geared just for kids.

Television

One cannot turn on the television today without learning something about current apparel fashions. The fashion industry obtains invaluable publicity from the simple fact that everyone who acts in a show or hosts or appears on a newscast or talk show wants to—and usually does—wear the latest fashions.

Because of the technical expertise and high level of quality required for network television, outside advertising agencies are usually hired to produce television advertising. Agencies develop an idea, present it in storyboard form to their client, photograph the advertisement, obtain or create the music, and provide tapes to individual stations for on-air viewing. Daytime talk shows and television commercials are another avenue of promotion for national brands of apparel. There is also a website, WornOnTV.net, that provides retailer information on products from celebrity looks "seen on" TV. For example, a customer could find an outfit that was worn on *Almost Family*, and where it is available for purchase, with a link to the purchase site.[2]

Cable Television

Cable television has become an increasingly attractive option for fashion advertisers, largely because it costs so much less than network television. Many more outlets also exist for cable television, which reduces the competition to buy space. Cable television is also the home of the infomercial, the extended commercial in which a sponsor presents information about its product in a program format. Several celebrity-owned or franchised cosmetics lines have relied on this advertising medium (see Figure 12.2). The 1982 debut of the Home Shopping Network (HSN) marked the beginning of a new outlet for sales as well as advertising. (See Chapter 11 for more information on HSN and QVC.) Fashion-inspired shows on cable television include *The Rachel Zoe Project* and *Project Runway* both on Bravo.

Radio

While television and print are unsurpassed as a fashion advertising medium because of its visual qualities, radio is popular because it is inexpensive and can reach large but targeted audiences. Stations exist that serve only the youth market; others, such as classical radio stations, are geared to an older market. Others broadcast news and can deliver a virtual captive audience during the morning and evening commutes, the so-called drive time.

Commercials announcing sales and other storewide events can use radio effectively because they do not

Figure 12.2 The television set of "The Beauty Report with Amy Morrison," on HSN.

depend on visual appeals. To attract advertisers, stations provide assistance with the preparation of copy, which may be delivered by disc jockeys and other announcers. Radio is also a source of publicity as products and fashion news are discussed on regular shows.

The Internet and Social Media

Smart marketers acknowledge they need to be where the customer is—whether that's on a website, mobile device, Twitter, Facebook, or YouTube.

A web page is a reflection of a firm's identity, and in the fashion industry especially it is necessary to have a website that is well-designed and user-friendly (see Figure 12.3). Web pages also allow the company to reach selected market segments and respond to their specific needs at any given moment. For example, retail customers can locate the nearest outlet of a favorite chain store, job applicants can find out about available positions and submit their résumés, and employees can communicate with one another, as well as with customers and vendors. Customers also have the ability to view and purchase products online within minutes.

Besides creating a whole new vocabulary, social media has managed to make the global fashion industry seem small. **Social media** are forms of electronic communication in which users create online communities and share information, including photos, videos, and messages. What the fashionable are wearing all over the world can be discovered with a push of a button or click of the mouse. Companies have responded to the social media explosion by jumping onto social networking sites and accumulating fans on Facebook, while promoting new products and delivering instant information via Twitter. And many design houses "tweet" about their fashion brands. By 2018, the top five most followed "tweeting" brands were Chanel, Victoria's Secret, Marc Jacobs, H&M, and Burberry (see Figure 12.4).[3] The bloggers, who have become just as famous as the designers themselves, send their reviews from the front row of fashion shows straight to the rest of the world. YouTube is another medium used to show off collections and related fashion videos.

According to e-Marketer, digital marketing expenditures account for half of total media advertising spending worldwide. It is expected that digital marketing will grow to $517.51 billion and represent 60.5 percent of all marketing spending by 2023.[4]

Everyone with a networked computer, smartphone, or tablet is able to find like-minded others, to share and publish, to create an audience or a market, and to collaborate with others to create things. The phenomenon is changing the world from a one-to-many broadcast format to a many-to-many interactive conversation.

Advertising, Publicity, and Public Relations Agencies

Advertising, publicity, and public relations agencies do far more for the fashion industry than prepare and sell advertising. An agency in any of these three areas

Figure 12.3 H&M, like all modern retailers, has a strong Internet presence.

Figure 12.4 "Connect at the Speed of Fashion." Hashtag promotions help brands spread the word through the efforts of faithful and enthusiastic followers.

INSPIRING BEAUTY: 50 YEARS OF EBONY FASHION FAIR

Eunice Walker Johnson, wife of John Johnson, CEO of Johnson Publishing and founder of *Ebony* and *Jet* magazines, showcased high fashion for African American audiences for over fifty years through the Ebony Fashion Fair. From 1958 to 2009, the Ebony Fashion Fair traveled the United States in what was billed as "the world's largest traveling fashion show."

Fashions were personally selected by Johnson on her annual buying trips to Paris. She spent as much as $1.5 million on the looks and styles for each year's event, including creations from iconic designers:

"Inspiring Beauty: 50 Years of Ebony Fashion Fair," first held at the Chicago History Museum, features over sixty garments from icons of the fashion industry, and now travels to select communities throughout the United States.

Pierre Cardin, Emanuel Ungaro, Courreges, Givenchy, Christian LaCroix and Paco Rabanne, Balizza, Emilio Pucci, Angelo Marani Valentino, Bob Mackie, Bill Blass, Lagerfeld, Eric Gaskins, McQueen, Valentino, Guy LaRoche, Halston, and Dior.

Produced in every type of venue across the United States, from school gymnasiums to hotel ballrooms to civic arenas, the fashion fair featured black models and full music and light productions that brought high fashion alive for the audience. "My mother often spoke about the importance of African American women feeling beautiful," said Linda Johnson Rice, chairman of the Johnson Publishing Company. "The Ebony Fashion Fair legacy represents an important part of the rich African American cultural experience in America." The fashion fair not only helped Johnson Publishing reach its audience, but the event helped raise millions of dollars for charities through the years.

The fashion fair and its legacy inspired an exciting exhibit showcasing sixty iconic fashions, produced by the Chicago History Museum. The exhibit was carefully curated to showcase three essential themes:

Vision looks at themes of power, affluence, influence, use of color, risk taking, and celebration of the female body.

Innovation examines boldness and experimentation, and Johnson's response to the desires and influence of youthful audiences.

Power reflects the glamour and showmanship.

Since Johnson's death in 2009, the fashion fair has been on hiatus, but her legacy, showcased in "Inspiring Beauty: 50 Years of Ebony Fashion Fair," was celebrated in collaboration with the Chicago History Museum and then toured selected US cities for about four years to follow.

may be deeply involved in creating a multimedia campaign designed to shape the public's image of a client company. These campaigns are used for ongoing maintenance of a company's image as well as for an image change.

Advertising Agencies

Advertising agencies provide many services, all of which are tied to the selling of commercial advertising space and/or time. Some agencies are specialized and deal only with one medium or one type of client, while others are general, offering a full range of services for many different types of clients. Agencies vary from one-person shops to giant agencies that employ hundreds of people around the world. Small agencies claim to offer personal attention, but even large agencies divide their staff into creative teams so they, too, promise and often deliver a specialized service.

Public Relations Agencies

Public relations firms are involved in the creation of publicity as well as in public relations. Publicity and

public relations require that the agency work closely with its client, keeping abreast of what is new and newsworthy and announcing it to the world, either through press releases, often accompanied by photographs, or with story ideas presented to trade and consumer magazines and newspapers. As noted, public relations also involves, on a much deeper level, the shaping of a company's image. To this end, a public relations agency may suggest or help to plan and coordinate an event or activity, such as the rendering of a public service or gift to a charity or community or the presentation of a scholarship or endowment to an institution or foundation.

Other Advertising and Public Relations Services

Maintaining the corporate image of a fashion producer or retailer requires the services of a number of "creative" specialists, who may be company employees, agency employees, or freelancers. For example, fashion stylists may select and coordinate the apparel and accessories for store catalogs and print ads, for magazine articles, or for commercials. The job of the stylist involves juggling

SO, YOU WANT TO WORK IN FASHION!

FASHION. As we have explored throughout these pages, it is a diverse industry ranging from major international retailers to small, exclusive boutiques; brick-and-mortar and e-commerce; legendary, heritage brands to new, trendy start-ups; luxury to budget-friendly. Production and sourcing span the globe, utilizing an ever-growing, ever-evolving complex of technology, trade agreements, and more. And every level of the process involves a wide range of interesting and challenging job opportunities.

In a recent study released by the United States Congress Joint Economic Committee, fashion is a $2.5 trillion global industry, and in the U.S. we spend $380 billion each year on the fashion industry. Across the entire continuum of fashion and apparel jobs, 1.8 million people are employed in the United States.

Fashion manufacturing has declined significantly over the past two decades, from about 940,000 in 1990 to about 123,000 in 2019, with significant production moving overseas. But according to a report by the California Fashion Association, manufacturing is a very small part of the modern apparel industry. The modern industry is a sophisticated mix of market research, licensing, intellectual property rights, design engineering, sourcing, product development, information technology, multiplatform marketing, and distribution. According to this same report, in Los Angeles, the strongest job growth across all creative industries, came in digital media, with many of these jobs involving creative design or promotion for the fashion industry.

Jobs in fashion can be found throughout the country. However the lion's share of fashion jobs are found in New York and California. New York is one of four of the world's fashion capitals, which also include Paris, Milan, and London. One third of those employed as a designer in the U.S. work in New York, and as of 2017, the New York City fashion industry employed 4.6 percent of the city's total private sector workforce, generating $11.3 billion in wages. In addition, New York is home to prominent fashion schools, leading fashion publications, and costume collections. In California, the Los Angeles metro area fashion industry ranked second behind the entertainment industry, employing 87,600 with a payroll totaling $4.4 billion annually.

About 79 percent of all US employees in fashion work for an apparel or fashion retailer, at an annual salary of $26,650. The average salary increases, however in retail marketing and sales management to an average salary reaching $84,600, and these professionals are among the highest paid throughout the entire industry. Opportunities in the retail sector also include financial management, purchasing, shipping and receiving.

The message is that while manufacturing jobs have left the US, new, high-value jobs have emerged. And jobs in these fields require more education, more training—and offer the prospect of higher earnings. This diverse industry holds opportunities for a wide range of skills and interests, from creative, to scientific, to business, to financial, to legal, and more.

Even with this changing landscape of opportunity, competition remains high for positions in the fashion industry. One strategy available to students are internships. This provides an opportunity to do professional-level work for a short period of time to gain exposure to the industry, day-to-day experience in the field, and to network with potential colleagues. One controversy of this practice is that this work is often unpaid, and several top brands have fallen under fire as exploiting this "free labor." Some argue that unpaid internships unfairly discriminate against lower income students who cannot afford to relocate to expensive locations like New York, Los Angeles, or elsewhere and work for no compensation.

Gain the best possible advantage in a competitive job market with great training, and present yourself in a positive, professional manner.

Others argue that part of educating professionals is to ensure that they understand that their skills are valuable and should be fairly compensated. Unfortunately, however, a significant amount of low-level work is done by very elaborate and well-planned internship programs throughout a profit-driven industry.

In her recent book "The Most Beautiful Job in the World," author Giulia Mensitieri exposes how professionals far beyond the level of apprentice or intern, such as stylists, models, designers, photographers, hair and make-up artists, and more are exploited by the French fashion industry, often receiving merchandise as payment, or going unpaid altogether. Mensitieri explains the rationale. "The message is, you don't have to be paid because you are lucky to be here at all." This phenomenon is not unique to the French industry. A wide variety of professionals in the U.S. tell of working for very little or for free, with claims of experience, exposure, and the general thrill of participating as compensation.

As future fashion professionals, what are your thoughts on compensation, unpaid internships, and being asked to work for free? Does the glamour and creative opportunity warrant such practice toward young, hopeful professionals?

many tasks in one day and often includes charming celebrities into posing in outfits they dislike. Many stylists work in either Los Angeles or New York, but more job opportunities are growing across the country. Hollywood's top stylists include Tim Eerebout & Sandra Amador, Ilaria Urbinati, Rebecca Corbin-Murray, Elizabeth Stewart, Petra Flannery, Kate Young, Erin Walsh, Jessica paster, Karla Welch, and Wayman Bannerman & Micah McDonald. Stylists must work cooperatively with the rest of the team: the photographers, the makeup artist, the hairdresser, the magazine editor, and the celebrity's agent or publicist (see Figure 12.5).

Fashion illustrators' and photographers' work appears in advertising and in the editorial pages of consumer and trade publications. Skilled fashion photographers command creative control of a shoot as well as high pay. Independent fashion show production companies offer their services to producers, retailers, and trade organizations (see Figure 12.6).

Store Design and Visual Merchandising

Two important on-site promotional activities that support the selling of fashion merchandise are store design and visual merchandising. The term **visual merchandising** includes the arrangement and presentation of merchandise in store windows and on the selling floor. It covers the arrangement of items that are on sale as well as the display and sample items on mannequins and other props. The layout and design of any retail business have an impact on sales. For the traditional retailer operating in a store, the selling floor serves the critical purpose of presenting the merchandise to the customer, a function that is essential in selling fashion goods, for which appearance is a primary feature. Manufacturers' and designers' showrooms are their selling floors and, thus, require the same attention to interior design and visual merchandising.

Signs and Graphics

Signs and graphics enhance merchandise presentations both in windows and on the selling floor. Temporary signs to announce a sale or special event or inform shoppers of a price could be produced easily with computer software. More permanent signage, such as directional signs for elevators, escalators, departments, and restrooms, are more typically prepared by professionals. Like other aspects of visual merchandising, signs should be in keeping with the store's image.

Figure 12.5 Celebrity stylists to Lady Gaga, Sandra Amador and Tom Erebout, attending the Jimmy Choo Power Stylist Dinner.

Figure 12.6 Models, buyers, designers, event producers, photographers, hair and make-up artists, and any number of other fashion professionals work together to produce a fashion runway event.

Information Resources

The fashion business is so huge and complex that no one individual or company can keep abreast of everything that is happening in it. It is a business made up in large part of trends and news in addition to its products. As a result, the auxiliary service provided by fashion consultants and research agencies, whose role is to supply information, is vital to the industry.

Fashion Consultants and Information Services

Fashion consultants are individuals and groups who provide information and services to producers and retailers. The most famous pioneer in fashion consulting was Tobé Coller Davis, who founded her agency, Tobé Associates, in 1927. Now called TOBE, it has continued to be an important source of information for the industry for decades. Other well-known consultants include retail veteran Walter F. Loeb. Additionally, firms working in the fashion and retailing consulting area include Accenture Strategy, Retail Management Consultants, and WSL Strategic Retail.

The Fashion Group International, Inc.

Another vital source of industry information is the Fashion Group International, Inc., a nonprofit global association of professional women who work in the industry and the associated beauty and home fashions industries. It was founded in 1930 to create executive jobs for women. Over the ensuing decades, however, it has become an important consulting and research agency. Its services are offered to members and, in some instances, nonmembers. Originally a group of seventeen fashion leaders in New York, it now has more than 5,000 members in chapters in fashion centers across the world.

The Fashion Group is known for its exciting and prophetic fashion presentations. Through lavish fashion shows and fiber displays, it offers the fashion industry its expert and insightful analysis of upcoming trends. It covers the US, European, and Far Eastern fashion scenes. The Fashion Group also publishes monthly news bulletins and maintains a valuable website (www.fgi.org), an online information service featuring directories of industry executives and professional services, calendars of events, trend reports and forecasts, classified job listings, public announcements, and conferences.

Specialized Information Services

A number of services disseminate reports on various segments of the fashion industry. For example, Pantone, The *International Colour Authority*, and the Color Association of the United States (CAUS) specialize in reporting on color trends in womenswear and menswear.

Market Research Agencies

Because knowing what is new and what is now is at the very heart of fashion, businesses in all segments of the industry avidly consume the raw data and trend analyses published by market research agencies. The services of these professional prophets are expensive, but many of their findings are made public in time to be useful to a larger following. Among the better-known agencies is Kurt Salmon, known for its extensive work with textile and apparel manufacturers and softgoods retailers.

The major accounting firms also have special divisions devoted to the fashion industries. Ernst & Young, Deloitte & Touche USA, and Management Horizons (a division of PricewaterhouseCoopers) all offer respected management consulting services on a global basis.

A new breed of researchers and forecasters who rely on a variety of resources—including their own anecdotal observations and gut instincts as well as polls and surveys—is epitomized by Faith Popcorn. BrainReserve, the company she founded in 1974, currently has a staff of thirty, but it also retains its "TalentBank" of 5,000 authorities in a variety of businesses whom it consults regularly. BrainReserve's public opinion surveying technique involves hour-long face-to-face interviews. Popcorn boasts a 95 percent accuracy rate in her predictions.

Exemplifying a trend themselves, a number of trend-forecasting agencies specialize, and the youth culture is a well-studied specialty. The fashion industry, instead of attempting to dictate what will be worn next season, is actively seeking out the influential consumers and taking a cue from them. Fashion forecasters follow these influencers throughout their daily activities: school, concerts, sports events, shopping, the gym, and so on. Interviews, observations, and photo and video documentation are compiled, culminating in trend reports available to subscribers and clients. Some trend-

forecasting firms include the Doneger Group, Trendstop, Fashion Snoops, and Mudpie.

Trade Associations and Trade Shows

Associations of manufacturers and retailers assist fashion buyers in many ways. The nature and frequency of assistance available, however, are not uniform throughout the industry, and buyers soon learn how much assistance will be forthcoming from their particular trade.

Retailers Group

The National Retail Federation (NRF) is the largest retail trade association in the United States, counting among its members all the major department and specialty stores. It disseminates information and advice through its monthly magazine, *Stores*, and other periodicals and through regional and national meetings. An annual general convention is sponsored by the NRF in New York City in January. Vendors of products and services as diverse as market research, management software, and shopping bags exhibit at this meeting. Members gather at seminars and workshops to learn from retailing authorities and from one another. A special feature at this convention is a session devoted to outstanding fashion promotions during the previous year.

Buyers Groups

Specialized associations or buying clubs provide an opportunity for an exchange of opinions and ideas among members. Retail buyers' groups also transmit the preferences of their members on matters as varied as the dates when lines should be opened and the appropriate sizes of stock boxes for specific products. Trade associations are often subsidized by outside sources—either the industry itself or a trade publication.

Trade Shows

Retail and manufacturing groups, as well as independent organizations, sometimes sponsor trade shows at which many exhibitors gather to show their products and lines in one place, usually a hotel or convention center. Trade shows save time that would otherwise be spent trudging from showroom to showroom and provide buyers with a chance to meet and exchange ideas with one another. They are especially helpful in fashion areas made up of many small firms. Exhibitors also find them a place to meet their counterparts from other regions or countries.

Buying, Merchandising, and Product Development Organizations

Another type of auxiliary service—one developed especially for the fashion industry—is the **buying, merchandising, and product development organization**. This type of organization evolved from a service called a resident buying office (RBO), and to understand the function of a buying, merchandising, and product development organization, one must first know something about RBOs. The buying offices came into being to serve the ongoing needs of a store or group of stores for a steady supply of new merchandise. Because a store's buyers worked out of the store and made only occasional market trips, they came to rely on a service located at the market centers for ongoing, daily attention to the store's needs. Originally, RBOs existed only for out-of-town retailers to place orders. Today, their functions and their clients have become so diverse that the term *resident buying office* is no longer complete or accurate.

Although their main job remains buying and coordinating orders, buying offices provide many support services—not just to retailer buyers but also, in some instances, to wholesalers and apparel manufacturers. They watch and report on fashion trends, help with strategic planning, make vendor recommendations, coordinate imports, and assist in product development. They help to organize fashion weeks and ensure that they go smoothly for their client stores' buyers. A good buying office continually adds to its list of services, and many have even expanded into areas such as sales promotion and advertising, personnel operations, and computer processing.

Functions of the Buying, Merchandising, and Product Development Organization

Even with instant communication by e-mail and the Internet, the buying function benefits from the services of a representative and adviser who is actually at the market. Some of the functions that buying offices perform on behalf of their clients are purchasing, preparing for market weeks, importing, and developing products (see Figure 12.7).

Purchasing

Buying offices offer store buyers advice and support in various buying situations. For example, an office can place an order large enough to qualify for a manufacturer's quantity discount and then divide the goods among several small clients. The organization's staff can visit manufacturers' showrooms and make recommendations to their clients about specials, trends, and hot items. Size and location give the buying office clout with vendors when it comes to reordering in midseason or making sure the right goods are delivered on schedule.

Preparing for Market Weeks

Market weeks are hectic times for fashion buyers, filled with many showroom visits and other information-gathering events. A buying office can provide services

Figure 12.7 This computer rendering previews the look of *Teen Vogue*'s booth at the upcoming WWD Magic convention.

EILEEN FISHER: Winner of the 2019 CFDA Positive Change Award

Eileen Fisher, winner of the 2019 CFDA Positive Change Award.

"We actually think maybe we don't have to sell so many clothes," said no designer, ever! That is, until now.

In the quest for greater sustainability, one could argue that the most sustainable product is something that lasts so long that a customer doesn't have to buy a replacement for years.

Designer Eileen Fisher is known for elegant, timeless garments styled from fine linen, wool and cotton. Her clothing is meant to last as long as possible, and instead of "replacing" ones wardrobe each year or each season, her styles are meant to be kept, add to, and enhance a woman's wardrobe.

With this focus on sustainable design, the company continues to look for ways to enhance their responsible practices. All of the cotton and linen is organic. As for the wool, the company works with ranchers who use regenerative practices to raise sheep. Designers are beginning to use recycled plastic bottles to make dresses and shoes, and they are shifting to more environmentally responsible dyes. Improvements to their operations activities include limiting air shipments of goods to as few as possible.

But Eileen Fisher takes it even a step further. Americans discard about seventy pounds of "old" clothing each year and Eileen Fisher has been a leader in circular design. This is the practice of using and reusing materials to create new clothing,

Eileen Fisher is a brand known for casual, elegant styles—seasonless and timeless!

rather than dumping, burying, or discarding. Circular design sounds like a good idea, but in reality, it is difficult, time-consuming, and expensive, making it something tough to actually accomplish on a large-scale basis. However, through the Eileen Fisher Tiny Factory in Irvington, New York, the company executes an elaborate and organized system of organizing, sorting, cataloguing, and storing old clothing for the purpose of creating new.

The company has been recapturing its own used product since 2009, resulting in about 1 million items collected. About half of the items are nearly new and can be re-sold as is through their RENEW program.

The other half is used to make new garments, and about 1,000 garments a year are produced through this facility.

Eileen Fisher was awarded the 2019 CFDA Positive Change Award, celebrating and recognizing her remarkable steps toward sustainable initiatives.

New clothes made from old, through the Eileen Fisher RENEW program. Using garments from the company's collection program, garments are sorted, cleaned, dismantled, and remade into new pieces which are sold alongside fashions from the regular collection.

similar to those of a tour guide to make the buying trip smooth and efficient. Staff members visit the showrooms in advance and assess each manufacturer's lines on behalf of their various clients. When the store buyers arrive, the buying office may give presentations to let them know what to expect. Sometimes personnel from a buying office accompany visiting buyers to vendors' showrooms and offer on-the-spot advice about orders.

Importing

In response to the increasingly global nature of the fashion business, many buying offices maintain divisions in key foreign cities or affiliate with a commissionaire overseas. (A commissionaire is an agent that represents stores in foreign markets. See Chapter 10 for further discussion.) Overseas divisions and commissionaires work closely with the merchandising division and with client stores. In addition to performing the buying functions of a domestic buying office, these services deal with the unique challenges of importing, such as quotas, tariffs, long lead times for delivery, and interpretation of the buyers' orders for vendors who speak a different language. Having an adviser and consultant overseas is especially beneficial for buyers who are attending a market week or trade show or having private-label goods produced in a foreign country.

Developing Products

Buying offices have played an important role in the development of private labels. Most corporate-owned buying offices have a private label program for their member stores.

Corporate offices have also aggressively pursued private-label business and product development. Macy's has a well-established product development and private-label program. It employs more than 500 people in more than eighteen countries to design, develop, and identify manufacturers for its product development private-label business.

Summary and Review

Fashion producers and retailers depend on a variety of auxiliary services to support the merchandising function. Depending on the size and resources of a company, it may rely on its own staff for these services or hire outside firms to perform them.

The media regard fashion businesses as clients and offer assistance in preparing and placing advertising in newspapers, in consumer and trade magazines, and on the Internet. They also air commercials on television and radio. Today, the use of social media is a fast-growing marketing tool for the industry. To attract advertisers, the media offer fashion businesses color and style forecasts and other trend information. Advertising and public relations agencies also provide auxiliary services in placing paid advertisements and free publicity in the media. Store design and visual merchandising are other promotional services that may be performed by staff members or independent suppliers.

For information about industry trends and fashion forecasts, retailers and producers can take advantage of the services offered by fashion consulting firms, market research agencies, trade associations, and trade shows.

A source of information unique to the fashion industry is the buying, merchandising, and product development organization. This type of business began as resident buying offices, representing out-of-town retailers in the major markets. Some firms were independent, selling their services to noncompeting retailers. Others were corporate owned, either as cooperatives owned by several retailers or as divisions of large retail chains. Resident buying offices have evolved into businesses that include wholesalers and producers among their clients and that provide a full range of services, including liaisons with vendors, advice and assistance in buying and merchandising, and forecasting and other information services.

FOR REVIEW

1. What is the difference between advertising and publicity/public relations?
2. Describe the contents of *Women's Wear Daily*.
3. What are the advantages of television, radio, the Internet, and social media for fashion exposure? Do you prefer one instead of another? Why?
4. What tasks do public relations firms undertake for their clients?
5. What advantages does a website or social media offer as a promotional medium?
6. How does a store design contribute to the store's image?
7. Describe the research methods that trend forecasters use.
8. What is the major function of buying, merchandising, and product development organizations? What additional services do they perform?
9. What are the similarities and differences between independent and corporate buying, merchandising, and product development offices?

FOR DISCUSSION

1. As a consumer, where do you get your information about fashion? How does each medium influence your buying decisions?
2. You own a small boutique that caters to upscale young women. What services of a buying, merchandising, and product development organization would be most useful to you? Why?

Trade Talk

Define or briefly explain the following terms:

advertising
buying, merchandising, and product development organization
editorial credit
public relations
publicity
social media
trade publications
visual merchandising

GLOSSARY

activewear The sector of sportswear that includes casual attire worn for sports such as running, jogging, tennis, and racquetball. Sometimes called active sportswear. (Chapter 8)

adaptations Designs that have all the dominant features of the styles that inspired them but do not claim to be exact copies. (Chapter 1)

advertising The paid use of space or time in any medium. This includes newspapers, magazines, direct-mail pieces, shopping news bulletins, theater programs, catalogs, business cards, billboards, radio, TV, and the Internet. (Chapter 12)

anchor A design from a previous season reworked in a different color of fabric. (Chapter 7)

apparel contractor A producer whose sole function is to supply sewing services to the industry; here it is sometimes called an outside shop. (Chapter 7)

apparel jobber (manufacturing) A firm that handles the designing, planning, and purchasing of materials and usually the cutting, selling, and shipping of apparel, but not the actual garment sewing. (Chapter 7)

apparel manufacturer Performs all the operations required to produce apparel, from buying the fabric to selling and shipping the finished garments. (Chapter 7)

auxiliary level Composed of all the support services that work with primary producers, secondary manufacturers, and retailers to keep consumers aware of the fashion merchandise produced for ultimate consumption. (Chapter 4)

bootleg goods Quality products made by the same manufacturer that produces the genuine branded products; these are sold to the black market. (Chapter 10)

boutique A shop associated with few-of-a-kind merchandise, generally of very new and extreme styles, with an imaginative presentation of goods. French word for *shop*. (Chapter 10)

brand names Words, names, symbols, etc., especially those legally registered as trademarks, used by a manufacturer or merchant to identify its products distinctively from others of the same type and usually prominently displayed on its goods, in advertising, etc. (Chapter 5)

bridge jewelry Merchandise ranging from costume to fine jewelry in price, materials, and newness of styling. (Chapter 9)

bundling Assembling the cut pieces of each pattern—sleeves, collars, fronts, and backs—into bundles according to their sizes. Usually done by hand. (Chapter 7)

buyer's directory A list (and often a map) of the manufacturer's showrooms in a particular market or mart; it is furnished to retail buyers to assist them in "working the market." (Chapter 10)

buying, merchandising, and product development organization *Associated/cooperative*: One that is jointly owned and operated by a group of independently owned stores. *Private*: One that is owned and operated by a single, out-of-town store organization, and which performs market work exclusively for that store organization. *Salaried, Fee*, or *Paid*: One that is independently owned and operated and which charges the stores it represents for the work it does. *Syndicate/Corporate*: One that is maintained by a parent organization that owns a group of stores and that performs market work exclusively for those stores. (Chapter 12)

carat A measure of weight of precious stones equal to 200 milligrams or 1/142 of an ounce. See also *karat*. (Chapter 9)

category or classification buying A practice whereby a chain store buyer located in a central buying office is usually assigned to purchase only a specific category or classification of merchandise instead of buying all categories carried in a single department. See also *departmental buying*. (Chapter 11)

category killer Superstores or category specialists who so dominate a market that they drive out, or kill, smaller specialty stores. (Chapter 11)

chain organization A group of twelve or more centrally owned stores, each handling somewhat similar goods that are merchandised and controlled from a central headquarters office (as defined by the US Bureau of the Census). (Chapter 11)

chargebacks Financial penalties imposed on manufacturers by retailers. (Chapter 7)

classic A style or design that satisfies a basic need and remains in general fashion acceptance for an extended period of time. (Chapter 1)

collection A term used in the United States and Europe for an expensive line. (Chapter 7)

commissionaire (pronounced *ko-mee-see-oh-NAIR*) An independent retailer's service organization, usually located in the major city of a foreign market area. It is roughly the foreign equivalent of an American resident buying office. (Chapter 10)

computer-aided design (CAD) A computer program that allows designers to manipulate their designs easily. (Chapter 7)

computer-aided manufacturing (CAM) Stand-alone computerized manufacturing equipment, including computerized sewing, patternmaking, and cutting machines. (Chapter 7)

computer-integrated manufacturing (CIM) Many computers within a manufacturing company are linked from the design through the production stages. (Chapter 7)

corporate licensing The use of a company's name on (sometimes) related merchandise. (Chapter 7)

costume jewelry Mass-produced jewelry made of brass or other base metals, plastic, wood, or glass, and set with simulated or nonprecious stones. Also called fashion jewelry. (Chapter 9)

cotton A natural fiber produced from the substance that is attached to the seed of a cotton plant. It is the most widely used of all the natural fibers. (Chapter 5)

couture house (pronounced *koo-TOUR*) An apparel firm for which the designer creates original styles. (Chapter 10)

couturier (male) or couturière (female) (pronounced *koo-tour-ee-AY* and *koo-tour-ee-AIR*) The proprietor or designer of a French couture house. (Chapter 10)

créateurs (pronounced *kray-ah-TOURS*) French ready-to-wear designers. (Chapter 10)

culmination (stage) See *fashion cycle*. (Chapter 1)

custom-made Clothing fitted specifically to the wearer. (Chapter 8)

decline (stage) See *fashion cycle*. (Chapter 1)

demographics Studies that divide broad groups of consumers into smaller, more homogeneous target segments; the variables include population distribution, age, sex, family life cycle, race, religion, nationality, education, occupation, and income. (Chapter 2)

department store As defined by the US Bureau of the Census, a store that employs twenty-five or more people and sells general lines of merchandise in each of three categories: home furnishings, household linens and dry goods (an old trade term meaning piece goods and sewing notions), and apparel and accessories for the entire family. (Chapter 11)

departmental buying A practice whereby a department buyer is responsible for buying all the various categories of merchandise carried in that department. See also *category buying*. (Chapter 11)

design A specific version of a variation of a style. In everyday usage, however, fashion producers and retailers refer to a design as a *style*, a *style number*, or simply a *number*. (Chapter 1)

details The individual elements that give a silhouette its form or shape. These include trimmings; skirt and pant length and width; and shoulder, waist, and sleeve treatment. (Chapter 1)

discount store A departmentalized retail store using many self-service techniques to sell its goods. It operates usually at low profit margins, has a minimum annual volume of $500,000, and is at least 10,000 square feet in size. (Chapter 11)

discretionary income The money that an individual or family has to spend or save after buying necessities such as food, clothing, shelter, and basic transportation. (Chapter 2)

disposable personal income The amount of money a person has left to spend or save after paying taxes. It is roughly equivalent to what an employee calls *take-home pay* and provides an approximation of the purchasing power of each consumer during any given year. (Chapter 2)

diversification The addition of various lines, products, or services to serve different markets. (Chapter 4)

Dominican Republic-Central American Free Trade Agreement (CAFTA-DR) Passed in July 2005. Eliminated most trade barriers between the United States and Costa Rica, the Dominican Republic, El Salvador, Guatemala, Honduras, and Nicaragua. (Chapter 10)

downward-flow theory The theory of fashion adoption, which maintains that to be identified as a true fashion, a style must first be adopted by people at the top of the social pyramid. The style then gradually wins acceptance at progressively lower social levels. Also called the trickle-down theory. (Chapter 3)

e-commerce Commercial transactions conducted electronically on the Internet. (Chapter 11)

editorial credit The mention in a magazine or newspaper of a store name as a retail source for merchandise that is being editorially featured by the publication. (Chapter 12)

electronic data interchange (EDI) The electronic exchange of machine-readable data in standard formats between one company's computers and another company's computers. (Chapter 7)

environment The conditions under which we live that affect our lives and influence our actions. (Chapter 2)

erogenous Sexually stimulating. (Chapter 3)

export When a country provides goods to another country. (Chapter 10)

fabrics Materials formed from knitted, woven, or bonded yarns. (Chapter 5)

factor Financial institution that specializes in buying accounts receivable at a discount. (Chapter 7)

factory outlet store Manufacturer-owned store that sells company products at reduced prices in austere surroundings with minimum services. (Chapter 11)

fad A short-lived fashion. (Chapter 1)

fashion A style that is accepted and used by the majority of groups at any one time. (Chapter 1)

fashion business Any business concerned with goods or services in which fashion is an element—including fiber, fabric, and apparel manufacturing; distribution; advertising; publishing; and consulting. (Chapter 1)

fashion cycle The rise, widespread popularity, and then decline in acceptance of a style. *Rise*: The acceptance of either a newly introduced design or its adaptions by an increasing number of consumers. *Culmination*: The period when a fashion is at the height of its popularity and use. The fashion then is in such demand that it can be mass-produced, mass-distributed, and sold at prices within the reach of most consumers. *Decline*: The decrease in consumer demand because of boredom resulting from widespread use of a fashion. *Obsolescence*: When disinterest occurs and a style can no longer be sold at any price. (Chapter 1)

fashion industries Those engaged in producing the materials used in the production of apparel and accessories for men, women, and children. (Chapter 1)

fashion influential A person whose advice is sought by associates. A fashion influential's adoption of a new style gives it prestige among a group. (Chapter 3)

fashion innovator A person first to try out a new style. (Chapter 3)

fast fashion A strategy of constantly changing fashion to keep it fresh by basing the collections on the most recent fashion trends presented at Fashion Week and manufacturing it quickly in an affordable way to the mainstream consumer, allowing retailers to develop ways to create and officially manage a variety. (Chapter 1)

fiber A threadlike unit of raw material from which yarn and, eventually, textile fabric is made. (Chapter 5)

first cost The wholesale price of merchandise in the country of origin. (Chapter 10)

flash-sale An e-commerce business model in which a brand or retailer offers a single product for sale for a period of twenty-four to thirty-six hours to promote new merchandise. These promotions involve a limited inventory, offering an extraordinary deal to the consumer. (Chapter 11)

flax Comes from the stem of a flax plant. It is used to make linen. (Chapter 5)

floor ready Merchandise that has been ticketed with a bar-coded price and packed in labeled cartons with all shipping documents attached. If the merchandise is a garment, it has been pressed and folded or hung on a hanger with a plastic bag over it. (Chapter 7)

franchise A contracted agreement in which a firm or individual buys the exclusive right to conduct retail business within a specified trading area under a franchiser's registered or trademark name. (Chapter 4)

fur farming The breeding and raising of fur-bearing animals under controlled conditions. (Chapter 6)

general merchandise retailer Retail stores that sell a number of lines of merchandise—for example, apparel and accessories; furniture and home furnishings; household linens and dry goods; and hardware, appliances, and smallwares—under one roof. Stores included in this group are commonly known as mass-merchandisers, department stores, variety stores, general merchandise stores, or general stores. (Chapter 11)

generic names Nontrademarked names assigned by the Federal Trade Commission to twenty-three manufactured fibers. (Chapter 5)

geographics Population studies that focus on where people live. (Chapter 2)

geotextiles Manufactured, permeable textiles currently used in reinforcing or stabilizing civil engineering projects. (Chapter 5)

global sourcing Term used to describe the process of shopping for and purchasing imported goods. (Chapter 10)

graded Adjustment of a style's sample pattern to meet the dimensional requirements of each size in which the style is to be made. Also referred to as sloping. (Chapter 7)

gray market goods Goods not intended for sale in the country in which they are being sold, often with an invalid warranty. (Chapter 10)

greige goods (pronounced *gray*) Fabric that has received no preparation, dyeing, or finishing treatment after having been produced by any textile process. (Chapter 5)

group A subdivision of a line, linked by a common theme such as color, fabric, or style. (Chapter 7)

haute couture (pronounced *oat-koo-TOUR*) The French term literally meaning "fine sewing" but actually having much the same sense as our own term *high fashion*. (Chapter 10)

hemp A cellulose fibrous plant. (Chapter 5)

hides Animal skins that weigh over twenty-five pounds when shipped to a tannery. (Chapter 6)

high fashion Styles or designs accepted by a limited group of fashion leaders—the elite among consumers—who are first to accept fashion change. (Chapter 1)

high-tech fabric A fabric that has been constructed, finished, or processed in a way that gives it certain innovative, unusual, or hard-to-achieve qualities not normally available. (Chapter 5)

horizontal-flow theory The theory of fashion adoption that holds that fashions move horizontally between groups on similar social levels rather than vertically from one level to another. Also called the mass-market theory. (Chapter 3)

horizontal growth A company expands on the level on which it has been performing. See also *vertical growth*. (Chapter 4)

import When a country buys goods from a foreign country. (Chapter 10)

inflation A substantial and continuing rise in the general price level. (Chapter 2)

item house Contractors that specialize in the production of one product. (Chapter 7)

karat A measure of the weight of the gold content of jewelry; abbreviated as *K*. (Chapter 9)

kips Animal skins weighing from fifteen to twenty-five pounds when shipped to a tannery. (Chapter 6)

knockoff A trade term referring to the copying, at a lower price, of an item that has had good acceptance at higher prices. (Chapter 1)

leased departments A department ostensibly operated by the store in which it is found but actually run by an outsider who pays a percentage of sales to the store as rent. (Chapter 11)

let out (furs) A cutting and resewing operation to make short skins into longer-length skins adequate for garment purposes. (Chapter 6)

licensing An arrangement whereby firms are given permission to produce and market merchandise in the name of the licensor, who is paid a percentage of sales for permitting his or her name to be used. (Chapter 4)

line An assortment of new designs offered by manufacturers to their customers, usually on a seasonal basis. (Chapter 4)

line-for-line These are exactly like the original designs except that they have been mass-produced in less expensive fabrics in standard size measurements. (Chapter 7)

m-commerce Consumer purchases researched or made over mobile devices, such as smartphones or tablets. (Chapter 11)

magalogs Catalogs that have editorial content, not just advertising. (Chapter 11)

marker (apparel manufacturing) A long piece of paper upon which the pieces of the pattern of a garment in all its sizes are outlined and that is placed on top of many layers of material for cutting purposes. (Chapter 7)

market A group of potential customers. Also the place or area in which buyers and sellers meet for the purpose of trading ownership of goods at wholesale prices. (Chapter 10)

market center A geographic center for the creation and production of fashion merchandise, as well as for exchanging ownership. (Chapter 10)

market segmentation The separating of the total consumer market into smaller groups known as market segments. (Chapter 2)

market week Scheduled periods throughout the year during which producers and their sales representatives introduce new lines for the upcoming season to retail buyers. (Chapter 10)

marketing A total system of business activities designed to plan, price, promote, and place (distribute) products and services to existing and potential customers. (Chapter 1)

mart A building or building complex housing both permanent and transient showrooms of producers and their sales representatives. (Chapter 10)

mass customization The idea to tailor the product to fit one particular customer—not one-size-fits-all—and to supply thousands of individuals, at mass prices, not custom-made prices. (Chapter 7)

mass or volume fashion Styles or designs that are widely accepted. (Chapter 1)

masstige When luxury designers apply their creativity to create apparel intended for mass market. (Chapter 8)

merchandising Sales promotion as a comprehensive function including market research, development of new products, coordination of manufacture and marketing, and effective advertising and selling. (Chapter 1)

merger A sale of one company to another with the result that only one company exists. (Chapter 4)

microfiber A fiber two or three times thinner than a human hair and thinner than wool, cotton, flax, or silk fibers. It has a texture similar to silk or cashmere but is wrinkle resistant. (Chapter 5)

millinery The women's hat industry. (Chapter 9)

mom-and-pop stores Small stores run by the proprietor with few or no hired assistants. (Chapter 11)

multichannel Access to more than one way to purchase goods from a company. Such options include physical stores, online stores, mobile app stores, telephone sales, catalogs, and any other method of transacting between customer and merchant. (Chapter 11)

natural fibers Fibers found in nature that originate from a plant or animal source. (Chapter 5)

North American Free Trade Agreement (NAFTA) An agreement that eliminated quotas and tariffs for goods shipped among Canada, the United States, and Mexico. This agreement is being replaced by the United States-Mexico-Canada Agreement (USMCA). (Chapter 10)

obsolescence (stage) See *fashion cycle*. (Chapter 1)

off-price retailing The selling of brand name and designer merchandise at lower-than-normal retail prices when they are at the late rise or early peak in the fashion cycle. (Chapter 11)

offshore production The importation of goods by domestic apparel producers, either from their own plants operating in cheap, labor-rich foreign areas or through their long-term supply arrangements with foreign producers. (Chapter 7)

omni-channel A seamless approach to multichannel commerce. A customer uses more than one channel to research and shop from a retailer for any given transaction. (Chapter 11)

outside shop See *apparel contractor*. (Chapter 7)

pelt The skin of a fur-bearing animal. (Chapter 6)

per capita personal income The wages, salaries, interest, dividends, and all other income received by the population as a whole, divided by the number of people in the population. (Chapter 2)

personal income The total or gross amount of income received from all sources by the population as a whole. It consists of wages, salaries, interest, dividends, and all other income for everyone in the country. See also *disposable personal income* and *discretionary income*. (Chapter 2)

PETA People for the Ethical Treatment of Animals; a nonprofit organization devoted to animal rights. (Chapter 6)

piecework A production method in which each operator sews only a section of the garment to speed the production process. See also *section work*. (Chapter 7)

prêt-à-porter (pronounced *preht-ah-por-TAY*) A French term meaning "ready-to-wear." (Chapter 10)

price zones A series of somewhat contiguous price lines that appeal to specific target groups of customers. (Chapter 8)

primary level Composed of the growers and producers of the raw materials of fashion—the fiber, fabric, leather, and fur producers—who function in the raw materials market. (Chapter 4)

primary suppliers Producers of fibers, textile fabrics, finished leathers, and furs.

private label Merchandise that meets standards specified by a retail firm and belongs to it exclusively. Primarily used to ensure consistent quality of products as well as to meet price competition. (Chapter 5, 7)

product development The teaming of market and trend research, with the merchandising, design, and technical processes that develop a final product used by both wholesale manufacturers, who develop products for signature brands, and retailers, who use it for private-label development at their own stores. (Chapter 7)

product lifecycle management (PLM) An advanced software technology that helps manage the lifecycle of a product from concept through manufacture.

product manager See *specification manager*. (Chapter 7)

profit The amount of money a business earns in addition to its expenses; net income. (Chapter 4)

prophetic styles Particularly interesting new styles that are still in the introductory phases of their fashion cycles. (Chapter 3)

psychographics Studies that develop fuller, more personal portraits of potential customers, including personality, attitude, interests, personal opinions, and actual product benefits desired. (Chapter 2)

public relations Works to improve a client's public image and may develop long-range plans and directions for this purpose. (Chapter 12)

publicity The mention of a firm, brand, product, or person in some form of media. (Chapter 12)

purchasing power The value of the dollar as it relates to the amount of goods or services it will buy. A decline in purchasing power is caused by inflation. (Chapter 2)

quality assurance (QA) Inspection of each component of a garment to ensure that it meets the standards established for it. (Chapter 7)

quick response (QR) A strategy used by manufacturers to shorten the ordering cycle to compete with foreign imports. (Chapter 7)

radio frequency identification (RFID) Uses electronic tags for storing data, using a unique serial number that allows the tracking of products, cartons, containers, and individual items as they move through the supply chain. They hold more data than bar codes and can be read many times faster. (Chapter 7)

ramie A minor natural cellulosic fiber from a woody-leafed plant grown mostly in China. (Chapter 5)

ready-to-wear Apparel made in factories to standard size measurements. Sometimes referred to as RTW. (Chapter 8)

recession A low point in a business cycle when money and credit become scarce and unemployment is high. (Chapter 2)

regenerated fibers A fiber created in a laboratory combining natural cellulosic materials with chemical compounds. (Chapter 5)

retail level The ultimate distribution-level outlets for fashion goods directly to the consumer. (Chapter 4)

rise (stage) See *fashion cycle*. (Chapter 1)

royalty fee Percentage of licensee sales paid to the licensor. See also *licensing*.

sales representatives Company representatives who exhibit merchandise to potential customers. (Chapter 4)

sample hand The designer's assistant who sews the sample garment. (Chapter 7)

secondary level Composed of industries—manufacturers and contractors—that produce the semi-finished or finished fashion goods from the materials supplied by the primary level. (Chapters 4, 10)

section work The division of labor in apparel manufacturing whereby each sewing-machine operator sews only a certain section of the garment, such as a sleeve or hem. (Chapter 7)

showcase stores A manufacturer's or designer's store that sells merchandise at the introductory and early rise stages of the fashion cycle. (Chapter 11)

silhouette The overall outline or contour of a costume. Also frequently referred to as *shape* or *form*. (Chapter 1)

silk Comes from a cocoon formed by a silkworm. It is best known for its luxurious feel; it is a breathable fabric that can be worn year-round. (Chapter 5)

skins Animal skins that weigh fifteen or fewer pounds when shipped to a tannery. (Chapter 6)

social media Forms of electronic communication in which users create online communities and share information, including photos, videos, and messages. (Chapter 2, 12)

social mobility When an individual or group moves within a social hierarchy. There is also an effort to associate with a higher class by imitation. (Chapter 2)

specification buying A type of purchasing that is done to the store's rather than to the manufacturer's standards. See also *private label*. (Chapter 7)

specification manager Manager who oversees the purchasing and manufacturing process for a private label. Also called a product manager. (Chapter 7)

spinnerette A mechanical device through which a thick liquid base is forced to produce fibers of varying lengths. (Chapter 5)

spreader A laying-up machine that carries material along a guide on either side of a cutting table, spreading the material evenly, layer upon layer. (Chapter 7)

sterling silver A term used for jewelry and flatware with at least 92.5 parts of silver; the remaining 7.5 parts are usually copper. (Chapter 9)

style A characteristic or distinctive mode of presentation or conceptualization in a particular field. In apparel, style is the characteristic or distinctive appearance of a garment, the combination of features that makes it different from other garments. (Chapter 1)

style number The number manufacturers and retailers assigned. The number identifies the product for manufacturing, ordering, and selling. (Chapter 1)

suit separates (menswear) Sports jacket and trousers worn much as the tailored suit used to be. (Chapter 8)

sumptuary laws Laws regulating consumer purchases (for example, dress) on religious or moral grounds. (Chapter 3)

supply chain management (SCM) Allows companies to share forecasting, point-of-sale data, inventory information, and the supply and demand for materials or products. (Chapter 7)

sustainable use An environmental program that encourages landowners to preserve animal young and habitats in return for the right to use a percentage of the grown animals. (Chapter 6)

synthetic fibers A fiber produced from basic raw materials such as petroleum or minerals and manufactured in a laboratory. The original form does not resemble a fiber. (Chapter 5)

tailored suit A structured suit that is designed to fit close to the body, rather than being loose. (Chapter 8)

tanning The process of transforming animal skins into leather. (Chapter 6)

target market A specific group of potential customers that manufacturers and retailers are attempting to turn into regular customers. (Chapter 2)

taste The recognition of what is and is not attractive and appropriate. Good taste in fashion means sensitivity not only to what is artistic but also to these considerations. (Chapter 1)

textile fabric Cloth or material made from fibers by weaving, knitting, braiding, felting, crocheting, knotting, laminating, or bonding. (Chapter 5)

texture The look and feel of material, woven or nonwoven. (Chapter 1)

trade associations Professional organizations for manufacturers or sales representatives. (Chapter 10)

trade publications Newspapers or magazines published specifically for professionals in a special field, such as fashion. (Chapter 12)

trade shows Periodic merchandising exhibits staged in various regional trading areas around the country by groups of producers and their sales representatives for the specific purpose of making sales of their products to retailers in that area. (Chapter 10)

trend A general direction or movement. (Chapter 1)

trimmings All the materials—excluding the fabric—used in the construction of a garment, including braid, bows, buckles, buttons, elastic, interfacing, padding, self-belts, thread, zippers, etc. (Chapter 5)

trunk show A form of pretesting that involves a designer or manufacturer sending a representative to a store with samples of the current line and exhibiting those samples to customers at scheduled, announced showings. (Chapter 8)

United States-Mexico-Canada Agreement (USMCA) A trade agreement between the US, Mexico, and Canada meant to replace the North American Free Trade Agreement (NAFTA). Once fully enacted, the agreement proposes to balance trade between the economies of North American countries. (Chapter 10)

universal product code (UPC) One of a number of bar codes used for automatic identification of items scanned at retail cash registers. UPC is the symbol that has been most widely accepted by retailers and manufacturers. (Chapter 7)

upward-flow theory The theory of fashion adoption that holds that the young—particularly those of low-income families as well as those of higher income who adopt low-income lifestyles—are quicker than any other social group to create or adopt new and different fashions. (Chapter 3)

vermeil (pronounced *vur-MAY*) A composite of gold over sterling silver.

versioning The ability to tailor versions of a catalog to different customer segments based on age, income, and product preferences. (Chapter 9)

versioning The practice of tailoring different versions of a catalog to different customer segments, allowing catalog marketers to focus on consumers by age, income, geographic region, lifestyle, and interests. (Chapter 11)

vertical growth When a company expands on a level different from its original one. (Chapter 4)

visual merchandising Everything visual that is done to, with, or for a product and its surroundings to encourage its sales. This includes display, store layout, and store decor. (Chapter 12)

wicking Fabrics that are capable of transporting moisture; have resistance to radiation, corrosive chemicals, and other stresses; and adjust to extreme weather changes. (Chapter 5)

wool The protein fiber that comes from the fleece coat of sheep. (Chapter 5)

yarn A continuous thread formed by spinning or twisting fibers together. (Chapter 5)

TOP 100 FASHION INFLUENCERS

What makes top 100 lists so much fun? The intense debate, evaluation, and reevaluation they inspire; it's also what makes them such a valuable learning experience. Iconic fashion influencers are not only designers. Brands, models, muses, entertainers, photographers, writers, and others contribute to what we wear and why we wear it. Influencers move fashion culture in every era, and in a wide variety of ways. So enjoy the list. Is this the last word on who is hot and who is not in terms of key influencers? Not at all! Someone not listed who you think should be there? Add it! Someone on the list who you think doesn't belong? Subtract it! And be ready to support your ideas with reasons for your choices. Have fun!

	Name	Decades Of Influence	Profession	Defining Characteristics
1	Richard Avedon	1950s–1980s	Photographer	Deceptively simple images, exposing the emotions and spirit of the subject.
2	Azzedine Alaia	1980s–2000s	Designer	Famous for seductive clothes. "King of Cling."
3	Giorgio Armani	1980s–2000s	Designer	Impacted men's and women's fashions. Fluid tailoring and luxurious fabrics.
4	Cristobal Balenciaga	1940s–1960s	Designer	Considered one of the greatest designers of the 20th century. Inspired work of many later designers—Givenchy, Ungaro, and Courrèges.
5	Josephine Baker	1920s–1930s	Entertainer	African American expat Paris entertainer who became famous for her exotic dance costumes.
6	Brigitte Bardot	1950s–1970s	Entertainer	French trendsetter and muse of Andy Warhol. Popularized bikini by wearing it in several films; sparked trends for wide-collared knit tops and ballerina flats.
7	The Beatles	1960s–1970s	Entertainers	Beatlemania! Worldwide cultural phenomenon. Along with records, they sold trends; copycat fans copied mop-top hair, mod clothing, bright colors, Cuban heels, mustaches.

	Name	Decades Of Influence	Profession	Defining Characteristics
8	Bill Blass	1970s–1990s	Designer	Mr. Sophistication. Refined cut. Innovative use of fabric.
9	Manolo Blahnik	1970s–1990s	Designer	Revived the stiletto in the 1970s. Known for creative styles while always using the classic heel.
10	Guy Bourdin	1960s–1970s	Photographer	Highly controlled images famous for a mysterious sense of danger and sex. Bourdin's models often appeared dead or injured.
11	David Bowie	1970s–1980s	Entertainer	Rebellious androgyny.
12	Christie Brinkley	1980s–1990s	Model	25 years as the "face" of Cover Girl and has appeared on over 500 magazine covers.
13	Hattie Carnegie	1930s–1940s	Entrepreneur	Translated French couture for American audience. Gave a career start to many future designers—for example, Norell, Trigère, and McCardell.
14	Gisele Bündchen	1990s–2000s	Model	Supermodel sought after by numerous brands and designers to sell their fashions.
15	Naomi Campbell	1980s–1990s	Model	Broke racial barriers as the first black model on the covers of French and British *Vogue*.
16	Bonnie Cashin	1940s–1950s	Designer	Championed the active lives of women through American sportswear; separates, layered look, stretch ski pants, capris, or "pedal pushers."
17	Jacques Cartier	1940s–1950s	Brand	Grandson of the famous jewelry-making family. Established company as iconic brand in WWII during Occupation through symbolic designs.
18	Hussein Chalayan	2000s	Designer	Internationally regarded designer; famous for his innovative use of materials.
19	Gabrielle "Coco" Chanel	1920s–1930s and 1950s–1970s	Designer/ Brand	Timeless classics born out of innovation and chic comfort; sweaters, tweeds, sailor looks.
20	Grace Coddington	1980s–2000s	Editor	Creative director, American *Vogue*.
21	Cindy Crawford	1980s–2000s	Model/ Entrepreneur	Supermodel. Translated fame into a fitness and cosmetic empire.
22	André Courrèges	1960s–1970s	Designer	First couturier to raise hemlines to mid-thigh. White boots, tough chic.
23	James Dean	1950s	Entertainer	Antiprep—jeans, T-shirt, and well-worn jacket.
24	Christian Dior	1940s–1950s	Designer	The "New Look" in 1947.
25	Linda Evangelista	1980s–1990s	Model	Supermodel of the 1980s and 1990s.
26	Patricia Field	1990s–2000s	Stylist	Costume designer and stylist for *Sex & the City* series and films, earning multiple awards and nominations.

	Name	Decades Of Influence	Profession	Defining Characteristics
27	Domenico Dolce & Stefano Gabbana	1990s–2000s	Designers	Inspired the young to dress up. Lingerie look is a signature. Emphasis on female physique.
28	Farrah Fawcett	1970s–1980s	Entertainer	The first "must-have" celebrity hairstyle. Highest-selling poster of all time.
29	Tom Ford	1990s–2000s	Designer	Design voice of Gucci. Left to direct films and won an Academy Award.
30	Jean Paul Gaultier	1980s–2000s	Designer	Trendy and controversial. Punk look. Daring and avant-garde.
31	Robin Givhan		Writer	First writer to win a Pulitzer Prize for fashion commentary.
32	Hubert de Givenchy	1950s–1980s	Designer	Audrey Hepburn was his fashion muse. Introduced chemise and sack dress.
33	Edith Head	1930s–1950s	Costume designer	Head designer for Paramount and Universal Studios; 35 Oscar nominations, 8 Oscar wins.
34	Jean Harlow	1930s	Entertainer	Blonde hair and dripping satin gowns.
35	Halston	1970s–1980s	Designer	Unconstructed separates. Lush cashmeres. Studio 54.
36	Audrey Hepburn	1950s–1960s	Entertainer	Iconic gamine on-screen look and the muse of devoted couturiers like Hubert de Givenchy, who dressed her for several films.
37	Katharine Hepburn	1930s–1940s	Entertainer	The famously feisty star showed the world that a woman could care about her looks and still look like herself. Wide-leg trousers, menswear-inspired fashions, and comfortable shoes.
38	Carolina Herrera	1980s–2000s	Designer	Caters to high-society clientele. Luxurious fabrics.
39	Horst P. Horst	1930s–1950s	Photographer	Captured an era of European and American glamour on film. Black-and-white portraits of 20th-century icons include Coco Chanel, Rita Hayworth, Andy Warhol, and Jackie Kennedy. Photography known for its drama, enchantment, and classical inspiration.
40	Iman	1970s–1980s	Model	Among the first black supermodels. Owns a line of cosmetics for skin colors underserved by mainstream makeup.
41	Marc Jacobs	1990s–2000s	Designer	Exceptional in leather and fur design. Designed for Perry Ellis label.
42	Beverly Johnson	1960s–1970s	Model	Most famously, the first black model to appear on the cover of American *Vogue*. Appeared on over 500 covers. Outspoken about demands on models to maintain unrealistic and unhealthy weight. Leveraged her name to expand into other industries.
43	Donna Karan	1980s–2000s	Designer/ Brand	Elegant sportswear. Simple silhouettes. Easy-fitting dresses.

	Name	Decades Of Influence	Profession	Defining Characteristics
44	Rei Kawakubo	1980s–1990s	Designer	Avant-garde clothes challenged classic idea of femininity.
45	Grace Kelly	1950s–1960s	Entertainer	Could make the simplest of fashions look glamorous. Epitomized 1950s style. Fairytale marriage to Prince of Monaco. Used a Hermes bag to conceal her "baby bump," which became known as the Kelly bag. Still inspires designers.
46	Calvin Klein	1970s–2000s	Designer	King of minimalism. Designer jeans. Sexually charged advertising.
47	Michael Kors	1990s–2000s	Designer	Shape and line, devoid of ornament.
48	Heidi Klum	1990s–2000s	Model/ Entrepreneur	Producer of *Project Runway*.
49	Nick Knight	2000s	Photographer	A thought leader in incorporating the Internet and video into the world of fashion photography.
50	Lady Gaga	2000s	Entertainer	Outrageous stage style and has written a fashion column for *V Magazine*.
51	Karl Lagerfeld	1980s–2000s	Designer	Produces 16 collections a year! Excellent technique and witty design. Resurrected the Chanel brand.
52	Eleanor Lambert	1930s–1940s	Publicist	One of the first fashion publicists. Founder of the Council of Fashion Designers of America and creator of New York Fashion Week.
53	Jeanne Lanvin	1920s–1930s	Designer	Early Paris couturier.
54	Ralph Lauren	1980s–2000s	Designer/ Brand	Reinvents classic American style.
55	Annie Leibovitz	1970s–2000s	Photographer	Iconic, powerful images. Regularly produces cover images for *Vogue*, *Vanity Fair*, and exhibits around the world.
56	Christian Louboutin	1990s–2000s	Designer	Red-soled shoes trademark this iconic brand.
57	Madonna	1980s–2000s	Entertainer	Iconic and irreverent personal style.
58	Claire McCardell	1940s–1950s	Designer	Leading voice in the American sportswear look.
59	Alexander McQueen	1990s–2000s	Designer	Started as a Savile Row tailor in London. Under design direction of Sarah Burton, designed Kate Middleton's gown for her wedding to Prince William.
60	Steven Meisel	1990s–2010s	Photographer	Photographed every cover and lead editorial for Italian *Vogue* over 20 years.
61	Martin Munkácsi	1920s–1930s	Photographer	Captured movement in fashion images at a time when photography was about stillness and poses.

	Name	Decades Of Influence	Profession	Defining Characteristics
62	Helmut Newton	1960s–1990s	Photographer	Controversial and influential. His photography coupled androgyny and conflict with classic fashion silhouettes.
63	Michelle Obama	2000s	Public figure	Sleeveless fashions and mix of high-end and mass retail. Champions young, little-known designers.
64	Jacqueline Kennedy Onassis	1960s–1970s	Public figure	Iconic First Lady, she represented the style and sophistication of 1960s America. Championed couture designers to prepare her public wardrobe as one of the first to experience politics in front of TV cameras.
65	Bettie Page	1950s–1960s	Model	Defined the bold and innocent bad-girl pinup look of the era.
66	Barbara "Babe" Paley	1930s–1960s	Public figure/ socialite	Socialite who possessed great style and flawless appearance.
67	Jean Patou	1920s–1930s	Designer	Elegant, ladylike couture clothes. Successful businesswoman and showman.
68	Irving Penn	1950s–1970s	Photographer	Minimal yet graceful style. Used plain background, focusing on the subject.
69	Paul Poiret	1920s–1930s	Designer	First Paris couturier of the 20th century to become a trendsetter. Designed corset-free fashions.
70	Miuccia Prada	1990s–2000s	Designer	Global trendsetter of clothing and accessories. Miu Miu as a secondary line for youth.
71	Princess Diana	1980s–1990s	Public figure	Transformed the traditional regal look into something altogether more inviting and modern.
72	Mary Quant	1960s–1970s	Designer	Distinctive style and subculture of the 1960s. Popularized miniskirt and other styles of the era for the young consumer.
73	Herb Ritts	1970s–1990s	Photographer	Classic photography to film director. Known for black-and-white photography. Classic and elegant images.
74	Carine Roitfeld	2000s	Editor	*Vogue Paris.*
75	Yves Saint Laurent	1960s–1990s	Designer	Pantsuits, pea jackets, safari, peasant styles, Rive Gauche.
76	Jil Sander	1990s–2000s	Designer	Highest-quality materials and craftsmanship. Expert tailoring.
77	Elsa Schiaparelli	1930s–1940s	Designer	Surrealism.

	Name	Decades Of Influence	Profession	Defining Characteristics
78	Jean Shrimpton	1960s–1970s	Model	One of the world's first supermodels. Embodied the swinging London of the 1960s.
79	Franca Sozzani	1990s–2000s	Editor	Editor in Chief, *Vogue Italia*.
80	Edward Steichen	1910s–1940s	Photographer	First fashion photographer.
81	Levi Strauss	1880s and beyond	Brand	Durable work wear—the blue jean—transitioned to fashion and high fashion throughout the 20th century and beyond.
82	Mario Testino	1990s–2000s	Photographer	Favored by celebrities. Shot Prince William and Kate Middleton's engagements photos. Numerous covers.
83	Tiffany & Company	1840s to current era	Brand	A storied and iconic brand. Iconic blue box. Established flagship store in New York in 1940.
84	Liz Tilberis	1970s–1990s	Editor	British *Vogue* and *Harper's Bazaar* in New York.
85	Twiggy (Lesley Hornby)	1960s–1970s	Model	Her name became synonymous with short pixie haircut and the mod look of London in the 1960s.
86	Gianni Versace	1980s–1990s	Designer	Kinetic prints. Metallic garments. King of fashion for rock-and-roll genre.
87	Madeleine Vionnet	1920s–1930s	Designer	Considered the "Queen of Bias" and "the architect among dressmakers." Continues to influence designers.
88	Diane von Furstenberg	1970s–2000s	Designer	Best known for wrap dress and prints. DVF has grown into global luxury brand.
89	Ellen von Unwerth	1980s–1990s	Photographer	Model-turned-photographer. Women have a realness and sense of humor.
90	Diana Vreeland	1960s–1970s	Editor	Editor of American *Vogue* and consultant at the Costume Institute of the Metropolitan Museum of Art.
91	Louis Vuitton	1850s to current era	Designer/ Brand	Status-symbol luggage.
92	Vera Wang	1990s–2000s	Designer/ Brand	Senior editor for *Vogue* for 16 years. Started wedding gown business in 1990. Now a global luxury brand expanded to ready-to-wear at various price levels.
93	Andy Warhol		Artist	Fashion and art merged. Championed the "Factory Girl" look inspired by Edie Sedgwick.
94	Bruce Weber	1980s–1990s	Photographer	Calvin Klein underwear campaign. Classic photography of all-American male.
95	Vivienne Westwood	1980s–1990s	Designer	Punk rock fashion.

	Name	Decades Of Influence	Profession	Defining Characteristics
96	Edna Woolman Chase	1910s–1950s	Editor	Editor of *Vogue* from 1914 to 1952. Started the Fashion Group (FGI) in 1928.
97	Charles Frederick Worth	1860s	Designer/ Father of French Couture	Created the "designer name" concept. Established a pattern of regular seasonal fashion showings.
98	Jason Wu	2000s	Designer	First fashion collection won Fashion Group Rising Star Award. First Lady Michelle Obama commissioned him to create both of her inaugural gowns.
99	Anna Wintour	1980s–2010s	Editor and creative director	Editor-in-chief of *Vogue* since 1988. In 2013 named creative director of Conde Nast, *Vogue*'s publisher.
100	Yohji Yamamoto	1980s–1990s	Designer	Sparse, understated fashions. Asymmetrical cuts.

Adapted from a variety of sources, including *WWD: 75 Years in Fashion 1910–1985*; *WWD Century*, September 1998; *WWD 100 Years | 100 Designers*, November 1, 2011; and *Time, All-TIME 100 Fashion Icons*, April 2, 2012.

NOTES

Chapter 1

1. *Merriam-Webster's Collegiate® Dictionary*, 11th ed. (Springfield, MA: Merriam Webster, 2004), 455.
2. Ibid., 776.
3. Agnes Brooke Young, *Recurring Cycles of Fashion: 1760–1937* (New York: Harper & Brothers, 1937; reprint, New York: Cooper Square Publishers, 1966), 30.
4. Caro, Felipe and Martinez de Albeniz, Victor, "How Fast Fashion Works: Can It Work for You, Too?" *IESE Insight*, 2014. https://www.ieseinsight.com/doc.aspx?id=1606&ar=14
5. Maryam Banikarim, "Seeing Shades in Green Consumers," *Adweek*, April 19, 2010, p. 18. Full text copyright © 2010 Nielsen Business Media, Inc.

FEATURES

Spotlight on Innovators: Out-of-This-World Designs of Iris van Herpen

Gregory, Alice. *T Magazine: Iris van Herpen's Intelligent Design* [blog]. *The New York Times*. https://www.nytimes.com/2015/04/08/t-magazine/iris-van-herpen-designer-interview.html

Iris Van Herpen [blog]. The Business of Fashion. http://www.businessoffashion.com/community/people/iris-van-herpen

Spotlight on Sustainability: Levi's: They Can Take a Little Dirt

Annie Sciacca. "Threads of Change: Levi Strauss Exec Weaves Social Responsibility into Company's Mission." *San Francisco Business Times*. Last modified June 12, 2015. http://www.bizjournals.com/sanfrancisco/print-edition/2015/06/12/threads-of-change-levi-strauss-exec-weaves-social.html.

"Engaging Customers—The Next Evolution in Sustainability." *Unzipped*. Last modified April 22, 2015. http://www.levistrauss.com/unzipped-blog/2015/04/engaging-consumers-the-next-evolution-in-sustainability/.

"Inside the Global Giants. Levi's—Dilemmas in Denim." BBC Worldservice.com. http://www.bbc.co.uk/worldservice/specials/151_globalgiants/page6.shtml.

Behbehani, Mandy. "Are Your Clothes Killing the Planet? Levi's, Everland among leaders stepping up to sustainability challenge." San Francisco Chronicle. Last modified November 19, 2018. https://www.sfchronicle.com/style/article/Can-fashion-survive-radical-new-model-of-reduce-13373068.php

Chapter 2

1. "Lifestyle and Behavior Segmentation: Nielsen PRIZM," Nielsen Corporation, 2010, http://www.nielsen.com.
2. "US Framework and VALS Types," *Strategic Business Insights*, http://www.strategicbusinessinsights.com/vals/ustypes.shtml, accessed October 2019.
3. US Department of Commerce, Economics and Statistics Administration, "Middle Class in America," February 2010, https://obamawhitehouse.archives.gov/sites/default/files/microsites/100226-annual-report-middle-class.pdf, accessed October 2019.
4. *Merriam-Webster's Collegiate Dictionary*, 11th ed. (Springfield, MA: Merriam-Webster, 2004), 641.
5. The National Bureau of Economic Research, "The NBERs Recession Dating Procedure." Last modified August 19, 2020. https://www.nber.org/cycles/r/recessions.html#:~:text=A%20recession%20is%20a%20significant,the%20economy%20reaches%20its%20trough, accessed August 2020.
6. US Census Bureau, "2017 National Population Projections Tables: Table 1-Projected population size and births, deaths, and migration." Last modified September 6, 2018. https://www.census.gov/data/tables/2017/demo/popproj/2017-summary-tables.html, accessed October 2019.
7. US Census Bureau, "Quick Facts United States." Last modified July 2019. https://www.census.gov/quickfacts/fact/table/US/RHI125218. Accessed October 2019.

8. US Census Bureau, "Projections of the Size and Composition of the U.S. Population: 2014 to 2060" (released March 2015), https://www.census.gov/content/dam/Census/library /publications/2015/demo/p25-1143.pdf, accessed October 2019.

9. United States Census Bureau, "Quick Facts United States." Last modified 2019. https://www.census.gov/quickfacts/fact /table/US/RHI125218, accessed October 2019.

10. United States Census Bureau, "Quick Facts United States." Last modified 2019. https://www.census.gov/quickfacts/fact /table/US/RHI125218, accessed October 2019.

11. US Census Bureau, "2014 National Population Estimates," http://factfinder.census.gov/faces/tableservices/jsf/pages /productview.xhtml?src=bkmk, accessed August 2015.

12. Pew Research Center "Key Facts About Asian Americans: A Diverse and Growing Population." Last modified September 8, 2017. https://www.pewresearch.org/fact-tank/2017/09/08 /key-facts-about-asian-americans/, accessed October 2019.

13. US Department of Labor, US Bureau of Labor Statistics, "Highlights of Women's Earnings in 2017," Report 1075, August 2018. https://www.bls.gov/opub/reports/womens -earnings/2017/home.htm, accessed October 2019.

14. US Department of Labor, US Bureau of Labor Statistics. "Highlights of Women's Earnings in 2017," Report 1075, August 2018. https://www.bls.gov/opub/reports/womens -earnings/2017/home.htm, accessed October 2019.

15. Paul H. Nystrom, *Economics of Fashion* (New York: The Ronald Press, 1928), 66–81.

FEATURES

Spotlight on Innovators: Donna Karan

Leslie Bennetts. "Donna's NEW Direction." *Town & Country*, July 2010, pp. 74–79, 106.

Marc Karimzadeh. "Karan Brings Her Touch to the Table." *WWD*, October 4, 2010, p. 15.

Nancy Jo Sales, "Donna Karan's Journey." *Harper's Bazaar*, September 21, 2010, pp. 342–354.

Spotlight on Sustainability: Thrifted Is the New Black—Thrift, Vintage, and Consignment Shopping Is on the Rise!

Maryalene LaPonsie. "6 Top Online Consignment Stores for Selling Your Clothes." *U.S. News & World Report.* Last modified February 21, 2019. https://money.usnews.com /money/personal-finance/saving-and-budgeting/articles/6-top -online-consignment-shops-for-selling-your-clothes, accessed October 2019.

Leonela Leon. "Why Thrifting is Good for the Planet, Not Just Your Wallet." SERC. March 12, 2019. https://serc.berkeley. edu/why-thrifting-is-good-for-the-planet-not-just-your-wallet/, accessed October 2019.

"With 9 Million Users and an Online Advantage, The RealReal is Widening its Net," *The Fashion Law.* September 19, 2018. http://www.thefashionlaw.com/home/with-9-million-users-and -an-online-advantage-the-realreal-is, accessed October 2019.

Glenda Toma. "The RealReal IPO: First Startup From Resale's New Wave to Go Public Sees Shares Soar." *Forbes.* June 28, 2019. https://www.forbes.com/sites/glendatoma/2019/06/28 /the-realreal-ipo-luxury-reseller-latest-retailer-to-go-public /#7c60e6496289, accessed October 2019.

Jessica Tully. "Recession Has Many Looking Thrift Store Chic." *USA Today.* Last modified July 5, 2012. http://usatoday30. usatoday.com/money/industries/retail/story/2012-07-05/thrift -shopping-trend/56037332/1, accessed October 2019.

"Industry Statistics & Trends." National Association of Resale Professionals. Last modified 2019. http://www.narts.org/i4a /pages/index.cfm?pageid=3285, accessed October 2019.

Chapter 3

1. Kate Dwyer, "How to Watch New York Fashion Week On Your Phone," *Fortune*, September 6, 2019. https://fortune .com/2019/09/06/how-to-watch-new-york-fashion-week -youtube-com-fashion-and-nyfw-all-access/, accessed October 2019.

2. Pearl Binder, *Muffs and Morals* (London: George G. Harrop & Co., 1953), 162–164.

3. James Laver, *Taste and Fashion*, rev. ed. (London: George G. Harrop & Co., 1946), 201.

4. Nicole Fritton, "The Top 13 Collections From The Spring 2020 Runway," *Harper's Bazaar*, October 16, 2019. https:// www.harpersbazaar.com/fashion/fashion-week/g29478395 /top-runway-collections-this-season/, accessed October 2019.

5. Madge Garland, *The Changing Form of Fashion* (New York: Praeger Publishers, 1971), 11.

6. J. C. Flügel, *The Psychology of Clothes* (New York: International Universities Press, 1966), 163.

7. James Laver, *Taste and Fashion*, rev. ed. (London: George G. Harrop & Co., 1946), 200.

8. Ibid., 201.

9. Yamarie Grullon, "The Rise of Personalized Products in Retail," Apparel, July 11, 2018. https://apparelmag.com/rise -personalized-products-retail, accessed October 2019.

10. "Power to the People," *WWD*, July 26, 2010, p. 20.

11. Charles King, "Fashion Adoption," 124.

12. Edward Sapir, "Fashion," *Encyclopedia of the Social Sciences*, vol. 6 (London: Macmillan & Co., 1931), 140.

13. "Kenneth Cole's 10 Rules of Style," *Upscalehype.com*, http:// www.upscalehype.com/2009/08/interesting-reading-kenneth -coles-10-rules-of-style/, accessed October 2019.

FEATURES

Spotlight on Innovators: Barbie Turns 60!

Mary Bellis, "Biography of Ruth Handler, Inventor of Barbie Dolls," *ThoughtCo.*, May 6, 2019. https://www.thoughtco.com /history-of-barbie-dolls-1991344, accessed October 2019.

"Fast Facts," Barbiemedia.com. Last modified 2016. http:// www.barbiemedia.com/about-barbie/fast-facts.html, accessed October 2019.

Lisa Lockwood, "2019 CFDA Fashion Awards to Honor Barbie With Board of Directors' Tribute Award," *WWD*, May 16, 2019. https://wwd.com/fashion-news/fashion-scoops/2019-cfda-fashion-awards-to-honor-barbie-with-board-of-directors-tribute-award-1203132160/, accessed October 2019.

"'Out of Touch' Barbie Doll Gets a Major Makeover," *CBS News*, January 28, 2016. https://www.cbsnews.com/news/barbie-doll-mattel-major-makeover-ethnic-diversity-body-types/, accessed October 2019.

Katherine Rosman, "The Chic Octogenarian Behind Barbie's Best Looks," *The New York Times*, April 24, 2019. https://www.nytimes.com/2019/04/24/style/barbie-fashion-clothing-designer.html, accessed October 2019.

Spotlight on Careers: Weddings! Big Business and Getting Bigger

Sandy Malone, "What Being a Wedding Planner is Really Like," *Brides*. Last modified November 18, 2016. https://www.brides.com/story/what-being-a-wedding-planner-is-really-like-sandy-malone, accessed October 2019.

Maggie Seaver, "The National Average Cost of a Wedding is $33,931," *The Knot*. 2018. https://www.theknot.com/content/average-wedding-cost, accessed October 2019.

Spotlight on Business: Express Your Sole—The Rise of Sneaker Culture

Ilya Martiz. "New Exhibit Laces Together Sneakers And History." NPR.org. Last modified July 14, 2015. http://www.npr.org/2015/07/14/422681151/new-exhibit-laces-together-sneakers-and-history, accessed October 2019.

Rich Lopez. "Nike Is Selling Way More Sneakers Than Adidas in the U.S." *Complex: Sneakers*. Last modified May 12, 2015. http://www.complex.com/sneakers/2015/05/nike-is-dominating-the-sneaker-market-adidas-is-third, accessed October 2019.

Eliza M. Dumais. "How Sneaker Culture Democratized Fashion." *The Observer*. Last modified July 13, 2015. https://observer.com/2015/07/how-sneaker-culture-democratized-fashion/, accessed October 2019.

"The Rise of Sneaker Culture." The Brooklyn Museum. https://www.brooklyn museum.org/exhibitions/rise_of_sneaker_culture, accessed October 2019.

Adrian Uthayagumaran and Steven Lo. "Sneakeromics: Sizing up the Growing Sneaker Market." *Ivey Business Review*. Last modified December 1, 2013. http://iveybusinessreview.ca/cms/4437/sneakernomics/, accessed October 2019.

Chapter 4

1. The Economic Impact of the Fashion Industry," *Joint Economic Committee, United States Congress*, February 6, 2015, p. 1, https://maloney.house.gov/sites/maloney.house.gov/files/documents/The%20Economic%20Impact%20of%20the%20Fashion%20Industry%20—%20JEC%20report%20FINAL.pdf, accessed October 2019.

2. Isabel Isidro, "Private Shopping Clubs: A Different Way of Selling on the Web," *PowerHomeBiz.com* Online, March 30, 2010, https://www.powerhomebiz.com/blog/2010/03/private-shopping-clubs-a-different-way-of-selling-on-the-web/, accessed October 2019.

3. "Franchise Business Economic Outlook for 2018," *Franchise Education and Research Foundation*, p. 2, January 2018, https://www.franchise.org>sites>default>files>Franchise_Business_Outlook_Jan_2018%20(2).pdf/, accessed October 2019.

4. "Global Sales of Licensed Products and Services Reach $280.3 Billion, Fifth Straight Year of Growth for the Licensing Industry," *Licensing International*, June 4, 2019, https://licensinginternational.org/news/global-sales-of-licensed-products-and-services-reach-us-280-3-billion-fifth-straight-year-of-growth-for-the-licensing-industry/, accessed October 2019.

5. Dwight E. Robinson, "Fashion Theory and Product Design," *Harvard Business Review*, 36 (November–December 1958): 129.

FEATURES

Spotlight on Business: Personalization is the New Black

DeLoitte, "The Deloitte consumer review: Made-to-order," 2019, https://www2.deloitte.com/content/dam/Deloitte/ch/Documents/consumer-business/ch-en-consumer-business-made-to-order-consumer-review.pdf

Nicasio, F., "9 examples of personalization to try in your retail store," *Vend Blog*, January 1, 2019, https://www.vendhq.com/blog/examples-of-personalization-retail/, accessed October 2019.

Roberts, J.J., "The diamond industry is obsessed with the blockchain," *Fortune*, September 12, 2017, http://fortune.com/2017/09/12/diamond-blockchain-everledger/, accessed October 2019.

Tekscan, "Dr. Scholl's kiosks," https://www.tekscan.com/applications/dr-scholls-kiosks, accessed October 2019.

Wassel, B., "The evolving luxury industry embraces social media and personalization," *Retail Touchpoints*, September 13, 2018, https://www.retailtouchpoints.com/features/trend-watch/the-evolving-luxury-industry-embraces-social-media-and-personalization, accessed October 2019.

Spotlight on Innovators: Rent the Runway! A Closet in the "Cloud"

Mara Leighton, "How Rent the Runway is Changing the Way Women Get Dressed – and Why It's Been Called One of the Most Disruptive Companies in the World, Alongside Uber, Airbnb, and SpaceX," *Business Insider*, August 7, 2018. https://www.businessinsider.com/rent-the-runway-membership-2018-8, accessed October 2019.

Sam Hollis, "How Rent the Runway Built an $800 Million Business in a Mom-and-Pop Industry," *Jilt.com*, September 2018. https://jilt.com/blog/rent-the-runway-logistics/, accessed October 2019.

"Our Story," *renttherunway.com*, 2019. https://www.renttherunway.com/about-us/story?action_type=footer_link, accessed October 2019.

Chapter 5

1. Jane Dorner, *Fashion in the Forties and Fifties* (New Rochelle, NY: Arlington House, 1975), 38.

2. "Extra-Fine Cotton Update," Supima, February 28, 2017, https://supima.com/wp-content/uploads/2017/03/Xfinefeb2017.pdf, accessed October 2019.

3. Mohammad R.M. Jamir and Azduwin Khasri, "Synthetic Fiber," *Science Direct*, 2018, https://www.sciencedirect.com/topics/materials-science/synthetic-fiber, accessed October 2019.

4. National Council of Textile Organizations, http://www.ncto.org/about-ncto/, accessed October 2019.

5. Marty Moran, "2019 State of the U.S. Textile Industry," *Textile World*, https://www.textileworld.com/textile-world/features/2019/05/2019-state-of-the-u-s-textile-industry/, accessed October 2019.

6. National Council of Textile Organizations, http://www.ncto.org/facts-figures/economic-impact/, accessed October 2019.

7. National Council of Textile Organizations, http://www.ncto.org/facts-figures/trade/, accessed October 2019.

8. "9 Recycled and Upcycled Clothing Brands You Shouldn't Pass In 2019," https://compareethics.com/9-recycled-and-upcycled-clothing-brands-you-shouldnt-pass-in-2018/, accessed October 2019.

9. Patagonia, *Worn Wear*, https://wornwear.patagonia.com/faq, accessed October 2019.

10. Manik Hehta, "Sourcing Shifts Creates New Players, Challenges," *Apparel*, September 10, 2014, http://apparel.edgl.com/news/Sourcing-Shift-Creates-New-Players,-Challenges95229, accessed October 2019.

11. "Textile Industry in India: Latest Facts, Figures, and Government Schemes," India Today, October 1, 2018, . https://www.indiatoday.in/education-today/gk-current-affairs/story/textile-industry-in-india-latest-facts-figures-government-schemes-1353406-2018-10-01, accessed October 2019.

12. "Trade in Goods with CAFTA-DR," United States Census Bureau, https://www.census.gov/foreign-trade/balance/c0017.html, last modified August 2019, accessed October 2019.

13. "Textile Industry & Market Growth in India," India Brand Equity Foundation, September 2019, https://www.ibef.org/industry/textiles.aspx, accessed October 2019.

14. "Threading Your Way Through the Labeling Requirements Under the Textile and Wool Acts," *Bureau of Consumer Protection*, http://business.ftc.gov/documents/bus21-threading-your-way-through-labeling-requirements-under-textile-and-wool-acts, accessed October 2019.

15. "Digital Textile Printing Market – Global Outlook and Forecast 2018-2023," *Artizon*, April 2018, https://www.arizton.com/market-reports/digital-textile-printing-market, accessed October 2019.

16. "The Future of 3-D Printing to 2027," *The Smithers Group*, https://www.smithers.com/services/market-reports/printing/the-future-of-3d-printing-to-2027, accessed October 2019.

17. Anna Brismar, "Seven Forms of Sustainable Fashion," *Green Strategy*, 2019, http://www.greenstrategy.se/sustainable-fashion/seven-forms-of-sustainable-fashion/, accessed October 2019.

FEATURES

Spotlight on Innovators: Rothy's: A shoe made from a recycled plastic bottle . . .

Campanelli, Melissa, "Game Changers: Stephen Hawthornthwaite, Co-Founder and CEO; Roth Martin, Co-Founder and Chief Creative Officer, Rothy's," *Total Retail*, October 2, 2018, https://www.mytotalretail.com/article/game-changers-stephen-hawthornthwaite-roth-martin-rothys/, accessed October 2019.

Chen, Connie, "Women in New York and San Francisco are Obsessed With These Comfortable Flats Made From Recycled Water Bottles—Here's What They Feel Like," *Business Insider*, September 19, 2019, https://www.businessinsider.com/rothys-comfortable-work-flat-review-2018-6, accessed October 2019.

Johns, Nikara, "How Two Shoe Outsiders are Making Rothy's One of the Most Talked-About New Footwear Brands," *Footwear News*, March 25, 2019, https://footwearnews.com/2019/business/entrepreneurs/rothys-shoes-interview-roth-martin-stephen-hawthornthwaite-1202763598/,accessed October 2019.

"3D Knitting: A Close Look at How Rothy's are Made," Rothy's, May 8, 2017, https://rothys.com/blog/behind-the-scenes/articles/3d-knitting-a-close-look-at-how-rothys-are-made, accessed October 2019.

Spotlight on Business: Recycled Fashion—Old Clothes, New Life

"Textiles." *The Environmental Protection Agency*. Last modified June 17, 2015. http://www.epa.gov/osw/conserve/materials/textiles.html.

SMART: Secondary Materials and Recycled Textiles. http://www.smartasn.org, accessed October 2019.

Celia Stall-Meadows and Gina Peek. "Recycled Household Textiles and Clothing." *Oklahoma Cooperative Extension Service.* http://pods.dasnr.okstate.edu/docushare/dsweb/Get/Document-7411/T-4318web.pdf, accessed October 2019.

Beth Stewart. "Upcycling: The New Wave of Sustainable Fashion." *Triple Pundit: People Planet Profit*, May 8, 2014, http://www.triplepundit.com/special/sustainable-fashion-2014/upcycling-new-wave-sustainable-fashion/, accessed October 2019.

"The Life Cycle of Secondhand Clothing." *Council for Textile Recycling*, October 30, 2015, https://ecogoodz.com/the-life-cycle-of-secondhand-clothing/, accessed October 2019.

Chapter 6

1. Robin Givhan, "Equine Finery for Fall, Designers Gallop Toward the Tony Pony," *Washington Post*, October 23, 1996, p. D1.

2. "AAC Annual Report," Alligator Advisory Council, December 2017, https://www.louisianaalligators.com /uploads/1/0/4/8/104800207/alligatorannual17.pdf, accessed November 2019.

3. "Guandong Market for Leather Weathers Storm, Spells Demand for American Hides and Finished Leather," USDA Global Agricultural Information Network, Guangzhou, China, November 16, 2009.

4. Leather Industries of America, https://www.leatherusa.com /i4a/pages/index.cfm?pageid=1&pageid=3267, accessed November 2019.

5. "About Us," APLF website, https://www.leatherfair.aplf.com /en-us/, accessed November 2019.

6. LINEAPPELLE, https://www.lineapelle-fair.it/en/lineapelle, accessed November 2019.

7. "Breeding Records Destroyed at Largest Bobcat Farm in the U.S., Animal Liberation Frontline, March 22, 2014. https:// animalliberationfrontline.com/?p=6550, accessed November 2019.

8. "Pelt Production down 9 Percent," National Agricultural Statistics Service, USDA, July 23, 2019, downloads.usda. library.cornell.edu, accessed November 2019.

9. "About NAFA Labels," North American Fur Auctions, https://www.nafa.ca/webcenter/portal/Auction/pages_buying /newnafalabels, accessed November 2019.

10. Fur Information Council of America, http://www.fur.org/fica -facts, accessed November 2019.

11. "About NAFA Home," *North American Fur Auction*, https:// www.nafa.ca/webcenter/portal/Auction/pages_aboutnafaa /aboutnafacopy, accessed November 2019.

12. Fur Commission USA, "U.S. Fur Sales Hurt by Economic Concerns in 2007," https://furcommission.com/u-s-fur -retail-sales-hurt-by-economic-concerns-in-2007/, accessed November 2019.

13. "Humane Decisions," http://www.humanedecisions.com /category/about-humane-decisions/, 2019, accessed November 2019.

14. Bridget Foley, "The Fur Debate," *WWD*, April 26, 2018, https://wwd.com/fashion-news/fashion-features/the-fur -debate-1202660445/, accessed November 2019.

15. Bridget Foley, "The Fur Debate," *WWD*, April 26, 2018, https://wwd.com/fashion-news/fashion-features/the-fur -debate-1202660445/, accessed November 2019.

16. Bridget Foley, "The Fur Debate," *WWD*, April 26, 2018, https://wwd.com/fashion-news/fashion-features/the-fur -debate-1202660445/, accessed November 2019.

17. Fur Information Council of America, "FICA Facts," http:// www.fur.org/fica-facts/, 2013, accessed November 2019.

18. Bridget Foley, "The Fur Debate: What Designers Say," WWD, April 26, 2018, https://wwd.com/fashion -news/fashion-features/the-fur-debate-what-designers -say-1202648059/, accessed November 2019.

19. International Fur Trade Federation, http://furcommission. com/iftf-global-retail-sales-increase-by-600-million/, accessed November 2019.

FEATURES

Spotlight on Innovators: Synthetic Leather – It might just be your cup of tea!

"Clothing Made From Tea Byproduct Could Improve Health of Fashion Industry," Iowa State University News Service, April 26, 2016, https://www.news.iastate.edu/news/2016/04/26 /sustainableclothing, accessed November 2019.

Spotlight on Business: Faux Real

Courtney Iseman. "It's 2015. Fashion is Full of Vegans. So Why Is Fur Still Trendy?" *Racked*. Last modified February 11, 2015. http://www.racked.com/2015/2/11/7986839/fashion-industry -fur-veganism, accessed November 2019.

Alice Hines. "The History of Faux Fur." *Smithsonian.com*. Last modified January 22, 2015. http://www.smithsonianmag. com/history/history-faux-fur-180953984/?no-ist, accessed November 2019.

"FICA Facts." *FICA: The Fur Information Council of America.* Fur.org. Last modified 2012. http://www.fur.org/fica-facts/, accessed November 2019.

Kellie Ell, "WWD List: Designers Warming Up to Faux Fur," *WWD*, March 13, 2019, https://wwd.com/business-news /business-features/wwd-list-designers-ditching -fur-1202994502/, accessed November 2019.

Chapter 7

1. Susan S. Nichols, "Product Development, Innovation in Demand from Top-Tier Retailers: (Exclusive Report From SPESA)," *Apparel*, July 2010, p. 28.

2. Muditha M. Senanayake and Trevor J. Little. (Sprint 2001), "Measures for New Product Development," *Journal of Textile and Apparel Technology and Management*, 1(3): 9.

3. American Apparel and Footwear Association, "AAFA Concerns Remain Despite Administration Plan to Pause Tariff Rate Increase," October 11, 2019. https://www .aafaglobal.org/AAFA/AAFA_News/2019_Press_Releases /AAFA_Concerns_Remain_Despite_Pause_in_Tariff_%20 Increase.aspx, accessed November 2019.

4. NAICS Association, "History of the NAICS Code," 2016, http://www.naics.com/history-naics-code/, accessed November 2019.

5. "Is 3D Body Scanning the Future of Fashion?" *Verdict.com*, July 23, 2018, https://www.verdict.co.uk/3d-body-scanning -fashion-future/, accessed November 2019.

6. "Why Transparency Matters," *Fashion Revolution*, 2019, https://www.fashionrevolution.org/about/transparency/, accessed November 2019.

7. "Why Transparency Matters," *Fashion Revolution*, 2019, https://www.fashionrevolution.org/about/transparency/, accessed November 2019.

FEATURES

Spotlight on Innovation:

"Top 10 Fashion-Tech Innovations of 2018," Techpacker, 2019, https://www.techpacker.com/blog/top-10-fashion-tech -innovations/, accessed November 2019.

Spotlight on Business: Power Suit, Indeed!

Joe Pinsker. "Wearing a Suit Makes People Think Differently." *The Atlantic*. Last modified April 30, 2015. http://www .theatlantic.com/business/archive/2015/04/wearing-a-suit -makes-people-think-differently/391802/, accessed November 2019.

Andrew Jensen. "Does Workplace Attire Affect Productivity?" *Andrew Jensen: Efficiency, Growth & Marketing*. Last modified September 4, 2019. http://www.andrewjensen.net/how-does -workplace-attire-affect-productivity/, accessed November 2019.

Chapter 8

1. Rachel Lubitz, "These are the Designers Working Hard to Make Stylish Clothes for Wheelchair Users," Mic, January 14, 2016, https://www.mic.com/articles/132453/these-are -the-designers-working-hard-to-make-stylish-clothes-for -wheelchair-users, accessed November 2019.

2. Destination Maternity Corporation, October 21, 2019, http://investor.destinationmaternity.com/investor- relations?c=72323&p=irol-irhome, accessed November 2019.

3. Miles Socha, "Masstige Gains Power," *WWD*, October 5, 2010, https://wwd.com/fashion-news/designer-luxury /masstige-gains-power-3326578/, accessed November 2019.

4. "Casualization Drives Growth in the US Menswear Market." *Coresight Research*, July 25, 2019, https://coresight.com /research/casualization-drives-growth-in-the-us-menswear -market/, accessed November 2019.

5. "Global Kidswear Market Insights, Forecast to 2025," Market Insights Reports, February 2019, https://www .marketinsightsreports.com/reports/02271115613/global -kidswear-market-insights-forecast-to-2025, accessed November 2019.

6. Allison Golub, "Size Matters," *Earnshaw's*, February 2007.

7. Craig M. Hale, "Prevalence of Obesity Among Adults and Youth: United States, 2015-2016," Centers for Disease Control and Prevention, pg. 3, October 2017, https://www .cdc.gov/nchs/data/databriefs/db288.pdf, accessed November 2019.

FEATURES

Spotlight on Innovation: Petit Pli—Origami Children's Clothing

Emily Matchar, "These Origami Clothes Grow With Your Child," *Smithsonian.com*, September 25, 2017, https://www .smithsonianmag.com/innovation/origami-clothes-grow-your -child-180965010/, accessed September 2019.

Oliver E. LaCrouts and Laura Drouet, "Ryan Mario Yasin's Folding Fashion of the Future," *Elle Décor*, July 31, 2019, https://www.elledecor.com/it/best-of/a28596751/ryan-mario -yasin-petit-pli-childrens-clothes/, accessed November 2019.

Spotlight on Careers: Communicating with the Customer—A Career in Social Media

Baer, J., "42 Percent of Customers Complaining in Social Media Expect 60 Minute Response Time," *Convince & Convert*, https://www.convinceandconvert.com/social-media-research/42 -percent-of-consumers-complaining-in-social-media-expect-60 -minute-response-time/.

Carter, R., "8 tips to build customer relationships with social media," *Sprout Social*, February 26, 2019, https://sproutsocial .com/insights/build-customer-relationships/.

"Converting customers: User-generated content vs professional content," *Photoslurp*, https://info.photoslurp.com/hubfs /Converting%20Customers%20-%20Photoslurp%20Research .pdf.

"The Sprout Social Index, edition XII: Call-out culture," *Sprout Social*, https://sproutsocial.com/insights/data/q3-2017/.

Nikki Gilliland, "A Day in the Life of the Social Media Manager at Oasis Fashion," Econsultancy, March 29, 2018, https:// econsultancy.com/a-day-in-the-life-of-social-media-manager -at-oasis-fashion/.

Spotlight on Business: Marketing to Teens—an elusive but powerful consumer demographic!

Lauren Thomas, "Teens are Spending $2,600 a year on Food and Clothes. Here's Where They Like to Shop," *CNBC*, April 8, 2019, https://www.cnbc.com/2019/04/08/teens-spend-2600 -a-year-on-food-clothes-heres-where-they-shop.html, accessed November 2019

"The 10 Most Popular Things for Teens in 2019," *Cision PR Newswire*, January 24, 2019, https://www.prnewswire .com/news-releases/the-10-most-popular-things-for -teens-in-2019-300783768.html, accessed November 2019.

"Study Provides Bridge to an Elusive but Powerful Consumer Demographic: Teen Girls," *Cision PR Newswire*, March 8, 2010, https://www.prnewswire.com/news-releases/study- provides-bridge-to-an-elusive-but-powerful-consumer -demographic-teen-girls-86866797.html, accessed November 2019.

Chapter 9

1. "Nike, Inc. CI B: Annual Financials for Nike Inc. CI B," *MarketWatch*, https://www.marketwatch.com/investing/stock /nke/financials, accessed December 2019.

2. "Apparel Stats and Shoes Stats 2018," American Apparel and Footwear Association, 2018, https://www.aafaglobal.org /AAFA/Media.aspx, accessed December 2019.

3. IBIS World, "Online Shoe Sales in the U.S.: Market Research Report," June 2019, https://www.ibisworld.com/united-states /market-research-reports/online-shoe-sales-industry/, accessed November 2019.

4. Madeline Fass, "Throw Some Shade With Summer's Best Sunglasses Trends," *Vogue*, May 21, 2019, https://www.vogue.com/vogueworld/article/shop-best-sunglasses-trends-spring-summer, accessed November 2019.

5. "Guide to Diamond Cut," Jewelry Information Center, https://www.jewelers.org/education/diamond-buying-guide/diamond-cut, November 2019.

6. "Fashion Company Nine West Emerges From Bankruptcy as 'Premier Brands,'" *Reuters*, March 20, 2019, https://www.reuters.com/article/us-ninewest-bankruptcy/fashion-company-nine-west-emerges-from-bankruptcy-as-premier-brands-idUSKCN1R127X, accessed November 2019.

7. The Swatch Group, Ltd., "The Swatch Group History (today)," https://www.swatchgroup.com/en/swatch-group/swatch-group-history, accessed December 2019.

8. Liam O'Connell, "Luxury Watch Market Value Worldwide from 2018 to 2020 (in billion U.S. dollars)," *Statista*, October 21, 2019, https://www.statista.com/statistics/940452/luxury-watch-market-value-worldwide/, accessed December 2019.

FEATURES

Spotlight on Innovators: Colleen Atwood: Academy Award-Winning Costume Designer

Abrams, B., "Three-time Academy Award winning costume designer Colleen Atwood talks shop," *The Credits*, November 4, 2014, https://www.mpaa.org/2014/11/three-time-academy-award-winning-costume-designer-colleen-atwood-talks-shop/, accessed October 2019.

Blair, E., "Colleen Atwood: To design the costume, understand the character," *NPR*, September 30, 2016, https://www.npr.org/2016/09/30/496119928/costume-designer-colleen-atwood-took-unlikely-path-to-hollywood-royalty, accessed October 2019.

Galas, M., "Colleen Atwood on designing Into the Woods costumes," *Variety*, February 13, 2015, https://variety.com/2015/artisans/production/colleen-atwood-on-designing-into-the-woods-costumes-1201432677/, accessed October 2019.

Kilcooley-O'Halloran, S., "Colleen's costume change," *Vogue*, June 17, 2014, https://www.vogue.co.uk/gallery/colleen-atwood-costume-designer-bag collection-interview, accessed October 2019.

Murphy, D., "Dumbo costume designer Colleen Atwood reveals the secrets behind her circus creations," *ET*, March 29, 2019, https://www.etonline.com/dumbo-costume-designer-colleen-atwood-reveals-the-secrets-behind-her-circus-creations-exclusive, accessed October 2019.

Spotlight on Sustainability: Gucci: Sustainability and Social Media

Bezamat, B., "Gucci launches online platform to promote sustainable purpose," *The Current Daily*, June 6, 2018, https://thecurrentdaily.com/2018/06/06/gucci-equilibrium-platform-sustainable-purpose/, accessed November 2019.

Primo, D., "What can luxury brands learn from Gucci about millennials?" *Forbes*, November 2, 2018, www.forbes.com/sites/forbesagencycouncil/2018/11/02/what-can-luxury-brands-learn-from-gucci-about-millennials/#3a9ce5c5e5ba, accessed November 2019.

"Sustainable Raw Materials," *Gucci Equilibrium: Leather*, http://equilibrium.gucci.com/environment/sustainable-raw-materials/animal-based-materials/, accessed December 2019.

Chapter 10

1. "Key Facts About LA County's Creative Design Industries," *Los Angeles Economic Development Corporation*, https://laedc.org/industries/creative-design/, accessed December 2019.

2. "Denim: California State Fabric," *State Symbols USA*, https://statesymbolsusa.org/symbol-official-item/california/cultural-heritage/denim, accessed December 2019.

3. Ibid.

4. Dallas Market Center Fact Sheet, http://dallasmarketcenter.com/assets/cms/files/DMC%20Fact%20Sheet.pdf, accessed December 2019.

5. Mode à Paris, http://www.modeaparis.com/spip.php?rubrique8#toppage8, accessed December 2019.

6. "Welcome to Paris!," *Federation Francaise du Prêt à Porter*, https://www.pretaporter.com/en/2019/01/21/welcome-to-paris/, accessed December 2019.

7. Marjorie van Elven, "Sales, Employment and Profits Growing in the Italian Fashion Sector," *Fashion United*, February 18, 2019, https://fashionunited.uk/news/business/sales-employment-and-profits-growing-in-the-italian-fashion-sector/2019021841643, accessed December 2019.

8. Madge Garland, *The Changing Form of Fashion* (New York: Praeger Publishers, 1971), 73.

9. Sarah Gray, "These are the Biggest U.S. Trading Partners," *Fortune*, March 7, 2018, https://fortune.com/2018/03/07/biggest-us-trade-partners/.

10. Grace I. Kunz and Myrna B. Garner, *Going Global: The Textile and Apparel Industry*, 2nd ed. (New York: Fairchild Books, 2011), 325–329.

11. Ibid., 284–385.

12. "The Best Street Style from Tokyo Fashion Week Spring 2019," *Vogue*, October 22, 2018, https://www.vogue.com/slideshow/tokyo-fashion-week-street-style-spring-2019, accessed December 2019.

13. "Organic Cotton Market Report 2018," *Textile Exchange*, p. 6, https://textileexchange.org/wp-content/uploads/2018/11/2018-Organic-Cotton-Market-Report.pdf, accessed December 2019.

14. Daniel Workman, "Cotton Exports by Country," *World's Top Exports*, http://www.worldstopexports.com/cotton-exports-by-country/, accessed December 2019.

15. "Textile industry and Market Growth in India," *India Brand Equity Foundation*, March 2017, https://www.ibef.org/archives/detail/b3ZlcnZpZXcmMzcxMTAmMTEy, accessed December 2019.

16. World Trade Organization, "World Trade Statistical Review 2019," https://www.wto.org/english/res_e/statis_e/wts2019_e/wts19_toc_e.htm, accessed December 2019.

17. S. Schoenian, "Real Men Wear Wool. Wool Production—Top 10 Countries and States," October 20, 2019, http://www.sheep101.info/wool.html, accessed December 2019.

18. Grace I. Kunz and Myrna B. Garner, *Going Global: The Textile and Apparel Industry*, 2nd ed. (New York: Fairchild Books, 2011), 384–385.

19. "Textiles and Apparel," The United States-Mexico-Canada Agreement Fact Sheet, https://ustr.gov/sites/default/files/files/Press/fs/USMCA/USMCA-Textiles.pdf, accessed December 2019.

20. "CAFTA-DR," Free Trade Agreements: Office of the United States Trade Representative, https://ustr.gov/trade-agreements/free-trade-agreements/cafta-dr-dominican-republic-central-america-fta, accessed December 2019.

21. "Textiles: Back in the Mainstream," World Trade Organization https://www.wto.org/english/thewto_e/whatis_e/tif_e/agrm5_e.htm, accessed December 2019.

22. Marty Moran, "2019 State of the U.S. Textile Industry," *Textile World*, May 15, 2019, https://www.textileworld.com/textile-world/features/2019/05/2019-state-of-the-u-s-textile-industry/, accessed December 2019.

23. "Exports Hit Their Stride," *WWD*, August 7, 1996, p. 28.

FEATURES

Spotlight on Innovators: Claire McCardell—The American Look

Richard Martin. "American Ingenuity: Sportswear, 1930s–1970s." In *Heilbrunn Timeline of Art History* (New York: The Metropolitan Museum of Art, 2000–). http://www.metmuseum.org/toah/hd/amsp/hd_amsp.htm (October 2004), accessed December 2019.

J. Le Zotte. "What a 1950s Fashion Maven Might Teach Us about What to Wear." *Smithsonian.com*. http://www.smithsonianmag.com/smithsonian-institution/1950s-designer-claire-mccardell-might-teach-us-about-what-wear-180955520/?no-ist (June 2015), accessed December 2019.

Kohle Yohannan and Nancy Nolf, *Claire McCardell: Redefining Modernism* (New York: Harry N. Abrams, Inc., 1998), 34-103.

Spotlight on Sustainability: The United Nations: Putting the Brakes on Fast Fashion

UN Alliance for Sustainable Fashion, https://unfashionalliance.org/, accessed December 2019.

"Putting the Brakes on Fast Fashion," UN Environment Assembly, http://web.unep.org/environmentassembly/putting-brakes-fast-fashion, accessed December 2019.

Chapter 11

1. Peter H. Lewis, "Attention Shoppers: Internet Is Open," *New York Times*, August 12, 1994, http://www.nytimes.com/1994/08/12/business/attention-shoppers-internet-is-open.html, accessed December 2019.

2. "Quarterly Retail e-Commerce Sales 3rd Quarter 2019," *U.S. Census Bureau News*, November 19, 2019, https://www.census.gov/retail/mrts/www/data/pdf/ec_current.pdf, accessed December 2019.

3. "45 Ecommerce Statistics You Need to Know in 2019," *The WordStream Blog*, August 27, 2019, https://www.wordstream.com/blog/ws/2019/04/04/ecommerce-statistics, accessed December 2019.

4. Stastia, "Retail e-commerce sales in the United States from 2017 to 2023," https://www.statista.com/statistics/272391/us-retail-e-commerce-sales-forecast/, accessed December 2019.

5. The Athlete's Foot, "About," https://www.theathletesfoot.us/aboutus.html, accessed December 2019.

6. Direct Selling Association, "2018 Direct Selling Statistics," https://www.dsa.org/docs/default-source/action-alerts/2018industryoverview-06032019.pdf?sfvrsn=9709c0a5_0%27, accessed December 2019.

7. "Top Direct Sales Clothing Parties Companies for 2019," *The Best Direct Sales Companies*, https://thebestdirectsalescompanies.com/clothing-parties-companies/, accessed December 2019.

8. "About Qurate Retail, Inc.," https://jobs.hsn.com/cornerstone-careers, accessed December 2019.

9. "Fashion Brands," *Home Shopping Network*, https://www.hsn.com/brands/by-category-fashion/fa, accessed December 2019.

10. "About QVC FAQs," https://www.qvc.com/FAQAboutQVC.content.html?viewType=gallery&pageSize=96&redirh=t, accessed December 2019.

11. "About EVINE, Inc.," *Shop HQ*, https://www.evine.com/p/help/evine-live/about-evine-live/?cm_re=gft-_-companyoverview, accessed December 2019.

12. Statista, "Apparel, Footwear and Accessories Retail e-commerce Revenue in the United States from 2017 to 2023," https://www.statista.com/statistics/278890/us-apparel-and-accessories-retail-e-commerce-revenue/, accessed December 2019.

13. Amelia Lucas, "Cyber Monday Online Sales Hit Record $9.4 billion, Boosted by Late-night Spending Spree, Adobe Says," *CNBC*, December 3, 2019, https://www.cnbc.com/2019/12/03/cyber-monday-online-sales-hit-record-9point4-billion-adobe-says.html, accessed December 2019.

14. "Most Popular Online Stores in the Fashion Segment in the United States in 2018, by e-commerce Net Sales," *Statista*, https://www.statista.com/statistics/646097/top-online-stores-fashion-united-states-ecommercedb/, accessed December 2019.

15. Tracey Wallace, "Omni-Channel Retail Report: Generational Consumer Shopping Behavior Comes Into Focus and Its Importance in Ecommerce," BigCommerce, https://www.bigcommerce.com/blog/omni-channel-retail/#why-us-consumers-shop-where-they-shop, accessed December 2019.

16. Lazar, Michael-Jon, "Retailers: Don't Ignore These Mobile Commerce Statistics for 2019," Ready Cloud, September 27, 2019, https://www.readycloud.com/info/retailers-dont -ignore-these-mobile-commerce-statistics-for-2019, accessed December 2019.

17. Alexa Lardieri, "Social Media Use Mostly Unchanged from 2018," *U.S. New and World Report*, April 10, 2019, https:// www.usnews.com/news/national-news/articles/2019-04-10 /survey-social-media-use-mostly-unchanged-from-2018, accessed December 2019.

18. James Reinhart, "ThreadUp 2019 Resale Report," *ThreadUp*, https://www.thredup.com/resale, accessed December 2019.

19. Rahul Thakur, "Online Clothing Rental Market is Expected to Reach $1,856 Million, Globally, by 2023," Cison PR Newswire, April 6, 2017, https://www.prnewswire.com /news-releases/online-clothing-rental-market-is-expected-to -reach—1856-million-globally-by-2023—-allied-market -research-618522543.html, accessed December 2019.

FEATURES

Spotlight on Business: Social Media and How People Really Shop!
Arthur, R., "10 fashion brands nailing their Snapchat strategy," *Forbes*, November 30, 2016, https://www.forbes.com/sites /rachelarthur/2016/11/30/10-fashion-brands-nailing-their -snapchat-content-strategy/#35413d0b4e9e, accessed December 2019.

"52 fascinating and incredible YouTube statistics," *Brandwatch*, July 15, 2019, https://www.brandwatch.com/blog/youtube -stats/, accessed December 2019.

"Social media's effect on the fashion industry," *GreenBuzz*, June 21, 2018, greenbuzzagency.com/social-media-effect-fashion -industry, accessed December 2019.

Tracey Wallace, "Omni-Channel Retail Report: Generational Consumer Shopping Behavior Comes Into Focus and Its Importance in Ecommerce," BigCommerce, https://www .bigcommerce.com/blog/omni-channel-retail/#why-us -consumers-shop-where-they-shop, accessed December 2019.

Spotlight on Innovators: Fashion Bloggers
Meghan Blalock, "Find out which fashion bloggers are making millions," *WhoWhatWear*, October 10, 2016, https://www .whowhatwear.com/how-do-bloggers-make-money, accessed December 2019.

Jessica Chandra, "These are the top 10 fashion influencers in the world, according to Forbes," *Bazaar*, October 3, 2017, https:// www.harpersbazaar.com.au/fashion/top-10-fashion-influencers -forbes-14532, accessed December 2019.

Chapter 12

1. *InStyle* Media Kit, https://www.instyle.com/promo/2019 -media-kit/instyle_media_kit_2019.pdf, accessed December 2019.

2. *WornOnTV*, http://www.wornontiv.net, accessed December 2019.

3. "Leading Fashion Brands on Twitter as of July 2018, By Followers," *Statista*, https://www.statista.com /statistics/242143/twitter-number-of-followers-of-popular -apparel-brands/, accessed December 2019.

4. Jasmine Enberg, "Global Digital Ad Spending 2019," *e-Marketer*, March 28, 2019 https://www.emarketer.com /content/global-digital-ad-spending-2019, accessed December 2019.

FEATURES

Spotlight on Innovators: Inspiring Beauty—50 Years of Ebony Fashion Fair
"Inspiring Beauty: 50 Years of Ebony Fashion Fair." http:// chicagohistory.org/inspiring beauty/index.html, retrieved July 15, 2015.

Jacki Lyden. "The Ebony Fashion Fair: Changing History on the Catwalk." *NPR.org*. Last modified February 15, 2014. http://www.npr.org/2014/02/15/276987206 /the-ebony-fashion-fair-changing-history-on-the-catwalk.

Spotlight on Careers: So You Want to be in Fashion
"Global Fashion Industry Statistics – International Apparel," *Fashion United*, January 2020, https://fashionunited.com /global-fashion-industry-statistics/, accessed January 2020.

"The 2018 Los Angeles Fashion Report," The California Fashion Association, https://www.cit.com/uploadedFiles/citcom /contents/articles/commercial_articles/Los%20Angeles%20 Fashion%20Report%202018.pdf, accessed December 2019.

"The Economic Impact of the Fashion Industry," *Joint Economic Committee Democrats*, February 22, 2019, https://www.jec .senate.gov/public/index.cfm/democrats/2019/2/the-economic -impact-of-the-fashion-industry, accessed December 2019.

"The Most Beautiful Job in the World," Bloomsbury – Academic and Professional, 2018, https://www.bloomsbury.com/uk/the -most-beautiful-job-in-the-world-9781350110137/, accessed December 2019.

Stephanie Marsh, "Chanel Shoes, But No Salary: How One Woman Exposed the Scandal of the French Fashion Industry," *The Guardian*, September 2, 2018, https://www.theguardian. com/fashion/2018/sep/02/academic-exposing-ugly-reality-high -fashion-giulia-mensitieri, accessed December 2019.

Spotlight on Sustainability: Eileen Fisher
Adele Peters, "How Eileen Fisher Thinks About Sustainable Consumption," *Fast Company*, October 31, 2019, https://www .fastcompany.com/90423555/how-eileen-fisher-thinks-about -sustainable-consumption, accessed December 2019.

Whitney Bauck, "Factory Tour: Eileen Fisher Helps Make the Eco-Fashion Dream of Circularity Come True," *Fashionista*, July 9, 2018, https://fashionista.com/2018/07/eileen-fisher -clothing-factory-tour, accessed December 2019.

"All the Winners from the 2019 CFDA Awards," *Fashionista*, June 10, 2019, https://fashionista.com/2019/06/2019-cfda -fashion-awards-winners, accessed December 2019.

CREDITS

frontis: Dominique Charriau/WireImage/ Getty Images

Part Opener 1: Victor VIRGILE/Gamma-Rapho via Getty Images

Chapter 1

1.0: THOMAS SAMSON/AFP/Getty Images

1.1: Pascal Le Segretain/Getty Images

1.2: Ericksen / WWD / © Conde Nast

1.3: Michael Ochs Archives/Getty Images

1.4a: Achard / WWD / © Conde Nast

1.4b: Giannoni / WWD / © Conde Nast

1.5: Fairchild Books

1.6: Betsie Van Der MeerMore/Getty Images

1.7–1.9: Fairchild Books

1.10: Tommaso Boddi/Getty Images for hulu

1.11: Daniel Zuchnik/WireImage/Getty Images

1.12: Centeno / WWD / © Conde Nast

1.13: Giannoni / WWD / © Conde Nast

1IVH1: Andrew Toth/Getty Images

1IVH2&3: Victor VIRGILE/Gamma-Rapho via Getty Images

1IVH4: Vittorio Zunino Celotto/Getty Images

1CS1: Courtesy of Judy Dawainis

1LS1: Michael Gottschalk/Photothek via Getty Images

1LS2: Mark Metcalfe/Getty Images

1LS3: Sathit/Shutterstock.com

Chapter 2

2.0: David Benito/Getty Images

2.1: CPI.org and Sheryl Farnan

2.2: Fairchild Books

2.3: H. Armstrong Roberts/ClassicStock/Getty Images

2.4: Chaz Niell/Getty Images

2.5: U.S. Census Bureau

2.6: Victor VIRGILE/Gamma-Rapho via Getty Images

2.7: Estrop/Getty Images

2.8: U.S. Census Bureau

2.9: Jacopo Raule/Getty Images

2DK1: Brian Ach/Getty Images for Urban Zen

2DK2: Jimi Celeste/Patrick McMullan via Getty Images

2DK3: Iannaccone / WWD / © Conde Nast

2DK4: Antonov / WWD / © Conde Nast

2CS1: Courtesy of Cally Carbone

2TNB1: Paul Aiken/Digital First Media/Boulder Daily Camera via Getty Images

2TNB2: Katie Falkenberg/Los Angeles Times via Getty Images

2TNB3: Kelly Sullivan/Getty Images for Rent the Runway

2TNB4: PAUL J. RICHARDS/AFP/Getty Images

Chapter 3

3.0: Jeff Spicer/BFC/Getty Images For BFC

3.1: WWD / © Conde Nast

3.2: Sean Drakes/WireImage/Getty Images

3.3a&b: Giannoni / WWD / © Conde Nast

3.4: Fairchild Books

3.5: Francois Durand/Getty Images

3.6: Tim P. Whitby/Getty Images

3.7: Keenan / WWD / © Conde Nast

3.8: Carlos R. Alvarez/WireImage/Getty Images

3B1-4: Thierry Chesnot/Getty Images

3CS1: CARL COURT / AFP / Getty Images

3SC1: Jordan Brand via Getty Images

3SC2: Bobby Metelus / Getty Images

3SC3: Jeff Kravitz/FilmMagic/Getty Images

3SC4: Chris Trotman/Getty Images

3SC5: Redux Images

Chapter 4

4.0: Randy Brooke/WireImage
4.1: Fairchild Books
4.2: Anna Bryukhanova / iStock
4.3 & 4.4: WWD / © Conde Nast
4.5: Fairchild Books:
4RTR1: Bennett Raglin/WireImage/Getty Images
4RTR2: Rick T. Wilking/Getty Images
4RTR3: Astrid Stawiarz/Getty Images
4RTR4: Thos Robinson/Getty Images for WeWork:
4SC1: Courtesy of Kate McConnell
4PB1: Jaap Arriens/NurPhoto via Getty Images
4PB2: Tim Johnson/MCT/Tribune News Service via Getty Images
Part 2 Opener: Richard Bord/Getty Images

Chapter 5

5.0: Lonely Planet Images/ Getty Images
5.1: Victor VIRGILE / Gamma-Rapho via Getty Images
5.2: Image Courtesy of The Advertising Archives
5.3 & 5.4: Fairchild Books
5.5: Image Courtesy of The Advertising Archives
5.6: LAKRUWAN WANNIARACHCHI / AFP / Getty Images
5.7: Maestri / WWD / © Conde Nast
5.8: WWD / © Conde Nast
5.9: Nagi / WWD / © Conde Nast
5.10 & 5.11: Giannoni / Maitre / WWD / © Conde Nast:
5RO1: Vivien Killilea/Getty Images for Rothy's
5RO2: Pool/Samir Hussein/WireImage
5CS1: Courtesy of Dani Locastro
5RS1: Courtesy of Council for Textile Recycling; rendered by QBS

Chapter 6

6.0: VCG/Getty Images
6.1: Randy Brooke / WireImage
6.2: Mitra / WWD / © Conde Nast
6.3: Zhang Jingtao/Visual China Group via Getty Images
6.4a & b: Man / WWD / © Conde Nast:
6SL1-3: Christopher Gannon, Iowa State University News Service.
6CS1: Courtesy of Audrey Cervellio
6FR1: Rabbani and Solimene Photography/Getty Images
6FR2: Vittorio Zunino Celotto/Getty Images for Dsquared2
6FR3: Estrop/Getty Images
6FR4: Vanni Bassetti/Getty Images
6FR5: Frazer Harrison/Getty Images for Mercedes-Benz Fashion Week
6FR6: Vanni Bassetti/Getty Images
PO3: Mark Sagliocco/Getty Images for Mercedes-Benz Fashion Week

Chapter 7

7.0: BJI/Blue Jean Images/Getty Images"
7.1: Mark Sagliocco/Getty Images for Mercedes-Benz Fashion Week
7.2a–d: Caroline McCredie/Getty Images
7.3: Amed / WWD / © Conde Nast
7.4: Maitre / WWD / © Conde Nast
7.5: Chinese / WWD / © Conde Nast
7.6: Lee / WWD / © Conde Nast
7.7: GREGOR FISCHER/DPA/AFP via Getty Images
7FT1-3: Tannis Toohey/Toronto Star via Getty Image
7CS1: Courtesy of Kanani Mahelona
7PS1: Carlos R. Alvarez/WireImage/Getty Images
7PS2: Jon Furniss/WireImage/Getty Images
7PS3: Dan MacMedan/Contour by Getty Images
7PS4: Kevin Mazur/Getty Images for iHeartMedia
7PS5: Jennifer Graylock/FilmMagic/Getty Images

Chapter 8

8.0: andresr/iStock
8.1: Pietro D'Aprano/Getty Images
8.2: Frazier Harrison/Getty Images for Mercedes-Benz
8.3: Ira L. Black/Corbis via Getty Images
8.4: BEN STANSALL/AFP/Getty Images
8.5: Pool/Samir Hussein/WireImage/Getty Images
8.6: Ericksen / WWD / © Conde Nast
8.7: Rindoff/Charriau/Getty Images
8.8: Astrid Stawiarz/Getty Images for John Varvatos
8.9: John Sciulli/Getty Images for Kenneth Cole
8.10: Jon Kopaloff/Getty Images
8.11: Maestri / WWD / © Conde Nast
8.12: Peter Sabok/NurPhoto via Getty Images
8.13: WWD / © Conde Nast
8.14: WWD / © Conde Nast
8.15: WWD / © Conde Nast
8PP1a-c, 2: Courtesy of Ryan Yasin
8PP3: Paul Grover/James Dyson Award
8SM1: iStock / Getty Images Plus
8TM1: William Perugini/Image Source/Getty Images
8TM2: John Shearer/AMA2019/Getty Images for dcp
8TM3: JEWEL SAMAD/AFP via Getty Images
8TM4: fitimi/iStock

Chapter 9

9.0: John Phillips/Getty Images for MBFW
9.1: Estrop/Getty Images
9.2: Kasuga / WWD / © Conde Nast
9.3a: WWD / © Conde Nast
9.3b: Christian Vierig/Getty Images
9.3c: WWD / © Conde Nast
9.4: Christian Vierig/Getty Images
9.5: Iannaccone / WWD / © Conde Nast
9.6 & 9.7: WWD / © Conde Nast
9.8 & 9.9: WWD / © Conde Nast
9.10: Michael Mauney / The LIFE Picture Collection / Getty Images
9.11: Bob Levey/WireImage/Getty Images
9.12: Jacopo Raule/Getty Images for Gucci
9SS1: Johnny Louis/Getty Images
9SS2: Mindy Small/FilmMagic/Getty Image
9CS1: Courtesy of Dr. Sara Marcketti
9CA1: FREDERIC J. BROWN / AFP / GettyImages
9CA2: Jeffrey Mayer / WireImage
9CA3: Jesse Grant/Getty Images for Vanity Fair
9CA4: Courtesy of Photofest
Part 4 Opener: Vostok/Moment/Getty Images

Chapter 10

10.0: VCG/VCG via Getty Images
10.1: WWD / © Conde Nast
10.2a: MIGUEL MEDINA / AFP / Getty Images
10.2b: MIGUEL MEDINA / AFP / Getty Images
10.3: Carsten Koall/Getty Images
10.4: YOSHIKAZU TSUNO / AFP / Getty Images
10.5: WWD / © Conde Nast
10CM1: Bettmann/Getty Images
10CM2 & 3: Genevieve Naylor
10CS1: Courtesy of Caroline Bartek
10C1: John Phillips/Getty Images for NEONYT
10C2: Fishman/ullstein bild via Getty Images

Chapter 11

11.0: EDUCATION IMAGES/GETTY
11.1: Ericksen / WWD / © Conde Nast
11.2: Getty Images / Image Source
11.3a & b: Coulter / WWD / © Conde Nast
11.4: PATRICK McMULLAN / Getty Images
11.5: Neilson Barnard/Getty Images for QVC
11.6: WWD / © Conde Nast
11.7: GUSTAVO CABALLERO/Getty Images
11.8: Maiatre / WWD / © Conde Nast
11SM1: Chesnot/Getty Images
11SM2: INA FASSBENDER/AFP via Getty Images
11SJ1-3: Shellie Jeffrey
11FB1: Rosdiana Ciaravolo/Getty Images
11FB2: Monica Schipper/Getty Images for Vionic
11FB3: Jonathan Leibson/Getty Images for Westfield

Chapter 12

12.0: Anna Webber/Getty Images for alice + olivia
12.1: David_Ahn / iStock / Getty Images
12.2: Tim Boyles / Getty Images for HSN
12.3: Deepblue4you/Getty Images
12.4: Donald Bowers/Getty Images for TRESemme
12.5: Stefanie Keenan/Getty Images for The Hollywood Reporter
12.6: Victor VIRGILE/Gamma-Rapho via Getty Images
12.7: WWD / © Conde Nast
12EF1: Dimitrios Kambouris/Getty Images
12EF2: Robert Alexander/Getty Images
12EF3: Vincent Tullo for The Washington Post via Getty Images
12CS1: Joe Raedle/Getty Images
12EB1: Helen H. Richardson / The Denver Post via Getty Images
12EB2: Lyn Alweis / The Denver Post via Getty Images
12EB3: Helen H. Richardson / The Denver Post via Getty Images

INDEX

body scanning, 147
bootleg goods, 216
boredom, 40
Bottega Veneta, 179
boutique, 206, 234
Bow, Clara, 59
Bowie, Iman, *26*, 27
brand names, 90, 140–1, 143
Branquinho, Veronique, 208
bridal wear, 155, 228
bridge jewelry, 188
bridge market, 77
Brinkley, Christie, 59, 235, 269
broadcast media, auxiliary fashion
    services, 248–9
Brooklyn Museum, 61, *61*
Brummel, Beau, 56
Bugg, Pippa, 164–5
bundling, 138
Burberry, 78, 125, 183, 184, 236
Burch, Tory, 184
Bureau of Consumer Protection, 105
Burlington Industries, 93
Burton, Sarah, *155*
Burton, Tim, 181
Bush, Barbara, 187
business
    diversity and competition, 67, 70
    e-commerce, 224
    importing by US, 215
    ownership, 72
business spotlights
    faux real, 116–117
    marketing to teens, 168–9
    personalization, 78–9
    power suit, 146
    recycled fashion, 101
    sneakers, 60–1
    social media and shopping, 240–1
buyer's directory, 199
buying, 257
    organization for, 225
    store-owned foreign, 214
buying power, 44, 48–9

C

cable television, 248
Calliston RTKL, 78
Cambodia, 219
Camilleri, Izzy, 137, 155
Campbell, Naomi, 116, 269
Canada, fashion market, 209
Canada Fox Breeders Association (CFBA),
    124

Canada Mink Breeders Association
    (CMBA), 124
carat, 185
Carbone, Cally, 30
career spotlights
    accessory designer (Audrey Cervellero),
        122
    consultant (Kanani Mahelona), 142–3
    costume designer (Shellie Jeffrey),
        230–1
    creative development (Cally Carbone),
        30
    creative director (Caroline Bartek),
        212–13
    designer (Kate McConnell), 74
    fashion industry, 252–3
    patternmaker and historian (Judi
        Dawainis), 13
    social media manager (Pippa Bugg),
        164–5
    surface design/illustrator (Jill
        McDonald), 96–7
    teacher, researcher, and historian (Sara
        Marcketti), 190
    wedding planner (Sandy Malone), 54
Care Labeling of Textile Wearing Apparel,
    71, 104
Caribbean Basin, fashion market, 209–10
Carlos Miele of Brazil, *234*
Carpet America Recovery Effort (CARE),
    100
Cartier, 186
Cartier, Jacques, 269
Cartier, Louis-Joseph, 189
casual living, 31
catalog(s), 171
catalog retailers, 235
category buying, 232
category killers, 234
Cavalli, Roberto, 154
Cedar Fair Entertainment Corporation, 230
Cellar-Kefauver, 71
Cervellero, Audrey, 122
CEW (Cosmetic Executive Women), 30
chain organizations, 229, 232
Chalayan, Hussein, *103*, 208, 269
Chambre Syndicale de la Couture
    Parisienne, 206
Chanel, 8, 79, 125, 183, 184, 206
    handbags, *179*
    leather gloves, *182*
    runway, *157*
    suit, *8*
Chanel, Coco, 56, 187, 269

character licensing, 167, 170
chargebacks, 145
Charter Club, 140
Chicago History Museum, *250*, 251
children's, tweens', and teens' apparel, 163,
    165–7, 170–1
    catalogs, 171
    industry trends, 170–1
    licensing, 167, 170
    merchandising and marketing, 167
    organization and operation, 163–4
    resale of childrenswear, 171
    role of fashion in, 166
    separate stores, 171
    shoes, 177
    size categories, 164–6
    specialization, 166
China, fashion market, 211
Choo, Jimmy, 184, *254*
Cintas, 212–13
Claiborne, Liz, 140, 156
classic, term, 8
classification buying, 232
Clayton Act, 71
Clements, Suzanne, 208
Clinton, Hillary Rodham, 27
Coach, Sabrina bag, *178*
Cole, Kenneth, 52, 62, 75, *159*, 184
collection, 132
color, 10
Color Association of the United States
    (CAUS), 256
Color Marketing Group, 10, 51
commissionaires, 214
communication, career in social media,
    164–5
communications, 39
companionship, desire for, 40
competition, 67, 70
computer-aided design (CAD), 132, 135–6
computer-aided manufacturing (CAM), 136
computer-integrated manufacturing (CIM),
    136, 145
conformity, 62
consulting, career spotlight, 142–3
consumer buying cycle, 14, *15, 80*
consumer income, 28–9
consumer use cycle, *15*
contractors, 133–4
Converse, Inc., 177
Converse Rubber Shoe Company, 60
Cooper, Bradley, *146, 159*
corporate licensing, 143
corporation, 72